MACROECONOMICS:
ANALYSIS AND POLICY

MACROECONOMICS:
ANALYSIS AND POLICY

James L. Cochrane
University of South Carolina

Samuel Gubins
Haverford College

B. F. Kiker
University of South Carolina

Scott, Foresman and Company
Glenview, Illinois   Brighton, England

Library of Congress Catalog Card Number: 73–85876
ISBN 0–673–07639–3

Regional offices of Scott, Foresman and Company are located
in Dallas, Texas; Glenview, Illinois; Oakland, New Jersey;
Palo Alto, California; Tucker, Georgia; and Brighton, England.

EDITOR'S FOREWORD

Ever since the Keynesian revolution, most undergraduate students of economics have found macroeconomics more satisfying than microeconomics. Although microeconomics is more logical and abstract, macroeconomics relates more closely to the world around them. Its data are concepts like GNP and personal income which one can read about in newspapers and whose values one can find in easily available data sources; whereas the basic data of microeconomics are concepts such as utility and marginal revenues, most of which are foreign even to the economic agents assumed to use them in routine decision making. More important, macroeconomics deals directly with issues of great urgency to students and others in society. It sets out to explain why our society has been afflicted periodically with mass unemployment and what the government might do to prevent such episodes. It deals with the division of the society's productive resources between the public and private sectors, and with the determinants and consequences of long-run economic growth.

In recent years, students have begun to feel that macroeconomics is less than satisfactory in helping them to understand the issues which it attempts to elucidate. Foremost among the reasons for this dissatisfaction is the apparently increasing tendency for our economy to be plagued simultaneously with high unemployment and rapid inflation, an issue about which traditional Keynesian theory has little to say. Students are also concerned about the persistence of extremely high unemployment rates and poverty levels in rural areas and urban ghettoes at times when the rest of the economy is near full employment. And they are concerned with persistent imbalance in the foreign sector which appears to limit our ability to achieve domestic goals. Perhaps most important, they are concerned by claims of noneconomists that economic growth may pose a threat to the global environment and perhaps to man's continued existence.

These and other contemporary macroeconomic issues are ignored or slighted in most macro textbooks. Of course, economists do not have complete or satisfactory answers to all these problems. But they do have more useful things to say about them than one would infer from reading available texts. Studies which have appeared in technical journals, but have not yet found their way into texts, supply some evidence and analysis to dispel misunderstandings and to place limits on the extent of our ignorance about solutions. After a thorough exposition of neoclassical and modern macroeconomic theory, the authors of this new text turn to discussion of a range of macroeconomic problems of the 1970s. In each case, they try to show what light can be shed on the problem by the theory, how the theory might be modified or extended to improve our understanding of the problem, and where the theory fails in its attempts to shed light on some problems.

The problem of manpower training programs is a useful illustration. Most texts have extensive discussions of full employment, but they say little about ways to modify the theoretical models to account for persistent ghetto unemployment in an otherwise fully employed economy. Such modifications are discussed in the present text, along with an analysis of manpower training programs designed to improve the situation. Finally, the authors frankly indicate the limited effect that manpower programs have had.

It is hoped, then, that the book will provide students not only a basic grounding in modern macroeconomic ideas and models, but also a better indication of the strengths and weaknesses of macroeconomics in helping to solve urgent social problems.

Edwin S. Mills   Advisory Editor in Economics
Princeton University

PREFACE

During the last few years we have found our courses in macroeconomics departing from the material available in current texts in several ways. We shortened our treatment of neoclassical and Keynesian analysis in order to make room for topics that are critical to an understanding of a modern macroeconomy: the relationship between inflation and unemployment, monetarist and fiscalist approaches to stabilization, the use of incomes policies both in the United States and abroad, the potential of manpower planning for shifting the Phillips curve leftwards, the evolving international monetary system and its consequences for macroeconomic policy, and input-output analysis as a planning tool. At the same time we found ourselves returning to a rigorous statement of neoclassical theory in order to explain the origins of the monetarist approach to macroeconomics. This text represents our ideas on how to combine traditionally taught topics with newer ones in a one-semester macroeconomics course.

The text is divided into three parts. Part I provides a brief treatment (two chapters) of neoclassical macroeconomics. The discussion begins with a review of the microeconomic foundations of macro theory. Part II is concerned with the modern formulation of macroeconomics and provides an understanding of the Keynesian approach to policy. Nevertheless, explicit treatment of modern monetary theory is incorporated in Chapters 9 and 10 in which the supply of and demand for money and the monetary base are discussed. The chapters have been arranged so that extended treatment of consumption behavior (Chapter 6) and the monetary base (Chapter 10) can be omitted in a course in which other topics are emphasized.

Part III includes the most recent topics in modern macroeconomics and is organized around the theme of government planning to achieve stabilization. It is our view that modern economies are turning, increasingly, to collective solutions to the complex problems of achieving acceptable rates of inflation and unemployment—recent wage and price controls are an example of this development.

Although Chapter 13 on Unemployment and Inflation is probably essential in a macroeconomics course, the remaining Chapters in Part III stand alone and the instructor could easily choose among them.

In addition to verbal descriptions of analysis, graphical and simple algebraic treatments are provided. High school algebra should be sufficient preparation. We have, however, agonized over the use of calculus and concluded that it is warranted in one specific instance. Accordingly, in a discussion of an aggregate production function, we have used one rule of calculus—differentiation—and have explained its use and significance in the text. It should take the instructor no longer than a half hour to explain this technique to the uninitiated.

To those who have aided us by suggestions and criticisms, we thank you. Our students at Bryn Mawr College, Haverford College, and the University of South Carolina have gone through the text at various stages, and their comments and queries have been of immense benefit. Our debts to colleagues are too extensive to acknowledge them all, but the following colleagues have been particularly helpful and we wish to cite, with gratitude, their service: Noel J. J. Farley of Bryn Mawr College, Russell Shannon of Clemson University, Vernon Dixon and Holland Hunter of Haverford College, Daniel Hamermesh of Michigan State University, Michael Wachter of the University of Pennsylvania, Edwin S. Mills of Princeton University, Eleanor Gubins of Rosemont College, Robert Carlsson, Susan Hill Cochrane, and C. Glyn Williams of the University of South Carolina, William Cook of Tulane University, and M. A. Stephenson of Wofford College. We want to specially thank Robert Runck of Scott, Foresman for services far beyond the usual call of editors. In addition, many useful comment on the manuscript were obtained from the following critical readers:

    Robert Barro, Brown University
    William Brainard, Yale University
    John Cornwall, Tufts University
    Thomas M. Humphrey, Federal Reserve Bank of
      Richmond
    Robert R. Keller, California State University at Long
      Beach
    John G. Ranlett, Sacramento State College
    Robert Haney Scott, University of Washington
    Lester D. Taylor, University of Michigan

Pamelia Stowers Waddell provided secretarial help, and assistance in proofreading was supplied by Lloyd R. Drown and Pamelia Stowers Waddell. Barbara K. Atrostic, a graduate student in economics at the University of Pennsylvania, did an excellent job preparing the index.

Contents

Introduction

MICROECONOMICS AND MACROECONOMICS

Economists use the terms *macroeconomics* and *microeconomics* to designate two areas of inquiry which have much in common but are distinguishable from each other. Macroeconomists study the workings of the economy as a whole, focusing on such aggregates as the level of output, the rate of unemployment, the price level, and the rate of growth of output. Microeconomists study parts of the economy, focusing on individual markets, consumers, behavior of individual business firms, and other such parts of the economic system.

Much of microeconomics is based on "partial equilibrium analysis." The first step in microeconomic analysis is to set up the relevant environment, or "model," of the particular aspect of the economy in question, such as the monopolistic firm. A microeconomist would then be concerned with the impact on one or more of the variables (for example, output and employment) within this environment of a change in one of the variables (for example, an increase in the costs of production). The key to this kind of work is the expression *ceteris paribus*, "everything else being equal." While inspecting the environment itself or the effect of a change in one or more of its structural relationships, everything outside the environment is held constant. There is no attempt to emphasize the interrelationships among the various segments of an economic system. Macroeconomics, in contrast, does emphasize some of these interrelationships. But, in the process of enlarging its focus, some of the inner workings are obscured. For example, in examining the relationship between national income and total consumption expenditures, we are not concerned with the particular goods and services consumed by the class of families whose incomes are between $5000 and $7000 per year.

Economics is often associated with the "scarcity problem": (unlimited) wants cannot all be satisfied, given (limited) available resources. Therefore, analysis of scarcity problems faced by individuals, such as how a manager of a firm can satisfy stockholders, given his firm's internal and external situation, is generally considered to be "microeconomics." A great deal of "macroeconomics," on the other hand, consists of analysis of scarcity problems faced by society as a whole, such as how government officials, acting on behalf of society, can satisfy defense and nondefense needs, given expected tax receipts and prevailing attitudes toward changes in the public debt.

One major reason for the existence of macroeconomics as a separate subject is that functions expressing economists' views of *aggregate* "behavior" cannot always be obtained by summing the functions expressing economists' views of *individual* behavior. In most cases, what is true for an individual economic unit is true for society, but not always. If we could simply investigate the operations of individual firms and assume that society is one large firm whose operations are similar to the individual firm, there would be no need to study macroeconomics or to develop a theoretical framework within which to study aggregate phenomena.

Although economists have a fairly good idea of the kinds of problems one is likely to study as a macro- or microeconomist, there are subjects of inquiry which are on the borderline between these two, and on the borderline the distinction breaks down. For example, an analysis of the impact of levying a tax on auto sales could be a microeconomic inquiry, if it is concerned with the automobile manufacturing industry and car consumption. Or it could be a macroeconomic inquiry, if it is concerned with the level of consumer demand, national product, and employment. In general, however, the terms "macro" and "micro" are helpful in identifying the kinds of questions raised.

POLITICAL PHILOSOPHY
AND ECONOMIC THEORY

Economic theories are securely anchored to the political philosophy of the society for which they are developed. In this book we try to make explicit the relationship between macroeconomic theory and political values. The cataclysmic swings in national economic activity which characterized the nineteenth and early twentieth centuries, the booms and busts of the past, are no longer tolerated in a society which prizes economic stability and seeks to minimize the hardships resulting from such crises.

As the economy suffered through the long and hard years of the Great Depression of the 1930s, economic theory was reworked to enable us to understand how to avoid such catastrophe in the future. In the wake of the Depression, economists were open to new integrating theories which could explain the forces creating depressions, and could suggest how the central government's economic power could be used to achieve stability. Prior to the Depression, and, for that matter, during most of it, macroeconomic models were in harmony with the political philosophy which says, "that government is best which governs least." *Laissez-faire* in economics was complemented by *laissez-faire* in politics.

Society has become increasingly less willing to permit economic hardship, and has taken on collectively, through government, the responsibility of securing stability. The history of government in the post-World War II period is a history of increasing sophistication in using the power of government to achieve economic stability, and it is also a history of expansion of government intervention in matters formerly deemed purely private. At present we are witnessing government intervention in economic matters on many levels, including that of making individual price and wage decisions.

STRUCTURE OF THE BOOK

From the perspective of the 1970s, it is apparent that macroeconomic theory has passed through three periods. The neoclassical economists (economists before John Maynard Keynes, and modern economists who are persuaded of the theoretical superiority of the neoclassical model) hold a view of the economy as a self-regulating mechanism which, in equilibrium, is characterized by full employment and the absence of inflation. In fact, we can infer from the neoclassical theoretical model that the presence of unemployment or inflation is itself evidence of temporary disequilibrium. The significance of the neoclassical model for public policy is that it rejects an active role for government in maintaining macroeconomic balance. Since the economy is presumed to be self-regulating, there is no reason for central governments to actively intervene to bring about equilibrium.

In Chapters 3 and 4 of this book we explore the theoretical framework of the neoclassical school. Since the distinction between macroeconomics and microeconomics was much less pronounced before Keynes than it is now, special attention is devoted to the microeconomic foundations of neoclassical theory.

It is important to understand neoclassical macroeconomics for several reasons. There has been a revival of interest in the neoclassical model for its focus on the role of money in the economy. During 1969 and 1970, in fact, U.S. national economic policy followed the policy recommendations of economists persuaded that models of neoclassical orientation have superior explanatory power. In addition, special attention is now being paid to microeconomic relationships which underlie macroeconomic models. The role of labor is under examination, and we devote a chapter to manpower and macroeconomic models. Thus, our excursion into neoclassical macroeconomics and the review of microeconomic theory which accompanies it is particularly important.

The second period for macroeconomic theory dates from 1936, when Keynes' *The General Theory of Employment, Interest, and Money* was published. To be sure, elements of Keynes' ideas can be found in the works of earlier economists. But it was not until *The General Theory* appeared that a framework was provided which explicitly took account of the stabilizing role of government. We refer to Keynes' ideas and those of his disciples (not all of whom agreed with the details of Keynes' model) as Keynesians.

The conclusion of the Keynesian model is that unemployment could be a permanent condition of an economy. Even though the economy could be in equilibrium, in the sense that no forces are present which would lead to changes in the economy, it could have a high level of unemployment. Where the neoclassical model pointed to the temporary nature of unemployment, the Keynesian model concluded that unemployment could be compatible with stability. The policy prescription is for government intervention in the economy to insure sufficient demand to call forth the unemployed resources of the economy. Part II of this book is concerned with Keynesian economics, and amounts to a statement of the "received doctrine" which is widely held among modern economists.

By the end of the 1960s, economic reality had outpaced economic theory. Both the Keynesian and neoclassical theories are inadequate to the task of explaining the persistence of simultaneous inflation and unemployment. During the 1960s, a series of manpower programs were brought into existence to deal with the special problems of the unemployed. In 1971, the U.S. government adopted a wage and price policy. These developments in controls and manpower programs suggest that the role of government in achieving macroeconomic balance has become more pronounced.

In Part III of this book we turn to post-Keynesian economic analysis, dealing with governmental planning aimed at macroeconomic balance. We leave the well-ordered theoretical framework of the neoclassical and Keynesian economists for the uncertainty of the current frontiers of public policy and economic theory. Since we detect an augmented role for government, we call this period of macroeconomic theorizing the "planning" period, reflecting the fact that government regulation is an increasing part of policies to achieve stabilization. The chapters of Part III are devoted to unemployment and inflation, manpower and national labor-market policy, incomes policies, foreign economic relations of the United States, economic growth, and input-output analysis.

GOALS OF MACROECONOMIC POLICY

What macroeconomic objectives should government economic policy be designed to achieve? Although there is certainly not universal agreement about all the objectives of economic policies, several major goals have widespread support. Economists, very much a part of the society from which these goals emerge, have adopted them and pointed economic models in the direction of their achievement.

Full Employment

Full employment calls for adequate jobs for all those able and willing to work. The work ethic is surely one of the cornerstones of contemporary ideology. As a result, society provides only minimal support for those unable or unwilling to work. With the single exception of social security, welfare payments are made grudgingly and gracelessly, even where there are clearly no work opportunities for the beneficiaries of welfare. National policies beginning in the early 1970s have attempted to link welfare benefits to employment. Society places a very high value on employment for all. As a result, models of the national economy have as one of their objectives the minimization of unemployment.

The national commitment to full employment was first expressed in 1946, with the passage of the Employment Act, which placed with government the responsibility "to promote maximum employment, production, and purchasing power." Exactly what "full employment" means is not clear. At various times the Council of Economic Advisers, established by the Employment Act of 1946, has defined full employment as 96–97% of the total labor force. We consider this issue in Chapter 13, *Unemployment and Inflation*.

Price-Level Stability

Avoiding severe short-run fluctuations and long-run upward shifts in prices (inflation) is very high on most lists of goals for the economy. There are many adverse consequences of inflation, but perhaps the most serious is the necessity for individuals to "relearn" prices as prices move upward. When prices are stable, or fluctuate within a narrow range, individuals form expectations of what "normal" prices are, based on past experience. When prices are rising, individuals' expectations of the prices they must pay are disappointed. The predominant reaction to this is frustration, and occasionally anger. Even when wages are rising more rapidly than prices, which means that real purchasing power is increasing, consumers register strong dissatisfaction with rising prices.

Stable prices are clearly in the interests of creditors. Under inflation, creditors are repaid with dollars of lower purchasing power. It is not so clear that those in debt (for most homeowners, the major debt is a house mortgage), whose money wages are rising as rapidly as prices, are better off under price stability, because a mortgage calls for monthly payments stated in a fixed number of dollars. Since the dollars represent reduced purchasing power as inflation occurs, the debtor is making repayments with "cheaper" dollars than he originally contracted for. Nevertheless, there is a widespread dislike of rising prices, and public policy reflects this sentiment. Macroeconomic models are designed to consider explicitly the rate of upward price changes and to provide an understanding of how to keep that rate low.

Economic Security

On the individual level, economic security means uninterrupted employment. On a national level, it means the absence of periods of recession. By keeping a national economy stable, without wide swings in performance, uncertainty is reduced and economic security is increased. Therefore, one of the aims of macroeconomic models is to show how the economy can be maintained on a course which does not cause disruption in employment or production.

Standard of Living

Like economic security, standard of living is a difficult goal to specify. Most people would agree that the standard of living in the United States is higher than in virtually any other country in the world, and that this is a good thing. More is better than less. Only recently, in the face of increased consciousness of environmental destruction, has the issue of "*less is more*" been given serious consideration. We treat this issue in Chapter 17. Leaving the environmental issue aside, however, one of the goals clearly articulated for an economy is producing as much goods and services as its capacity permits. Macroeconomic models are formulated to reveal how output can be maximized.

Economic Growth

Not only should a society enjoy a high standard of living, many would urge that this standard be raised continuously, and as rapidly as technological changes will permit. As indicated above, those concerned with the environment question this goal, especially as it is believed that economic growth is inevitably accompanied by adverse environmental effects.

Equitable Distribution of Income

Although most people would not favor complete equality of incomes, most do accept that the spread between the very rich and those living in stark poverty should be diminished. This value is articulated through public policies which have as their professed aim reducing poverty and providing for equality of opportunity. These public policies are based on the assumption that income is unequally distributed because people have unequal opportunity, rather than unequal abilities.

Very little attention is paid, in macroeconomic models, to the distribution of income and whether or not it is equitable. Unlike the goals of price stability and low unemployment, on which there is common agreement, the judgment of what is the "best" distribution of income is essentially a moral one, rather than an economic one. However, the empirical question of what the distribution *is*, and would be under varying assumptions about the future of a national economy, is clearly an economic one, and can be answered.

Economic Freedom

Perhaps the most ambiguous of all policy goals, economic freedom is one everyone immediately agrees on—until it comes to defining it. The basic issue is the extent to which decisions traditionally thought of as "private" ones can and should be molded by public policies. At one extreme there are those who argue that virtually *all* economic decisions should be made in the private sector, implying a minimal economic role for public policy.

Stemming from nineteenth-century liberal political economics, this view is currently identified with the "Chicago" school of economics, and that school's most distinguished theorist, Milton Friedman. At the other extreme are those who see a wider role for public policy than is presently played, and a diminished reliance on free markets for determining allocation of resources.

It is perhaps obvious that some of these goals conflict with others. For example, it has proven difficult to maintain full employment and price-level stability. Many economists agree that there is a "trade-off" between these two goals—the closer the economy gets to using all of its available productive resources, the greater is the pressure on prices. (See the discussion in Chapter 13 on the Phillips curve.) Some economists believe that national central planning may permit an economy to develop faster than it would without central planning. Hence the goals of maximum growth and economic freedom may conflict.

The goals of macroeconomic policy are introduced here because models of the national economy are constructed on the basis of these goals. Even though the goals often are not explicit in the model, they are there, and you will want to be aware of them. In the quest for "objectivity," model builders take as "given" certain economic goals. Remember that these objective models rest on ideological premises.

BASIC CONCEPTS

Throughout the book we refer to a variety of concepts, which are described below. You should check back to this section to refresh your understanding of their meaning as you come upon them in the text.

Variables

A variable is a quantity that can have different values at different points in time. Aggregate consumer expenditure is an example of a variable. Macroeconomic models seek to predict a value (a specific amount) of this variable for periods in the future, as well as to explain levels which prevailed in the past.

Stock Variables

A variable defined for a *point* in time is a stock variable. For example, the money supply is a stock variable because it is measured for a given time. Inventory on a specific date is a stock variable; the number of single-family dwellings at the close of a year is a stock variable.

Flow Variables

A variable defined over a *period* of time is a flow variable. Income, investment, and saving are all flow variables referring to magnitudes observed over a period of time. The values of stock variables change as a result of flows. The flow of net investment during a quarter, for example, augments the capital stock.

Functional Relationships

The relationship of changes in the value of one variable to changes in the value of another variable is called a functional relationship. For example, in simple demand analysis

$$D = f(P)$$

which says that quantity demanded (D) is a function of price (P). P is the price at which the good might be sold in the marketplace. The law of demand says that as the price increases (as the value of the variable P becomes larger), the quantity demanded decreases (the value of the variable D becomes smaller), all other things being equal.

A simple macroeconomic functional relationship exists between consumption (C) and disposable income (Y_d):

$$C = f(Y_d)$$

As disposable income increases, so do consumption expenditures, all other things being equal. When this function is specified, as in the linear form

$$C = a + b Y_d$$

a and b are referred to as *parameters* or *coefficients*. These parameters are constant—so long as all the other variables which might affect the functional relationship between C and Y_d are held constant. If the other variables are allowed to change, the parameters would have different values.

Economic Models and Types of Functional Relationships

An economic model is a framework for saying something about a relationship in the economy. The demand and consumption functions above are examples of very simple economic models. The macroeconomic models we develop in this book consist of a series of relationships in the economy. These relationships are described in words, with graphs, and as sets of algebraic equations. The relationships involved are one of the three following kinds:

1) A *definitional* relationship, also called an *identity* or a *tautology*, expresses a linkage among variables that is established by the way they have been defined. For example,

$$Y = C + I + G + X$$

where Y is net national product, C is consumption expenditures, I is net investment, G is government expenditure, and X is the excess of exports over imports. Or $S = D$ is a definitional relationship if we mean by S the quantity sold and by D the quantity bought in a given marketplace. In each case the variables on the left of the equal sign are *defined* as equal to the variables on the right of the sign.

2) A *behavioral* relationship is one that expresses a relationship resulting from the voluntary arrangements of economic actors. For example, the consumption function expresses a voluntary relationship. If disposable income rises, consumers will respond by raising their consumption expenditures because they want to.

3) A *structural* (*institutional*) relationship, or a *constraint*, is given to the economic model builder by the structure of the economy. For example, a tax law which says that for every dollar of national income twenty cents will be collected in taxes is a structural relationship. (It takes the form $T = tY$, where T is tax collections, t is the tax rate—equal to 20%—and Y is national income). Another example of a constraint is government expenditures. If national economic policymakers decide that G will be a certain amount, this decision is a constraint which then gets built into the economic model.

Types of Equilibrium

What values do variables have when all the forces described by the model are operating? If there are forces which would disturb equilibrium, does the model seek out a new equilibrium or return to the old one? Recall from simple supply and demand analysis that a disturbance away from equilibrium supply and demand (say a price ceiling below equilibrium price) results in strong pressures to return to equilibrium. Such a model has the property of *stable* equilibrium.

A simple way to think of stable equilibrium is to picture a marble in a bowl. It will roll to the lowest point in the bowl. Any disturbance from that center point will result in swings back and forth in ever decreasing arcs until the marble comes to rest again at the lowest point.

If we place the marble on a level plane and push it away from the spot on which it is resting, it will move to a new spot on the plane and remain there. We refer to this as *metastable* equilibrium.

Finally, if the marble is gingerly balanced on the top of an inverted bowl, any disturbance moving the marble away from the top will send it rolling rapidly down the side of the bowl. This is an example of *unstable* equilibrium.

Statics and Dynamics

Most of the models used in this book are of the static variety—they are concerned with equilibrium at a point in time and in the forces which are operating. Ignored in static analysis is how the economy reached the equilibrium position and where it might be going. Comparative static analysis takes two points in time, describes the equilibrium position at each point, and describes the mechanism whereby the economy moved from one point to the other. Occasionally used are dynamic models (as in Chapters 17 and 18 on growth theory) which explicitly incorporate time as a variable.

SUGGESTED READING

Mark Blaug, *Economic Theory in Retrospect*, rev. ed. (Irwin, 1968). In his "Notes on Further Reading" (pp. 682–684), which follows an introduction to the method and scope of economics, Professor Blaug lists and briefly abstracts the extensive body of journal articles and monographs devoted to past and present controversies over economic methodology.

Milton Friedman, *Essays in Positive Economics* (University of Chicago Press, 1953). The first essay in this collection, "The Methodology of Positive Economics" (pp. 3–43), is now considered to be one of the major twentieth-century pronouncements on economic methods.

Daniel R. Fusfeld, *The Age of the Economist*, rev. ed. (Scott, Foresman, 1972). This 200-page paperback is an excellent and entertaining review of the history of economic thought. A good book to start with in getting oriented to the subject of economics.

Sherman Roy Krupp, ed., *The Structure of Economic Science* (Prentice-Hall, 1966). There are a number of outstanding essays in this volume. See, especially, Martin Bronfenbrenner's "A Middlebrow Introduction to Economic Methodology," pp. 5–24.

Richard G. Lipsey and Peter O. Steiner, *Economics*, 2nd ed. (Harper & Row, 1969). Part I, "Scope and Method" (pp. 2–63), is excellent. Careful reading of the first few chapters of this outstanding introductory textbook would aid in more readily understanding the material presented in our book. The Appendix to Chapter 3, "Some Common Techniques," for example, introduces just about all of the graphical and mathematical concepts employed in the chapters to follow in our book.

D. C. Rowan, *Output, Inflation and Growth* (London: Macmillan, 1968). Chapters 1–3 of this British macroeconomics textbook are an excellent introduction to "the process of economic analysis" within the context of an introduction to the "circular flow" of aggregate production and income.

Paul A. Samuelson, "Economists and the History of Ideas," *American Economic Review*, Vol. 52 (March 1962), 1–18. This essay, Professor Samuelson's 1961 presidential address to the American Economic Association, might be, even for readers with little prior knowledge of the history of economics, a helpful, highly entertaining excursion into the work of past economists.

Joseph A. Schumpeter, *History of Economic Analysis* (New York: Oxford University Press, 1954). Part I (pp. 3–47) is an excellent, historically-oriented introduction to economics.

National Income
and
Product Accounts

We mentioned in Chapter 1 that the production of more and better goods and services is one of the major goals of an economic system. The task of determining whether or not the United States is achieving this goal at any given time rests on timely and accurate quantitative measures of national output and income. Such estimates tell us, for example, how rapidly production is increasing, how rapidly incomes are increasing, and how heavily we are being taxed to pay for the goods and services being provided by government. In addition, although there may be differences in definitions, estimating procedures, and accuracy of estimation among countries, measures of national output and income give us some idea of how our aggregate income compares with those of other countries.

National income and product accounts, however, do more than simply satisfy our statistical curiosity. The most important function of income and product accounts is to aid government policymakers in influencing the performance of the economy—presumably toward the goals mentioned in Chapter 1. National income accounts are also useful in formulating and testing theoretical models. Most economists agree that for theories or models to be meaningful, it should be possible to verify them by testing them against reality. Hence, the variables, parameters, and relationships of a model must be observable and accurately measurable. If they are not measurable, there is no way to test the theories or models.

This chapter is designed primarily to explore those measures of economic variables which describe aggregate economic activity in the United States. The major responsibility for formulating and publishing these data rests with the National Income Division of the Office of Business Economics, U.S. Department of Commerce. Although its publication, the *Survey of Current Business*, is the originating source of most national income data, other good sources of data include *National Economic Trends*, prepared by the Federal Reserve Bank of St. Louis, the *Federal Reserve Bulletin*, published by the Board of Governors of the Federal Reserve System, and *Economic Indicators*, published by the Joint Economic Committee of Congress.

Attempts at estimating national income go back to Sir William Petty and his efforts in the seventeenth century to estimate the wealth of the United Kingdom. However, it was not until the 1930s that national accounts were first prepared elsewhere. In 1932 Congress directed the Department of Commerce to prepare studies identifying the composition and point of origin of U.S. income. The results of these studies, directed by Simon Kuznets, were published in 1934, and gave estimates of "national income"—defined as the sum of the earnings of the labor and property used to produce (final) goods and services—for the years 1929–1932.

Although the Department of Commerce published annual estimates of national income and related data throughout the 1930s, others formulated a broader concept. In 1934 the notion of the "value of GNP (Gross National Product)" was developed. The "value of GNP" differed from the concept of national income in that GNP included the replacement of depreciated capital equipment and indirect business taxes (sales and other taxes that enter into product price). GNP was given official status in 1942 when the Department of Commerce began to publish GNP estimates. Since 1947 it has provided both quarterly and annual estimates.

There are two ways to determine the value of GNP. One method, called the "product flow" approach, is to estimate the value of *final* goods and services produced during a given time period. The other method, called the "income flow" approach, is to estimate the *gross* income generated in producing the nation's goods and services during a given time period.

GROSS NATIONAL PRODUCT

In the product flow approach, GNP is defined as the *value* (evaluated at current market prices) of all *final* goods and services produced in a nation during *a given time period* expressed at an annual rate.[1] GNP is a flow, so a time dimension is required. GNP includes the purchases of all goods and services by domestic consumers, all goods and services by government (even, for reasons to be explained below, labor services), gross private domestic investment (including the change in business inventories), and net

1. Much of this discussion is based on two excellent sources of information about national accounting procedures in the United States: (1) Sheldon W. Stahl, "The U.S. National Income and Product Accounts," *Federal Reserve Bank of Kansas City Review* (May-June 1967), 11–19; and (2) *The National Income and Product Accounts of the United States*, 1929–1965, Office of Business Economics, U.S. Department of Commerce (U.S. Government Printing Office, 1966), viii–xi.

exports (exports minus imports). Although this definition of GNP seems simple enough, there are some conceptual difficulties.

Notice that we emphasize the word "value." The relative importance of each good or service (except government services) that enters into the GNP estimate is measured by its market price, and the sum of these prices (times the quantities produced) is GNP. The values of government goods and services (most of which do not have a market price) are determined by the cost of inputs used to produce them.

Final Goods
and Intermediate Goods

Another word emphasized is the word "final." It is necessary to distinguish between final and *intermediate* goods and services. Goods and services sold for resale during a given year, either in the same or modified form (for example, flour, steel, free-lance services), are intermediate goods. These goods and services are not counted in GNP. Final goods, on the other hand, do not re-enter the market. They are purchased by the ultimate consumer, and hence are part of GNP.

When all final goods are consumer goods, the distinction between final and intermediate goods is reasonably unambiguous. However, a portion of a nation's output is not currently consumed, but is nevertheless a final good. These goods form current capital, and the distinction between them and intermediate goods *is* perhaps ambiguous. An intermediate good is *always* resold during the given year in either the same or a modified form. A final capital good is *not* resold during the given year. For example, if Bethlehem Steel had a net increase in its steel inventory in a given year, the value of this increase would enter GNP. If, however, this steel were sold in the same year to General Motors to produce new automobiles, the steel would be an intermediate good and hence not included in GNP. The value of the steel would be included in the price of the new automobiles—which *would* be included in GNP.

Double Counting

Inclusion of the value of intermediate goods in gross national product would be *double counting*. It would result in a serious overstatement of GNP. If we add to the value of a final consumer good—bread, for example—the intermediate market value of its ingredients, we are including the same product at several stages. In growing wheat, value was produced; more value was added when the wheat was made into flour; and still more value was added when the flour was baked into bread. The GNP value of the product is not the added-up market prices of wheat, flour, and bread. It is the *value added* at each stage in the production process, or the *market value* of the bread alone (assuming it is purchased for family use and not for resale with meals at a restaurant). If properly computed, value added and market value are identical.

GNP measures only those goods and services that are currently sold in a market. Hence, nonmarket goods and services—for example, do-it-yourself child care, housekeeping, and home repair—are excluded from GNP, although the value of these services *would* be included if performed by paid nurses, maids, or plumbers. In fact, it was suggested several years ago that GNP in the United States would increase by over 25% if "imputed" values for housewives' services were included, which could be valued at the wages paid to domestics.

Leisure Time Activity

The GNP accounts also disregard the value of leisure time. For the average member of the work force in the United States, leisure time has doubled over the last century. Accompanying this increase in leisure time has been more do-it-yourself, nonmarket production. This neglected output is perhaps as important quantitatively as housewives' services. In addition, since the output from illegal activities and incomes generated from such activities are generally not divulged, they are also not included in GNP. One might argue, however, that if illegal activities could be accounted for they should be included, "since there is little logic to including the services of the hangman employed by the state but excluding the services of Murder, Inc."[2]

Imputed Values

Intangible items such as sports events, outdoor activities, and concerts which command a price are included in GNP. If, however, similar intangible services are free, they are not captured in GNP, although they provide satisfaction to the consumer in the same way as the intangibles that enter the marketplace. Failure to calculate an imputation for nonmarket activities poses a problem in interpreting GNP data if these imputed values vary significantly over the long run. If, for example, there is a long-run shift from housewives' services (a nonmarket activity) to professional housecleaning services and daycare centers (both market activities), then there would be an upward bias to GNP figures. For the short run, most of these

2. Myron H. Ross, *Income: Analysis and Policy* (McGraw-Hill, 1969), 49.

biases may be insignificant for the purpose of predicting national economic aggregates one to two years into the future.[3]

The "current-sales" orientation of GNP is the general rule, although there are exceptions. Prior to 1947, the rental paid to owners of rented dwellings was included as property income in GNP. Yet no corresponding inclusion was made for owner-occupied dwellings. Since rent represents the value of shelter produced by economic resources, ignoring the rental value of owner-occupied dwellings (a substantial portion of total dwellings) led to serious underestimation of the value of resources devoted to shelter. Hence, GNP accounts now include an imputed rental value for owner-occupied dwellings in the GNP estimate. That is, owners are now thought of as renting to themselves. The value of goods produced and consumed on farms is also given an imputed value and included as part of the GNP.

Table 2-1 shows GNP as it appears in official publications. The sum at the top of the current-dollar column represents the total spending on the nation's output, valued at current prices. Since "GNP in current prices" is obtained by valuing all currently produced final goods and services using current prices, when the general price level changes, current GNP also changes. In an inflationary period, for example, GNP in current dollars may rise, even though the volume of final goods and services produced remains the same. Hence, in order to measure *real* changes in GNP, it is necessary to adjust for changes which might occur in the general price level. In Table 2-1, the constant-dollar column shows the composition of GNP expressed in 1958 dollars.

Price Index

Adjustment for changes in the general price level is made by using a *price deflator* or *price index*. To illustrate how a price index is computed, assume that a given group of the many goods and services consumed by an "average" family is represented by x. This is called a "market basket" of goods and services. It might, for example, be twenty goods and services, including bread, milk, oranges, housing, dental care, and so forth. Let

$$P_1, P_2, \ldots, P_k, \ldots P_x$$

be the prevailing prices of these goods and services during a "base period" —some past period selected because it was a "normal" period. Let

$$C_1, C_2, \ldots C_k, \ldots C_x$$

be the quantities of the x goods and services consumed by the family during the base period. Multiplication of these x "consumption weights" by the

3. For a discussion of the complex problems of construction and interpretation of the National Income Accounts, see Martin J. Bailey, *National Income and the Price Level* (McGraw-Hill, 1971), Chapter 12.

Table 2-1   Gross National Product in Current and Constant Dollars 1972[a] (in Billions)

	Current Dollars	Constant (1958) Dollars
Gross National Product	1,151.8	789.5
Personal consumption expenditures	721.0	524.6
Durable Goods	116.1	102.8
Nondurable goods	299.5	220.5
Services	305.4	201.3
Gross private domestic investment	180.4	124.0
Fixed investment	174.5	119.4
Nonresidential	120.6	84.4
Structures	42.2	22.9
Producers' durable equipment	78.3	61.4
Residential structures	54.0	35.0
Nonfarm	53.2	34.5
Farm	.7	.5
Change in business inventories	5.9	4.6
Nonfarm	5.6	4.3
Farm	.3	.3
Government purchases of goods and services	254.6	142.8
Federal	105.8	61.6
National defense	75.9	
Other	29.9	
State and local	148.8	81.3
Net exports of goods and services	−4.2	−1.9
Exports	73.7	56.8
Imports	77.9	58.7

a) *Summed components may not equal totals, because of rounding.*
Source: *U. S. Department of Commerce, Office of Business Economics,* Survey of Current Business, *Vol. 53 (June 1973), p. 4.*

corresponding x prices yields this family's x cash flows, expressed at annual rates, for these goods and services. For the base period, the sum of goods and services consumed, multiplied by their prices, can be computed as follows:

$$\sum_{k=1}^{x} C_k P_k = C_1 P_1 + C_2 P_2 + \ldots + C_k P_k + \ldots + C_x P_x$$

This number will be a dollar amount, say $3940.0.

We next choose to identify this number with unity. That is, we let the base-period sum of the products of the consumption weights and the market prices be associated with an aggregate price level of 1.000.

Let $P_k{'}$ be the *current*-period market price of the kth product. Assuming that the quantities of the x products consumed by the representative family do not change much between the base period and the current period, they may be used again. Using the same base year, consumption weights will ensure that *all* of the change in the price index is due to price changes.

The sum of the $C_k P_k'$ term can be computed for the current period:

$$\sum_{k=1}^{x} C_k P_k'$$

This number might turn out to be 4018.8. If the base-period sum of 3940.0 is associated with unity—1.000—then the current-period sum of 4018.8 should be associated with 1.02. That is, $y = 1.02$ in the following equality:

$$\frac{4018.8}{y} = \frac{3940.0}{1.00}$$

Thus the prevailing level of the price index is 1.02. That is, given that base-period prices are unity, current prices are 1.02. Conventionally, price indexes are reported as price index times 100. So instead of reporting 1.02, we would report 102.0.

Real GNP (or the real value of any of the macroeconomic variables we refer to in this book) can be derived by dividing GNP in current dollars by the price index and multiplying by 100. For example, if the total expenditure on the collection of goods and services included in the sample market basket increases by 20% from the base period to the later period, the price index increases from 100 to 120. If GNP in current dollars were $800 billion in the base year with a price index of 100, and $1000 billion now, with a price index of 120, then real GNP would have increased from $800 billion to approximately $833 billion. The remainder of the apparent increase in GNP resulted from inflation.

The price index itself may be one of the three major U.S. price indexes: the consumer price index (CPI), the wholesale price index (WPI), and the GNP deflator. These indexes are discussed in greater detail in Chapter 13.

Components of GNP

The expenditure components shown in Table 2-1 encompass the four major demand sectors of the economy and the major uses of GNP. These include personal consumption expenditures, gross private domestic investment, government purchases of goods and services, and net exports of goods and services.

Personal consumption expenditures are broken into three categories—durables, nondurables, and services—on the basis of the durability of the product purchased. Goods normally lasting more than a year are considered durable goods. Nondurables are those goods which are normally consumed within a year of the time of purchase. Products consumed at the time of purchase are classified as services.

The national income accounts define personal consumption expenditures to include expenditures made by nonprofit institutions (for example, hospitals, churches, schools). The rental value of owner-occupied dwellings is also included in this component of GNP; the purchases of dwellings are included in investment.

Gross private domestic investment consists of the purchases of new capital goods by private business firms and nonprofit institutions. It includes commissions (brokerage fees to real-estate agents, for example) on the purchase of new and existing fixed assets (the most important of which is real estate). In addition, it includes the net change in the value of business inventories and the value of *all* newly constructed private dwellings.

Gross private domestic investment does not include the purchase of a newly produced asset that does not maintain or enhance the nation's capital stock, although selling costs associated with the purchase enter GNP as services rendered. The purchase of a share of stock, for example, is simply the transfer of ownership of an asset from one owner to another. Since such transactions do not maintain or add to the nation's capital stock, they are not included in GNP accounts as part of gross private domestic investment—although they are an "investment" from the point of view of the purchaser. Even if the share of stock were newly issued, it would not enter into GNP. However, if the funds received from the sale of the share of stock were used to purchase new productive equipment, the value of that purchase would enter the investment component of GNP.

A portion of the fixed-investment category (see Table 2-1) of the investment component of GNP consists of outlays made to replace that part of the nation's capital stock that has been "used up" in production during the given year. This part of investment spending covers the depreciation of the nation's capital stock, and is referred to as *capital consumption allowance*.

Depreciation estimates of nonfarm capital are computed on an original cost basis, while depreciation estimates of farm capital (tractors and other machinery) are computed on a replacement basis. Nonfarm capital is greater than farm capital. Hence, estimating depreciation on an original cost basis during an inflationary period understates depreciation costs and thus overstates profits, which, of course, causes GNP to be overestimated. To a certain extent this overestimation of GNP is compensated for by technological advances: since a given number of new machines can often do the job of a larger number of old ones, replacement costs are reduced.

Government expenditures represent the third portion of GNP. As shown in Table 2-1, government expenditures consist of purchases of goods and services, both military and civilian. These purchases are made from domestic and foreign businesses. Government expenditures also include the salaries paid to government employees.

While goods and services sold in the market command prices which presumably represent the values consumers and businesses place on them, government-provided goods and services, such as health, education, and protection, are measured by salaries paid to doctors, teachers, policemen, and military personnel, and the costs of drugs, supplies, equipment, police cars, guns, tanks, and so forth. It is quite likely that the cost of the inputs used to produce the services mentioned above "undervalue" the actual output, which would include time otherwise lost through illness, knowledge and skills gained by students in school, and the social and economic value of crimes and wars prevented.

Government expenditures not made for currently produced goods and services are not included in GNP. Such expenditures are called "transfer payments," and consist of unemployment compensation, relief payments, veteran's benefits, social security benefits, government interest payments, and grants-in-aid to local and state governments, to give some examples. Expenditures for these purposes represent merely a transfer of money from one group of the economy to another, the recipients of transfer payments, e.g., taxes and payments for social security. Such payments should not be included in GNP, since they are not a measure of a nation's economic output.

Net exports of goods and services is the remaining component of GNP. This component (also called *net foreign investment*) is the difference between the value of exports and the value of imports. Exports are domestically produced goods and services sold abroad. Imports are goods and services produced abroad, but consumed domestically. Expenditures on imports are included in the expenditures of the various spending units in the GNP breakdown. Since imports represent output produced abroad (and hence generate income abroad), while exports represent output produced domestically (and hence generate income domestically), the former must be deducted from the latter to determine "net exports."

NATIONAL INCOME

In the income flow approach, the *gross* income generated in producing the nation's output equals GNP. However, the value of GNP is not synonymous with the remuneration received by the owners of the resources used in producing the nation's output. Non-income charges are the difference. They consist of capital consumption allowances (depreciation) and indirect business taxes. When non-income charges are excluded, income-flow measurement yields an estimate of "national income" which is less than that estimated by the product-flow approach.

National income is the aggregate labor and property earnings generated in the production of the nation's goods and services during a given year. Table 2-2 illustrates the major components.

Table 2-2   National Income by Type 1972[a] (in Billions of Current Dollars)

National Income	935.6
Compensation of employees	705.3
Wages and salaries	629.5
Private	491.9
Military	20.6
Government civilian	114.0
Supplements to wages and salaries	78.8
Employer contributions for social security	38.5
Other labor income	40.3
Proprietors' income	75.2
Business and professional	55.6
Farm	19.6
Corporate profits	88.2
Before taxes	94.3
Tax liability	41.3
After taxes	53.0
Dividends	26.4
Undistributed profits	26.6
Inventory valuation adjustment	−6.0
Rental income of persons	25.6
Net interest	41.3

a) *Summed components may not equal totals, because of rounding.*
Source: *U. S. Department of Commerce, Office of Business Economics*, Survey of Current Business, *Vol. 53 (June 1973), p. 5.*

Components of National Income

Compensation of employees consists of wages, salaries, commissions, tips, and bonuses. Payment in kind—for example, the value of food and housing provided to employees as part of the remuneration for their work—is also included, as are employer contributions to social security and private pension funds.

Proprietor income and corporate profits are the earnings, both monetary and *in kind*, of sole proprietorships, partnerships, corporations, and producers' cooperatives before taxes.

Rental income and *net interest* are the remaining major components. Rental income consists of the earnings of persons from the rental of real property, including rental imputed to owner-occupied nonfarm dwellings. Net interest includes all actual and imputed interest received by individuals and governments. Interest paid by the government is excluded since it is a transfer payment.

Relationship Between National Product and National Income

We define GNP as the value of goods and services currently produced. Net National Product (NNP), as shown in Table 2-3, is GNP less capital consumption allowances (depreciation). From the point of view of economic welfare or economic growth, NNP is perhaps a more useful measure of how the economy has performed during a given year. Worn-out machines that are no longer used in production should not be considered as currently available to the economy.

The difference between GNP when it is estimated by the product-flow approach and when it is estimated by the income-flow approach (including non-income charges) is called *statistical discrepancy*. Since incomes are estimated primarily from income-tax reports, and since many incomes (for example, farm and professional) are understated, the income approach often produces a lower estimate of GNP than the product approach.

Disposable Personal Income

National income is *not* a measure of the income available to consumers to spend. To determine consumer "spendable" income, or *disposable personal income*, it is necessary to adjust the estimate national income in the following way (see Table 2-4).

We determine *personal income* by deducting from national income all corporate profits, business inventory evaluation adjustments, and employer contributions to social security; and by adding all government transfer payments to individuals, net interest paid by all consumers, dividends, and

Table 2-3   Relation of Gross National Product and National Income 1972 (in Billions of Current Dollars)

Gross National Product	1,151.8
Less: Capital consumption allowances	103.7
Equals: *Net National Product*	1,048.1
Less: Indirect business tax and nontax liability	110.1
Business transfer payments	4.9
Statistical discrepancy	−.8
Plus: Subsidies less current surplus of government enterprises	1.7
Equals: *National Income*	935.6

Source: *U. S. Department of Commerce, Office of Business Economics,* Survey of Current Business, *Vol. 53 (June 1973), p. 5.*

Table 2-4   Disposable Personal Income, 1972 (in Billions of Current Dollars)

National Income	935.6
Less: Corporate profits and inventory valuation adjustment	88.2
Contributions for social security	74.0
Plus: Government transfer payments to individuals	99.1
Interest paid by government (net) and by consumers	31.6
Dividends	24.4
Business transfer payments	4.9
Equals: *Personal Income*	935.9
Less: Personal Contributions for Social Security	35.5
Less: Personal Tax Payments	140.8
Equals: *Disposable Personal Income*	795.1

Source: *U. S. Department of Commerce, Office of Business Economics,* Survey of Current Business, *Vol. 53 (June 1973), p. 5.*

business transfer payments. To get *disposable personal income*—what actually gets into the hands of consumers—we must subtract workers' contributions to social security, and personal taxes—federal, state, and local.

NATIONAL ACCOUNTS AND TRUE ECONOMIC WELFARE

Although the national income accounts provide a useful tool for analyzing the state of the U.S. economy, the accounts are not precise measures of economic activity. This should be obvious from our brief discussion of the conceptual difficulties associated with developing the account estimates. Without them, however, it would be difficult to know the "state of the national economy," both now and in the past, and it would be exceedingly difficult to formulate policies that would guide the economy toward desirable future goals.

Even if the national income accounts did provide precise measures of economic activity, these measures cannot be regarded as an index of the economic well-being of the nation's population. One reason for this is that total GNP estimates alone can be misleading. A more useful measure than GNP of economic well-being is *per capita* or *per family* GNP. However, even when per capita measures are used, various difficulties of measuring economic well-being arise. Some nations may have a high per capita GNP with a large percentage of the population living below the poverty level. Kuwait, for example, enjoys a very high per capita income, but a substantial percentage of the people live in poverty.

Table 2-5   Gross National Product and MEW, Various Years, 1929–1965 (Billions of Dollars, 1958 prices)

	1929	1935	1945	1947	1954	1958	1965
1. Gross national product	203.6	169.5	355.2	309.9	407.0	447.3	617.8
2. Capital consumption, NIPA	−20.0	−20.0	−21.9	−18.3	−32.5	−38.9	−54.7
3. Net national product, NIPA	183.6	149.5	333.3	291.6	374.5	408.4	563.1
4. NIPA final output reclassified as regrettables and intermediates							
a. Government	−6.7	−7.4	−146.3	−20.8	−57.8	−56.4	−63.2
b. Private	−10.3	−9.2	−9.2	−10.9	−16.4	−19.9	−30.9
5. Imputations for items not included in NIPA							
a. Leisure	339.5	401.3	450.7	466.9	523.2	554.9	626.9
b. Nonmarket activity	85.7	109.2	152.4	159.6	211.5	239.7	295.4
c. Disamenities	−12.5	−14.1	−18.1	−19.1	−24.3	−27.6	−34.6
d. Services of public and private capital	29.7	24.2	31.0	36.7	48.9	54.8	78.9
6. Additional capital consumption	−19.3	−33.4	−11.7	−50.8	−35.2	−27.3	−92.7
7. Growth requirement	−46.1	−46.7	−65.8	+5.4	−63.1	−78.9	−101.8
8. Sustainable MEW	543.6	573.4	716.3	858.6	961.3	1,047.7	1,241.1

NIPA = national income and products accounts.
Source: *W. Nordhouse and J. Tobin, "Is Growth Obsolete?"* Fiftieth Anniversary Colloquium, V, *NBER, Columbia Univ. Press, 1972.*

Even a real increase in per capita GNP more equitably distributed does not necessarily mean that a society is better off. A proportionate increase in "disproducts" (undesirable side effects) may have accompanied the rise in real GNP, resulting in little or no net improvement in economic well-being. Such side effects are common in a modern economy. Examples include mine slag, piles of junked cars, mountains of garbage, polluted air and water, and urban decay.

(It is ironic that the elimination of disproducts generates products. If, in the process of producing steel, a steel mill pollutes a lake and then uses additional resources to clean it up, two items enter GNP: the output of the steel mill and the expenditure to clean up the lake. In fact, any expenditure on reducing environmental deterioration would enter GNP as increased real output!)

The desire for a better measure of economic well-being than our present GNP has prompted a group of social scientists to recommend the development of several measures to supplement the national income and product accounts.[4] These "social indicators" would tell us the true health of society, the extent of social mobility, the extent of poverty, and the impact of crime on our lives. Such a comprehensive set of statistics would tell us whether society is progressing or not, much as the national income and product accounts tell us by how much output is increasing.

One challenge to our way of computing national income and national product has come from William Nordhaus and James Tobin, who presented a methodology for computing a "measure of economic welfare" (MEW).[5] The MEW is an adjustment to GNP to account for shifts in preference for leisure, the disamenities of pollution and much of urban life, and other disproducts. The adjustments to GNP show, as might be expected, that GNP is rising more rapidly than MEW, and the gap is widening. Nevertheless, MEW *is* rising on a per capita basis—in other words, economic growth, as measured by GNP, is still a real improvement in our economic well-being, as measured by MEW. Table 2-5 shows the relationship among GNP and the adjustments recommended by Nordhaus and Tobin.

CIRCULAR FLOW

National output, expenditures, and income can be summarized as a circular flow, shown in Figure 2-1. The circular flow diagram displays three of the four types of spending on gross output of the economy: personal consumption expenditures, gross private domestic investment, and government expenditures. Net exports are excluded from the flow diagram because the macroeconomic models that we present in the first two parts of the book are representative of *closed* economies, that is, economies in which net exports are assumed to be zero. Reasons for this assumption are given below.

The symbols given in Figure 2-1 are consistent with the symbols used throughout the book, although there is more detail in the circular flow than in subsequent models. Summarized below are some of the relationships and notation that appear frequently in the book.

4. See *Toward A Social Report*, U.S. Department of Health, Education, and Welfare (U.S. Government Printing Office, January 1969).
5. W. Nordhaus and J. Tobin, "Is Growth Obsolete?" *Fiftieth Anniversary Colloquium*, V, National Bureau of Economic Research (Columbia University Press, 1972).

Figure 2-1 Circular flow diagram

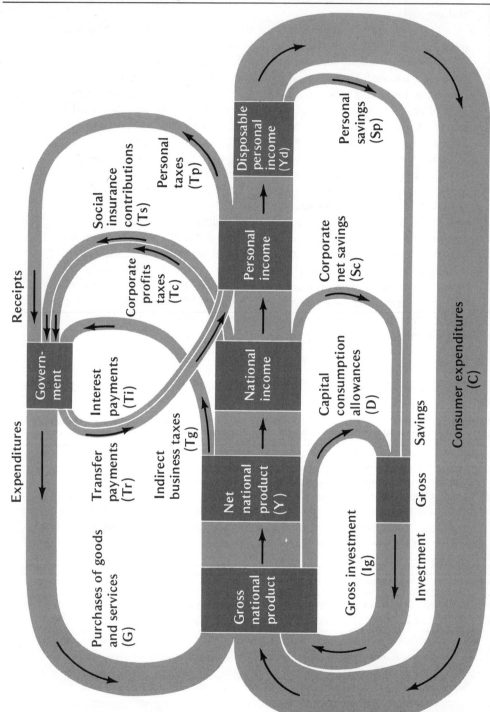

C = consumption expenditures

I_g = gross investment

G = government expenditures

I = net investment

D = depreciation

T = net taxes

T_p = personal taxes

T_g = indirect business taxes

T_s = social insurance contributions

T_c = corporate profits taxes

T_r = transfer payments

T_i = interest payments

S_p = personal savings

S_c = corporate savings

Gross National Product: $\text{GNP} = C + I_g + G$

Net National Product: $Y = C + I + G$

Net Investment: $I = I_g - D$

Disposable Personal Income: $Y_d = Y - T$

Net Taxes: $T = T_p + T_g + T_s + T_c - (T_r + T_i)$

Consumption Expenditures: $C = Y_d - S_p$

Saving: $S = S_p + S_c$

If we assume a closed, *private* economy, that is, an economy without government, as well as without foreign trade, our system of equations becomes:

Gross National Product: $\text{GNP} = C + I_g$

Net National Product: $Y = C + I$

Net Investment: $I = I_g - D$

Disposable Personal Income: $Y_d = Y$

Consumption Expenditures: $C = Y - S$

Saving: $S = S_p + S_c$

The variables in these equations are flow variables.

Stocks and Flows

Economic variables are either "stocks" or "flows."[6] A flow variable requires a time dimension, such as output *per* day or output *per* year. In contrast, a "stock" simply requires a *date*, such as the amount of coins, currency, and demand deposits held by the nonbank public in the United States at 3 p.m. on May 31, 1974. A stock is often an average, such as the average quantity of money managers of the commercial and central banking systems want to supply during the third quarter of 1974.

Data is often reported on a quarterly basis, so economists often use a quarter of a year as a "period of analysis" but express data on an annual basis. Thus the expression "quarterly totals at annual rates" is used

---

6. Economists often use variables which are *ratios* of stocks, flows, or stocks and flows. An interest rate, for example, is the ratio of a flow (so many dollars of interest per year) to a stock (so many dollars of principal).

throughout this book. Whenever a flow variable appears, it is a quarterly total, expressed at an annual rate.

The aggregate output of goods and services (GNP) is viewed here as a flow, a steady stream of goods and services from the beginning to the end of the period. The concept of output as a flow can be thought of in terms of someone sitting in a factory watching a continuously moving assembly line. If this person were asked to describe the flow of commodities in dollar terms, his answer would be largely meaningless unless he attached a time dimension to the number. A *given*, smoothly continuous flow could be defined as $100 worth per hour, $2400 worth per day, or $219,000 worth per quarter. All these statements are descriptions of the same flow. For our purposes, however, we would want the man to reply, "During this quarter, $876,000 worth of goods flowed by, expressed at an annual rate."

A Note on Flow of Funds

The national income accounts can be extended to include the financial sector—the flow of money and other financial assets and the occurrence of debt. The purpose of such an extension is to emphasize the interdependence between financial flows and the flows of goods and services.

Flow-of-funds accounts are a method of measuring financial flows throughout the nation's economy. Flow-of-funds accounts are published quarterly in the *Federal Reserve Bulletin*, and the information is used regularly by the Federal Reserve System. By dividing the economy into sectors, we can record the sales and purchases of all goods and services by sectors, capital flows among sectors, and changes in liquid assets (and financial positions in general) of each sector. Included in flow-of-funds accounts are *all* transactions that are affected by the use of money or credit. They include, for example, the purchases of old assets, as well as newly produced goods and services. In addition, the accounts reflect purely monetary transactions, such as payments made on mortgages or purchases of securities. Hence, flow-of-funds accounts contain more information than do national income accounts.

Flow-of-funds accounts classify sectors in the following way: households, businesses, state and local governments, federal government, the rest of the world, and the financial sector. The financial sector consists of the monetary authorities (including the Treasury), commercial banks, and nonbank financial institutions. Each sector's account records the *sources* and *uses* of money and credit resulting from economic activity. In addition, flow-of-funds data are divided into *assets* and *liabilities*.

The "source-use" classification refers to flows, and the "asset-liability" classification to stocks of funds. Perhaps an analogy with business accounting statements will clarify the use of these terms. The income statement of a firm lists the income and costs of operation for a given time period;

hence, it is a *flow* concept. The balance sheet gives a picture at a given moment in time of the financial condition of the firm. Sources and uses of funds are analogous to the income statement. These data measure increments in financial holdings of each sector. Assets and liabilities are analogous to the balance sheet; these accounts portray a picture of the stock of financial holdings outstanding at a given moment in time (at the end of some specified period) for each sector.

Since flow-of-funds accounts provide a measure of money and credit flows and stocks, as well as the flows and stocks of goods and services, they should be of value to policymakers, both federal and private.

SUGGESTED READING

William I. Abraham, *National Income and Economic Accounting* (Prentice-Hall, 1969). This informative book provides an exploration of all the different national accounting systems now in use in the world. National income accounts, input-output tables, flow of funds, and national wealth balance sheets are discussed.

Morris A. Copeland, *Study of Money Flows in the United States* (National Bureau of Economic Research, 1952). Copeland developed the first flow-of-funds accounts. His book is a landmark in this area of analysis.

For general summaries of this alternative approach to measuring aggregate economic activity, see Sumiye Okubo, "The Flow-of-Funds Accounts," *Federal Reserve Bank of Richmond Review* (June 1970), 8–12; and Basil J. Moore, "National Flow-of-Funds and Balance-Sheet Accounts," in *An Introduction to the Theory of Finance* (The Free Press, 1968), 19–27.

John W. Kendrick, *Economic Accounts and Their Uses* (McGraw-Hill, 1972). This text provides a thorough treatment of the measurement and interpretation of the hundreds of items in the National Income Accounts.

Simon Kuzents, *National Income and Its Composition*, 1919–1938 (National Bureau of Economic Research, 1954). Part I of this book consists of an excellent discussion of the concept of national income, its distribution, and its methods of measurement.

Richard and Nancy Ruggles, *National Income Accounts and Income Analysis*, 2nd ed. (McGraw-Hill, 1956). The first part of this book builds up the national income concept from the accounts of individual firms, governmental units, and households.

Paul A. Samuelson, *Economics*, 9th ed. (McGraw-Hill, 1973). The last part of Chapter 10 contains a discussion of how economists can begin to adjust the GNP numbers in an effort to get a more meaningful estimate of economic growth and welfare. In an effort to arrive at an estimate of Net Economic Welfare (NEW), Samuelson suggests that we adjust the GNP number for certain items such as the value of leisure, housewives' services, and other items summarized as "disamenities of modern urbanization." Samuelson's discussion borrows heavily from the pioneering study by William Nordhaus and James Tobin, "Is Growth Obsolete?" *Fiftieth Anniversary Colloquium, V* (National Bureau of Economic Research, Columbia University Press, 1972).

David L. Sills, ed., *The International Encyclopedia of the Social Sciences*, (London: Macmillan, 1968). John W. Kendrick's "National Income and Product Accounts" (Vol. 11, pp. 19–33) is an excellent summary of the subject. Richard Ruggles' "Economic Data" (Vol. 4, pp. 365–369) treats very briefly the following topics: (1) types of economic data available; (2) problems of measurement and reliability; and (3) validity of measurement and operationalism.

Sheldon Stahl, "The U.S. National Income and Product Accounts," *Federal Reserve Bank of Kansas City Review* (May–June 1967), 11–19. This article gives a brief historical review of the present U.S. national income and product accounts, and discusses two of the major measures of aggregate economic activity: gross national product (GNP) and national income.

A NEOCLASSICAL APPROACH TO MACROECONOMIC UNDERSTANDING

PART

In the next two chapters we present a summary of neoclassical macro-economics. As with any such summary, it is a bit of a caricature. But we hope it is a helpful way of viewing the approach to economics *which Keynes attacked*. We begin with a discussion of neoclassical *micro*economics, which provides a foundation for understanding the central neoclassical conclusion: that a national economy is at equilibrium only under full employment of resources.

Chapter 3 reviews microeconomic theory, and presents the theory of the aggregate demand for labor, which stems from the assumption of profit maximization of firms, and from the technological relationship between inputs and outputs known as the aggregate production function. Chapter 4 introduces the theory of the supply of labor, and generates an aggregate labor supply curve. With the introduction and development of these micro-economic constructs, it is possible to develop a neoclassical macroeconomic model in which real output and employment is shown to be independent of the quantity of money and the general price level.

The neoclassical belief that the quantity of money only affected the general price level—that it had no direct effect on real output and employment—was critically examined by Paul Samuelson:

> From January 2, 1932, until an indeterminate date in 1937, I was a [neo]classical monetary [macro]theorist. . . .
>
> Essentially, we believed that in the longest run and in ideal models, the amount of money did not matter. Money could be "neutral" and in many conditions the hypothesis that it was could provide a good first or last approximation to the facts. To be sure, Hume, Fisher, and Hawtrey had taught us that, under dynamic conditions, an increase in money might lead to "money illusion" and might cause substantive changes—e.g., a shift to debtor-entrepreneurs and away from creditor-rentiers, a forced-saving shift to investment and away

from consumption, a lessening of unemployment, a rise in wholesale prices relative to sticky retail prices and wage rates, *et cetera*.

But all this was at a second level of approximation, representing relatively transient aberrations. Moreover, this tended to be taught in applied courses on business cycles, money and finance, and economic history rather than in courses on pure theory. In a real sense there *was* a dichotomy in our minds; we were schizophrenics. From 9 to 9:50 a.m. we presented a simple quantity theory of neutral money. There were then barely ten minutes to clear our palates for the 10 to 10:50 discussion of how an engineered increase in M would help the economy. In mid-America in the mid-1930s, we neoclassical economists tended to be mild inflationists, jackasses crying in the wilderness and resting our case essentially on sticky prices and costs, and on expectations.

Returning to the 9 o'clock hour, we thought that *real* outputs and inputs and price ratios depended essentially in the longest run on real factors, such as tastes, technology, and endowments. The stock of money we called M (or, to take account of [demand] bank deposits, we worked in effect with a velocity-weighted average of M and M'; however, a banking system with fixed reserve and other ratios would yield M' proportional to M, so M alone would usually suffice). An increase in M—usually we called it a doubling on the ground that after God created unity he created the second integer—would cause a proportional increase in *all* prices (tea, salt, female labour, land rent, share or bond prices) and values (expenditure on tea or land, share dividends, interest income, taxes). You will hardly believe it, but few economists in those days tried to write down formal equations for what they were thinking. Had we been asked to choose which kinds of equation system epitomized our thinking, I believe at first blush we would have specified:

A. Write down a system of real equations involving *real* outputs and inputs, and *ratios* of prices (values), and depending essentially on real tastes, technologies, market structures, and endowments. Its properties are invariant to change in the stock of money M.

B. Then append a fixed-supply-of-M equation that pins down (or up) the absolute price level, determining the scale factor that was essentially indeterminate in set A. This could be a quantity equation of exchange—$MV = PQ$—or some other non-homogeneous equation. . . .*

The goal of the next two chapters is to present a model in which the above two-part specification is carefully and explicitly developed. We are not concerned with the "business cycles, money and finance, and economic

* Paul A. Samuelson, "What Classical and Neoclassical Monetary Theory Really Was," *Canadian Journal of Economics*, Vol. 1 (February 1968), 1–2.

history" contributions to macroeconomic understanding offered by the preKeynesian writers. We focus on their "ideal model."

Although our primary objective in the next two chapters is to present the core of a single "neoclassical" macroeconomic model, we should first point out that it is difficult to get people to agree on just how the adjective "neoclassical" should be used in economics. First, the ascendency of neoclassical economics was the ascendency of *micro*economic theory. Most economic theory developed *before* the 1870s would today be considered macroeconomic. But from the 1870s to the 1930s, the period during which neoclassical macroeconomics was developed, microeconomics was dominant. The theories of the firm, household, and industry developed during the last few decades of the nineteenth century and the first few decades of the twentieth century are taught today as *the* theories. In fact, microeconomics courses are frequently described in many college and university catalogs as "a study of neoclassical value and distribution theory." Thus, our task here is a little difficult because we must present a neoclassical macroeconomic model which is to some extent a consolidation of relevant portions of neoclassical microeconomic analysis.

Second, neoclassical macroeconomics was developed on a broad front by a large number of writers, many of whom were totally unaware of the existence of their "colleagues." The major developments associated with the "neoclassical school" cut across "school" and national boundaries. The theory of money, interest, and the general price level associated with neoclassical economics, for example, had strong roots in the earlier, *classical* school of (among others) David Ricardo (1772–1823) and John Stuart Mill (1806–1873). Also, it was developed simultaneously by (among others) Alfred Marshall, 1842–1924 (English); Léon Walras, 1834–1910 (French-Swiss); Knut Wicksell, 1851–1926 (Swedish); and Irving Fisher, 1867–1947 (American), all of whom are placed in different "schools."

Third, while the key features of *other* past macroeconomic systems have been almost completely replaced, absorbed into modern work, or accepted but never really expanded, the basic propositions of neoclassical macroeconomics are even today being refined and expanded. The system is very much alive. It is still the source of fresh insights into the workings of a modern economy. During the 1960s and 1970s there has been a general revival of neoclassical macroeconomics. Some very important neoclassical results are being proved again, as is discussed later in this book. The propositions underlying the dynamic version of neoclassical macroeconomics have been refurbished and combined with more recent propositions (and worked on with recently developed empirical techniques) to increase our understanding of the *growth* process of an economy. The same is true of the static version of neoclassical macroeconomics. The propositions underlying the key results of the static aggregate neoclassical model (discussed in the next two chapters) have been continually refined and clarified.

Neoclassical
Microeconomics (I)

NEOCLASSICAL MACROECONOMICS
AND PERFECT COMPETITION

Neoclassical macroeconomic doctrine, that is, the macroeconomic ideas which represent the generally accepted wisdom before the Keynesian revolution, is based on a belief in the "natural" economy's ability to achieve full employment of the nation's resources. The "natural" economy is one which is free from governmental manipulation or monopoly elements in any significant sense; it is an economy of free markets. In fact, the foundation upon which neoclassical macroeconomics is built is the theoretical context of perfect competition. Since understanding the theory of perfect competition is basic to the development of our neoclassical model, it is necessary to introduce its five basic characteristics.

First, all members of the economy must qualify as "rational," according to economists' standards. That is, each person must act to advance his own self-interest. This assumption is not designed to preclude the possibility of charitable or sympathetic behavior. It does serve, however, to make behavior predictable. Irrational, possibly even masochistic, economic behavior—such as people buying a product for $200 when the same product is available from the same supplier for $150—is ruled out.

Second, all members must know about past performances, present alternatives, and future potentialities. This assumption of "perfect knowledge" does not necessarily require *total* certainty about a future event. The assumption in its most general form simply means that events during a given period of time, such as a quarter of a year, can be predicted. An example of this is a case where the managers of a firm know that if they hire 25 men to work with 900 units of capital equipment, the firm will, *without a shadow of doubt*, produce 30,000 units of output during a quarter of a year. It is in the same class of argument to say that, under these conditions, the firm can be 95 % confident of producing between 25,000 and 35,000 units of output per quarter.

A particularly difficult problem for economists is *uncertainty*, which must be distinguished from *risk*. "Risk" is something capable of actuarial calculation, such as computing with statistical techniques that the managers of a firm can be 95 % "confident" that the actual result will be within a certain range. "Uncertainty" is when we simply do not know—when there are no grounds for an actuarial calculation.

Third, all elements of the economy must be "atomistic." That is, an individual buyer or seller of a good or service (including those used as factors of production) must be such a negligible portion of the total market in which he is operating that his actions, alone, cannot affect the market as a whole. For example, when *one* person quits smoking cigarettes, the tobacco growers, cigarette manufacturers, wholesalers, and so forth never notice his decision. More importantly, from the standpoint of perfect competition, a single buyer of cigarettes must accept the market-determined price (determined by industry-wide supply and demand) as a fact of life. By purchasing more or fewer packs of cigarettes (or none at all), a single buyer will not influence the market. When this assumption is assumed to hold for every buyer and seller of every product and service, all individuals in the economy are "price takers": they must all accept market-determined prices as given.

Fourth, all resources and final products must be free to move in time and space. That is, the costs and frictions associated with transporting factors of production and final products from one place to another as well as from one point in time to another are ignored. This is done for convenience as well as to allow the assumption to be made that resources will always be used in the most efficient way and that final goods and services will always be delivered to those who can and want to buy them.

Fifth, the economy must be "planned" by the market. Most goods and services are assumed to be produced by firms in business to make profits. Public authorities are assumed to limit their activities to the "traditional" duties of government, such as providing for national defense, public health, widows, orphans, and perhaps education.

SAY'S LAW

The cornerstone of the neoclassical approach to macroeconomics is the notion that in a perfectly competitive model, after any "temporary disequilibrium" that might exist has worked itself out, full utilization of labor as well as other resources will always prevail.

If we decide to accept perfect competition as defining our basic theoretical context—our first, most "ideal" approximation of reality—we must then, by extension, assume that during some future time interval, say a year or a quarter of a year, *all incomes will be consumed or saved*. This is not the same as saying that after the fact, or *ex post*, all national income during a past period *has been* consumed or saved. Such a statement is true by definition, because any portion of national product not consumed by households or added to capital by business will add up as unintended investment in the form of unexpected inventory accumulation. The neoclassical statement is that all incomes *will be* consumed or saved. It is a behavioral statement, not an accounting identity. It is a statement about next quarter, not last quarter.

Since uncertainty, as opposed to risk, has been assumed away, *no incentives exist to hoard purchasing power*. There is no rational justification for stuffing wages into mattresses or holding profits in company safes. Furthermore, there are no barriers constraining the movement of resources in time or space. Perfect competition also implies the absence of income recipients who are on the one hand satiated with consumer goods and on the other hand do not have any investment outlet for their savings. Hence *all savings will flow into investment*.

The result of this assumption, that all incomes will be consumed or invested, is called *Say's law*. It is attributed to Jean Baptiste Say (1767–1832), a French popularizer of Adam Smith's *Wealth of Nations* (1776). Say's law is usually summarized as *supply creates its own demand*. The assumption and result are, of course, related in an "if ... then ..." fashion. *If* all incomes generated during some future time period will be either consumed or invested, *then* all goods produced during the time period will, taken together, be sold. In a perfectly competitive economy, so the argument goes, shortages as well as gluts of national product are impossible.

Given the existence of perfect competition in the economy, the neoclassical model consists of (1) a theory of aggregate demand, (2) a theory of aggregate supply, and (3) a model of the determination of the general price level. Say's law and the flexibility of all prices assures sufficient aggregate demand. Aggregate supply is determined in the labor market (and by past investment decisions). Since wages are flexible, labor unemployment is ruled out. The general price level is determined by the quantity of money supplied and the demand for money. Combining these three analytical constructs yields a simplified, but essentially accurate, neoclassical model.

In the remainder of this chapter and in the next, while we are developing a noeclassical macroeconomic model, we work in what may seem to be a backward fashion. We work first with the *real* output of each firm (which may cut across industry lines) and use this concept to determine the *equilibrium* level of real aggregate output, Y^*. We then introduce the concept of money, and with Y^*, determine the *equilibrium* level of the aggregate price index, P^*. After all this is done, we go back and express our relevant aggregative variables in current-period dollars. For example, current "nominal" aggregate output—that is, current aggregate output valued at current prices—would be P^*Y^*.

PRODUCTION

The production or supply "side" of neoclassical macroeconomics is based on the assumption that there are n perfectly competitive firms, each producing one or more final products. To avoid the problem of "double counting," we concentrate solely on the production of *final* goods and services. That is, the output of any of our n firms cannot be counted toward aggregate output as a final product—such as flour—and *also* be counted as an intermediate product (an input) to produce another product—such as bread—during the current period. *All* our firms produce *only* final goods and services. All inputs used by the managers of each of these n firms are categorized as either labor (N) or capital (K). Both labor and capital are assumed to be homogeneous—it is impossible, for example, to distinguish among various units of labor.

In reality, a firm's capital stock—its machinery, buildings, goods in process, inventories of raw materials and finished goods—is constantly changing. Additions and deletions are made almost every working day. In Parts I and II of this book, however, each firm is assumed to hold a known endowment of capital at the beginning of the period of analysis, and it is assumed that no noticeable net changes in these initial holdings occur during the period. The period of analysis is assumed to be so short that *all* deletions and additions from the capital stocks of each of the n firms can be ignored. These simplifying assumptions about capital allow us to avoid certain analytical complexities, such as those associated with the average age of capital or with the amortization funds needed to replace depleted or depreciated capital. Yet the results that are shown in this and the following chapters—the key results in static neoclassical and Keynesian macroeconomics—can still be obtained.

The ith Firm's Production Function

The base-period dollar value of the quarterly output of any firm (at an annual rate)—say, the "ith" firm, where i could be any number from 1 to n—may be denoted as Y_i. Thus, Y_i, the contribution of the ith firm to aggregate output, depends on the ith firm's given endowment of capital ($\bar{K}_i$)—where the bar over K is simply a way of denoting that it is a predetermined variable—and the amount of labor (N_i) its managers decide to hire. The various maximum amounts of real output (the dependent variable) the managers of the ith firm can get "depends on," or is a function of, the prevailing levels of labor and capital (the two independent variables).

The dependency of real output on inputs can be expressed as

$$Y_i = F_i(N_i, \bar{K}_i) \tag{3-1}$$

Table 3-1

N_{26}	Y_{26}
4	120,000
9	180,000
16	240,000
25	300,000
36	360,000
49	420,000

Equation 3-1, which is a production function in general form, should be read "the real output of the ith firm is some (unspecified) function of the amount of labor its managers employ and a given amount of capital." Capital as well as output are assumed to be measured in base-period dollars. The managers of the firm must accept this capital stock as a fact of life and do the best they can with it.

For some particular firm, say the 26th, the *explicit* production function might be

$$Y_{26} = AN_{26}^{\alpha}\bar{K}_{26}^{1-\alpha} \qquad (3\text{-}2)$$

where A and α are constants determined by the 26th firm's prevailing technology.

If $A = 60$, $\alpha = \frac{1}{2}$, and $\bar{K}_{26} = \$1$ million (base period), the 26th firm's production function would become

$$Y_{26} = (60)(N_{26}^{1/2})(1,000,000^{1/2})$$

$$Y_{26} = 60,000\,N_{26}^{1/2} \qquad (3\text{-}3)$$

By substituting levels of N_{26} between zero and fifty which have "nice" (easy to compute) square roots into Equation 3-3, we obtain Table 3-1. These combinations of N_{26} and Y_{26} are graphed in Figure 3-1.

The curve drawn in Figure 3-1 through the points given in Table 3-1 is simply a graphical version of our numerical production function, Equation 3-2. It shows the maximum amounts of output, expressed in base-period dollars per year, which can be obtained from between zero and fifty employees—if $A = 60$, $\alpha = \frac{1}{2}$, and $\bar{K}_{26} = \$1$ million (base period). It should be clear from inspecting Equation 3-2 that a larger level of $\bar{K}_{26}$ would produce an entirely different curve in Figure 3-1, even if α and A remain the same. With more capital, a given number of employees would be able to produce more output than they could before. Also, inspection of Figure 3-1 should show that as N_{26} increases, Y_{26} increases, but at a decreasing rate. That is, a 10% increase in the 26th firm's labor force *will* bring about an increase in its output, but by less than 10%.

Figure 3-1

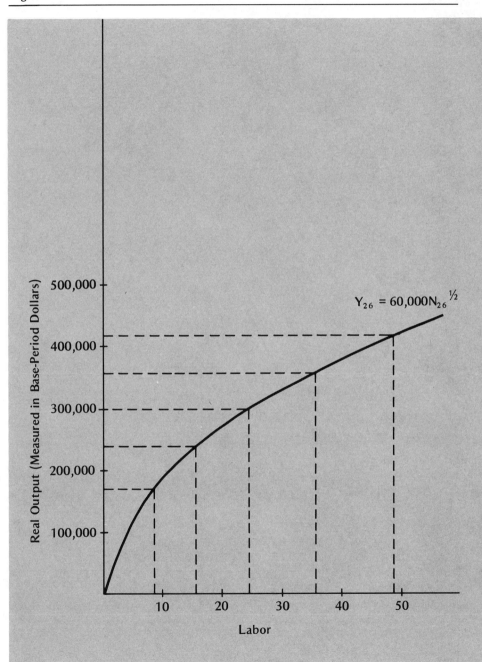

$Y_{26} = 60,000N_{26}{}^{1/2}$

Figure 3-2

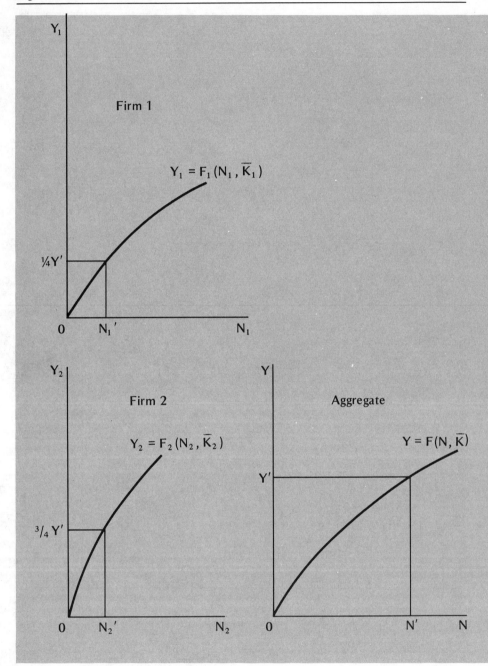

An Aggregate Production Function

Obtaining a theoretical production function for an economy as a whole involves major difficulties associated with going from individual to aggregate relationships. An aggregate production function cannot be obtained simply by adding the n firms' production functions together, because the functions are nonlinear. Assume that the economy is composed of only two firms and that their production functions are

$$Y_i = A_i N_i^{\alpha_i} \bar{K}_i^{1-\alpha_i}$$

where $i = 1, 2$. Assume also that $\alpha_1 = \frac{1}{2}$ and $\alpha_2 = \frac{2}{3}$. Therefore

$$Y_1 = A_1 N_1^{1/2} \bar{K}_1^{1/2}$$

$$Y_2 = A_2 N_2^{2/3} \bar{K}_2^{1/3}$$

Even if we have numerical values for A_1, A_2, $\bar{K}_1$, and $\bar{K}_2$, we cannot add the left-hand sides of the above two equations together to get an expression connecting aggregate output ($Y_1 + Y_2$) to aggregate employment ($N_1 + N_2$). But we do want an aggregate production function in which short-run aggregate output is dependent upon the (variable) total quantity of labor employed and the (fixed) total stock of capital. An aggregate production function *can* be obtained if each level of aggregate output corresponds to a unique distribution of this output among all firms.

Assume that the two firms' production functions are as depicted in Figure 3-2. Also, assume that when aggregate output is Y' (so many billions of base-period dollars) the firms contribute 25% and 75%, respectively, to the nation's total output. If aggregate output is Y', the aggregate level of employment can be deduced from the two firms' production functions. Figure 3-2 shows that firm 1 would contribute $\frac{1}{4}$ Y' to aggregate output and employ N_1' units of labor. Firm 2 would contribute $\frac{3}{4}$ Y' to total output and employ N_2' units of labor. Hence, if aggregate output were Y' billion (constant dollars), $N' = N_1' + N_2'$ units of labor would be employed. This gives us one point on our aggregate production function, drawn in the lower panel of Figure 3-2. Other points can be obtained in the same way.

The ith Firm's Marginal Productivity of Labor

The "slope" or "first derivative" of any continuous function with *one* independent variable, such as $y = f(x)$, is expressed as dy/dx. This expression should be read "the small change in y resulting from a small change in x." The general rule for finding the "first derivative" of an explicit function such as $y = ax^m$ is

$$\frac{dy}{dx} = max^{m-1}$$

All that has to be done to obtain a first derivative from some explicit function (such as $y = ax^m$) is "to bring down" the exponent (m), multiply it by any constant term which might appear in the original function (a), repeat the independent variable just as it appeared in the function (x^m), and subtract 1 from its exponent. The first derivative is not affected by constant terms which are not attached to the independent variable. For example, in the equation

$$y = ax^m + b$$

where b, as well as a and m, are constants, we can "hypothetically" attach an x^0 term to the constant b, since anything raised to the zero power is equal to unity:

$$y = ax^m + bx^0$$

Using our rule to find the "first derivative" of the above function, we get

$$\frac{dy}{dx} = max^{m-1} + 0bx^{0-1}$$

or, since anything multiplied by zero vanishes,

$$\frac{dy}{dx} = max^{m-1}$$

Thus the constant term does not affect the "slope" or "first derivative" of the function.

The slope of our explicit production function

$$Y_{26} = 60{,}000 N_{26}^{1/2}$$

is

$$\frac{dY_{26}}{dN_{26}} = (1/2)(60{,}000)N_{26}^{(1/2)-1}$$

or

$$\frac{dY_{26}}{dN_{26}} = 30{,}000 N_{26}^{-1/2} \tag{3-4}$$

For any value of N_{26}, there is a corresponding level of dY_{26}/dN_{26}. For example, if $N_{26} = 25$, the prevailing level of the first derivative of our production function would be 6000. In general, the slope of a production function—in this case, the change in the 26th firm's level of production resulting from a very small change in the quantity of labor its managers hire, everything else remaining constant—is called "the marginal productivity of labor."

By substituting into Equation 3-4 the same values of N_{26} used in Table 3-1, we obtain the table of values given in Table 3-2. These combinations of N_{26} and dY_{26}/dN_{26} are graphed in Figure 3-3.

Table 3-2

N_{26}	dY_{26}/dN_{26}
4	15,000
9	10,000
16	7500
25	6000
36	5000
49	4286

Viewing Figures 3-1 and 3-3 together: if the managers of the 26th firm hire 16 full-time men, the *total* quarterly output (at an annual rate) is $240,000 (base period) worth of product. The *average* productivity of labor at this volume of activity Y_{26}/N_{26} is $15,000 (base period) worth of goods per quarter. The *marginal* productivity of labor at this level of employment is 7500. This means that making a very small addition to the work force will add 7500 to the base-period dollar value of total quarterly output, expressed at annual rate. For example, if the firm hired 17 employees it would produce $247,386.30. The 17th employee would have added $7,386.30 to the annual receipts of the firm. The marginal productivity of labor we computed—$7500—is at a point right *at* the employment level of 16, rather than over a *range* of the production function in the neighborhood of 16 and 17. This difference in what is being measured accounts for the difference between the marginal productivity of labor at an employment level of 16 ($7500) and the "marginal productivity" of the 17th man ($7,386.30).

The inverse property between the marginal productivity of labor and the quantity of labor employed is basic to neoclassical economics. It was built into the production function of our 26th firm by assuming α to be greater than zero and less than one (specifically, equal to $\frac{1}{2}$). Generally it is incorporated, *by assumption*, into all "neoclassical" production functions to denote "diminishing returns to factor proportions." We are simply trying to account mathematically for the technical fact of life that, as more and more men are employed with a given capital stock, output increases, but at a decreasing rate.

CAPITAL, SAVING, INVESTMENT, AND INTEREST

The many alternative theories of capital, saving, investment, and interest attributed to "neoclassical" economists are difficult to compress into a single "model." Some aspects of these theories, especially multiperiod aspects, are discussed in Part II. The discussion here is designed to be consistent with the monoperiodic nature of the basic neoclassical model.

Figure 3–3

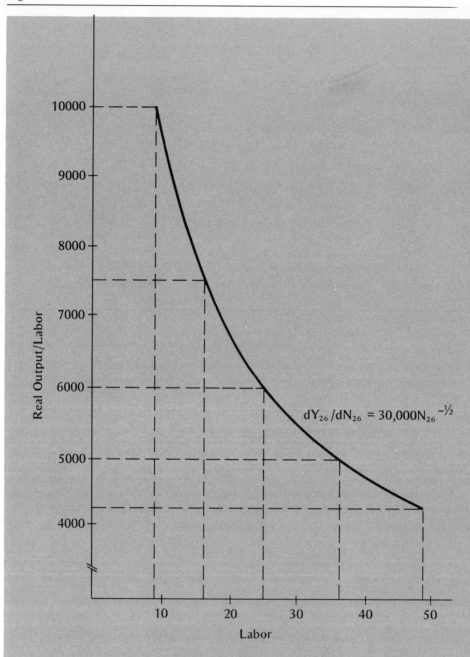

$dY_{26}/dN_{26} = 30{,}000N_{26}^{-\frac{1}{2}}$

Saving versus Investment

Economists define "saving" as the *act* of abstaining from consuming all of income. "Investment"—we will focus on *net* investment—is the *act* of making additions or deletions to capital stock. Households *and* businesses save (businesses retain profits). Households *and* businesses invest (households buy residential dwellings which are counted as part of the nation's capital).

There are two major sources of funds destined to be used by businesses to carry out aggregate net investment activity. First, businesses may retain a portion of current profits and use this purchasing power to make net additions to their capital holdings.

The other major source of purchasing power for net investment is saving done by households. The amount currently saved by *one* individual, however, does not necessarily lead to aggregate saving. For example, if he manages to save $1000 during the time period and buys a few shares of IBM common stock (a financial asset) from another individual, IBM has not (yet) got any additional purchasing power to undertake a capital expansion. If the second individual uses the first individual's purchasing power to buy a fur stole for his mistress, *aggregate* saving has not taken place. The act of the second individual (who has *dis*saved, that is, eaten into his personal wealth) had so far canceled out the act of the first individual.

On the other hand, the *seller* of the fur stole might have read an ad in the *Wall Street Journal* announcing that the management of the Nuclear Toy Corporation want to sell new shares in their company. If the seller of the fur stole gives the $1000 to the management of this company (in turn receiving, say, a certificate specifying that he owns 100 shares of Nuclear Toy common stock), and NTC management uses the funds to add to the capital holdings of the firm, and if these additions to the company's capital stock do not come from buying other domestic firms' capital, *investment will occur*. Of course, the management of Nuclear Toy might use the $1000 for a big weekend in Cleveland, so that the saving of the first individual would *not* eventually become investment. Remember, net investment is the act of making additions or deletions to the capital stock.

Interest

Interest is usually thought of as a payment for a loan of money over a period of time. The loans can be for a day or for a decade, but interest is generally expressed at an annual rate. In reality, hundreds of interest rates prevail simultaneously. A loan shark handling "juice" loans for a crime syndicate may charge 200% per year, while a neighborhood commercial bank charges 10%. Yet most macroeconomic models, such as the neoclassical one being developed here, are based on the existence of a single interest rate, "the" rate of interest. This rate is often an average of representative rates which are readily available to economic analysts. When this notion of "the" rate of interest is used, however, it should be kept in mind that at any moment in time different rates of interest prevail. These individual rates reflect risk, time to maturity of the loan, and other considerations which are submerged by the aggregation process.

As noted earlier, in this chapter it is desirable to delay discussing variables expressed in current-period dollars as long as possible. So we will deal here with a "real," rather than a "money," rate of interest. The real rate of interest (r) is the rate of interest on loans of constant purchasing power, that is, on loans in which the principal as well as the associated interest payment are expressed in base-period dollars.[1]

The "money" rate of interest (the payment for loans in which all amounts are expressed in current-period dollars) is the real rate plus the percentage change in the general price level anticipated for the coming period. Thus, if the real (annual) rate of interest is 8% (the corresponding quarterly rate being 2%)—i.e., if one had to promise to deliver 1.02 "base-period" dollars at the end of the quarter to borrow one at the beginning— and if the general price level were expected to fall by 2% during the quarter, the money rate of interest would be zero.

The Supply of and Demand for Loanable Funds

The existing capital stock held by n firms at the beginning of the quarter is assumed to be known. All profits made during the time period are assumed to be passed on to stockholders. Managers of the n firms may make net additions to the current stock of capital by acquiring some of the purchasing power obtained by households during the period (real wage, interest, and dividend payments). Households offer some of their purchasing power *temporarily* to businesses. That purchasing power which managers actually choose to acquire will be sunk into investment projects which will probably last for many time periods. The firms will have to pay a rate of return on this borrowed purchasing power every period and return the same "base-period dollars' worth" at the contracted terminal date of the loan.

The supply side of the neoclassical or "loanable funds" theory of interest may be introduced in the following way. The greater the reward for offering funds—the rate of interest—the greater the volume of purchasing power offered to be used as capital. The owners of commodities receive a market-determined percentage (r). As this percentage increases, more and more purchasing power will be forthcoming. The higher rates increasingly compensate for the discomfort of having to wait many periods before con-

1. We are ignoring the effect of price changes on the interest payment. For a discussion of the proper computation of the real rate of interest, see Stephen W. Rousseas, *Monetary Theory* (Knopf, 1972), 29–31.

suming. At very high rates, even those individuals who place a high premium on current consumption may decide to *save*, that is, to *offer* purchasing power to be used as investment.

Many of the neoclassical economists, especially Irving Fisher, used utility analysis to show exactly how much savings would be forthcoming under various conditions. The simplest possible way of presenting this approach is to view a potential saver as balancing the utility of consuming one base-period dollar's worth of goods and services at the beginning of a time period against the utility of consuming one base-period dollar's worth of goods and services plus interest at the end of the period.

The demand side of the theory of loanable funds rests on the proposition that the volume of purchasing power demanded by businesses will be greater, the lower the rate of interest. While interest to households is income, to firms it is a cost. (Although consumption loans and business savings are here ignored, the basic nature of this discussion would not be changed if they were taken into account.)

An addition to capital, or an act of investment, is productive if one unit added to capital at the end of the current time period will, everything else being constant, add more to next period's output than it itself depreciates, or, if we ignore depreciation, if it adds anything at all to the next period's output. The lower the market-determined cost (r) of borrowing the commodities, the more of these net additions will be made.

These notions of supply and demand, as well as the process of attaining equilibrium, can probably best be discussed with reference to a diagram. To keep up with standard notation, let S be the real value of commodities supplied and I the real value of commodities demanded this quarter for use as capital. The role of the interest rate in equilibrating these two quarterly flows is shown in Figure 3-4.

If the prevailing rate of interest was, for some reason, above r^* in Figure 3-4, the quantity of purchasing power to be used for capital formation would exceed the quantity demanded. A positive excess supply of savings would exist. Since the option to employ (or to borrow) rests with the managers of the firms, the actual addition to capital would be the quantity demanded. Those owners of capital who would want to supply purchasing power to lend at the artificially high rate of interest, but who cannot be satisfied, would compete among themselves for the small number of opportunities by accepting lower rates of return. Cuts in the rate of interest would occur until r^* eventually prevailed. The same competitive process is applicable if the rate of interest were initially below its equilibrium level. Savers would prefer a rate of interest above r^* and investors would prefer a rate of interest below r^*. But only at r^*, where S^* is equal to I^*, are both groups, taken together, satisfied.

One final point about this formulation should be made. If the investment function were I' in Figure 3-4, and the savings function S, the econ-

Figure 3-4

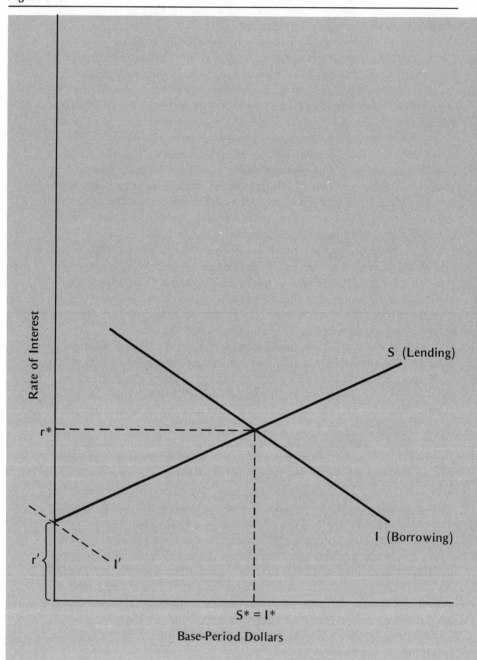

Rate of Interest

S (Lending)

r*

r'

I'

I (Borrowing)

S* = I*

Base-Period Dollars

omy would be at equilibrium with no net capital formation, but with a positive rate of interest. If nothing else were changing (for example, if there were a constant labor force and no technical change), the economy would be in a stationary state. The economy would be on a plateau with a positive rate of interest. "Real" interest would have to be paid. This interest rate would be r' in Figure 3-4. At this low rate, no net offerings would be made. The rate is such that it just balances the premium placed on consumption during this period, as opposed to the next period, for those individuals most apt to save, that is, for those individuals who place the lowest such premium on current consumption. If some individuals were indifferent between present and future consumption, the savings function would go through the origin.

PROFIT MAXIMIZATION
AND THE DEMAND FOR LABOR

As discussed above, the managers of the ith firm begin the current time period with capital holdings which they must accept as facts of life. What they have, they use. They do not add to or subtract from this stock. Yet it is helpful to think of the market-determined rate of interest introduced in the preceding section as an "opportunity cost" of the capital. It is also helpful to assume that the managers of the ith firm *could* have liquidated their capital holdings and loaned the money at interest. They would have received an annual rate of r^*. As long as the market for loanable funds is perfectly competitive, such a liquidation and injection of cash into the loan market would not affect r^*.

The "opportunity cost" of each base-period dollar's worth of the capital stock is r^*. We will treat this *implicit* cost as an *explicit* cost. Thus, the ith firm's capital cost is $r^*\bar{K}_i$. $\bar{K}_i$ is a stock without a time dimension, but since the rate of interest is a quarterly rate, $r^*\bar{K}_i$ is a quarterly total at an annual rate. The firm's capital cost is expressed in terms of its own output. Since depreciation during the time period has been assumed to be negligible, $r^*\bar{K}_i$ will be the firm's total capital cost no matter how intensively its managers use the fixed holdings at their disposal.

Let P be the current level of the general price index (as defined in Chapter 2). Let W be the "money wage"—the amount, expressed in current-period dollars, which a firm must pay for a person to work eight hours a day, five days a week, for thirteen weeks (but multiplied by four to get an annual rate). Although variables or constants expressed in terms of current-period dollars cannot be thoroughly discussed until the next chapter, we can here, just for purposes of clarification, assume that the managers of the individual firms know the market-determined levels of the money wage (W) and the current level of the general price index (P). For example, assume that the money wage is \$6120 and that the prevailing level of the general price index is 1.02. In terms of base-period purchasing power, this money wage is "really worth" $W/P = \$6000$.

The variable W/P—the "real" wage— is the cost of labor. After first discussing what determines the equilibrium level of this ratio, we will then work backward and discuss what determines the prevailing levels of its component parts, W and P. But for now, the presentation is limited to the ratio itself.

Profit Maximization by the ith Firm

The real profits of the ith firm, Π_i, is purchasing power against which the factors of production have no claim. Such real profits, or the portion of real output to be claimed by the shareholders, may be defined algebraically as

$$\Pi_i = F_i(N_i, \bar{K}_i) - (\overline{W/P}) N_i - r^* \bar{K}_i \qquad (3\text{-}5)$$

All four components of Equation 3-5 are expressed in terms of base-period prices. This equation rests on the assumption that the managers of the ith firm know three things, and that these three things do not change during the time period: *production techniques*, as embodied in Equation 3-1, $Y_i = F_i(N_i, \bar{K}_i)$; the *fixed stock of capital*, $\bar{K}_i$; and the prevailing, market-determined real factor prices, $(\overline{W/P})$ and r^*. Thus Equation 3-5 simply states that the real profit of the ith firm equals real output less the real wages and the real cost of capital. Hence it should be noted that the only *unknown* in Equation 3-5 is N_i, the amount of labor employed, while $\bar{K}_i$, $(\overline{W/P})$, and r^* are given to the firm.

The bar over the real wage denotes the fact it is a predetermined variable. That is, the managers of the firm must accept it as a fact of life. Given a perfectly competitive environment, in which the ith firm is responsible for only a small portion of the aggregate labor demand, a change in the quantity of labor its managers choose to hire will have such an infinitesimal effect on labor demand in the economy as a whole that it can be ignored.

One of the tasks of the managers of the ith firm is to select (and then to hire) that amount of labor which will, given the above three facts of life, make the real profits of their firm as large as possible. This maximizing behavior is "rational" in the sense that the managers are probably also shareholders and, even if not, the shareholders might seek a new set of managers if the results at the end of the period are not "satisfactory."

What the managers should do is set forth in Figure 3-5. The upper panel of the figure contains the output and real cost portions of Equation 3-5, plotted separately. The production function increases at a decreasing rate; that is, its slope (dY_i/dN_i) becomes less and less as N_i increases because of the assumption of diminishing returns to factor proportions. The real total cost function increases linearly with N_i because its slope is the

Figure 3-5

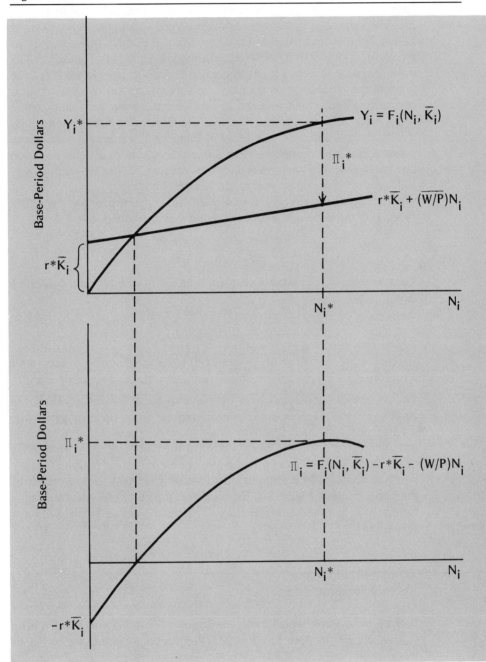

constant real wage. The vertical axis intercept of this cost function is $r^*\bar{K}_i$. Even at $N_i = 0$, the firm must pay the interest charges, $r^*\bar{K}_i$, on its capital.

The vertical distance between the two functions in the upper panel of Figure 3-5 is, as expressed in Equation 3-5, real profit. These vertical distances for all levels of N_i are plotted in the lower panel of Figure 3-5. The managers want to be at a point where real profit is as large as possible. The levels of the variables at such a point are noted with asterisks. These profit-maximizing levels could be found by careful visual inspection, but there are some purely analytical gains to be obtained from being more precise.

With regard to the lower panel of Figure 3-5, real profit is as large as possible at that level of N_i where very small changes in N_i in either direction do not increase Π_i. That is, the condition necessary for the N_i^* result to prevail is for the slope of the real profit function to be zero.

By taking the derivative of Equation 3-5 [remembering that $Y_i = F_i(N_i, \bar{K}_i)$], the slope of the profit function may be written as

$$\frac{d\Pi_i}{dN_i} = \frac{dY_i}{dN_i} - \left(\frac{\overline{W}}{P}\right)$$

Thus, real profit is at a maximum when employment has been adjusted so that

$$\frac{d\Pi_i}{dN_i} = \frac{dY_i}{dN_i} - \left(\frac{\overline{W}}{P}\right) = 0$$

or

$$\frac{dY_i}{dN_i} = \left(\frac{\overline{W}}{P}\right)$$

That is, profits are maximized when the marginal productivity of labor is equal to the real wage. In order to maximize real profit, the managers of the ith firm must hire that quantity of labor for which the addition to real output obtained from the last labor unit hired is equal to its real cost in terms of the firm's output. The firm would break even on this "marginal" labor unit but would make real profit on all the nonmarginal units. In terms of the upper panel of Figure 3-5, the condition for profit maximization is for the slope of the production function, dY_i/dN_i, to equal the slope of the cost function, $(\overline{W}/P)$.

A Numerical Example
of Profit Maximization

Perhaps an example would make the notion of profit maximization a little clearer. Recall the 26th firm's production function introduced earlier in this chapter:

$$Y_{26} = AN_{26}{}^\alpha \bar{K}_{26}{}^{1-\alpha}$$

where $A = 60$, $\alpha = \frac{1}{2}$, and $\bar{K}_{26} = \$1$ million (base period). Substituting these numerical values into the production function, we obtained

$$Y_{26} = 60{,}000N_{26}^{1/2}$$

For every specific value of N_{26}, there is a corresponding value of Y_{26}. We found earlier that, to maximize real profit, a firm should adjust its labor force so that

$$\frac{dY_i}{dN_i} = \left(\overline{\frac{W}{P}}\right)$$

that is, where the marginal productivity of labor is equal to the real wage. Recall the 26th firm's marginal productivity of labor function introduced earlier in this chapter:

$$\frac{dY_{26}}{dN_{26}} = 30{,}000N_{26}^{-1/2}$$

Assume that the prevailing real wage is $6000 (base period). The managers of the 26th firm will maximize real profit at that level of employment where

$$30{,}000N_{26}^{-1/2} = 6000$$

Solving the above equation for N_{26}, we find that the profit-maximizing level of labor is

$$N_{26}{}^* = 25$$

If the managers hire 25 full-time employees, their real receipts (Y_{26}) will be $300,000 (base period) per year. If the equilibrium rate of interest (r^*) were 6%, the firm's real capital cost ($r^*\bar{K}_{26}$) would be $60,000 (base period). Real labor cost $(W/P)N_{26}$ would be $150,000 (base period). On an annual basis, the firm's profit would be $90,000 (base period).

The ith Firm's Labor Demand Curve

With reference to Figure 3-5: if (for some reason external to the firm) the market-determined real wage fell, the cost line in the upper panel in Figure 3-5 would rotate downward from the fixed point $r^*\bar{K}_i$. The production function would, of course, remain the same. But, since the cost line has rotated downward, the level of real profit associated with each level of employment would be greater than before. Thus, with reference to the lower panel of Figure 3-5, there would be an entirely new profit function. In order to again maximize real profits, the firm's managers would have to increase the level of N_i until dY_i/dN_i fell to the level of the now lower real wage. In exactly this sense, the ith firm's marginal productivity of labor function (such as the specific one depicted in Figure 3-3) can be thought of as its labor demand function, N_{Di}, depicted in Figure 3-6.

For any given real wage, there is one level of employment which will

Figure 3-6

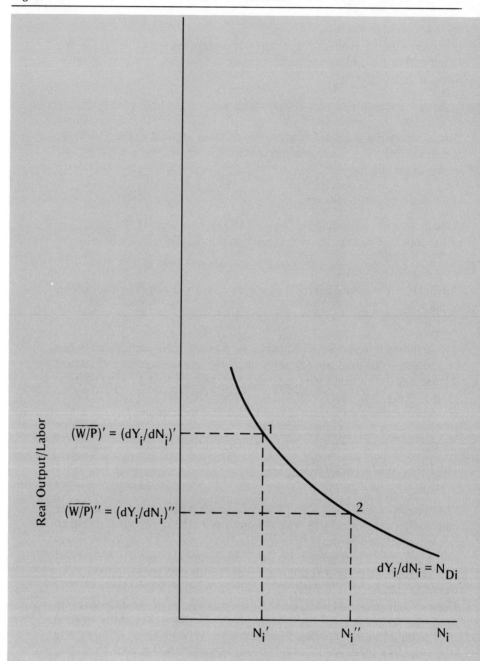

produce a maximum profit—that level of employment which yields a level of dY_i/dN_i equal to this particular real wage. With reference to Figure 3-6: if the prevailing real wage were $(W/P)'$, the managers must (assuming they are rational) hire N_i' units of labor, because only at that level of employment is $(dY_i/dN_i)'$ equal to $(W/P)'$. If the real wage for some reason fell to $(W/P)''$, employment would increase to N_i''.

It should be emphasized that the real-wage/quantity-of-labor-demanded combinations given by N_{Di} in Figure 3-6 are not equally preferable to the managers. Although combinations 1 and 2 are both profit-maximizing combinations, managers would, given different values of the real wage, prefer combination 2 to combination 1. With reference to the upper panel of Figure 3-5: if the real wage falls, the gap between real output and real cost widens for all levels of N_i, including the new profit-maximizing level. Thus, with reference to Figure 3-6, combination 2 yields a higher *total* real profit than combination 1.

The Aggregate Labor Demand Curve

An *aggregate* labor demand curve—the labor demanded to produce *all* final goods and services—can be obtained from the labor demand functions of the n individual firms. We simply have to pick some specific real wage, such as $(W/P)'$; adding up the quantities of labor demanded by all firms at that particular real wage, we have

$$\sum_{i=1}^{n} N_i' = N'$$

This would yield one point on the aggregate labor demand curve. The process could be repeated using another real wage, such as $(W/P)''$, and another point would be obtained. The aggregate labor demand function as a whole is the set of all such combinations.

Thus the aggregate demand for labor function is obtained by "horizontally" summing the individual firms' demand for labor functions as in Figure 3-7. There is no reason for this function to be linear. It has been drawn that way only for convenience. Having obtained this particular aggregate function, we will put it aside for the time being.

Thus far we have laid the microeconomic foundations for neoclassical macroeconomics. We have described how production and profit-maximizing behavior lead to an aggregate-demand-for-labor curve. And we have considered the role of the capital market in bringing together savers and investors. In the next chapter we turn to the supply side of labor so that we can determine the equilibrium level of employment and, therefore, output. This permits us to introduce money and prices into the neoclassical model and to show how these latter "monetary" concepts do not affect "real" concepts such as employment and output.

Figure 3-7

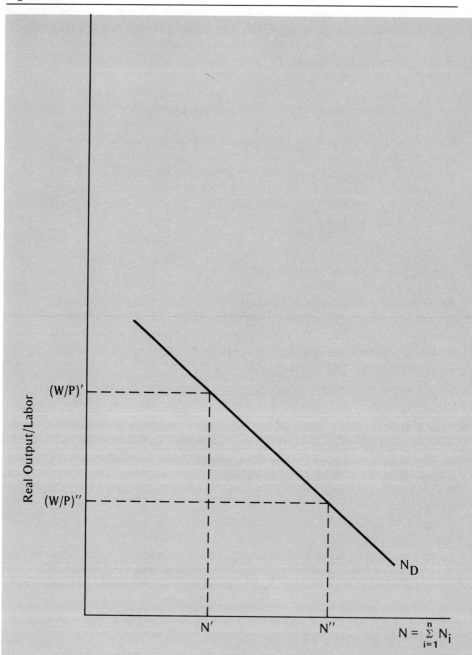

Neoclassical Macroeconomics (II)

UTILITY MAXIMIZATION AND THE SUPPLY OF LABOR

The neoclassical *supply* of labor function is based on the existence of a perfectly competitive market in which m workers offer labor services to n firms. The labor unit in which these services are measured must be identical to that used when discussing the demand side of the labor market. For example, if one labor unit demanded denoted one of the firms "owning" the services of one worker eight hours a day, five days a week, for thirteen weeks, a worker supplying exactly this amount of labor service must be thought of as supplying one labor unit. Workers are assumed to be able to supply, just as firms are assumed to be able to demand, fractional labor units.

The jth Worker's Line of Attainable Combinations

The fixed total time the jth worker has available for work (N_j) and leisure (LE_j) may be defined as $\bar{T}_j$. This relationship can be expressed algebraically as

$$\bar{T}_j = N_j + LE_j$$

As denoted by the bar, $\bar{T}_j$ is assumed to be a predetermined variable. For any given individual, it is determined by psychological and physiological (but not economic) factors. Given the labor unit used above, if the jth worker required eight hours every working day and two full days a week for recuperation (that is, for eating, sleeping, and "necessary" time off, not to be confused with leisure), he has sixteen hours a day and five days a week this quarter to be divided between work and leisure. Thus, in this case, $\bar{T}_j = 2$.

Expressed in real terms, the market-determined remuneration for offering one labor unit is the real wage, $(\overline{W/P})$. The bar over the real wage denotes the fact that the jth worker is such a small part of the total labor force that he must accept the prevailing real wage as a fact of life.

By definition,

$$-N_j = LE_j - \bar{T}_j$$

and

$$\left(\frac{\overline{W}}{P}\right)N_j = -\left(\frac{\overline{W}}{P}\right)[LE_j - \bar{T}_j] \tag{4-1}$$

Equation 4-1 gives the alternative combinations of real income $(\overline{W/P})N_j$, and leisure which can be obtained by the jth worker, given a market-determined real wage and a fixed amount of time available for both work and leisure.

Equation 4-1 is plotted in Figure 4-1. The slope of this "line of attainable or alternative combinations," or "constraint," is the real wage expressed as a negative value. That is,

$$\frac{d\ [(\overline{W/P})N_j]}{dLE_j} = -\left(\frac{\overline{W}}{P}\right)$$

Given the constraint, the jth worker must determine which of the continuous set of combinations of real income and leisure is in some sense "best."

The jth Worker's Utility Function

The jth worker's level of satisfaction or "utility" (U_j) may be thought of in this context as a function of his real income and leisure:

$$U_j = F_j\left(\frac{W}{P} N_j, LE_j\right) \tag{4-2}$$

The preference map generated by Equation 4-2 is drawn as in Figure 4-2. The three curves labeled U_j', U_j'' and U_j''' are three isoutility (equal satisfaction) curves. We will refer to these curves as indifference curves, since any single curve such as U_j' gives a continuous set of combinations of real income and leisure among which the jth worker is indifferent. Any point on a higher curve, however, such as U_j''' would be preferable to any point on a lower curve; that is, given a particular level of leisure, more income is always preferable to less.

There are two characteristics of any given indifference curve which should be discussed—its general downward-sloping property and its convexity with respect to the origin. The downward-sloping property of U_j' denotes the assumption that if the jth worker's real income is reduced, his leisure must be increased if his overall level of satisfaction is to remain con-

Figure 4-1

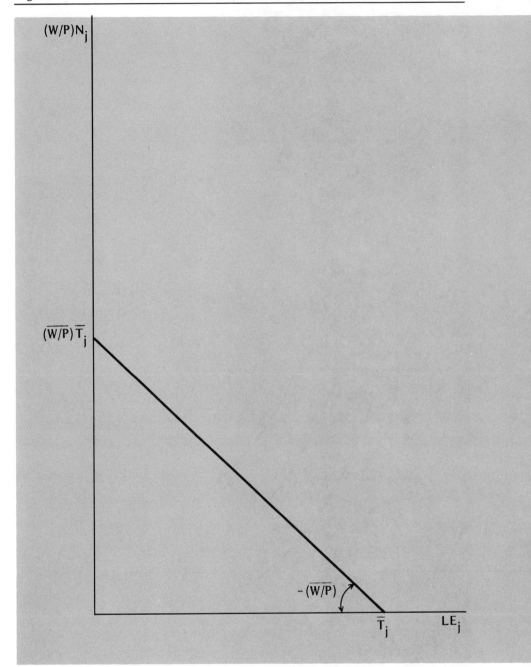

Figure 4-2

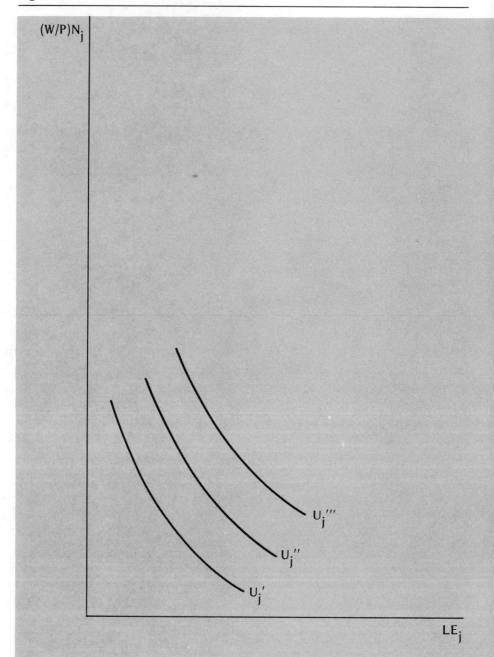

stant. To put it another way, this property implies that both leisure and real income are desirable.

The second property, convexity, results from the fact that as we move down along a given indifference curve, the slope of the curve increases toward zero. The slope of the curve, or the rate at which the *j*th worker trades off real income for leisure, is called the *marginal rate of substitution.* As the worker moves down the curve, he is willing to give up less and less of real income for a given increment in leisure, and therefore the marginal rate of substitution diminishes. It diminishes in the other direction as well; as the worker moves up the curve, he is willing to trade diminishing amounts of leisure for equal increments of real income.

Utility Maximization

The constraint presented in Figure 4-1 can now be superimposed over the preference map of Figure 4-2, as shown in Figure 4-3. The objective of the *j*th worker is to attain the highest level of satisfaction, given the line of attainable combinations. The space of Figure 4-3 is assumed to be continuously dense with indifference curves. The best the worker can do—that is, the highest indifference curve he can attain—is given by the point where the line of attainable combinations is tangent to some indifference curve. At this point, the worker is maximizing the satisfaction he can get from the various combinations of real income and leisure that are possible to him, *given the real wage* $(\overline{W/P})$ and the total amount of time he has available for work and leisure $(\overline{T}_j)$. Such a point, labeled $(\overline{W/P})N_j^*$ and LE_j^* in Figure 4-3, is unique because the constraint is linear and the indifference curves are convex from below.

As the real wage faced by the *j*th worker increases, the slope of the line of attainable combinations (which is the real wage) increases, thus rotating the line upward from the fixed point $\overline{T}_j$. It was generally assumed in neoclassical literature that the shape of most workers' preference patterns was such that higher lines of attainable combinations would be tangent to higher indifference curves at lower levels of leisure. Hence, with reference to Figure 4-3, as the real wage increases, the new levels of LE_j^* would be to the left of the original. The real wage and N_j^* would vary in the same direction, so that the labor supply curve for the economy as a whole would appear as depicted in Figure 4-4.

Aggregate Labor Supply Curve

Such a supply curve is obtained by adding up the amounts of labor supplied by all *m* individuals at varying levels of the real wage. It is possible that after

Figure 4-3

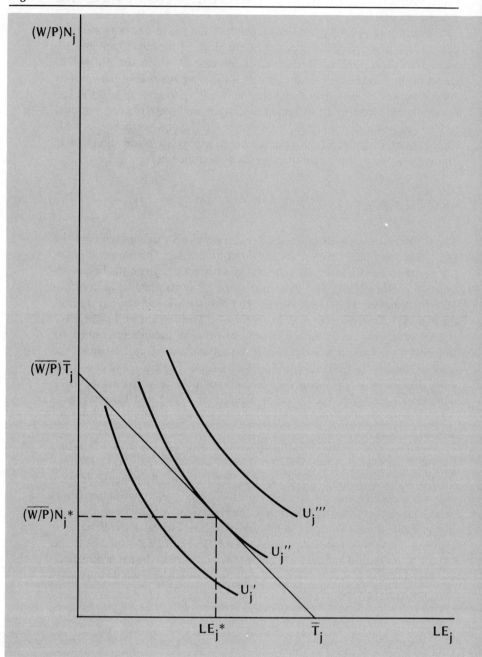

Figure 4-4

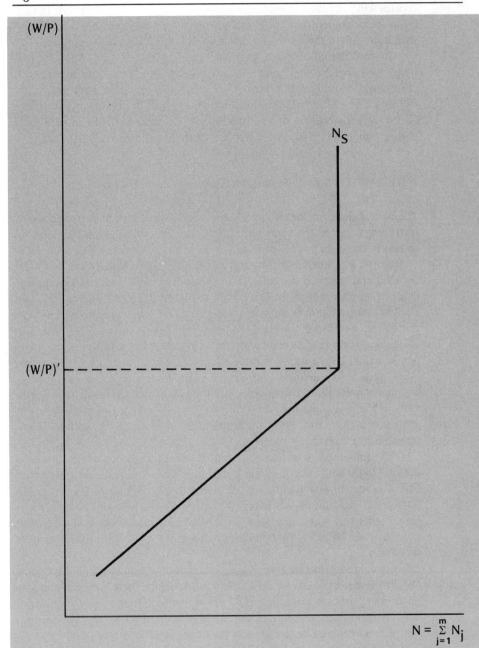

some level of real wage is attained, such as $(\overline{W/P})'$ in Figure 4-4, further increases will not result in increases in the quantity of labor supplied. In fact, it has been argued that the function might even be "backward bending," with increases in the real wage resulting in fewer labor units supplied.

It must be emphasized that the real-wage/labor-supplied combinations given by N_S in Figure 4-4 are not equally preferable to workers. Households would want to be as high as possible along the aggregate labor supply curve. All combinations along N_S *are* utility-maximizing positions (given different values of the real wage). But higher combinations yield higher *total* utility than lower combinations.

FULL-EMPLOYMENT EQUILIBRIUM

The next step in our development of a neoclassical macroeconomic model is to bring together the aggregate supply and demand schedules for labor as shown in the upper panel of Figure 4-5. "Full employment" of a factor of production is defined as a situation such that the quantities of the factor demanded and supplied are equal *at the prevailing factor price*. Full employment of labor, noted with asterisks in the upper panel of Figure 4-5, is an equilibrium position. If for some reason the real wage were above $(W/P)^*$, the quantity of labor supplied would exceed the quantity demanded. But since the option to hire rests with the managers, the quantity of labor *employed* would be the quantity demanded. Those who would want to supply labor units at the artificially high real wage, but who cannot be satisfied, would compete for the available positions by accepting lower real wages. Cuts in the real wage would occur until $(W/P)^*$ eventually prevailed. The same competitive process is applicable if the real wage were initally below its equilibrium level.

The full-employment result, which competitive forces will maintain, is optimal in the sense that this combination of real wage and aggregate quantity of labor employed is the only combination at which businesses maximize profit *and* households maximize utility. The *m* households would prefer a higher real wage and the *n* firms would prefer a lower real wage. But only at the $(W/P)^*,N^*$ combination are both groups taken together satisfied.

Given the prevailing aggregate labor supply and demand functions, $(W/P)^*$ is determined. In turn, the *n* firms select their respective profit-maximizing amounts of labor, N_i^*, which then determine the *n* amounts of Y_i^*. By summing these latter amounts, the full-employment national output, Y^*, is obtained, as depicted in the lower panel of Figure 4-5.

It should be pointed out that we are working with short-run models in which the capital stock is given and fully utilized. It is the utilization of labor that varies in the short run. As a result, we use the terms "full employment" and "full employment of labor" synonymously. How short is

Figure 4-5

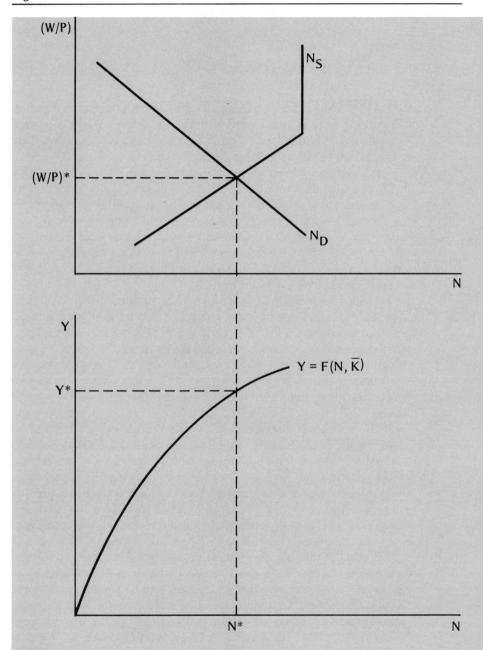

the short run? The answer is implicit in our assumption: the short run is that period of time in which the capital stock cannot be expanded.

Increasing Society's Real Output

If Y^* in Figure 4-5 is the equilibrium level of output in the current period, what can be done to make next period's equilibrium aggregate output greater than Y^*? Within the context of the n firms and m households, there are several ways such an increase might be achieved.

First, an improvement in production techniques would alter some or all of the production functions of the n firms and would cause the aggregate labor demand curve to shift to the right. If the aggregate labor supply curve were a straight vertical line, the aggregate level of employment would not change, but more output would result from the employment of this constant total work force. An improvement in production techniques would cause a decrease in aggregate output only if the aggregate labor supply curve were sufficiently backward-bending.

Second, an increase in T_j, the amount of time the jth worker decides he has available for work and leisure, would, if the increase were not entirely consumed in leisure, shift the aggregate supply of labor curve to the right. Even if T_j remained constant, a change in the household's preferences away from leisure in favor of real income would also shift the aggregate supply of labor curve to the right. This rightward shift, everything else constant, would cause the aggregate level of employment and therefore of output to increase.

Real aggregate output next period would probably be greater than Y^* if some or all of the n firms' capital stocks increased. Capital holdings would be increased if a portion of the stockholders' real income, Π^*, the workers' real income, $(\overline{W/P})N^*$, and the real income going to owners of capital, $r^*\overline{K}$, were offered to the n firms as capital and not consumed this time period. The increase in the aggregate capital stock would cause the aggregate labor demand curve to shift to the right, and unless the aggregate supply curve were sufficiently backward-bending, Y^* would increase.

The effect of this increase in the aggregate capital stock on a particular firm's level of output does not end here. An increase in K_i would cause the slope of the production function in Figure 4-6 to be greater at any given level of employment than it was before. The real wage—the per unit cost of labor—has also risen because of the rightward shift of the labor demand curve. Thus the *slope* of the cost line in Figure 4-6 would increase. Whether or not the new profit-maximizing level of employment for the ith firm would be different from the original level could only be determined by analysis of specific cases. It would depend on the relative sizes of the upward shifts in the production and cost functions. In any event, the larger

Figure 4-6

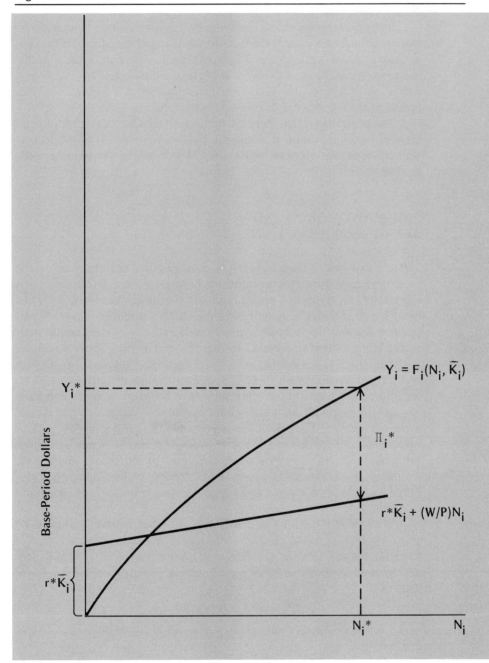

capital stock would cause the firm's output to increase unless its labor supply curve were backward-bending.

It should be noted that a change in the equilibrium rate of interest, r^*, would definitely not change the real output of any of the n firms. If the capital stock of the firms remained constant, neither portion of the n profit-maximizing conditions, $dY_i/dN_i = W/P$, would be affected. For example, a decline in r^* would only produce a redistribution of Y^* in favor of real profits at the full expense of income from capital.

The point here is that there are no magical tricks available for increasing real national output. It would take some improvement in production techniques or an increased willingness to sacrifice by foregoing present consumption.

SAY'S LAW, MONEY, AND THE GENERAL PRICE LEVEL

Up to this point in the development of our neoclassical macroeconomic model, we have shown that competition between workers and businessmen causes the prevailing real wage to be such that it equates the quantity of labor supplied with the quantity demanded. This equilibrium level of employment is also the full employment level. Full employment equilibrium in the labor market is depicted in Figure 4-5. Unemployment would be possible only if labor insisted on a real wage higher than the equilibrium real wage, a possibility which neoclassical economists discard. In addition, we showed in Chapter 3 that the competitive behavior of savers and businessmen results in an equilibrium interest rate at which saving and investment are equated. The role of the interest rate in equilibrating saving and investment is discussed in Chapter 3, with reference to Figure 3-4. Since all income is either spent on consumer goods or flows into investment, shortages and surpluses of commodities are impossible. Hence, full employment of labor is assured and all real income generated in the economy is spent.

With $(W/P)^*$ and N^* established in the labor market, and thus Y^* given by the aggregate production function (remember that the capital stock is assumed constant, that is, $K = \bar{K}$), and r^* established by the supply and demand for loanable funds, aggregate profit in the economy is known. That is,

$$\Pi^* = Y^* - (W/P)^*N^* - r^*\bar{K}$$

which is simply the aggregate of the n versions of Equation 3-5 in Chapter 3. Therefore,

$$Y^* = (W/P)^*N^* + r^*\bar{K} + \Pi^* \tag{4-3}$$

The full-employment levels of the variables in Equation 4-3 are all expressed in terms of billions of base-period dollars.

The next step in the development of our model is to introduce the concept of money, and with a given Y^*, determine the equilibrium level of the aggregate price level, P^*. After this is done, we can then express our relevant aggregate variables in current-period dollars. To accomplish this, we must discuss in more detail Say's law of markets.

Say's Law

According to Say's law, as discussed in Chapter 3, if all incomes are spent, then all goods that are produced will be sold. There is no reason in this model to expect any of the incomes not to be spent. There is no reason for profit or factor income receivers not to claim their portions of the national output. Thus, Say's law of markets *does* prevail in the present neoclassical model. Aggregate product is exactly matched by aggregate income and spending.

Two versions of Say's law have been developed. One of these formulations, referred to as "Say's identity," is today considered to be erroneous, while the other, referred to as "Say's equality," is not only "correct" (that is, internally consistent), but is also the basis for current work in monetary theory.

To obtain the erroneous, "identity" formulation of Say's law of markets, multiply both sides of Equation 4-3 by P:

$$P Y^* = P(W/P)^*N^* + Pr^*\bar{K} + P\Pi^* \qquad (4\text{-}4)$$

The term on the left-hand side of Equation 4-4, $P Y^*$, is the already-determined level of output expressed in current-period dollars. It is the dollar value of the aggregate supply of final goods and services. Let Z represent aggregate supply (expressed in dollar terms), or

$$Z = P Y^*$$

The term on the right-hand side of Equation 4-4

$$[P(W/P)^*N^* + Pr^*\bar{K} + P\Pi^*]$$

is the sum of the already-determined factor earnings, but expressed in current-period dollars. It is the dollar value of the aggregate demand for final goods and services. Let D represent aggregate demand (expressed in dollar terms), or

$$D = P(W/P)^*N^* + Pr^*\bar{K} + P\Pi^*$$

Equation 4-4 holds for any general price level P, no matter how arbitrarily chosen. In this form the neoclassical model shows that the current-period dollar value of goods and services demanded at any general price level is equal to the current-period dollar value of goods and services supplied. The current-period general price level, in consequence, cannot be obtained from this neoclassical model. The value of the aggregate supply, Z, equals the value of aggregate demand, D, regardless of the price level, P. Z is identical to D; that is, $Z \equiv D$.

In this simple, identity version of Say's law, some of the variables used, such as the real wage, have components with a monetary dimension, but this dimension is suppressed. Money is not thought of as something tangible which people can hold in their hands or burn. It is just a unit of account without any "utility" of its own. A theoretical economic environment based on this concept of money has all the characteristics of a barter economy.

Formulation of Say's law in this way is what modern writers refer to as "the invalid dichotomy." The dichotomy is that real factor prices such as (W/P) are determined by real forces, while the cash equivalents of these real prices are determined later. This dichotomy is invalid. We are unable to determine the current price level.

Money

To formulate Say's law in a validly dichotomized way, it must be assumed that money is something tangible, something that can be held in your hand. In the following discussion, money is a medium of exchange; for example, a United States Federal Reserve Note. In the Say's identity formulation, money is simply a unit of account—an abstraction, such as a dollar. In the Say's equality formulation, money is a unit of account as well as a medium of exchange.

Since money is assumed to be a medium of exchange, at any given time an aggregate amount of it will be held by all the households and business enterprises in the economy. We need to know the average total cash holdings over the three-month time period for the model under consideration. From the point of view of the work force as a whole, for example, the entire quarterly wage might be paid in three cash payments of $\frac{1}{12} P(W/P)*N*$ each. Recall that the wage is a quarterly total at an annual rate, so that the actual quarterly wage bill is $\frac{1}{4} P(W/P)*N$. The size of these monthly cash payments will vary proportionately with P, the as-yet-undetermined general price level. Assuming that each worker is paid at the beginning of each month, for any given level of P, the cash balances of the workers as a whole might follow the pattern depicted in Figure 4-7.

At the beginning of any month, or 0, 1, or 2 in Figure 4-7, the cash balances of workers are initially at $\frac{1}{12} P(W/P)*N*$, the sum of all their monthly paychecks. That is, the day after pay day, the workers are holding cash balances equal to the previous month's earnings. During the course of the month, the workers spend their income, reducing their cash balances. Perhaps most of the earnings are spent during the early part of the month, with some left over to pay for expenses during the latter part of the month.

Figure 4-7

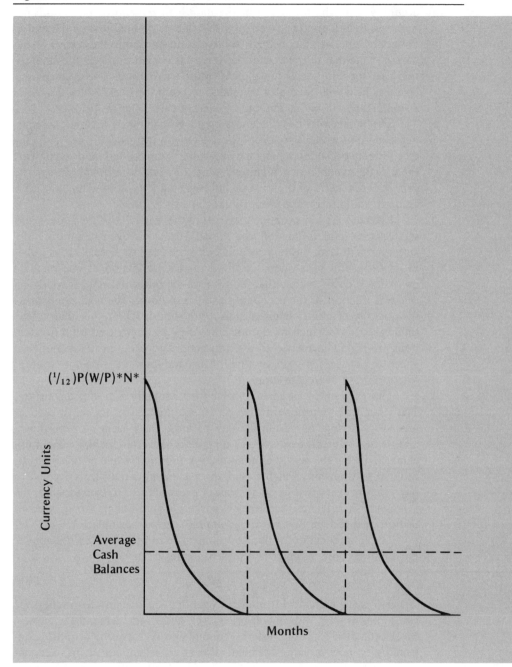

In Figure 4-7 we show the combined cash balances of all workers as declining from the beginning of the month to the end of the month for each month in a quarter. Average cash balances, represented by the dotted horizontal line, are the average holdings of cash during the course of the month. Note that the curves for declining cash balances reflect the assumption that spending behavior is identical in each month. The average cash balances held will obviously be related to the price level, P. The higher is P, the higher will be the amount of average cash balances held.

Similar average cash balances could be computed (again, the computed amount would vary proportionately with the general price level) for the other two classes of income receivers: shareholders and capitalists. Finally, the average cash balances required by business firms to bridge the gap between cash outflows and inflows could be computed, and this amount would also vary proportionately with P.

Even though Y^* has been restricted to the real value of *final* goods and services, the total volume of cash flows discussed above is a substantially larger amount than the value of the *final* goods and services. That is so because there are transactions involved in the production of intermediate products. We will assume that the value of all final goods and services is a *constant* fraction of the economy's total cash flows. Then we can express the quantity of money demanded as a function of PY^* rather than of the total cash flows (which we do not know). By assuming that total transactions are highly correlated to the transactions involved in the sale of final goods and services, we can say that the demand for money is some constant fraction (λ) of aggregate supply PY^*.

The fraction λ is assumed to be an institutionally determined constant. The value of λ depends on a web of institutional relationships, such as people's spending habits, firms' pay periods, check-clearing procedures, and the use of credit cards. We assume that these relationships remain unchanged during the period of analysis. (As an example of a change in institutional relationships which would affect λ, imagine that firms decided to pay workers every two weeks instead of every month. In consequence, the average cash balances required by workers would fall. It is this kind of institutional change that we are assuming does *not* take place.)

The total demand for units of money (we can think of a \$100 note as one hundred units of currency) may be expressed as

$$L = \lambda P Y^* \qquad (4\text{-}5)$$

where L is the demand for money. Note that the demand for money has two unknowns: P, the general price level, and L, the demand for money. Most estimates of λ for western economies vary between $\frac{1}{4}$ and $\frac{1}{2}$, depending on how money is defined. (For example, should savings account deposits be considered "money"?) For the United States, λ is approximately $\frac{1}{4}$.

Let the *actual* cash holdings—that is, the money supply that exists in the economy during the quarter—be represented by M. Assume that the supply (M) is a variable, the value of which ($\bar{M}$) is determined by the central bank. Thus $M = \bar{M}$. We now have a demand function for money and a supply function. For there to be an equilibrium in the market for money, L must equal M, or $\lambda P Y^* = \bar{M}$.

Consider a disequilibrium in the market for money, and assume that there is excess supply, or that $(M - L) > 0$. Individuals will reduce their holdings of money by buying goods and services. That will drive the prices of these goods and services upward, raising the price level, P. This spending behavior will not raise Y^* because Y^*, real output, is already as high as it can be—given the aggregate production function and the choice already made by workers regarding the division of their time between leisure and work.

As a result of rising P, the quantity of money demanded will rise, because $L = \lambda P Y^*$. This process—excess holdings of money leading to spending, which leads to rising prices—will continue as L rises until there is no longer an excess supply of money, or until $M = L$. At that point the money market will be in equilibrium. Notice that an excess supply of money in the economy is, in the neoclassical model, the very same thing as an excess demand for final goods and services.

We are now prepared to show how the neoclassical model determines the price level. And we are also prepared to show that Say's law—aggregate demand equals aggregate supply—is not an identity, but a condition which obtains only in equilibrium.

The dollar value of aggregate demand, D, is now equal to the sum of factor earnings (total wages, total interest, and total profit) plus the excess supply of money:

$$D = P(W/P)^*N^* + Pr^*\bar{K} + P\Pi^* + (M - L) \qquad (4\text{-}6)$$

If $(M - L) = 0$, there is no excess demand for final goods and services originating in the market for money. If $(M - L) < 0$, then the demand for money is greater than the supply, and a process which is the reverse of the one described above will occur. The excess demand for money will result in a reduction of expenditures for goods and services, which will lower the prices of final output and therefore the general price level, P.

As P falls, the demand for money, L, will fall, by the relationship $L = \lambda P Y^*$. P will fall until there is no longer an excess demand for money. As before, note that in the neoclassical model an excess demand for money in the economy is the very same thing as an excess supply of final goods and services.

At this point we can introduce the supply and demand for money into Equation 4-6 and factor out the price level, P:

$$D = P(W/P)^*N^* + Pr^*\bar{K} + P\Pi^* + (M - L)$$

$$D = P(W/P)^*N^* + Pr^*\bar{K} + P\Pi^* + \bar{M} - \lambda P Y^*$$

$$D = PY^* + \bar{M} - \lambda PY^*$$

$$D = P[Y^*(1 - \lambda)] + \bar{M} \qquad (4\text{-}7)$$

Since λ is less than 1, the expression in the parentheses on the right-hand side of Equation 4-7 is positive.

The General Price Level

If the value of aggregate supply of goods is defined as before $(Z = PY^*)$, and the value of the aggregate demand for goods is assumed to be given by Equation 4-6, $Z = D$ becomes an equilibrium condition. It is not true by definition, as in the "Say's identity" version of the neoclassical theory of money. The equilibrium condition, $Z = D$, can be used to solve for the equilibrium general price level, P^*.

The dollar value of aggregate supply, in equilibrium, is the equilibrium general price level P^*, times the level of real output, Y^*, or

$$Z = P^*Y^*$$

The dollar value of aggregate demand, in equilibrium, is given by Equation 4-7, with the difference that instead of P, the undetermined price level, we now have P^*, the equilibrium general price level.

$$D = P^*[Y^*(1 - \lambda)] + \bar{M}$$

In equilibrium, $Z = D$, so

$$P^*Y^* = P^*[Y^*(1 - \lambda)] + \bar{M}$$

$$P^*Y^* = P^*Y^* - P^*Y^*\lambda + \bar{M}$$

$$P^* = \bar{M}/Y^*\lambda$$

Since Y^*, $\bar{M}$, and λ are all given, the value of P^* is determined.

Perhaps a numerical example will help clarify this equilibrium position. Assume that equilibrium aggregate output is measured in billions of base-period dollars and that the quantity of money supplied is measured in billions of current dollars.

If $Y^* = 750$, $\lambda = 0.2586$, and $M = 198.24$, the aggregate supply function is $Z = 750P$ and the aggregate demand function is $D = 555.75P + 198.24$. Using Equation 4-5, the demand for money function would be $L = 194.25P$. These relationships are plotted in Figure 4-8. The equilibrium general price level is 1.02, and the equilibrium nominal aggregate product—that is, the aggregate product valued in current rather than base-period prices—is 765.

If the general price level were initially, for some reason, above 1.02 (with respect to Figure 4-8), the excess demand for cash at this particular

Figure 4-8

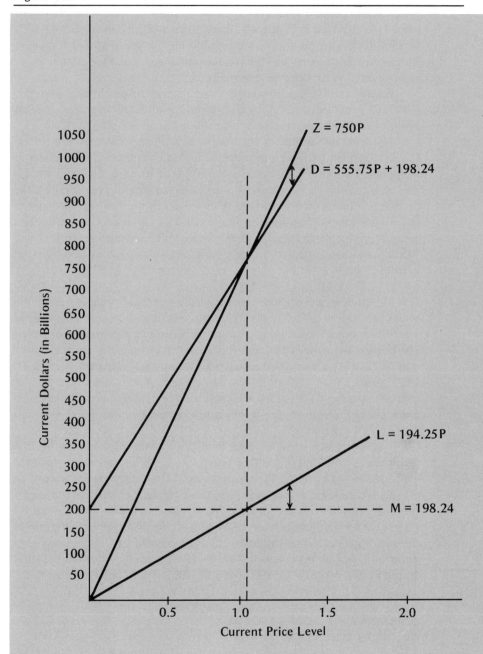

price level would be exactly equal to the excess supply of goods. The glut of goods would prompt price cutting by firms until the excess supply disappeared. As depicted in Figure 4-8, there is one and only one price level (P^*) which will yield supply and demand equilibrium for goods as well as money. The two markets must be equilibrated *simultaneously*. One cannot be in equilibrium and the other in disequilibrium.

When formulated as an equality, a monetary version of Say's law is not trivial. D is not equal to Z, by definition, for all levels of prices. It is an equilibrium condition, true only at a unique price level, P^*.

The main importance of the neoclassical theory of money and prices, called "the quantity theory of money," is that changes in the constants in the demand for money function, λ and Y^*, tend to be gradual and steady. The conclusion is that substantial changes in the general price level are the product of changes in the amount of cash held by individuals, M, which is largely determined by monetary authorities. If the monetary authorities cause M to change, the result will only be a change in the general price level. There is no way of affecting any *real* variable by changing the cash holdings of individuals.

The neoclassical economists discussed a great many refinements of the model presented here. This model, however, is the core of neoclassical macroeconomics, although it could be modified in many ways. For example, in the basic neoclassical model, changes in the actual cash holdings of individuals (M) do not by themselves affect any real variable, such as r^*, $(W/P)^*$, Y^*, and N^*. And it is these real variables that matter. An x percent change in the supply of money will cause an x percent change in money variables, such as causing r^* (the money rate of interest) to become $r^* + x$, and causing P^* to become $P^*(1 + x)$.

Yet there may be some interim effects on the economy before the change in cash holdings produces (only) a change in the variables which are expressed in money terms. The movement of the money rate of interest to $r^* + x$, for example, might be accompanied by some changes in the supply of or the demand for commodities to be used as investment, caused by people confusing the (constant) real rate with the (changing) money rate of interest. Such interim adjustments may be purely illusory, but possibly very important. In fact, many neoclassical writers, especially Knut Wicksell and Irving Fisher, made of them a foundation for a theory of business cycles.

SUMMARY OF NEOCLASSICAL MACROECONOMICS

The assumptions and results of the neoclassical macroeconomic model presented in Part I of this book are, we hope, a fair representation of macroeconomics as it was in the decades before World War II. There was, of course, a great deal of work done before Keynes' *General Theory* which does not fit this rigid mold. But enough of it does.

The neoclassical economists argued that saving and investment depend on the rate of interest and that the equilibrium level of the rate of interest is at any given time determined by the market interaction between savers and investors. The demand "side" of the neoclassical *labor* market is obtained from the conditions necessary for business managers to maximize profits. The quantity of labor demanded is inversely dependent upon the real wage. The supply side of the neoclassical labor market is obtained from the conditions necessary for workers to maximize utility. The quantity of labor supplied is directly dependent upon the real wage. The equilibrium real wage is determined by the market interaction between suppliers and demanders of labor. Once this equilibrium real wage, which is by definition the level corresponding to full employment (in the sense that $N_D = N_S$), is known, the levels of aggregate employment and real output are also known. The quantity theory of money—the theory that the quantity of money demanded varies directly with the nominal value of GNP—can then be used to determine the prevailing level of general prices.

All of these interactions are assumed to occur simultaneously, of course. We rather artificially separated them in Part I of this book for analytical convenience. These interactions are thought of as short-run relationships—that is, they are developed in a context in which the capital holdings of firms are constant. Also, these relationships are "ideal" relationships—they are developed and discussed in a context of perfect competition, a "laboratory" environment not unlike a perfect vacuum in theoretical physics. The main neoclassical result is that in a perfectly competitive environment, macroeconomic equilibrium is synonymous with full-employment equilibrium. The proper role of government is to ensure that the economy approximates the conditions defining perfect competition—by encouraging free mobility of inputs and outputs or discouraging the formation of cartels or unions. Other government activity, such as tinkering with the money supply, might lead to changes in variables expressed in nominal terms, but not those expressed in real terms.

SUGGESTED READING

R. G. D. Allen, *Macro-Economic Theory* (St. Martin's Press, 1967). An excellent, short treatment of neoclassical macroeconomics is provided in Chapter 6, "Classical Macro-Economic Theory." Like many "Keynesian" economists, Professor Allen uses the word "classical" to describe the doctrines and techniques referred to here as "neoclassical."

Professor Allen's usage follows from the fact that many "Keynesians," especially the English, don't believe that there is a great deal of difference between Ricardo and Marshall.

Joseph Ascheim and Ching-Yao Hsieh, *Macroeconomics: Income and Monetary Theory* (Merrill, 1969). Chapter 2, "Classical Theory of Income and Employment," is an extensively documented discussion of *Ricardian* economics. In Chapter 3, "Neoclassical Theory of Income and Employment," an abridged neoclassical model is presented. Chapter 7, "Classical Monetary Theory," is an extensive collection of quotations from the original classical texts. Chapter 8, "Neoclassical Monetary Theory," is a well-documented discussion of the various versions of the quantity theory of money.

For an excellent discussion of the Marshallian or "Cambridge" theory of money and the general price level, see Eprime Eshag's *From Marshall to Keynes: An Essay on the Monetary Theory of the Cambridge School* (Oxford: Basil Blackwell, 1963), Chapter 1, "The Internal Value of Money," pp. 1–25.

Mark Blaug, *Economic Theory in Retrospect*, rev. ed. (Irwin, 1968). An excellent analytical treatment of economics from the 1870s to the 1930s is offered in Chapters 8–14. This presentation is over 300 pages long, and is complete with readers' guides to the major neoclassical texts as well as annotated bibliographies.

The best encyclopedic reference to economics of the period is Joseph A. Schumpeter, *History of Economic Analysis* (New York: Oxford University Press, 1954), Parts IV and V.

Fine literary introductions to neoclassical economics are offered by Robert Lekachman, *A History of Economic Ideas* (Harper & Row, 1959), Part III; and Overton Taylor, *A History of Economic Thought* (McGraw-Hill, 1960), Chapters 12 and 13.

James L. Cochrane, *Macroeconomics Before Keynes* (Scott, Foresman, 1970). This book is a selective history of macroeconomics from the physiocrats (1750–1775) to the 1930s, up to but not including Keynes' *General Theory of Employment, Interest, and Money* (1936). Although it includes a discussion of the various neoclassical "schools" of economics, as well as detailed physiocratic, classical, and Marxian macroeconomic models, about one third of the book is devoted to developing a neoclassical macroeconomic model similar to the one developed in Part I of our book.

Joseph W. Conrad, *An Introduction to the Theory of Interest* (University of California Press, 1959). Among the many topics taken up by Conrad which are relevant to neoclassical macroeconomics is an excellent discussion of "Irving Fisher's Theory of Interest" (pp. 47–71).

Irving Fisher, *The Purchasing Power of Money*, rev. ed. (New York: Macmillan, 1913). Fisher's "transactions" approach to the "quantity" theory of money and prices is presented in Chapters 1, 2, 3, 4 and 8.

The best *classical* version of the "quantity theory" is John Stuart Mill, *Principles of Political Economy*, edited by W. J. Ashley (London: Longmans, Green, 1909), Book III, Chapters 7–14.

Some major original sources of other *neoclassical* versions of this theory are: Alfred Marshall, *Official Papers*, ed. John Maynard Keynes (London: Macmillan, 1926), 7–15, 34–53, and 267–269; and John Maynard Keynes, *A Tract on Monetary Reform* (London: Macmillan, 1923), Chapter ii, and Chapter iii, Section 1.

An excellent collection of selected passages from the major contributors to the quantity theory from the eighteenth century to the present day is provided by Edwin Dean, ed., *The Controversy Over the Quantity Theory of Money* (D. C. Heath, 1965).

John Maynard Keynes, *Essays in Biography* (W. W. Norton, 1951). Keynes was an extraordinarily fine writer of biography. His essays on Alfred Marshall (pp. 125–217), F. Y. Edgeworth (pp. 218–238), and William Stanley Jevons (pp. 255–309) are among the finest short English-language biographies in existence.

John Maynard Keynes, "The General Theory of Employment," *Quarterly Journal of Economics*, Vol. 51 (September 1937), 209–223. This summary of Keynesian economics is clear, precise, and can be successfully read *before* going on to modern restatements of Keynes' work.

In the words of G. L. S. Shackle: "In the *General Theory of Employment, Interest and Money* Keynes was still exploring. In 'The General Theory of Employment' he had arrived." G. L. S. Shackle, *The Years of High Theory: Invention and Tradition in Economic Thought 1926–1939* (England: Cambridge University Press, 1967), 132.

John Maynard Keynes, *The General Theory of Employment, Interest, and Money* (Harcourt Brace Jovanovich, 1936). The nonmonetary portions of Chapter 2 of our book follow Keynes' "The Postulates of Classical Economics" (pp. 4–22). His Chapter 14 contains a discussion of "The Classical Theory of the Rate of Interest," while Chapter 19 is devoted to showing how the neoclassical labor market is in a constant state of equilibrium through "Changes in Money-Wages."

Joan Robinson, *Economic Philosophy* (Aldine-Atherton, 1962). Mrs. Robinson provides an outstanding discussion of the transition from classical to neoclassical to Keynesian economics in Chapter II, "The Classics: Value"; in Chapter III, "The Neo-Classics: Utility"; and in Chapter IV, "The Keynesian Revolution."

A KEYNESIAN APPROACH TO MACROECONOMIC UNDERSTANDING

II
PART

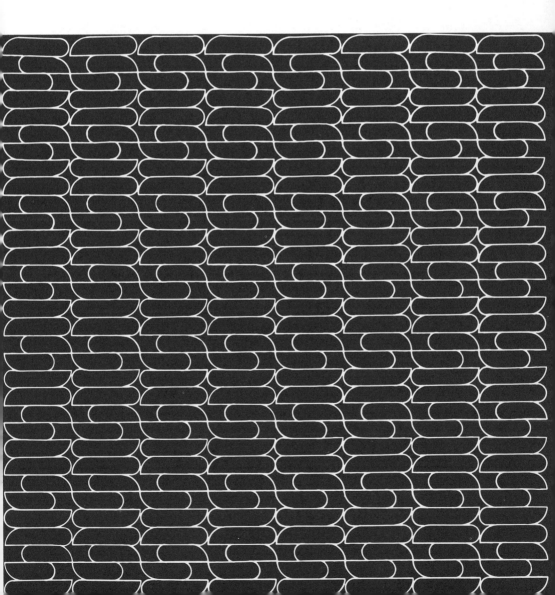

KEYNES' GENERAL THEORY

Even before the publication in 1936 of John Maynard Keynes' *The General Theory of Employment, Interest, and Money*, economic realities were demanding a more adequate explanation of economic phenomena than neoclassical theory could offer. In the United States, for example, unemployment had risen from slightly over 3% of the labor force in 1929 to 25% in 1933. Total United States real production had declined during this period by approximately one third. It was apparent to Keynes and others that economists attempting to explain economic phenomena using a model based on the automatic establishment of full-employment equilibrium were not facing the economic facts of life in the 1930s. Keynes believed that, in a private domestic economy, total spending (aggregate demand) might fall short of the level of receipts businesses required to induce them to hire the full employment level of labor. The system he developed showed how this might occur.

There has been a great deal of discussion about what Keynes really said, as well as about what Keynes really wanted to say. *The General Theory* can be interpreted in many different ways. Keynes wanted the word "General" to be underscored in the title of his book because he viewed his work as encompassing all of neoclassical macroeconomics and some other possibilities as well.

In Part II of our book we are concerned with presenting a single static model of a macroeconomy which contains certain elements we think should be part of a model of this sort. This model is "Keynesian" to the extent that it contains some assumptions and results also in *The General Theory*. Some of these assumptions, such as that the level of saving depends on the level of income, rather than on the rate of interest, are undeniably Keynesian. Other assumptions, such as that the level of the money wage is exogenously given, are debatably Keynesian. This is not particularly important. What is important is that the model explains certain general features of a macro-economy in a way which is relatively consistent with the views of most contemporary economists. Also, the model yields the one really important Keynesian result—that an economy as a whole, even under rather ideal conditions, can settle down to a macroeconomic equilibrium which is *not* consistent with full utilization of available factor resources.

"KEYNESIAN" MACROECONOMICS

Ever since the publication of Keynes' *The General Theory*, many economists have been interested in distilling the theoretical content of "Keynesian" macroeconomics. This interest has produced an enormous and continuously expanding body of written work. One portion of this work consists of basically static algebraic models of a capitalist economy, in which it is possible that, during the time span under consideration, the only variable productive input (labor) is going to be underutilized. These models are used to show that an economy's operating at less than full capacity, at full capacity with no pressure on prices, or at full capacity with built-in inflationary pressures depends on the exact relationship between aggregate supply and demand. The other major features of a "Keynesian" macro-economic model are also present in such treatments: the introduction of different independent variables in the saving and investment functions (income and interest, respectively, not just the rate of interest).

While these versions of Keynes' model were being developed, other economists were attacking the model itself. *The General Theory* had political and social overtones which did not appeal to everyone. Specifically, Keynes and his followers had advocated that a capitalist economy at any given moment did not necessarily operate at full capacity. Full capacity could be achieved by the private and public monetary authorities. But traditionally, such authorities deny that they have such power, and therefore the responsibility to act. Neoclassical economists and monetary authorities argue that changes in the supply of money only affect the general level of prices.

Keynes argued that in Britain, at least, the monetary authorities would fail to act because they were unwilling to accept long-run capital losses, which might be necessary to achieve stabilization. Bond prices would rise as the central bank added to the country's money supply by purchasing government bonds at the attractive prices required to coax at least a portion of the wealth-owning public to get out of government bonds and—at least at first—into cash. Conversely, Keynes and others would want central banks to sell government bonds during a period of excessive aggregate demand at prices low enough to coax purchasing power out of the economy. Such counter-cyclical activity is not compatible with the "sound business principles" so firmly entrenched in the minds of many individuals who control central banks.

Furthermore, Keynes argued that since the monetary authorities can be expected not to do their duty (as he saw it), and since wage cuts were to him a socially undesirable and perhaps institutionally infeasible method of achieving full capacity, fiscal policy was required to do the job. Placing such responsibility with the central *government* was, to many of Keynes' antagonists, very close to Bolshevism.

KEYNES AND THE KEYNESIANS

We refer to Part II of our book as "Keynesian Macroeconomics" because the model developed contains several aspects of a macroeconomy which Keynes emphasized in his *The General Theory*, and many aspects of what most economists view as a "Keynesian" macroeconomy. Yet, more and more economists have become convinced that the mechanistic *equilibrium* models, such as the ones presented in Part II *as well as* in Part I, were precisely what Keynes was reacting against.

In 1937 Keynes replied[1] to a few early criticisms of his *The General Theory*. He attempted to clarify the nature of his case against his predecessors. Anyone reading this essay now, more than thirty years after it was written, cannot avoid being shocked at the difference between the aspects of *The General Theory* Keynes wanted to emphasize and those which make up many contemporary orthodox presentations of "Keynesian" macroeconomics. The dominant theme of Keynes' essay was the distinction between risk and uncertainty.

According to Keynes, the perfectly competitive neoclassical system was based on the absence of uncertainty:

"It is generally recognized that the Ricardian analysis was concerned with what we now call long-period equilibrium. Marshall's contribution mainly consisted in grafting on to this the marginal principle and the principle of substitution, together with some discussion of the passage from one position of long-period equilibrium to another. But he assumed, as Ricardo did, that the amounts of the factors of production in use were given and that the problem was to determine the way in which they would be used and their relative rewards. Edgeworth and Professor Pigou and other later and contemporary writers have embroidered and improved this theory by considering how different peculiarities in the shapes of the supply functions of the factors of production would affect matters, what will happen in conditions of monopoly and imperfect competition, how far social and individual advantage coincide, what are the special problems of exchange in an open system and the like. But these more recent writers like

---

1. "The General Theory of Employment," *Quarterly Journal of Economics*, Vol. 51 (February 1937), 209–223.

their predecessors were still dealing with a system in which the amount of the factors employed was given and the other relevant facts were known more or less for certain. This does not mean that they were dealing with a system in which change was ruled out, or even one in which the disappointment of expectation was ruled out. But at any given time facts and expectations were assumed to be given in a definite and calculable form; and risks, of which, tho admitted, not much notice was taken, were supposed to be capable of an exact actuarial computation. The calculus of probability, tho mention of it was kept in the background, was supposed to be capable of reducing uncertainty to the same calculable status as that of certainty itself; just as in the Benthamite calculus of pains and pleasures or of advantage and disadvantage, by which the Benthamite philosophy assumed men to be influenced in their general ethical behavior." (Ibid., pp. 212–213.)

It should be undeniably clear that Keynes, as he asserted in the passage above, believed the major innovation of *The General Theory* to be the incorporation of (or the suggestion to incorporate) *uncertainty* into economic analysis. Keynes' use of uncertainty is the key to what Joseph Schumpeter, an eminent historian of economic thought, referred to as Keynes' "vision" —his *gestalt* conception of how a modern capitalist economy works.

The following quotation can serve to introduce Keynes' distinction between risk and uncertainty:

"By 'uncertain' knowledge, let me explain, I do not mean merely to distinguish what is known for certain from what is only probable. The game of roulette is not subject, in this sense, to uncertainty; nor is the prospect of a Victory bond being drawn. Or, again the expectation of life is only slightly uncertain. Even the weather is only moderately uncertain. The sense in which I am using the term is that in which the prospect of a European war is uncertain, or the price of copper and the rate of interest twenty years hence, or the obsolescence of a new invention or the position of private wealth owners in the social system in 1970. About these matters there is no scientific basis on which to form any calculable probability whatever. We simply do not know." (Ibid., pp. 213–214.)

The extent of our misunderstanding of Keynes' *The General Theory* has been noted by G. L. S. Shackle:

"Keynes' whole theory of unemployment is ultimately the simple statement that, rational expectation being unattainable, we substitute for it first one and then another kind of irrational expectation: and the shift from one arbitrary basis to another gives us from time to time a moment of truth, when our artificial confidence is for the time being dissolved, and we, as business men, are afraid to invest, and so fail to provide enough demand to match our society's desire to produce. Keynes in *The General Theory* attempted a rational theory of a field of conduct which by the nature of its terms could be only semi-rational. But sober economists gravely upholding a faith in the calculability of human affairs could not bring themselves to acknowledge that this could be his purpose. They sought to interpret *The*

General Theory as just one more manual of political arithmetic. In so far as it failed this test, they found it wrong, or obscure, or perverse."[2]

Professor Axel Leijonhuvud[3] has become one of the most persistent advocates of the view that economists must reconsider *The General Theory* as a declaration to economists of a few facts of life:

1. Adjustments to economic equilibria take time, and we live in the very uncertain interim during which the adjustments are taking place.
2. The process of adjustment is costly (the "higgling" required to get to supply and demand equilibrium is often done by professional "higglers").
3. Deals are going to be closed at other than the "equilibrium" price while the "higgling" is taking place.

Macroeconomists (and students of macroeconomics!) are left in a bit of a dilemma which should not, however, be too disturbing. *The General Theory of Employment, Interest, and Money* is now a "classic" itself. Like all the Great Books in the history of economics, it was not a perfectly formed, completed whole. Much was left for the reader to fill in himself. The book is now studied by scholars who are concerned with at least two questions: (1) What did Keynes really say? (2) Given some answer to the first question, what is "Keynesian economics," and how and why did its disciples arrive at "Keynesianism"? However, we simply want to present a relatively complete static model. The doctrinal issues are of secondary importance in this book.

INVOLUNTARY UNEMPLOYMENT

Perhaps it would be worthwhile to give a brief preview of the major Keynesian result, which he called "involuntary unemployment." The upper panel of Figure II-1 is the aggregate production function introduced in Part I. Aggregate real output (Y) is depicted as a function of the quantities of labor (N) and capital (K) employed. The quantity of capital employed is accepted as a datum (we are working with a short-run model), and a given increase in N causes Y to increase less than equiproportionately (diminishing returns occur, caused by the fixity of capital). If the prevailing level of the labor force is fully employed, the level of aggregate real

2. G. L. S. Shackle, *The Years of High Theory: Invention and Tradition in Economic Thought, 1926–1939.* (Cambridge University Press, 1967), 129.
3. Axel Leijonhuvud, *On Keynesian Economics and the Economics of Keynes: A Study in Monetary Theory* (Oxford University Press, 1968). Leijonhuvud has offered several summaries of his point of view. See, for example, "Keynes and the Keynesians: A Suggested Interpretation," *American Economic Review*, Vol. 57 (May 1967), 401–410; and "Keynes and the Effectiveness of Monetary Policy," *Western Economic Journal*, Vol. 6 (March 1968), 97–111. An excellent discussion of the "uncertainty" interpretation of Keynes' *The General Theory* is offered in Shackle, *op. cit.*, Chs. 11 and 12.

Figure II-1

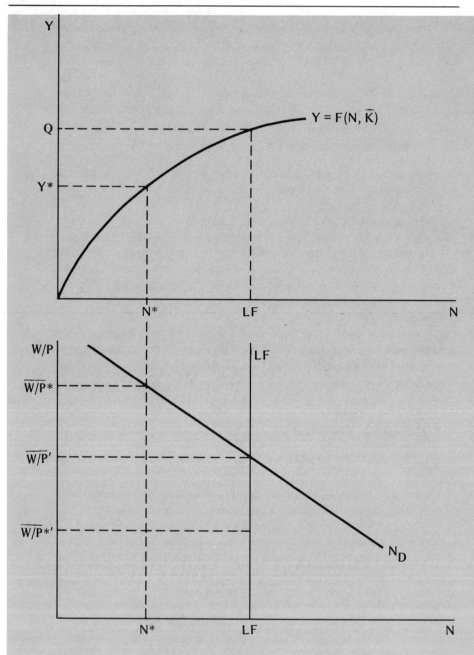

output is full-employment or capacity output (Q). Hereafter, we will denote this special level of real income as Q.

An aggregate labor demand function (N_D) is drawn in the lower panel of Figure II-1. It gives the various quantities of labor business managers as a whole will want to hire given any specific level of the real wage (W/P). It is a downward-sloping function because, as discussed in Chapter 3, the labor demand function is the marginal productivity of labor function, and the marginal productivity of labor declines as the quantity of labor employed increases.

The vertical line in the lower panel of Figure II-1 denotes the prevailing level of the labor force (WF). In Part II of this book we assume that the quantity of labor supplied during some given time period is a fact of life and does *not* vary with the real wage, as we assumed it did in Part I.

The final feature of Figure II-1 that should be clarified is that the money wage is assumed to be exogenously given, as denoted by the bar over the W terms. The wage expressed in current-period dollars is assumed to be determined by economic and noneconomic forces outside our "system" or frame of reference.

"Full employment" in this context is where the labor demand function intersects the vertical WF line. The real wage at this intersection, labeled $\bar{W}/P'$ in Figure II-1, is the real wage which must prevail if the entire labor force is to be employed. Although this view of the labor-production nexus is a little different from that developed in Part I, it is not *that* different.

In Part I we denoted the full-employment levels of variables and parameters with asterisks. Hereafter, variables denoted with asterisks will be "equilibrium" levels—not necessarily full-employment levels. The version of Keynesian "involuntary unemployment" developed in Part II of this book is based on macroeconomic equilibrium occurring at a real wage other that $\bar{W}/P'$. We show that there is no reason to expect this "full-employment" real wage to prevail automatically. The real wage can turn out to be anything, such as $\bar{W}/P^*$ or $\bar{W}/P^{*\prime}$, with reference to the lower panel of Figure II-1.

If the prevailing equilibrium real wage turns out to be $\bar{W}/P^*$, the aggregate quantity of labor employed will be N^* and the aggregate level of real output will be Y^*. In this case the economy is not producing all it can produce (Q). This situation is the one referred to in Part II as the involuntary unemployment case. Whether or not this is precisely what Keynes had in mind when he introduced the concept in 1936 does not concern us very much now. In Part II, we are concerned with "involuntary unemployment," as depicted in Figure II-1.

Keynesian
Equilibrium
and
Consumption

In the neoclassical model presented in Part I of this book, aggregate consumption did not play a prominent causal role. The major relationship in that macroeconomic model was the link between production and employment. Keynes reoriented macroeconomics from production-employment relationships to consumption-employment relationships. Keynes emphasized the demand rather than the supply side of macroeconomics, perhaps because he was writing during a period in which many Western economies were experiencing deficient aggregate demand.

Since 1936, economists have focused on the determinants of the components of aggregate demand, and more importantly, on the relationship between them and the level of aggregate economic activity. Consumer spending is the largest and generally the most stable component of aggregate demand, so we will begin our presentation of "Keynesian" models with a discussion of the determinants of this particular aggregate variable.

INCOME AND CONSUMPTION

Personal consumption expenditures (C), measured here in billions of base-period dollars, refer to the final goods and services which households plan to acquire during the current period for their personal use. This item includes planned purchases of services, nondurables, and durables (except new residential construction). As is discussed at length in Chapter 6, many factors affect the level of consumption. Yet by and large, the greater the level of current real income (Y), measured in base-period prices, that an individual, household, or an entire nation has, the greater will be the level of consumer demand and spending.

Certainly the amount of an individual's expenditures is influenced, or is at least limited, by his real income. It is true that purchases on credit as well as other factors permit the volume of consumption to exceed real income for varying lengths of time, but generally the magnitude of household real income places a distinct limitation upon consumption. Obviously, different households will spend varying amounts even with identical real incomes if they are differently situated (that is, some may have large families, large bank balances, or may view the future differently than others do). Furthermore, at a given level of real income, a large number of factors could alter the proportion of one's real income devoted to consumption.

Aside from differences in circumstances, however, empirical studies indicate that, at higher levels of real income, consumption increases, but the increase in consumption is less than the increase in real income. Keynes termed this relationship the "consumption function"—a behavioral function. Although the reasons why a given increase in real income results in a smaller increase in consumption are not absolutely clear, the following considerations are relevant: the diminishing marginal utility of increased quantities of goods; the increased incentive to speculate on the stock market as real incomes rise; a greater inclination to save for retirement (when real incomes become substantial for most persons, retirement is usually imminent and provision for retirement becomes more vital).

All of these are mere rationalizations of observed patterns and not much stress should be placed on them. It is the pattern which is significant. It indicates that there is a stable positive association between real income and consumption. Hence, if individual real income is a determinant of individual or household consumption, it follows that aggregate real income must affect aggregate consumption.

MARGINAL AND AVERAGE PROPENSITIES TO CONSUME

Let us examine briefly the aggregate consumption function. It may be written in general form as

$$C = f(Y)$$

Note that we are relating consumption to real income. This may appear unrealistic, since we know that consumers must pay taxes with a portion of Y and do not have the power to decide to spend or save that portion which is taxed away. (Public authorities make that decision for them.) In this chapter, however, we abstract from taxes, so that real income (Y) is the same as real disposable income (Y_d).

The function $C = f(Y)$ expresses the assumption that consumption (C) depends upon, or "is some function of," real income (Y). This general function may be expressed explicitly as a linear function:

$$C = a_1 + a_2 Y \quad \text{(with } a_1 > 0 \text{ and } 1 > a_2 > 0\text{)}$$

This form of the consumption function is used throughout this part of the book. There are two reasons for doing this: (1) it gives a reasonably accurate description of the consumption function *in the neighborhood of the equilibrium real income;* and (2) it simplifies the analysis.

The Marginal Propensity to Consume

In the above function, a_2 denotes the slope of the consumption function, dC/dY, and a_1 represents the intercept on the vertical axis. The change in consumption brought about by a change in real income $(dC/dY = a_2)$ is called the *marginal propensity to consume* (MPC).

Recall the concept of a "derivative" introduced in Chapter 3. In a function with only one independent variable, such as

$$y = ax^m + b$$

(in which a, m, and b are constants), the "first derivative" or slope (since there are only two variables and the function can be graphed in two-dimensional space) was expressed as

$$\frac{dy}{dx} = max^{m-1}$$

The consumption function

$$C = C(Y) = a_1 + a_2 Y$$

is an identical function. Since a_1 and a_2 are constants,

$$\frac{dC}{dY} = a_2 1 Y^{1-1} = a_2 Y^0 = a_2$$

We have already placed limits on the range of the coefficients in the algebraic version of the consumption function introduced above—that is

$$C = a_1 + a_2 Y \qquad \text{(with } a_1 > 0 \text{ and } 1 > a_2 > 0\text{)}$$

These limits mean we are assuming that the vertical intercept (a_1) of the consumption function is positive, and that its slope (a_2) is a positive fraction, as depicted in Figure 5-1.

The Average Propensity to Consume

The average propensity to consume (C/Y) is the fraction consumed of an average dollar of real income. The average propensity to consume at any particular level of income, such as Y' in Figure 5-1, can be obtained graphically by drawing a line from the origin to the relevant point on the con-

Figure 5-1

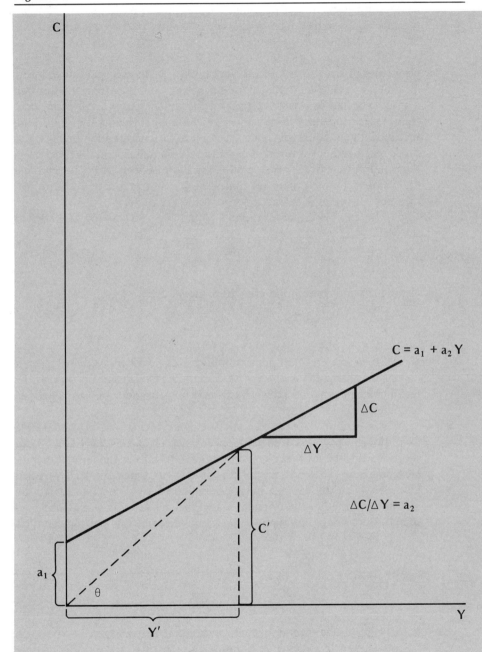

sumption function. The slope of this line is given by the tangent of the angle θ formed by its construction. The tangent of θ is obtained by dividing the side opposite the angle by the side adjacent. That is, the slope of this line is C'/Y', the average propensity to consume.

Note that this ratio, unlike our MPC, varies with the level of Y. It is clear from Figure 5-1 that, at very low levels of Y, the slope of this connecting line is greater than that of a line emanating from the origin and forming a 45° angle; that is, it is greater than unity. At these low levels of income, the average propensity to consume (APC) is greater than unity—indicating that individuals in the aggregate spend more for consumption than the nation's real income. However, at higher levels of real income, the APC is less than unity—that is, the consumption function lies below the line forming the 45° angle, which indicates that society is not spending all of its real income, but rather is saving a portion of it.

From our linear consumption function, we have already found that the MPC is

$$\frac{dC}{dY} = a_2$$

Using the same consumption function, the APC is

$$\frac{C}{Y} = \frac{a_1}{Y} + a_2$$

Hence, if we posit a linear consumption function with a positive a_1 term, it is clear that the MPC is *always* less than the APC. This means that, as the real income of a nation grows, its citizens consume less and save more, in relative terms.

Cross-section data—data obtained by surveying a sample of people from different portions of society concerning their spending activities—and short-run time-series data suggest that the APC falls as the level of real income increases. However, an analysis of long-run time-series data revealed that the APC in the United States has remained fairly constant (or, to say the same thing, that the fraction of real income saved has remained constant). A consumption function that would describe this phenomenon has $a_1 = 0$; that is,

$$C = a_2 Y$$

where

$$\frac{dC}{dY} = a_2 \quad \text{and} \quad \frac{C}{Y} = a_2$$

In this case, the MPC and APC are constant and equal.

As is seen in Chapter 6, a more comprehensive theory of consumer behavior is needed to resolve the contradiction between the evidence from short-run and cross-section data, and long-run data. In the present discussion we will continue to assume that $a_1 > 0$.

INCOME AND SAVING

If we use a linear form of the consumption function, then the relationship between consumption and saving is apparent:

$$S = Y - C$$
$$S = Y - a_1 - a_2 Y$$
$$S = -a_1 + Y - a_2 Y$$
$$S = -a_1 + (1 - a_2) Y$$

The slope of the saving function $(1 - a_2)$ is the marginal propensity to save (MPS), that is, the change in saving brought about by a change in real income (dS/dY). Note that the MPS is $1 - $ MPC.

The average propensity to save (APS) is defined as S/Y. In our case of a linear consumption function

$$\frac{S}{Y} = -\frac{a_1}{Y} + (1 - a_2)$$

A linear saving function is drawn in the lower panel of Figure 5-2. Note that the vertical intercept of the saving function is negative. At some low level of real income, such as Y' in the upper panel of Figure 5-2, the average propensity to consume (C/Y) becomes unity. That is, the line from the origin to the consumption function at this particular level of real income forms a 45° angle. The nation is consuming all of its real income at this level. Real saving is zero, as denoted in the lower panel of Figure 5-2. At levels of real income below Y', saving actually becomes negative. In such cases a portion of household consumption for the nation as a whole is financed out of accumulated past saving.

A DIGRESSION ON
NET CORPORATE SAVING

Businesses save, as well as households. They save in the form of "undistributed profits," corporate profits not paid to stockholders, which is called *net corporate saving* in the national income and product accounts. It and household saving constitute total private saving. Although net corporate saving and household saving are deducted from Y to obtain consumption, most of net corporate saving flows immediately into net corporate investment in inventories, plant, and equipment. Since consumption is assumed in this chapter to depend on the level of Y, the marginal propensity to consume, a_2, is smaller than it would be if our income variable were disposable personal income. The lower MPC is explained by the inclusion in Y of net corporate saving, a portion of Y over which the consumer has no control.

Figure 5-2

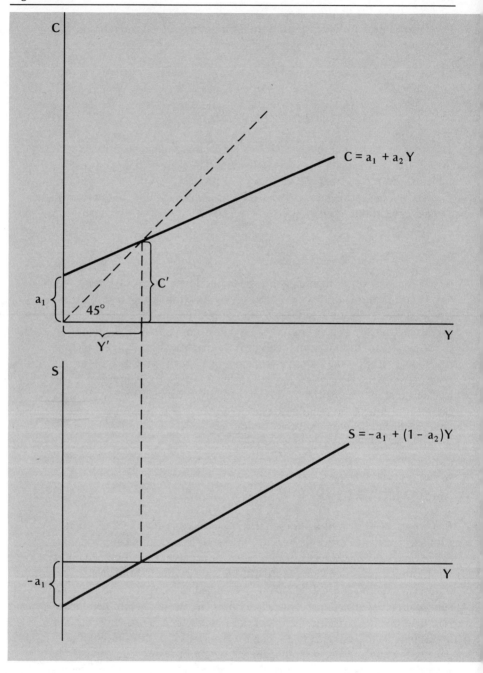

So far in this chapter we have presented the bare essentials of a simple consumption function. Because of the importance of the consumption function in Keynesian macroeconomics—some economists believe that the concept of the consumption function is Keynes's most important contribution—we return to the subject in Chapter 6.

AGGREGATE DEMAND

For analytical as well as accounting purposes, economists divide a macroeconomy into four institutional "sectors"—households, businesses, government, and foreign trade. We will use the letters C, I, and G to denote consumption, net investment, and government spending, respectively. "Net exports" (that is, exports minus imports) will be denoted by X. Therefore, the aggregate demand for final goods and services, excluding capital replacement, can be expressed as

$$Y = C + I + G + X$$

For purposes of simplification, we will assume in this chapter a closed private capitalistic economy. In other words, we will assume that we are dealing with an economy which has no government (and hence no taxes) and no foreign trade; that is, G and X are assumed to be zero. In Chapter 16 we expand this model to include foreign economic relations. Thus the expression for aggregate demand used is quite simple:

$$Y = C + I$$

The two components of the right-hand side of the above equation are the relevant demands for final goods and services.

In the neoclassical model developed in Part I of this book, the prevailing levels of both saving and investment are determined by the rate of interest. As discussed above, Keynes introduced into macroeconomic analysis the notion of a "consumption function" and equivalently a "saving function" where the prevailing level of consumption is depicted as a linear function of the level of income. Thus, one component in our aggregate demand function, consumption, depends on the level of income. The other component, net investment, that is, the level of net additions to capital that business managers want to make during the period, is assumed to be determined by factors beyond our consideration at the present time. Thus we write our expression for aggregate demand as

$$Y = C + \bar{I} \tag{5-1}$$

The bar over the investment term (I) in Equation 5-1 denotes that the level of net investment is assumed to be exogenously determined. That is, investment is an explicit variable in the present model, but its prevailing level is determined outside the confines of the model, and is accepted as a fact of life. In later chapters net investment is viewed in a different fashion; we allow it to become an endogenous variable, meaning that its prevailing level is determined within the confines of our models.

KEYNESIAN EQUILIBRIUM

Economists distinguish between planned, intended, or *ex ante* variables and actual, realized, or *ex post* variables. Equation 5-1 should be thought of as giving the *planned* levels of consumption and investment.

We are interested in discovering the more important factors that determine the equilibrium level of Y, and in turn, the volume of employment which this level of Y will support during any given time period. It is not unrealistic to assume that the spending plans of households are realized. However, it *is* quite possible that the plans of businesses to make a given addition to their capital stocks (which include finished goods) may go unrealized. Business managers might plan a certain level of investment activity (I), but it is possible that, among other things, positive or negative unexpected inventory investment will cause their plans to be unrealized.

The discrepancy between planned or intended investment and realized investment is resolved by business accepting unplanned inventory changes. (They cannot really keep customers from taking goods off the shelves if they are willing to pay for them.)

We have introduced the linear consumption function

$$C = a_1 + a_2 Y$$

This function is drawn in the upper panel of Figure 5-3. The corresponding linear saving function

$$S = -a_1 + (1 - a_2) Y$$

is drawn in the lower panel. I is an exogenously given level of planned investment. The $C + I$ line in the upper panel of Figure 5-3 is obtained by vertically adding I to the level of consumption corresponding to each level of income. This same level of investment is used to determine the position of the I line in the lower panel of Figure 5-3. For now we will ignore the upper panel of the diagram. It is drawn only to reinforce the connection between the saving function and the consumption function. We will, however, discuss the content of this upper panel when we get to Figure 5-4, which is equivalent to Figure 5-3.

Assume that, for some reason, the level of Y *in the beginning of the current period* is Y', with respect to both panels of Figure 5-3. The level of saving corresponding to this level of income (S') is simply read from the vertical axis in the lower panel of Figure 5-3. This level of saving is exceeded

Figure 5-3

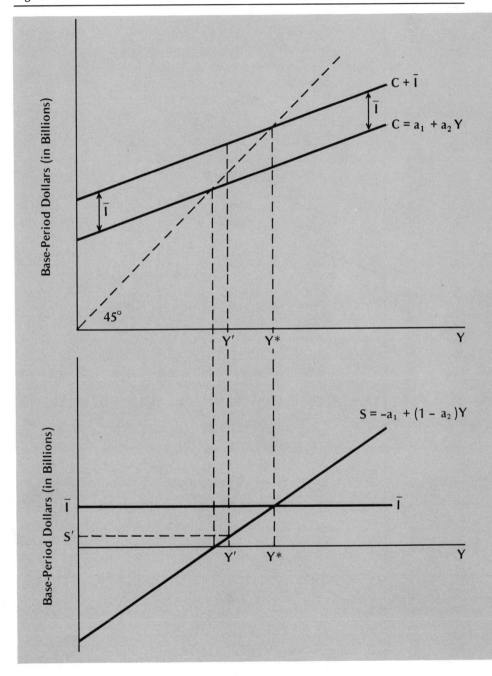

Figure 5-4

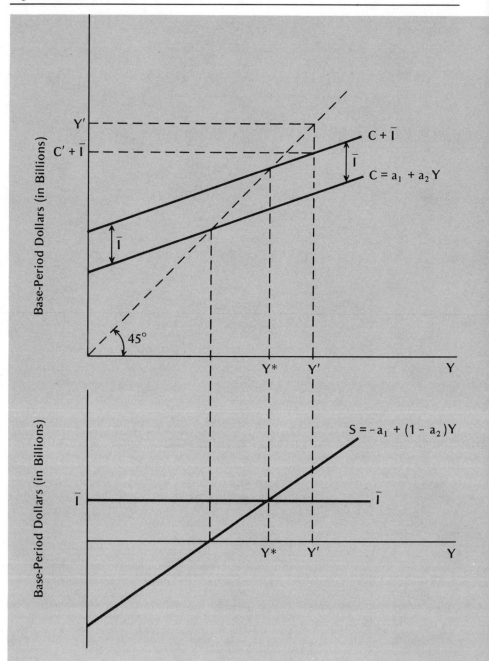

by the exogenously given level of planned investment $\bar{I}$ (which, by assumption, does not vary as income varies). Businesses have overestimated the amount of purchasing power households want to save—that is, not spend on current goods and services—during the current period, and are placed in a position of losing inventories which they had not expected to lose.

To increase their depleted stocks of inventories, businesses will probably increase current output (and employment). Such increases would increase current income and, hence, consumption. These increases will continue until the level of saving is equal to planned investment. The level of income at which this equality would occur is Y^* in Figure 5-3. Y^* is the equilibrium level of Y. It is the level of Y at which business in the aggregate has no incentive to expand or contract the current volume of real income (output) and employment. Y^* will be the level of Y during the current period if there is time enough for these adjustments to occur.

In reality, we may begin an accounting period with a level of Y at an annual rate of Y'. During the period, say a quarter, market forces are moving us to a Y^* level of activity. Of course we may not get there, so the level of Y reported by the Department of Commerce may be between Y' and Y^*. Also, Y^* itself—the target level of Y towards which we are moving—may itself change between the beginning and end of the period, because of a change in $\bar{I}$ or a_2, for example. This same adjustment process works if the level of income were, for some reason, initially above Y^*. Figure 5-4 is designed to help you see this adjustment process from the other direction and in the context of the *consumption* function rather than the *saving* function.

The dashed line forming the 45° angle in the upper panel of Figure 5-4 may be used to mark off equal constant dollar amounts on each axis. Therefore, if the current level of real income were for some reason at Y', this amount can be read, using the 45° line, from either the horizontal or the vertical axis. A Y' level of real income corresponds to a $C' + \bar{I}$ level of aggregate demand. This level of aggregate demand is less than Y'. The amount of the deficiency is marked off in the upper panel of Figure 5-4. Businesses have *over*estimated the amount of purchasing power households want to spend for goods and services during the current period, and are left with a corresponding amount of unsold products.

To reduce these stocks of undesired inventories, businesses will probably cut back on output. As has already been discussed, an inventory adjustment process forces the economy to the Y^* level of real income. Y^* is a stable equilibrium level of income. If the economy is not there, automatic market forces will force it there; and if it is there, it will stay there.

In short, differences between saving and investment are assumed to be eliminated by fluctuations in output. One of the key pillars of static, aggregate economics is the assumption that these adjustments have *fully worked themselves out during the current period, in every productive sector in the economy.*

CONCLUSION

The model presented in this chapter is the simplest possible macroeconomic model. This model and the one presented in Chapter 6 are probably familiar to you from your introductory course in economics. So far, our simple model consists of three equations. We have disregarded the government sector, the foreign trade sector, the money market, and the labor market. In addition, we have assumed that the value of net investment is predetermined and fixed.

In the next chapter we continue with this "Keynesian equilibrium" approach to macroeconomic analysis. Government activity, both spending and taxing, is brought into the picture, and government *policy* is discussed. In essence, we will add three more equations to our model, and in the following chapters additional equations are added as the money and labor markets are brought into the analysis. Our most complex, "complete" model (presented in Chapter 12) consists of twelve equations, and is constructed from the equations that we develop and explain in preceding chapters, including this one.

Economists today are increasingly interested in applying economic theories to real life, and this requires the development of highly sophisticated macro models. Numerous large-scale research projects are underway all over the world for the purpose of attempting to determine the actual causes and effects of macroeconomic activity and to determine ways to control their outcome. Economic theory, statistics, mathematics, and computers are being applied to this quest. The result has led to the development of complex macroeconomic models with 200 (or more) equations. These complex models, however, are similar in essentials to the models, particularly the "complete" model given in Chapter 12, which we use to illustrate macroeconomic relationships. The more sophisticated macro models may have four or five consumption equations which include many more variables than our single consumption equation. However, an understanding of the nature of the single consumption equation will prepare you to understand the more complex treatment of consumption in macro models. Accordingly, if you can understand the macro models developed in this text, you are prepared to comprehend the more sophisticated empirical models in use today.

The Consumption Function

Economists had been interested in the factors determining how a society divides its income between consumption and saving long before Keynes focused attention on the problem in *The General Theory*. As discussed in Chapter 5, the "consumption function" (equivalently, the "saving function") is a very important part of modern marcoeconomic theory. In his treatment, Keynes emphasized the delineation of four basic components of aggregate demand: consumption, investment, government spending, and net exports. Consumption, of course, is the largest component. In most countries, it is also a fairly predictable portion of aggregate demand. Keynes viewed the second portion of aggregate demand, investment, as highly volatile. He feared that western economies' inability to match *full employment* saving with the prevailing level of investment would lead to chronic unemployment.

Keynes made the following points about the consumption function:

1. "Men are disposed, as a rule and on the average, to increase their consumption as their income increases, but not by as much as the increase in their income."[1] That is, the marginal propensity to consume (MPC) is greater than zero but less than one.
2. The MPC is smaller than the average propensity to consume (APC).
3. The APC may decline with increases in income. The reason for this is that it may take time to change one's habits. In addition, as a nation becomes wealthier, its citizens tend to save more of an average dollar.
4. At low levels of income, consumption may exceed income; that is, the APC may exceed 100% and dissaving occurs. *Dissaving* is the consequence of consumption expenditures exceeding income receipts; it is accomplished either by using previously accumulated savings or by borrowing.

1. John Maynard Keynes, *General Theory of Employment, Interest, and Money* (Harcourt Brace Jovanovich, 1936), 96.

These propositions of Keynes have stimulated an enormous amount of research on the consumption function. Fortunately (and not by coincidence),
this stimulation occurred at a point in history when national accounting
systems were being developed in many western countries, providing data
for such research.

   An important goal of this chapter is to discuss whether or not these
propositions have been verified, and if not, why not. Also, it is important
to consider the propositions within the time context of the short run or
long run.

SHORT-RUN AND LONG-RUN CONSUMPTION FUNCTIONS

The two most prominent forms of the consumption function which we can
use to discuss Keynes' propositions are given in Figure 6-1. Both functions
are consistent with proposition 1 given above. The one in the upper panel
is a linear function passing through the origin:

$$C = a_2 Y \quad \text{(with } 1 > a_2 > 0)$$

The marginal propensity to consume (MPC) and the average propensity
to consume (APC) are both constant; that is,

$$\frac{dC}{dY} = \frac{C}{Y} = a_2$$

Hence, this function is inconsistent with the Keynesian propositions 2
through 4.

   The function in the lower panel of Figure 6-1, the form used in Chapter 5, has a positive vertical axis intercept:

$$C = a_1 + a_2 Y \quad \text{(with } a_1 > 0 \quad \text{and} \quad 1 > a_2 > 0)$$

where
$$\frac{dC}{dY} = a_2 \quad \text{and} \quad \frac{C}{Y} = \frac{a_1}{Y} + a_2$$

Although the MPC is constant in the latter function, the APC declines
with increases in real income. In addition, the APC exceeds the MPC. The
function in the lower panel of Figure 6-1 shows a declining APC as real
income increases. Hence, the fraction of an average dollar of equilibrium
real income which will be spent on current goods and services declines as
Y increases.

   Moreover, the consumption function in the lower panel of Figure 6-1
is one in which dissaving can occur at relatively low levels of Y. Hence, a
consumption function of this general form is consistent with all of the
basic Keynesian propositions mentioned above.

   The consumption function in the lower panel of Figure 6-1 has been
verified empirically, using two basic sets of data. First, research based on

Figure 6-1

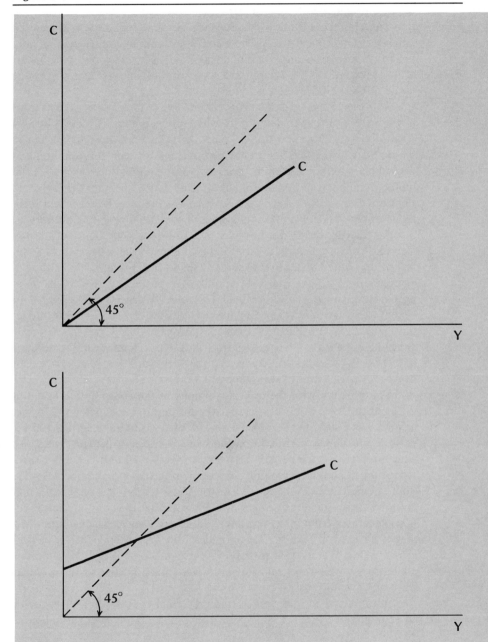

family-budget data indicates that current consumption expenditures are highly correlated with various measures of current (or recent) income, and that the APC exceeds the MPC. Second, *short-run* time series data lead to much the same conclusions.[2] These consumption functions (which we refer to as "cyclical" consumption functions) are ones in which dissaving occurs at low levels of Y. (Dissavings *did* occur in the United States during the worst of the 1930s Depression years.)

Short-run time series data that cover three different periods are shown in Figure 6-2, a scatter diagram in which consumption is plotted against disposable real income for given years. Straight lines are drawn through the points which reflect the trend relationships between consumption and disposable real income for the desired years. Although not all points fall on the trend lines, those that do not are very close. The lines themselves in Figure 6-2 are drawn freehand. To be more precise, the statistical technique of *regression analysis* could be used to determine their positions.

As early as the 1940s, however, a serious conflict of evidence arose. Derived from *long-run* time series data, Simon Kuznets' estimates of savings in the United States for the period 1869 to 1929 revealed that, although aggregate real income rose substantially, the average as well as marginal propensities to consume remained *constant*.[3] Kuznets' data, plotted in Figure 6-3, were verified by Raymond Goldsmith.[4] A consumption function consistent with Kuznets' findings is like the one shown in the upper panel of Figure 6-1. Hence, long-run data tend to refute the hypothesis that the APC would normally exceed the MPC, and that the APC would decline with increases in real income.

The problem with the cyclical versions of the consumption function is that they have not always predicted consumption adequately when real income was rising, nor have they always been accurate when used in reverse. For example, consumption functions based on short-run time series data available for the periods between World Wars I and II led to *under-*estimation of consumer spending based on projected postwar income levels. That is, the cyclical functions were for some reason too flat—the MPC given by these functions was too low. In addition, the consumption functions generated from interwar annual data were also very inaccurate when they were used in reverse. They forecast too *little* saving for the period *before* World War I—that is, the levels of pre-World War I consumption predicted by these "cyclical" functions were much greater than the actual levels of consumption.

It appears then, that to describe the actual consumption behavior of an economy, we need to distinguish the long-run and short-run relation-

2. See Robert Ferber, *A Study of Aggregate Consumption Functions* (National Bureau of Economic Research, 1953).
3. Simon Kuznets, *National Product Since 1869* (National Bureau of Economic Research, 1946). See also Kuznets' "Proportion of Capital Formation to National Product," *American Economic Review*, Vol. 42 (May 1952), 507–526.
4. Raymond Goldsmith, *A Study of Saving in the United States* (Princeton University Press, 1955).

Figure 6-2

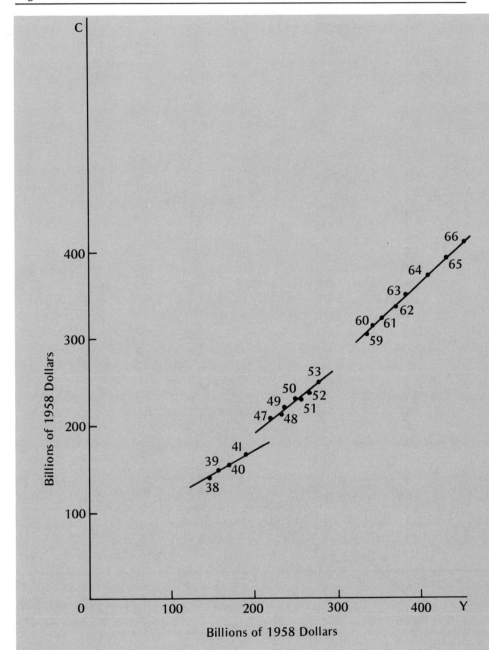

Figure 6-3

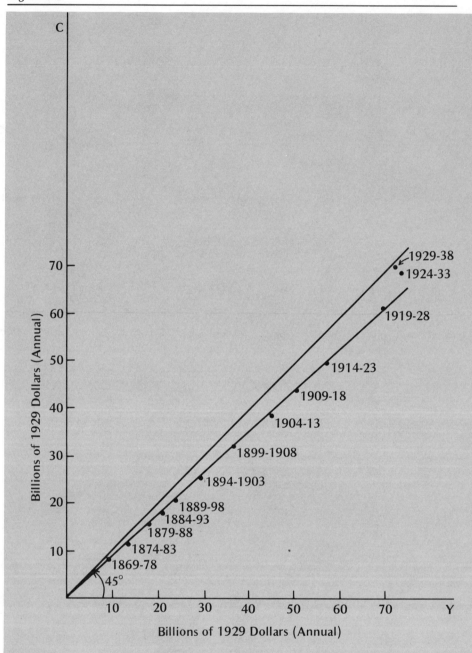

ships between consumption and income. Cross-sectional or relatively short-run time-series data obtained at three different points or periods of time might produce consumption functions such as those labeled 1, 2, and 3 in Figure 6-4 (similar to those presented in Figure 6-2). These consumption functions are assumed to have shifted over time as real income has increased. For the time period represented by consumption function 1, average income is Y_1 and average consumption is C_1; for period 2, average income is Y_2 and consumption is C_2; and so on. By connecting these points (C_1, C_2, C_3), we have a line (C) that is a theoretical representation of Kuznets' long-run time-series data. This C function would be a *long-run* consumption function, applicable to the study of an economy over a long span of time. Yet for short-run policymaking, the prevailing short-run consumption function (and hence the prevailing short-run MPC) would be relevant.

As this difference between short-run consumption functions (which could be relatively volatile, causing difficulties for monetary and fiscal policies on a *given* MPC) and long-run consumption functions became accepted as facts of life, economists next tried to answer the question— "*Why* are they different?" Accordingly, it was then suggested that a more comprehensive theory of consumer behavior was needed to resolve the contradiction between the evidence from long-run time-series data and short-run time-series and budget (cross-section) data. Attempted solutions to this contradiction have resulted in additional hypotheses about the relevant income variable in the consumption function and the influence of wealth on consumer behavior.

The remainder of this chapter examines several of these consumption function hypotheses. In addition, the impact of other variables on consumption is discussed.

THE RELATIVE INCOME HYPOTHESIS

Our analysis in Chapter 5 of the *absolute* income hypothesis (current real income as the independent variable in the consumption function) was implicitly based on the assumption that each individual consumer's behavior is independent of that of every other individual. Brady and Friedman suggest, however, that an individual's consumption depends not on absolute income, "but on the relative position of the individual on the income scale."[5] Thus the C/Y ratio (the average propensity to consume) for an individual is determined by emulation—"keeping up with the Joneses." It is *relative* position, not absolute position, on the current real-income scale which determines an individual's spending habits. Hence, for an individual, consumption becomes a function of the ratio of current income to average

5. Dorothy S. Brady and Rose D. Friedman, "Savings and the Income Distribution," *Studies in Income and Wealth*, Vol. 10 (National Bureau of Economic Research, 1947), 247–265.

Figure 6-4

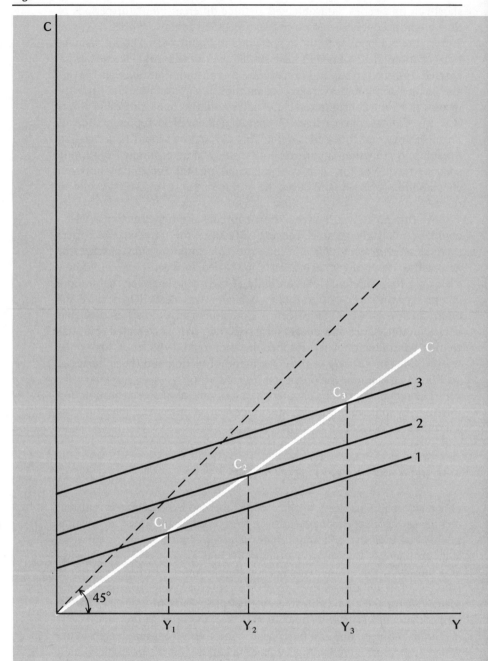

community income. Additional theoretical and empirical support for this relative income hypothesis was given by Modigliani[6] and Duesenberry.[7]

According to Duesenberry, in any *given period of time* an individual will consume a smaller fraction of his current real income, the higher is his position on the income scale. This behavior is consistent with evidence from family-budget data which show that as an individual's real income rises, his average propensity to consume declines. Yet if the individual remains in the same *relative position* on the income scale *as his current real income increases over time*, he will continue to consume the same percentage of his income. If *all* individuals remain in the *same* relative position as current aggregate real income increases, aggregate consumption will increase proportionately. Hence, the C/Y ratio will remain constant over time. Although some individuals may find their relative positions on the income scale changing, *in the aggregate* these changes will cancel each other, so that the C/Y remains constant. Hence, the relative income hypothesis explains the apparent conflict between family-budget data (which show a declining C/Y ratio over time as Y increases) and Kuznets' data (which show a constant C/Y ratio over time).

THE PREVIOUS-PEAK INCOME HYPOTHESIS

A closely related hypothesis is Duesenberry's *previous-peak income hypothesis*. Once the individual or family reaches a particular income level and the standard of living associated with it, any reduction of current real income will lead to efforts to maintain the level of consumption. Hence, when incomes fall, *individuals (or families) try to maintain the level of consumption and standard of living associated with the highest level of income previously reached.* On the basis of this reasoning and using time-series data, Duesenberry developed an aggregate consumption function that relates aggregate consumption to the ratio of current aggregate real income (Y) and an adjusted (deflated for changes in prices and population) measure of the highest level of aggregate real income previously reached (Y_m).

His consumption function can be represented by:

$$C = Y\left(a_1 + a_2\frac{Y}{Y_m}\right)$$

where

$$\frac{dC}{dY} = a_1 + 2a_2\frac{Y}{Y_m} \quad \text{and} \quad \frac{C}{Y} = a_1 + a_2\frac{Y}{Y_m}$$

6. Franco Modigliani, "Fluctuations in the Saving-Income Ratio: A Problem in Economic Forecasting," *Studies in Income and Wealth*, Vol. 11 (National Bureau of Economic Research, 1949), 371–443.
7. James Duesenberry, *Income, Saving and the Theory of Consumer Behavior* (Harvard University Press, 1949).

(with $a_1 > 0$ and $-1 < a_2 < 0$)

It is apparent from this function that changes in real income may cause the MPC and the APC to change. As Y increases, the C/Y ratio—the APC—declines. Hence, we can easily get the "short-run" variability. In the long run, however, if we have steady growth in real income, each year's current real income (Y) will be equal to last year's (Y_m) plus a *constant* percentage (g) of last year's income; that is,

$$Y = Y_m + g Y_m$$

$$Y = (1 + g) Y_m$$

$$\frac{Y}{Y_m} = (1 + g)$$

If we substitute $(1 + g)$ for the Y/Y_m ratio in the equations for the marginal and average propensities to consume given above, we find that

$$\frac{dC}{dY} = a_1 + 2a_2(1 + g)$$

$$\frac{C}{Y} = a_1 + a_2(1 + g)$$

Hence, in the long run (assuming steady growth) the APC and MPC are constant, while in the short run they vary with the Y/Y_m ratio.

Empirical consumption functions that have relative income as the independent variable have produced good statistical "fits." However, in such studies the long-run average propensity to consume is constant (which Kuznets' data showed), although in the short run the average propensity to consume depends on the ratio of current to previous-peak income.

THE PERMANENT INCOME HYPOTHESIS

Another attempt to reconcile the empirical findings about consumption behavior was made by Friedman.[8] In 1957 he set forth an hypothesis that has dominated research efforts since that date. Labeled by Friedman the *permanent income hypothesis*, the central idea is that individuals base their consumption on their levels of average *current* and *expected real income over a number of periods*, rather than on the level of current real income. Consumption is defined by Friedman to exclude the purchase of consumer durables but to include the value of services they yield each year.

The central idea of Friedman's hypothesis can be illustrated by paraphrasing one of his hypothetical examples. Consider a large group of individuals with weekly incomes of $100, each spending the entire $100 on current consumption. Assume that the individuals receive their pay once

8. Milton Friedman, *A Theory of the Consumption Function* (National Bureau of Economic Research, 1957).

a week and that the paydays are staggered so that one seventh are paid on Sunday, one seventh on Monday, and so on. Suppose that budget data are collected from a sample of these people for any one day chosen at random. If income were defined as cash receipts on that day, and consumption were defined as cash expenditures, one seventh of the sample would be recorded as having an income of $100, and six sevenths as having an income of zero. Although most individuals would probably spend more on payday than on any other day, they would also make expenditures on the other days. Accordingly, the one seventh with an income of $100 would be recorded as having positive savings, and the other six sevenths as having negative savings. It might appear that consumption rises with income, but with an MPC < 1.

According to Friedman, these results reveal nothing meaningful about consumer behavior. They simply reflect the use of inappropriate income and consumption concepts. As he points out, consumers do not adapt their consumption expenditures to their current receipts. In the above illustration, consumption expenditures might well be zero on Sunday. Accordingly, the central theme of Friedman's work is that the use of a "reporting period" even as long as a year does not make the error in actual data negligible, let alone eliminate it entirely.

In general form, Friedman's permanent income hypothesis can be summarized by a system of three simple equations:

$$c_p = a_3' y_p \qquad\qquad (6\text{-}1)$$

$$y = y_p + y_{tr} \qquad\qquad (6\text{-}2)$$

$$c = c_p + c_{tr} \qquad\qquad (6\text{-}3)$$

Equation 6-1 expresses an *individual's* planned or permanent consumption (c_p) as some fraction (a_3') of his planned or permanent real income (y_p). The parameter a_3' is thought by Friedman to depend on several variables; particularly the rate of interest (r); the ratio of nonhuman to total (nonhuman plus human) wealth (w_e); and a catchall variable (u), of which taste and preferences, age, race, and uncertainty attached to the receipt of income are important; that is:

$$a_3' = a_3'(r, w_e, u)$$

In addition, a_3' is thought to be independent of y_p and to be *relatively constant*.

Equation 6-2 defines the components of a consumer's current real income (y) in a given time period. Friedman treats this income as the sum of permanent real income (y_p) and transitory real income (y_{tr}). The permanent component (y_p) is estimated as the product of the present value of an expected future real income stream and the rate (r) at which this stream is discounted (you may find it helpful at this point to refer to the section in Chapter 8 on "Present Value and the Rate of Discount"); that is,

$$y_p = rv$$

where

$$v = \frac{R_1}{(1+r)} + \frac{R_2}{(1+r)^2} + \cdots + \frac{R_n}{(1+r)^n}$$

The R series represents the consumer's (subjective) view of his property and nonproperty real income stretching over a number of time periods (years), the end of which is denoted by n. The transitory component (y_{tr}) is interpreted by Friedman to reflect deviations of current income from permanent income. For example, any unexpected income gain or loss would be included in this component.

In Equation 6-3, current consumption (c) is the sum of permanent consumption (c_p) and transitory consumption (c_{tr}). Permanent consumption reflects the value of goods and services that an individual *plans* to consume during the time period in question, while transitory consumption reflects such factors as an especially favorable opportunity to purchase an item or a normal purchase deferred because of unavailability of the item.

Friedman assumes that y_{tr} and c_{tr} are uncorrelated *with each other* and with y_p and c_p, respectively. The former assumption means that *unexpected* increases or decreases in income are followed by no change in consumption. In other words, the marginal propensity to consume transitory income is zero.

Rewriting Equation 6-2 as

$$y_p = y - y_{tr} \tag{6-4}$$

and substituting Equation 6-4 into Equation 6-1 yields

$$c_p = a_3'(y - y_{tr}) \tag{6-5}$$

Substituting Equation 6-5 into Equation 6-3 yields a general expression of Friedman's consumption function:

$$c = a_3'(y - y_{tr}) + c_{tr} \tag{6-6}$$

Hence, an individual's current consumption is some fraction of the difference between his observed income and his transitory income, plus a "chance" occurrence (either positive or negative) of consumption.

Given certain simplifying assumptions, an *aggregate* consumption function has the same form as the individual consumption function described by Equations 6-1 through 6-3. It may be written as:

$$C = a_3(Y - Y_{tr}) + C_{tr} \tag{6-7}$$

where a_3 denotes the aggregate equivalent of the a_3' term discussed above, and the remaining variables in Equation 6-7 are the aggregate equivalents of the individual-level variables in Equation 6-6. The assumption that Y_{tr} and C_{tr} are uncorrelated with each other and with Y_p and C_p, respectively, continues to be held.

In the long run and for a large group of individuals, we could expect the transitory components of consumption and income to cancel each other out so that current consumption equals permanent consumption and current income equals permanent income. Hence, if

$$Y_{tr} = C_{tr} = 0$$

the marginal and average propensities to consume are equal:

$$\frac{dC}{dY} = a_3 = \frac{C}{Y}$$

Since a_3 (like a_3') is relatively constant, Friedman's theory of consumption behavior is consistent with Kuznets' findings that the long-run APC is constant.

In the short run, however, we would expect Y_{tr} and C_{tr} to be *nonzero*. Accordingly, the APC becomes

$$\frac{C}{Y} = a_3 - \frac{a_3 Y_{tr}}{Y} + \frac{C_{tr}}{Y}$$

If we assume that there is no systematic relation between C_{tr} and Y_{tr} (that is, if the marginal propensity to consume any transitory income is zero), the APC will fall as current real income. increases To see that this is true, let us assume that, during a period of prosperity, current real income (Y) rises above permanent real income. The increase is entirely an increase in transitory real income (Y_{tr}). All of Y_{tr} will be saved. In the equation above, if C_{tr} remains constant as Y and Y_{tr} increase, the C_{tr}/Y term will decline, and the $a_3 Y_{tr}/Y$ term will remain constant. Hence C/Y or the average propensity to consume will decline.

Although there is some evidence that C_{tr} and Y_{tr} are in fact nonzero in the long run and correlated (which would give a variable long-run APC),[9] the permanent income hypothesis is a major contribution to the theory of consumer behavior.[10]

POLICY IMPLICATIONS OF THE PERMANENT INCOME HYPOTHESIS

It should be apparent from the discussion of the permanent income hypothesis that economic policy decisions which suddenly or temporarily change the level of the nation's real income or disposable real income may have no effect on current consumption behavior. In an inflationary period, for example, a tax increase or surcharge may be appropriate. Yet if con-

9. See, for example, H. S. Houthakker, "The Permanent Income Hypothesis," *American Economic Review*, Vol. 48 (June 1958), 396–404.
10. In their article, "Consumption Patterns and Permanent Income" [*American Economic Review*, Vol. 47 (May 1957), 536–555] I. Friend and I. B. Kravis attempt to refute Friedman's hypothesis.

sumers expect continued inflation they may not reduce consumption, even though current disposable income falls with the tax increase. In fact, according to the permanent income hypothesis, a sudden tax increase would result in a decline in transitory income (Y_{tr}) and hence would have little or no effect on current consumption.

On the other hand, in a recessionary period, a tax reduction may be called for. If consumers believe that the tax reduction is a sign of continued recession (or worse), they may reduce consumption even though current disposable income will rise with the tax cut. Hence, if the desired results are to follow from a policy decision, it may be necessary to manage fiscal and monetary policies that affect real income so that adverse expectational effects are not generated, that is, so that desired changes occur in the permanent component of the consumption function.

WEALTH

Absolute Income Plus Wealth

The magnitude and composition of assets that individuals have accumulated may influence the level of current consumption.[11] In most cases, the more real wealth an individual has accumulated, and the easier it can be converted into cash, the greater will be his propensity to consume at any given level of income.

In fact, if consumer wealth is included as an independent variable (along with current real income) in the aggregate consumption function, the contradiction between Keynes' consumption hypothesis and Kuznets' data may be resolved. That is, the growth which has occurred in wealth in the United States may explain the historical constancy of the APC. If W_e denotes the total asset holdings, or wealth, of the nation's consumers, and the a terms are constant ($a_1 > 0$, $1 > a_2 > 0$, $1 > a_3 > 0$), an explicit consumption function with a wealth variable may take the form:

$$C = a_1 + a_2 Y + a_3 W_e$$

where

$$\frac{dC}{dY} = a_2 \qquad \text{and} \qquad \frac{C}{Y} = \frac{a_1}{Y} + a_2 + \frac{a_3 W_e}{Y}$$

If W_e grows over time (as it has in the United States), consumers spend more out of each period's (increasing) current real income. This is based on the presumption that the increase in wealth holdings in each period reduces the *need* for saving out of each period's current income. If the in-

11. See, for example, James Tobin, "Relative Income, Absolute Income, and Saving," in *Money, Trade, and Economic Growth, Essays in Honor of John Henry Williams* (Macmillan, 1951), 135–156.

crease in consumption out of W_e were large enough to offset the effect of an increase in Y, the APC would be constant. In the short run, however, the real wealth of households may not change enough to affect aggregate consumption sufficiently. Hence, W_e may be relatively *constant*, and we can obtain the short-run Keynesian effect of a declining APC.

Life Cycle

An hypothesis closely related to the permanent income hypothesis and one which explicitly includes a wealth variable in the consumption function was set forth by Ando and Modigliani.[12] This view of consumer behavior is referred to as the *life-cycle hypothesis*. It begins with an individual consumer possessing a given quantity of nominal wealth in period t (w_{et}). This individual knows his current nominal income obtained from his labor (y_t) as well as the present value of expected future *nonproperty* nominal income (v_t). He attempts to distribute his total consumption (c_t) over his lifetime so as to maximize total utility.[13] Expected future nonproperty income (v_t) is the beginning-of-the-period value of the current-period labor income, $y_t/(1 + r)$, which is assumed to be received at the end of the period, plus the discounted value (recall the discount formula given earlier) of the individual's income from labor to be received in future periods.[14]

This individual's consumption function can be represented as

$$c_t = a'_{1t} y_t + a'_{2t} v_t + a'_3 w_{et} \tag{6-8}$$

where the a_t terms are constant ($a'_{t1} > 0$, $1 > a'_{t2} > 0$, $1 > a'_{t3} > 0$) and depend on the consumer's age, his life expectancy, and his income pattern. This function can be aggregated to the form

$$C_t = a_{1t} Y_t + a_{2t} V_t + a_{3t} W_{et} \tag{6-9}$$

where the variables in Equation 6-9 are the aggregate equivalents of the variables in Equation 6-8. The a terms now depend primarily on the age distribution, life expectancies, and income pattern of the population.

The average propensity to consume (C/Y) in this formulation of the consumption function is

$$\frac{C_t}{Y_t} = a_{1t} + a_{2t} \frac{V_t}{Y_t} + a_{3t} \frac{W_{et}}{Y_t}$$

12. A. Ando and F. Modigliani, "The 'Life Cycle' Hypothesis of Saving: Aggregate Implications and Tests," *American Economic Review*, Vol. 53 (March 1963), 55–84. Ando and Modigliani, following Friedman, define consumption to exclude durables but to include their use value.
13. In the Ando-Modigliani formulation of the life-cycle hypothesis, all terms are defined in nominal (current) dollars rather than in the constant dollars used in the other studies summarized here.
14. Note that v_t includes only nonproperty income, while the v in the permanent income hypothesis formulation includes income from *all* sources.

If Y_t and V_t are assumed to change proportionally, it is apparent from this function that the constancy of the APC depends on the W_{et}/Y_t ratio. In the short run and during periods of rising income, we would expect the W_{et}/Y_t ratio to fall, since changes in W_{et} would be small during any given time period. Hence, the C_t/Y_t ratio would decline. In periods of declining income, we would expect W_{et}/Y_t to increase and hence the APC to rise. This behavior, of course, is consistent with Keynes' assumption about the APC.

Since the W_{et}/Y_t ratio has been approximately constant over long periods of time, the C_t/Y_t ratio would be constant. This hypothesis is also consistent with Kuznets' data.

THE INFLUENCE OF OTHER VARIABLES ON CONSUMPTION

From the foregoing analysis of the consumption function and from Chapter 5, we might conclude that consumers as a whole adjust their levels of consumption only when their wealth and/or incomes (however measured) change. However, there are various factors which *could* cause consumption to vary independently of income.

Rate of Interest

The response to a change in the rate of interest (r) may be an increase *or* a decrease in the amount of current consumption at the existing level of income. An increase in the rate of interest may induce households to reduce their consumption at any level of income. If they refrain from present consumption and earn real interest on the unspent funds, they will be able to purchase a larger market basket of consumer goods in the future than they can at present. Also, consumer durables are an important fraction of consumer spending, and many of these purchases are not currently paid for by the recipient. Higher rates of interest might be expected to cause people to postpone or forgo purchasing consumer durables.

It is conceivable, however, that households may increase their consumption at each level of income if the rate of interest rises. Suppose, for example, that a family is saving in preparation for the day when the head of the household retires. Suppose they expect retirement to be comfortable at a certain income, and are setting aside funds to achieve this goal. An increase in the rate of interest, everything else being equal, allows the household to consume a larger amount of current income and still achieve its goal. Although we might expect on balance a negative relationship between changes in consumption and changes in the interest rate, this relationship is not absolutely certain.

As a result of empirical studies, several economists have concluded that consumption and the rate of interest are slightly negatively related.

No empirical evidence, however, shows *significant* interest-rate effects on aggregate consumption.

Income Distribution

Both theory and empirical evidence suggest that a nation's consumption function is not independent of the distribution of income, although by postulating a single marginal propensity to consume in our models we have implied that it is. A change in the distribution of income among the various income classes *does* affect the real consumption of the three major income classes in the economy: wage and salary receivers, recipients of rents and interest (which are relatively fixed dollar amounts), and profit (primarily dividend) receivers.

An example of the effect on consumption caused by a change in the distribution of income is inflation (discussed in greater detail in Chapter 13). As prices rise, the real income—and hence the real consumption—of fixed income recipients (such as bond owners) will decline. If wages and salaries are increasing faster than prices, the real income and consumption of this particular income class will increase. The gains of wage and salary receivers may or may not be offset by the losses of fixed-income receivers, as well as possible losses to profit receivers. To the extent that the marginal propensity to consume wage and salary income is greater than the marginal propensity to consume rent and interest income as well as profit income, a redistribution of income in favor of wages and salaries results in an *increase* in consumption.

In fact, Lubell found that a totally equal distribution of U.S. income in 1941 would have produced a 5.82% increase in consumption.[15] However, using 1966 data, others[16] estimated that a 100% redistribution of income toward total equality would cause only a 10% change in consumption and that a 10% redistribution of income toward total equality would increase consumption by less than 1%.

Other Factors

Although individual household *tastes and preferences* may change drastically within a long period of time, tastes and preferences for the aggregate economy are relatively constant in the short run and can be disregarded as a determinant of consumption in the short run.

Socioeconomic characteristics include such characteristics as the num-

---

15. Harold Lubell, "Effects of Redistribution of Income on Consumers' Expenditures," *American Economic Review*, Vol. 37 (March 1947), 157–170; and his "Correction," *loc. cit.*, Vol. 37 (December 1947), 930.
16. Judith K. Schoenberg, Gertrude S. Weiss, and Natalie C. Strader, "Size and Composition of Consumer Savings," *Federal Reserve Bulletin* (January 1967), 32–50.

ber of persons in a family, the age composition of its members, race, and education. In general, the larger, the younger, and the better educated the family, the larger is the level of its consumption at any given level of income. These socioeconomic characteristics do not change over short periods of time, and can be disregarded as factors influencing consumption in the short run.

If *consumer credit* becomes easier to obtain, households may increase their credit-financed purchases and current consumption would rise. The ease of obtaining consumer credit may also lead consumers to spend a larger proportion of their income during prosperous periods. Consequently, the proportion of income spent during recessionary periods would decrease as households find themselves paying the debts incurred during the previous prosperity.

CONCLUDING NOTE

We have examined in this chapter alternative views on the relevant independent variable(s) to be included in the consumption function. However, no single variable or set of variables is generally accepted as defining *the* consumption function for the United States during recent times. We mentioned in Chapter 5 and reiterated here that Keynes believed a stable functional relationship existed between current real consumption and current real income. Most economists would probably agree that this relationship is sufficiently strong in the short run that current real income can be used as the independent variable in the consumption function. This dominance of current real income allows economists to develop meaningful static macroeconomic models in which the consumption function has the form assumed in Chapter 5:

$$C = a_1 + a_2 Y \qquad \text{or} \qquad C = a_1 + a_2 Y_d$$

Consumption is thus passive, responding only to changes in current real income (or disposable real income). Factors that might affect consumption (other than current real income) can be taken as unchanging. Hence, a_1 is assumed to be constant, and the location of the function can be taken as unchanging. In addition, the slope (a_2) can be assumed to be unaffected by nonincome factors.

Although current real income is perhaps the most important independent variable in the consumption function, and the only variable that appears explicitly in our consumption function in Chapter 5, it is important to keep in mind the emphasis of this chapter—that other forms of income (for example, relative and/or permanent) and nonincome variables may be important independent variables influencing consumption behavior.

Macroeconomic Multipliers and Fiscal Policy

FULL CAPACITY LEVEL OF OUTPUT
VERSUS EQUILIBRIUM LEVEL OF OUTPUT

As defined in Chapter 4, "full employment" is a situation in which the available work force (LF) is fully employed. Associated with this full employment level is a specific level of real output, which we have referred to as "full capacity" output (Q).

There is no reason to expect that the *equilibrium* level of real output introduced in Chapter 5 (Y^*) is the same as the *full employment* volume of output (Q). There is no reason to expect that Y^* of Figure 7-1 will support the available labor force. It is possible that even if problems of structural and frictional unemployment (people locked into an area or an industry, or people who will not or cannot move to where the jobs are, or people in the process of changing jobs) are assumed away, men may be *involuntarily* unemployed, in the aggregative, theoretical, and "ideal" sense of the word "unemployment." Indeed, this is the *leitmotif* of Keynes' General Theory.

The other type of Keynesian equilibrium—when aggregate demand exceeds the ability of the economy to produce goods and services—was not stressed by Keynes (he was writing during a nearly worldwide economic *depression*). If businesses and households have the ability to deliver $C + I$ in purchasing power during the current period, with reference to Figure 7-2, and full capacity output is Q, the economy will be tending toward a level of aggregate output (Y') which is unattainable. The actual level of Y (Y^*) will simply be the ceiling level (Q). The purchasing power (expressed in base-period prices) above and beyond what the economy can deliver, labeled "Gap" in Figure 7-2, will result in excessively high prices for the products the economy *can* produce.

But all our variables with a monetary dimension are measured in base-

Figure 7-1

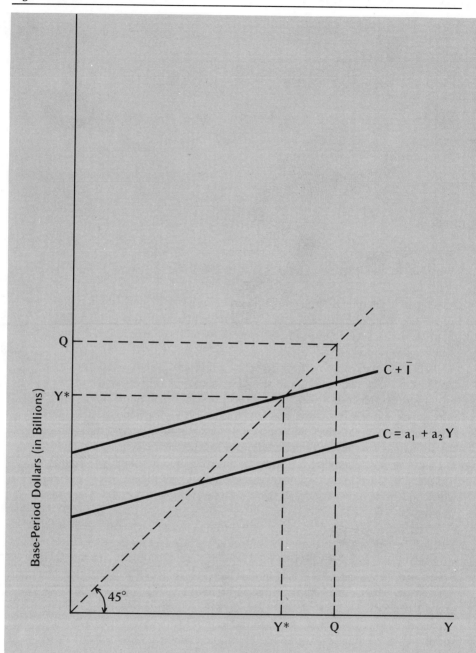

Figure 7-2

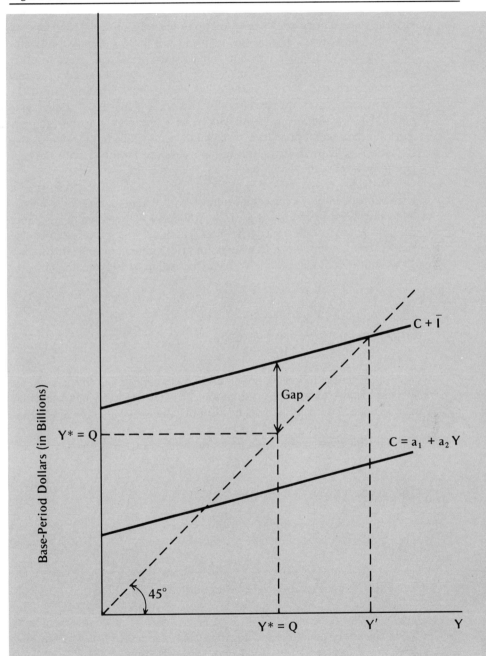

period prices. The current level of the general price index is suppressed. The presentation in this and the next few chapters is based on the assumption that the general price level is constant up to the point at which the economy reaches full capacity. Beyond this point, as in Figure 7-2, output and employment are at a maximum, but "inflationary pressures" exist. In other words, when there is unemployment, a change in aggregate demand merely results in a change in output; the price level remains constant. But if the economy's resources are already fully utilized, a higher level of aggregate demand during the current period will be reflected entirely by upward pressures on the general price level. We will delay a detailed discussion of this "inflationary" equilibrium until we have developed a model with the general price level explicitly included.

In reality, any increase in aggregate demand, if the economy is in a less-than-full-employment equilibrium, will probably increase *both* output and the general price level. Again, we will delay a discussion of this more complicated case until we have developed a model which is more amenable to investigating simultaneous changes in price and real output. In Chapter 13 we consider modern models which treat inflation and unemployment.

THE "MUTIPLYING" EFFECTS
OF A CHANGE IN INVESTMENT

We will begin the following presentation by assuming that the economy is in a less-than-full-employment situation. The first step in trying to see what can be done about this is to define algebraically the *equilibrium* level of income, Y^* in Figures 7-1 and 7-2.

The linear consumption function introduced earlier is

$$C = a_1 + a_2 Y \tag{7-1}$$

The exogenously given level of investment is

$$I = \bar{I} \tag{7-2}$$

The equilibrium level of income is defined as

$$Y^* = C + I \tag{7-3}$$

Substituting Equation 7-1 and Equation 7-2 into Equation 7-3 yields

$$Y^* = a_1 + a_2 Y^* + \bar{I}$$

Y^* in the above equation denotes the *equilibrium* level of Y. We can now solve this equation for the equilibrium level of income:

$$Y^* - a_2 Y^* = a_1 + \bar{I}$$
$$Y^*(1 - a_2) = a_1 + \bar{I}$$

$$Y^* = \frac{1}{1 - a_2}(a_1 + \bar{I}) \qquad (7\text{-}4)$$

The purpose of Equation 7-4, and other "reduced-form" equations like it, is to express the *solution* of a system of equations in terms of the predetermined variables or constants of the system.

For example, if $a_1 = 20$, $a_2 = 0.7$, and $\bar{I} = 50$, Equations 7-1, 7-2, and 7-3 above may be written as

$$C = 20 + 0.7\,Y \qquad (7\text{-}5)$$

$$\bar{I} = 50 \qquad (7\text{-}6)$$

$$Y^* = C + I \qquad (7\text{-}7)$$

The equilibrium level of income can be obtained by solving Equations 7-5, 7-6, and 7-7 simultaneously:

$$Y^* = 20 + 0.7\,Y^* + 50$$

$$Y^* - 0.7\,Y^* = 70$$

$$Y^*(1 - 0.7) = 70$$

$$Y^* = \left(\frac{1}{1 - 0.7}\right)70 = 233.33$$

Given the numerical values assigned to a_1, a_2, and $\bar{I}$ above, we can go directly to Equation 7-4 to obtain the prevailing equilibrium level of income:

$$Y^* = \frac{1}{1 - a_2}(a_1 + \bar{I}) = \frac{1}{1 - 0.7}(20 + 50) = 233.33 \qquad (7\text{-}8)$$

The basis for a graphical interpretation of Equation 7-4 is provided in Figure 7-3. The right-hand panel contains the same diagram used earlier. The consumption function ($C = a_1 + a_2 Y$) and the aggregate demand function ($C + I$) are plotted against Y. The aggregate demand schedule is drawn for an exogenously given level of investment ($\bar{I}$), and the equilibrium level of income is denoted by Y^*.

By clearing through the parentheses on its right-hand side, Equation 7-4 can be written as

$$Y^* = \left(\frac{1}{1 - a_2}\right)a_1 + \left(\frac{1}{1 - a_2}\right)\bar{I}$$

This equation is plotted in the left-hand panel of Figure 7-3. Equilibrium income (Y^*), the dependent variable in Equation 7-4, is measured along the vertical axis, and the exogenously given level of investment ($\bar{I}$) is measured along the horizontal axis. If $\bar{I}$ were equal to zero, Equation 7-4 would become

$$Y^* = \left(\frac{1}{1 - a_2}\right)a_1$$

Figure 7-3

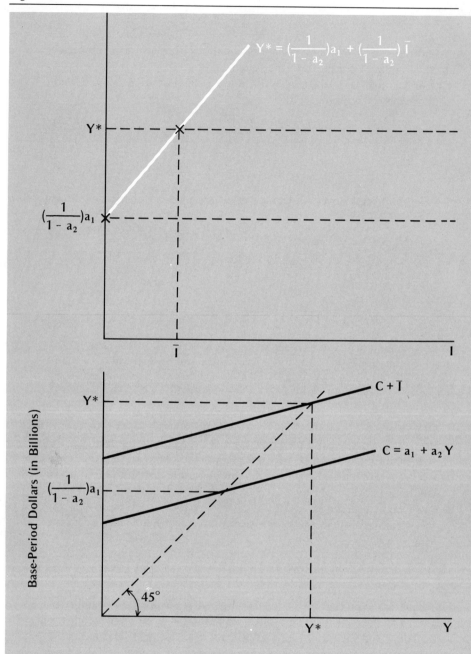

Thus the vertical intercept of Equation 7-4, when graphed, is $[1/(1 - a_2)]a_1$, while its slope is $1/(1 - a_2)$.

As discussed above, it is possible that Y^* is less than the full capacity level of real output (Q). Since we have assumed that a_1 and a_2 are constant (at least in the short run), the only way in the present context for the economy to get closer to Q is for business to increase the level of planned investment.

One key feature of Keynesian macroeconomics is that if investment is changed by x base-period dollars, equilibrium income will be changed by more than x. The "investment multiplier" is the change in Y^* caused by a change in $\check{I}$. That is, the investment multiplier is the slope of the line in the left-hand panel of Figure 7-3, or equivalently, the "first derivative"[1] ($dY^*/d\check{I}$) of Equation 7-4.

We have already written Equation 7-4 as

$$Y^* = \left(\frac{1}{1 - a_2}\right)a_1 + \left(\frac{1}{1 - a_2}\right)I$$

The slope, or the first derivative of this equation with respect to I, is

$$\frac{dY^*}{d\check{I}} = \frac{1}{1 - a_2}$$

That is, it is one divided by one minus the marginal propensity to consume. This "multiplying effect" of a change in investment can be discussed in the context of Figure 7-4.

If a_2, the marginal propensity to consume, is a positive fraction, the slope of Equation 7-4 is greater than one. Thus, a given change in investment, say $\Delta\check{I}$ of Figure 7-4, causes a larger change in equilibrium income (ΔY^*). If $a_2 = 0.7$, for example, the investment multiplier $1/(1 - a_2)$ is equal to 3.333. That is, a change in $\check{I}$ of, say, x billions of base-period dollars per year, will cause an increase in equilibrium income of $3.333x$.

FISCAL POLICY (TAXES EXOGENOUS)

We mentioned in Chapter 1 that one of the socially desirable goals of our economic system is the maintenance of full employment of labor or, equivalently, the maintenance of full capacity output. If equilibrium output (Y^*) is less than full capacity output (Q), and if a_1, a_2, and $\check{I}$ cannot be changed,

---

1. As explained in Chapter 3, for the function $y = a + bx^m$, where a, b, and m are constants, which can be written as

$$y = ax^0 + bx^m$$

the "first derivative" is

$$dy/dx = a0x^{0-1} + bmx^{m-1}$$

or

$$dy/dx = bmx^{m-1}$$

Figure 7-4

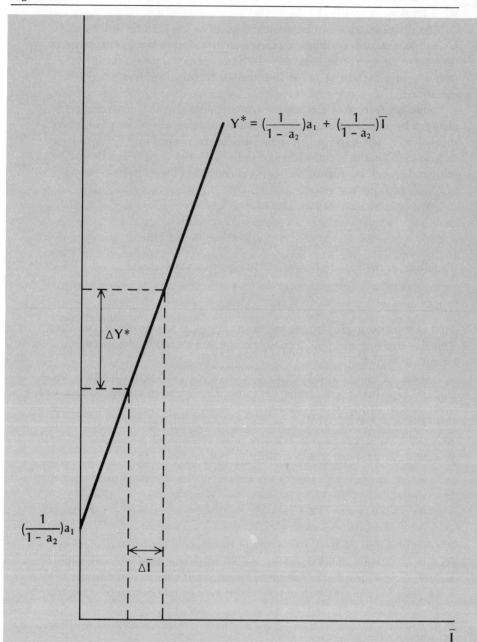

public authorities may be able to close the gap between actual and potential output. Thus far in this presentation of Keynesian equilibrium, we have assumed a completely private economy. Now is a good time to drop this assumption.

We will view government spending (purchases by state, local, and federal governments of goods and services) as a politically (and, we would hope, microeconomically) determined expenditure. We will consequently treat it as something determined outside our macroeconomic system. Tax receipts (T) will be assumed later in this chapter to vary with national income. But for now this variable will also be an exogenous one. The symbol T and the terms "taxes" and "tax receipts" are used throughout this book to represent net taxes, that is, the difference between gross tax receipts and government transfer payments.

A given, exogenously determined level of government spending $(\bar{G})$ might exceed the prevailing level of government tax receipts $(\bar{T})$. This "deficit" would have to be financed by the government issuing IOUs of some sort. The IOUs might be bought by the citizens of the country or by foreigners. Excluding the latter possibility, the deficit would be met by using a portion of the nation's current saving—the purchasing power supplied for capital expansion. This deficit would then become an addition to the national debt, from a public point of view, and an addition to personal wealth, from a private point of view.

In some future time period, of course, the government might have to tax its citizens to pay back the IOUs, with interest, to its citizens. This latter activity, however, is simply a redistribution of purchasing power from one portion of the economy (taxpayers in general) to another portion of the economy (the holders of the government IOUs). The government can also, of course, treat the debt as something permanent, and simply transfer some purchasing power within the economy by meeting only the interest payments on the debt. This last case, however, is based on the willingness of private wealth holders to continue holding their wealth in the form of government IOUs.

With the introduction of taxes, consumption can now be more realistically viewed as a function of disposable real income ($Y_d = Y - T$). Under these conditions, the consumption function can be written as

$$C = a_1 + a_2 Y_d \qquad (7\text{-}9)$$

The marginal propensity to consume, a_2, is now larger than the earlier marginal propensity to consume out of Y, although its value still lies between unity and zero. The other equations in our system are

$$Y_d = Y - T \qquad (7\text{-}10)$$

$$T = \bar{T} \qquad (7\text{-}11)$$

$$I = \bar{I} \qquad (7\text{-}12)$$

$$G = \bar{G} \tag{7-13}$$

$$Y^* = C + I + G \tag{7-14}$$

Equation 7-14 is an equilibrium condition. It expresses the condition that, if all necessary adjustments have worked themselves out (which, if the period is long enough and conditions do not change, they will), the spending plans of households (C), businesses (I), and government (G) will be matched by national output.

We now need to condense the above six equations into one equation. Substituting Equation 7-11 into Equation 7-10 yields

$$Y_d = Y - \bar{T}$$

Substituting this result into Equation 7-9 yields

$$C = a_1 + a_2(Y - \bar{T})$$

Substituting this result and Equations 7-12 and 7-13 into Equation 7-14 yields

$$Y^* = a_1 + a_2(Y^* - \bar{T}) + \bar{I} + \bar{G}$$

Solving this equation for Y^*, we obtain

$$Y^* - a_2 Y^* = a_1 - a_2 \bar{T} + \bar{I} + \bar{G}$$

$$Y^*(1 - a_2) = a_1 - a_2 \bar{T} + \bar{I} + \bar{G}$$

$$Y^* = \frac{1}{1 - a_2}(a_1 - a_2 \bar{T} + \bar{I} + \bar{G})$$

The above equation expresses the equilibrium level of income in terms of the predetermined variables and constants of the original six equations.

From this equilibrium formulation, three "multipliers" can be derived:

$$\frac{dY^*}{d\bar{I}} = \frac{1}{1 - a_2} \qquad \text{(investment multiplier)}$$

$$\frac{dY^*}{d\bar{G}} = \frac{1}{1 - a_2} \qquad \text{(government expenditure multiplier)}$$

$$\frac{dY^*}{d\bar{T}} = \frac{-a_2}{1 - a_2} \qquad \text{(tax multiplier)}$$

The important result in this context is to note that the "tax multiplier" $(dY^*/d\bar{T})$ is not only negative, but its absolute value is less than the government spending multiplier. A target increase in Y^* (designed, say, to get the economy closer to full-capacity output), could be obtained by a *decrease* in taxes of x dollars, but an *increase* in government spending of less than x dollars. This is due to the fact that the entire amount of the change in government spending immediately becomes income, while only a portion of the decline in taxes becomes spending and hence someone's income. While a change in government spending has a *direct* impact on aggregate demand, a change in taxes has an *indirect* impact by first changing disposable real income. As Y_d changes, consumption expenditures will change in the same direction, but since a_2 is less than unity, consumption will change by less than real disposable income.

Suppose, however, that the government budget is balanced prior to the target increase in Y^* and that it is thought to be politically desirable to maintain the balance while generating the increase in real income. To maintain the balance, the increase in government spending must equal the increase in taxes. That is, $\bar{G} = \bar{T}$ and $\Delta\bar{G} = \Delta\bar{T}$. Accordingly, the total combined effect of equal increases in government spending and taxes is given by

$$\Delta Y^* = \frac{1}{1 - a_2} \Delta\bar{G} - \frac{a_2}{1 - a_2} \Delta\bar{T}$$

or, since $\Delta\bar{G} = \Delta\bar{T}$,

$$\Delta Y^* = \left(\frac{1}{1 - a_2} - \frac{a_2}{1 - a_2}\right) \Delta\bar{G} = \left(\frac{1 - a_2}{1 - a_2}\right) \Delta\bar{G} = \Delta\bar{G}$$

Hence, simultaneous and equal increases (or decreases) in government spending and taxes will generate an increase (or decrease) in real income of an equal amount. In this case, an expansionary fiscal policy does not introduce a budget deficit. This proposition is known as the "balanced-budget multiplier."

FISCAL POLICY (TAXES ENDOGENOUS)

In the last section, tax receipts were assumed to be a predetermined variable. Of course, personal and business income taxes vary with the level of real income—the higher are individual and business real incomes, the higher tax payments probably will be. Also, as real incomes rise, people can be expected to purchase more goods covered by sales and excise taxes, resulting in an increase in tax receipts.

Therefore, a more realistic tax function is one in which taxes vary positively with the level of real income, as depicted in Figure 7-5. The level of tax receipts corresponding to a Y' level of real income is T'. The vertical distance between T' and $\bar{G}$ would be the prevailing tax deficit. The tax function depicted in Figure 7-5 can be written as

$$T = t_1 + t_2 Y \quad \text{(with } t_1 > 0 \text{ and } 1 > t_2 > 0)$$

where t_1 is its vertical intercept and t_2 is its slope. The slope of the tax function gives the change in tax receipts resulting from a very small change in income. For this reason, the slope (t_2) is referred to as the *marginal tax rate*. *Both* the slope and vertical intercept can be thought of as constants determined by tax laws and policies (which can be changed). For now, however,

Figure 7-5

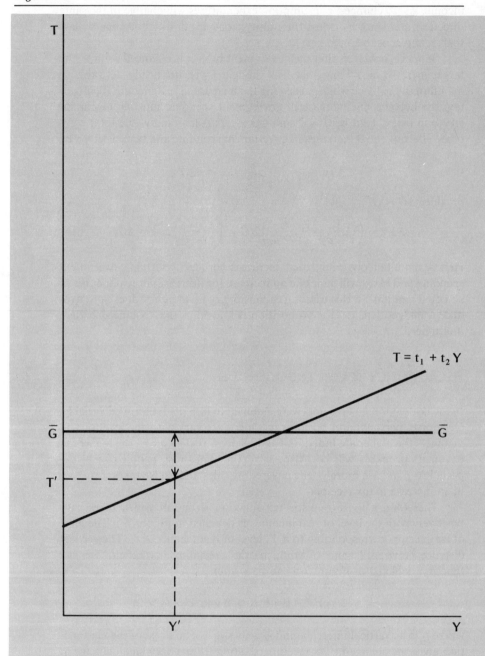

we will think of a change in tax policy as affecting only t_1, the vertical intercept of the tax function.

After this adjustment is made, our "Keynesian equilibrium" equations may be written in the following way:

$$C = a_1 + a_2 Y_d \tag{7-15}$$

$$Y_d = Y - T \tag{7-16}$$

$$T = t_1 + t_2 Y \tag{7-17}$$

$$I = \bar{I} \tag{7-18}$$

$$G = \bar{G} \tag{7-19}$$

$$Y^* = C + I + G \tag{7-20}$$

Our next task is to collapse the equations above into a single equation. This may be done by first substituting Equation 7-17 into Equation 7-16:

$$Y_d = Y - t_1 - t_2 Y$$

Then, substituting this result into Equation 7-15, we get:

$$C = a_1 + a_2(Y - t_1 - t_2 Y)$$

Now we need to substitute the above equation, as well as Equations 7-18 and 7-19, into Equation 7-20:

$$Y^* = a_1 + a_2(Y^* - t_1 - t_2 Y^*) + \bar{I} + \bar{G}$$

Finally, this equation may be solved for Y^*, the equilibrium level of real income:

$$Y^* = a_1 + a_2 Y^* - a_2 t_1 - a_2 t_2 Y^* + \bar{I} + \bar{G}$$

$$Y^* - a_2 Y^* + a_2 t_2 Y^* = a_1 - a_2 t_1 + \bar{I} + \bar{G}$$

$$Y^*[1 - a_2(1 - t_2)] = a_1 - a_2 t_1 + \bar{I} + \bar{G}$$

$$Y^* = \frac{1}{[1 - a_2(1 - t_2)]}(a_1 - a_2 t_1 + \bar{I} + \bar{G}) \tag{7-21}$$

The left-hand side of Equation 7-21 is the equilibrium level of income. The right-hand side consists entirely of the constants or predetermined variables of Equations 7-15 to 7-20.

As before, various "multipliers" can be derived from Equation 7-21:

$$\frac{dY^*}{d\bar{I}} = \frac{1}{[1 - a_2(1 - t_2)]} \quad \text{(investment multiplier)}$$

$$\frac{dY^*}{d\bar{G}} = \frac{1}{[1 - a_2(1 - t_2)]} \quad \text{(government expenditure multiplier)}$$

$$\frac{dY^*}{dt_1} = \frac{-a_2}{[1 - a_2(1 - t_2)]} \quad \text{(tax multiplier)}$$

Since $0 < t_2 < 1$, the investment and government-expenditure multipliers are now smaller than those derived earlier when we assumed tax receipts to be an exogenously given constant. The above tax multiplier is quite different from the one derived earlier, which gave the change in Y^* resulting from a very small change in the exogenously given level of tax receipts. Now the tax multiplier is the change in Y^* resulting from a very small change in t_1, the vertical intercept of the tax function.

A NUMERICAL EXAMPLE OF FISCAL POLICY

Perhaps a numerical example would clarify the nature of Equation 7-21 and the associated "multipliers." Let Equations 7-15 to 7-20 take the following numerical form:

$$C = 20 + 0.7Y_d \tag{7-22}$$

$$Y_d = Y - T \tag{7-23}$$

$$T = 22 + 0.2Y \tag{7-24}$$

$$\bar{I} = 50 \tag{7-25}$$

$$\bar{G} = 100 \tag{7-26}$$

$$Y^* = C + \bar{I} + \bar{G} \tag{7-27}$$

We *could* solve this numerical system following the same steps used to *obtain* Equation 7-21. However, we can also substitute the prevailing values of the relevant predetermined variables and constants *into* Equation 7-21.

$$Y^* \quad \frac{1}{[1 - 0.7(1 - 0.2)]}[20 - (0.7)(22) + 50 + 100] = 351.36 \tag{7-28}$$

Now that we know that the equilibrium level of real income is 351.36, we can go back to Equations 7-24, 7-23, and 7-22 to obtain the prevailing equilibrium values for tax receipts, disposable income, and consumption—all measured in billions of base-period dollars per year. Specifically, $T^* = 92.272$, $Y_d^* = 259.088$, and $C^* = 201.36$.

We should perhaps check to make sure the equilibrium level of output ($Y^* = 351.36$) can support the spending activity of households ($C^* = 201.36$), business ($\bar{I} = 50$), and government ($\bar{G} = 100$). This is done more to check our arithmetic than anything else. We have *built into* Equation 7-21 the fact that spending plans are realized. Of course, there is no reason to expect that $Y^* = 351.36$ is consistent with full employment. Also, a portion of household savings, $Y_d^* - C^* = 57.728$, will be required to finance the government deficit of 7.728.

Substituting the values of the predetermined variables and constants in Equations 7-22 to 7-27 into the second set of expressions for investment, government-spending, and tax multipliers derived earlier, we get

$$\frac{dY^*}{d\bar{I}} = \frac{1}{[1 - 0.7(1 - 0.2)]} = \frac{1}{0.44} = 2.27$$

$$\frac{dY^*}{d\bar{G}} = \frac{1}{[1 - 0.7(1 - 0.2)]} = \frac{1}{0.44} = 2.27$$

$$\frac{dY^*}{dt_1} = \frac{-0.7}{[1 - 0.7(1 - 0.2)]} = \frac{0.7}{0.44} = -1.59$$

Suppose again that $Y^* = 351.36$, and that the level of real income sufficient to employ all of the nation's resources is 402.36. Assuming that the above multipliers are relevant for our economy, what must be the increase in investment or government spending necessary to generate the additional real income ($\Delta Y^* = 51$) required to attain full employment?

An increase in $\bar{I}$ or $\bar{G}$ of x billions of base-period dollars per year will cause an increase in equilibrium real income by $2.27x$. Hence, if we want our *increase* in Y^* to be 51.00, then x, the increase in $\bar{I}$ or $\bar{G}$, must be

$$\Delta Y^* = 2.27x$$

$$2.27x = 51.00$$

$$x = 22.47$$

Achieving an increase in Y^* of 51.00 through tax policy is a bit more tricky. Public authorities would have to find that package of tax regulation changes which would produce an entirely new tax function—one with a vertical intercept consistent with a full-employment level of output. A decrease in t_1 by x billion dollars would cause Y^* to increase by $1.59x$. To achieve our goal through tax policy, the decrease in t_1 must be

$$\Delta Y^* = -1.59x$$

$$-1.59x = 51.00$$

$$x = -32.08$$

The above model gets at the core of Keynesian equilibrium and Keynesian macroeconomic policy. The equilibrium level of real income (Y^*) towards which an economy might be tending in any given period may not be consistent with the full utilization of resources. If this equilibrium level is recognized quickly enough, however, the levels of investment and government spending or the current tax policy could be changed to bring about a more desirable level of Y^*. Of course, the deficiency must be recognized quickly, the action must be taken quickly, and the action must be immediately effective. The real world is, alas, a world of lags. But at least by now you should have a rough idea of the basic interrelationships of the variables introduced in this chapter and the rudiments of "Keynesian" macroeconomic policy. In the next chapter we will explore ways of trying to make investment an endogenous rather than an exogenous variable.

Investment

In Chapter 3 we assumed that "investment"—the amount of purchasing power demanded by businesses for the purpose of making net additions to capital—varies with the rate of interest. This inverse relationship was used, but not really fully explained. We simply argued that households (and firms with uncommitted retained profits) consider interest as an *income*. But to firms desiring to borrow some of this purchasing power (to be paid back later, with interest), interest is a *cost*. As this cost rises, intuitively one would expect businesses to cut back on the volume of loans they take out. Higher interest rates will cause businesses to curtail some of their "marginal" proposed expansion ventures. By "marginal" ventures in this context we mean those ventures which managers believe have the least chance of "success," in the sense that they have lower "potential yields."

In Chapters 5 and 7, the prevailing level of planned net-investment expenditures was assumed to be exogenously determined. Although we will continue to maintain the other assumptions made in the previous two chapters, we now allow investment to become an endogenous variable in our models. We are returning to the inverse relationship between investment and the rate of interest introduced in Chapter 3. But we now want to explore this relationship in some detail.

COMPONENTS OF NET INVESTMENT

The net investment component of aggregate demand consists of expenditures on newly produced net additions to plant and capital equipment, residential dwellings, and on intended changes in business inventories, all of which are purchased by the private sector of the economy. For simplicity, we will lump these three components of real investment together. Although this is done to simplify our discussion, it is not wholly unrealistic, since, as is pointed out below, the volume of all three components depends at least in part on the interest rate. Certainly, if we think of the term "residential construction" as the construction of residential dwellings by businesses for sale to homeowners (a substantial portion of residential construction), then what is said below about plant and equipment applies in the short run also to this component of real investment. In the long run, however, investment in housing depends primarily on population growth. In addition, since "carrying costs" are an important consideration in inventory management, and since these costs are related to the interest rate, the decision criterion for planned inventory investment is somewhat similar to the decision process for investment in plant and equipment.

Although we do not include government capital formation as a component of net investment, the government sector is involved in what are, in fact, net investment activities. These activities range from the construction of hospitals and schools to the construction of training facilities for the military. However, since our national income and product accounts do not identify such activities as capital formation, it is difficult to analyze government investment activities very accurately. Recall from Chapter 2 that government expenditures, whether for consumer or capital goods, are lumped into one expenditure account, Government Purchases of Goods and Services.

It is important to distinguish between the purchase of *capital* and the purchase of financial assets, as we did in Chapter 3. Recall that the purchase of a new issue of equity or debt may not necessarily create additional capital, jobs, and output. Of course, when the funds received *are* used to purchase new net-investment goods (for example, plant and equipment), investment activity does occur. Also, we must distinguish between new real investment activity and the purchase of secondhand physical assets. This distinction is significant because new real investment expenditures create additional jobs and new output, while purchases of secondhand real assets have no direct effect upon these key variables.[1] In the latter case, physical assets, such as machines or warehouses, just like previously issued equity and debt, are merely transferred from one owner to another. It is *new real* net investment, measured in base-period dollars, in which we are interested.

PRESENT VALUE AND
THE RATE OF DISCOUNT

Why does business want to acquire capital assets? The answer is obvious— they expect to make profits by so doing. The meaning of "profit" in this context, however, needs to be clarified.

The decision to acquire new capital is based on two considerations, revenue and cost. The cost side of the decision is straightforward—from the

---

1. Unless, of course, the secondhand real assets had previously been idle and are now put to productive use.

point of view of a single, perfectly competitive firm, the market price for a unit of capital, whether it be a machine or a roll of copper wire, can be thought of as a fact of life. This cost is quoted to the buyer by the asset manufacturer. The buyer of the physical asset is thought of as such a negligible portion of the group of actual or potential buyers of the product that his actions (or changes in his actions) cannot affect the prevailing market price of a unit of capital. (Recall the discussion of "perfect competition" in Chapter 3.)

The revenue aspects of the decision to invest are a bit more complex. The revenue side involves a *stream* of expected receipts over (probably) many time periods. Also, there are costs associated with using the new capital (especially if it is equipment or buildings), such as maintenance costs, operating labor costs, and the cost of additional materials, fuel, power, and so forth. These expected "variable" costs (note that depreciation and interest cost are *not* included in this element of costs) should be subtracted from the expected per period receipts, to get an idea of the "profitability" of the purchase. The stream of expected per period receipts less expected per period variable costs (associated with using the new capital) is referred to from now on as "the expected net receipts" or "net revenue stream."

Because these expected net receipts will flow into the firm at different times, we must convert them into what they are worth at the point in time when the capital may be purchased—that is, we must compute their "present value"—in order to be able to add them together and compare them with the market price of the capital.

Assume you have a transferable (capable of being legally sold) promise from some person or institution to give you $1000, a year from today. Today, this promise (which is likely to be printed on expensive-looking paper, gilded with green gingerbread artwork, *circa* 1900) is worth "what the market will bear." Assume further that a buyer comes along and offers you $925.93 for the IOU. You might have accepted even less for it, but you are definitely willing to swap the IOU for cash at a price of $925.93. What rate of interest would the buyer have to get on his $925.93 to have it grow to $1000 by the end of the year? That is, what is r in the following equation?

$$\$925.93(1 + r) = \$1000$$

The answer is $r = 0.08$. An annual rate of return of 8% equates the desirability of a *promise* to pay $1000, a year from now, with the desirability, for the potential buyer, of holding the $925.93 *today*.

Assume that in the above context, you know instead that the promise was for $1000 and that you would sell the promise at an 8% discount. This percentage is *your* rate of discount on the IOU. This percentage incorporates your fears that the promise will not be kept and your preference to have the cash *now* rather than a year from now. One reason why having the cash now is probably preferable to you is your natural myopia towards consumption—most people would rather consume a base-period dollar's worth of goods now than a year from now. Under these conditions, you might want to deal with someone willing to pay you at least *your* "present value" of the IOU:

$$\text{Present value} = \left(\frac{1}{1 + 0.08}\right)\$1000$$

By solving the above equation for "present value," we are back to where we started—present value or price is equal to $925.93.

Let us now ask a slightly different question—what is the present value of an IOU promising two payments of $1000, each made at the end of each year for two consecutive years? Assume that a rate of discount of 8% is associated with the IOU. The present value of the $1000 payment to be made at the end of the second period, from the point of view of the beginning of the second period, is given by the following equation:

$$\text{Present value} = \frac{1}{1 + 0.08}\$1000 = \$925.93$$

That is, the payment to be made at the end of the second year is "worth" $925.93 at the beginning of the second year. But what is this second payment worth at the beginning of the first year—right now? The present value of the $925.93 at the beginning of the first period is given by:

$$\text{Present value} = \frac{1}{1 + 0.08}(\$925.93) = \$857.34$$

The present value of the first payment, the one to be made at the end of the first year—from the point of view of the beginning of the first year, right now—is our original $925.93. The present value of *both* payments, that is, the present value of this particular IOU itself, is

$$\text{Present value} = \left(\frac{1}{1 + 0.08}\right)\$1000 + \left(\frac{1}{1 + .08}\right)\$925.93 = \$1783.17$$

This IOU, if the "market agrees" that its proper rate of discount is 8%, should trade for $1783.17.

Another way of writing a present value equation involving many time periods takes into account the fact that the later period payments are really present values of cash amounts which are themselves present values. For example, we could write our above equation as

$$\text{Present value} = \left(\frac{1}{1 + 0.08}\right)\$1000 + \left(\frac{1}{1 + 0.08}\right)\left(\frac{1}{1 + 0.08}\right)\$1000$$

or as

$$\text{Present value} = \left(\frac{1}{1 + 0.08}\right)\$1000 + \left(\frac{1}{1 + 0.08}\right)^2\$1000$$

This method, of course, assumes that the same rate of discount is used for all periods.

INVESTMENT FROM A
MICROECONOMIC POINT OF VIEW

There are essentially two approaches to evaluating a new investment project: the present value and the marginal efficiency of investment approaches. Either approach is relevant for an investment criterion, whether the firm's sources of funds are internal (from retained earnings) or external (from borrowed funds). In addition, both approaches usually yield the same results when used to evaluate the same project.

Present Value

One procedure for assessing an investment project is to determine the present value of the net revenue stream (estimated total receipts less estimated variable cost) to be expected from undertaking a particular new investment project and comparing this present value with the cost of the project. The present value of an expected net revenue stream is determined by discounting the expected net revenue stream at the highest possible rate of return (adjusted for risk) r on alternative investment projects and/or financial assets and secondhand capital assets. The term r could be simply the market rate of interest at which the firm can either borrow or lend money. If the net revenues expected in future periods $1 \ldots n$ are $R_1, R_2, \ldots R_n$, and if the junk value of the asset is denoted by J, the present value (V) of the yields from the project can be determined as follows:

$$V = \frac{R_1}{(1+r)} + \frac{R_2}{(1+r)^2} + \cdots + \frac{R_n}{(1+r)^n} + \frac{J}{(1+r)^n}$$

If businesses seek to make profits and if funds are available, it will pay to invest in a new capital project so long as the present value (V) of a new capital asset exceeds its cost (P_K). If $V < P_K$, the project will be rejected. If $V = P_K$, the project is *marginally* acceptable (that is, the businessman is *just* willing to invest in the project).

Suppose, for example, a firm is considering the purchase of a new piece of machinery which it expects will yield an annual net revenue of $1000 ($R$ series) for five years ($n = 5$), at which time it becomes worthless (even for junk). Suppose, further, that either the cost of funds to the firm or the highest alternative rate of return on the cash that might be committed to this project is 16% per year. Will the new machine be purchased? From the equation above we can calculate the present value of the expected yields from the machine:

$$V = \frac{\$1000}{(1+0.16)} + \frac{\$1000}{(1+0.16)^2} + \frac{\$1000}{(1+0.16)^3}$$

$$+ \frac{\$1000}{(1+0.16)^4} + \frac{\$1000}{(1+0.16)^5} + \frac{0}{(1+0.16)^5}$$

$V = \$3275$

If the cost of the machine quoted by its manufacturer is less than $3275, the new investment will occur. In fact, in order to earn 16% on the expenditure, the *most* that the firm can afford to pay for the machine is $3275. If it had to pay more, the cost of the machine would exceed the present value of the expected yields from the machine, and the firm would be unwilling to make the purchase.

Marginal Efficiency of Investment

An alternative, and the most commonly used, procedure for assessing an investment project is the marginal efficiency of investment or internal rate of return approach. The rate of discount (d) which will equate the net revenue stream expected from an *additional unit* of *newly produced* capital to its price is referred to as the "marginal efficiency of investment (*mei*)." It is called *marginal* because it refers only to *additions* of new capital, and *efficiency* because it indicates an expected *rate* of return over cost. When d replaces r and P_K replaces V in the equation above, we have the following equation, which can be solved for d, the level of *mei* for this particular project:

$$P_K = \frac{R_1}{(1+d)} + \frac{R_2}{(1+d)^2} + \cdots + \frac{R_n}{(1+d)^n} + \frac{J}{(1+d)^n}$$

Continuing with the values given in the example above, suppose a given capital expenditure for a new machine will yield an annual expected net revenue stream of $1000 for five years, at which time the machine becomes worthless. If these values are substituted into the equation above and if we assume that the expected net revenue flows occur at the end of the year, we find the expected internal rate of return (d) on the $3275 expenditure:

$$\$3275 = \frac{\$1000}{(1+d)} + \frac{\$1000}{(1+d)^2} + \frac{\$1000}{(1+d)^3} + \frac{\$1000}{(1+d)^4} + \frac{\$1000}{(1+d)^5} + \frac{0}{(1+d)^5}$$

from which it follows that $d = 0.16$. The expected internal rate of return (16% in our example) is, in a sense, a measure of the expected profitability of the investment project, which costs $3275.

If the purchase of the machine results in an expected marginal efficiency of investment of 0.16, what would be the internal rate of return on two, three, or four machines? We would probably expect d to fall as more dollars are expended on such capital assets. If we drop our assumption of perfect competition, such a decline could occur because the firm is expecting the R series to fall as a result of a fall in the price of the output produced by the additional capital, and/or a rise in its expected variable cost—for example, the firm might foresee rising wages, as the demand increases for the labor necessary to operate and maintain the new capital.

A small firm in a perfectly competitive industry, whose output and work force are so small that changes in them do not affect the market price or wage rate might not foresee this outcome. Yet it might still have to limit its investment. The interest it must pay to acquire funds for investment purposes is a fixed cost. Even if the firm uses its own funds (retained earnings), the rate of return that it could earn on lending these funds or acquiring secondhand or financial assets is a fixed opportunity cost. For a small firm, however, retained earnings would probably be an inadequate source of large amounts of funds. The expected internal rate of return is subject to errors in estimation and, of course, could turn out to be much less than expected. Hence, the greater the dollar value of the level of investment, the greater the loss the firm would incur if expectations were not realized. A small firm might be able to incur a small loss, but a large loss could ruin it. The small firm, therefore, might make a greater reduction in the R series as an allowance for risk, the larger the constant dollar value of investment expenditures. This would cause the marginal efficiency of investment to fall with each additional capital expenditure.

The firm's *mei* thus falls with new capital investment. In the example given above, the *mei* of a new machine which costs $3275 is 0.16. This gives a point on the firm's *mei* schedule. This point is labeled 1 in Figure 8-1, which shows the base-period dollar value of new investment on the vertical axis, and the *mei* on the horizontal axis. For one or several of the reasons given above, the *mei* of an additional machine would decline, given that the first machine had been or would be purchased, so that the *mei* associated with the dollar value of purchasing *two* machines would be at the point labeled 2 in Figure 8-1. Other combinations of d and I can be obtained in the same manner. Hence, the firm's *mei* curve is established by adding the dollar volume of new investment at each particular expected rate of return (d) to the dollar value of investment at all higher expected rates of return.

The *mei* curve is equivalent to the *firm's demand curve* for new investment. Although we assume a smooth, continuous curve, the relationship between d and I in reality would probably be such that gaps would appear in the curve of Figure 8-1. The slope of this curve is clearly negative. The magnitude of the slope, however, cannot be deduced by *a priori* reasoning. That is, theory does not predict the value of the slope—it must be found empirically.

We have found that a project will be undertaken if $V > P_K$, rejected if $V < P_K$, and marginally acceptable if $V = P_K$. However, we can see from the equations above that when $V > P_K$, $d > r$; when $V < P_K$, $d < r$; and when $V = P_K$, $d = r$. We can conclude, therefore, that for any new investment project to be acceptable, the expected internal rate of return (d) must exceed some alternative rate (r), which is either the rate at which the firm

Figure 8-1

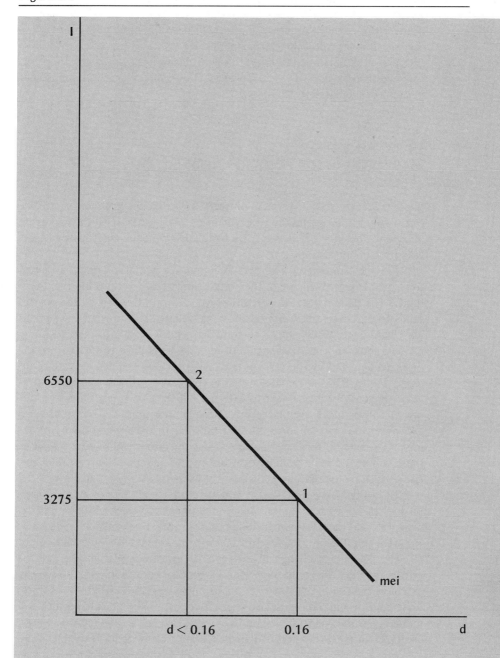

can borrow or the rate which could be earned with the funds if the project were rejected and the funds invested elsewhere. (The investment opportunity yielding this alternative rate should have the same degree of risk as the investment project under consideration.)

If the "opportunity cost" (r) to the firm is r', as depicted in Figure 8-2, net investment will be I'. At a lower level of r, say r'', the amount of net investment increases to I''.

INVESTMENT FROM A MACROECONOMIC POINT OF VIEW

If all firms assess new investment projects in the manner presented above, we can simply sum horizontally all of the firms' *mei* curves to get the aggregate marginal efficiency of investment schedule (*MEI*) equivalent to the aggregate investment demand curve.

For the economy as a whole, "the" market rate of interest is assumed to be an adequate measure of the "opportunity cost" involved in the use of funds. The market rate of interest (r) can be considered to be the cost of funds to purchase a new capital asset, as well as the rate of return obtainable from lending such funds to someone who is willing to pay the going rate. In addition, this market rate of interest is assumed to be given to the firms, as depicted by the vertical line in Figure 8-3. The market rate of interest is thus the cost element which is compared with the aggregate marginal efficiency of investment to determine if the situation is favorable for new net investment. Profitable investment opportunities exist whenever d exceeds r, and these opportunities are fully exhausted if, and only if, investing proceeds to the level at which $d = r$. At any rate where r and d are equal, there will be a certain volume of investment demanded, that amount precisely given by the marginal efficiency of investment (*MEI*) schedule.

If, in Figure 8-3, the market rate of return ("the" rate of interest) is r', businesses will wish to undertake all investment projects yielding a d in excess of r', and the base-period dollar value of investment demand will be I'. If r were to fall to r'', the level of investment demanded would increase to I''. The percentage change in the level of investment demanded may be greater, smaller, or equal to a given percentage change in r. Although the extent of the responsiveness of I to a change in the interest rate is a subject of dispute among economists,[2] it is generally believed that a change in r will induce a smaller percentage change in I. Hence, as is pointed out below, changes (shifts) in the marginal efficiency of investment curve may be more

2. Numerous empirical studies have been conducted in an attempt to shed light on this subject, but they have yielded conflicting results. See William H. White, "Interest Elasticity of Investment Demand—The Case from Business Attitude Surveys Re-examined," *American Economic Review*, Vol. 46 (September 1956), 565–587.

Figure 8-2

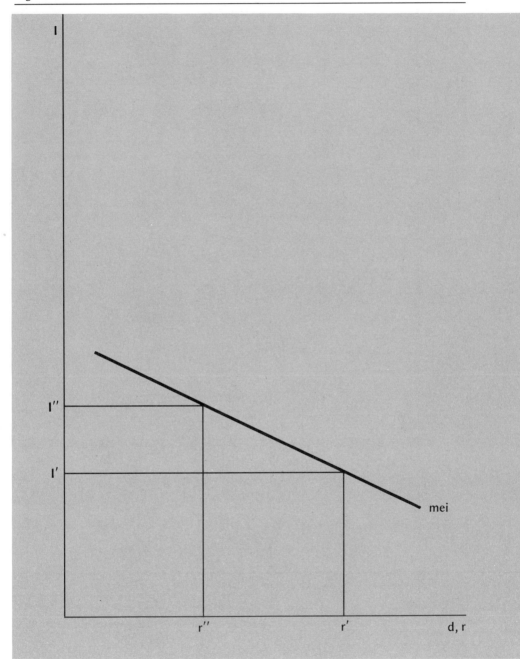

Figure 8-3

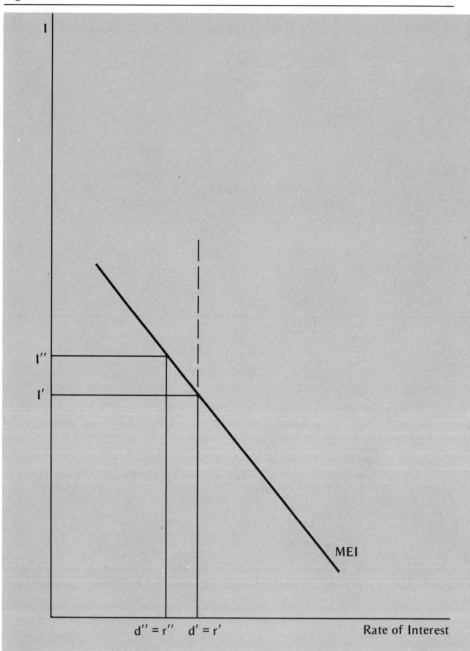

important in inducing investment than movements along an existing sched-ule that result from changes in the interest rate.

Since aggregate net investment is carried up to the point where $d = r$, we have the investment demand function, which may be written in general form as:

$$I = f(r)$$

or explicitly as

$$I = n_1 + n_2r$$

where n_1 and n_2 are predetermined constants with $n_1 > 0$ and $n_2 < 0$.

From now on, although the interest rate is a percentage, it is entered as $(r)(100)$. Thus a rate of interest of $8\frac{1}{2}\%$ or 0.085 will be written as 8.5. (This method of expressing rates of interest is used throughout the re-mainder of this book.) Assume that the investment function is

$$I = 45.38 - 1.3r$$

If r is 10.5%, net investment would be $31.73 billion (constant dollars).

Shifts in the Aggregate Investment Function

The difficulty with leaving the investment equation in the foregoing form is that it gives the appearance of emphasizing the interest rate as the signifi-cant determinant of real investment, a debatable proposition which many economists do not support.

The key determinant of investment is the marginal efficiency of invest-ment, and shifts in the *MEI* curve may *perhaps* be more important in ac-tually affecting investment than movements along an existing *MEI* sched-ule. Among the factors which may account for shifts in the *MEI* schedule are (1) changes in the level of aggregate demand, (2) changes in the existing capital stock, (3) innovation, and (4) the general state of confidence in the economy. An increase in aggregate demand would perhaps increase (shift to the right) the *MEI* schedule by increasing the expected future returns from an investment. If businesses believe that increases in aggregate demand will continue in the near future, they expect prices and/or sales to increase. To incorporate the favorable "state of expectations" into their investment-decision model, they will postulate higher expected net revenue streams (the *R* series) for their proposed investment projects. This assertion assumes that the extent of excess capacity (underutilized productive resources) is unimportant. Otherwise, output for expected enhanced sales could be pro-duced by greater utilization of the existing capital stock.

How net investment may be *induced* by increases in the level of aggre-gate demand is discussed in Chapter 17. This process, called the "accelera-tor principle," assumes that the current level of net investment depends on *changes* in the level of aggregate real income. For any net investment at all to occur, ΔY must be positive. For net investment to increase from one period to another, the level of ΔY in the second period must exceed the level of ΔY in the first period. Although empirical demonstrations of the accelerator principle have been unconvincing, it does offer some insight into certain features of the investment decision. Certainly, given full utilization of existing capital stock, an increase in real income would result in a higher *MEI* and thus an increase in net investment.

An increase in the existing capital stock (an increase in capacity this period resulting from last period's investment) may dampen current investment, owing to the effects of diminishing returns as new investment occurs—businesses knowing that additional capital applied to a complement of fixed factors may yield smaller increments in output than previous units—thereby lowering the expected net revenue stream on proposed investment projects. This effect would shift *MEI* to the left.

Innovation (defined as improvements in production processes, improved business techniques, and new products) and investment are usually concomitant. The impetus to such investment usually comes from the declining supply price of capital (P_K), brought about by improvements in business techniques and/or production processes. In addition, the impetus may come from an increase in the expected net revenue streams of proposed investment projects. The latter favorable effect on the *MEI* could be brought about by decreasing future expected variable cost through improved techniques and/or increasing expected total revenue by placing new products on the market. The effects of innovation mentioned above would result in a rightward shift in the *MEI*.

One of the most important determinants of the location of the marginal efficiency of investment schedule is the general state of confidence in the economy. This state of confidence is a highly volatile thing. It is naturally unstable, according to Keynes:

> due to the characteristic of human nature that a large proportion of our positive activities depend on spontaneous optimism rather than on a mathematical expectation. . . . Most . . . of our decisions to do something positive, the full consequences of which will be drawn out over many days to come, can only be taken as a result of animal spirits—of a spontaneous urge to action rather than inaction, and not as the outcome of a weighted average of quantitative benefits multiplied by quantitative probabilities.[3]

Thus, the stimulation of "animal spirits," the creation of a social climate appealing to the business community, becomes an economic necessity to prevent the *MEI* schedule from shifting leftward and, hence, preventing investment from falling off sharply. Whether or not public antirecessionary

3. J. M. Keynes, *The General Theory of Employment, Interest, and Money* (Harcourt Brace Jovanovich, 1936), 161.

policies are wise, from a purely rational point of view which ignores the delicate nature of "animal spirits," is of no great consequence. If businesses *think* the policies will be ineffective, the *MEI* schedule may shift to the left and the desired objective of generating income and employment may not be fulfilled. It is even possible that insistence upon a balanced budget during a recession may be quite stimulating if this policy has the effect of restoring confidence, thereby shifting the *MEI* schedule to the right. As Keynes suggests, "economic prosperity is excessively dependent on a political and social atmosphere which is congenial to the average businessman."[4]

Each of the factors mentioned above—changes in the level of aggregate demand, changes in the existing capital stock, innovation, and the general state of confidence in the economy—may change (shift) the *MEI* schedule through their effect on the relationship between the *expected* net revenue stream and the current supply price of capital goods. Accordingly, it is useful to summarize these factors under one heading: *the state of expectations*. If entrepreneurs expect conditions (economic, social, or political) more favorable to business, then the state of expectations may change and the *MEI* schedule will shift to the right. This would result in higher levels of investment at each interest rate.

While we are assuming that all new investment (new plant and equipment, planned inventories, and residential construction) is lumped together and that its volume depends upon the relationship between the marginal efficiency of investment and the interest rate, we should keep in mind that the level of planned inventories depends, perhaps principally, on the uncertainty surrounding the actual level of future sales. Since inadequate inventories result in the loss of sales, if businesses expect prosperity, they will want to hold relatively large inventory levels. However, since carrying inventories is expensive—among the cost items are storage, handling, clerical work, obsolescence, deterioration, and, most important, earnings foregone on funds tied up in inventories or interest costs on funds borrowed to finance inventory stocks—businesses want relatively low inventory levels if recession is expected. Since uncertainty, or the "state of expectations," is important in determining the shape and location of the marginal efficiency of investment schedule, changes (more favorable) in expectations of future sales will influence (increase) the level of inventories.

Carrying costs are very important in inventory management, and these costs are positively related to the interest rate; hence, inventory investment may, like investment in plant and equipment, increase along a given marginal efficiency of investment schedule with decreases in the interest rate. Accordingly, inventory investment may occur through movements *along* an existing *MEI* schedule as well as by *shifts* in the schedule.

The fact that the three components of real investment are responsive to many factors suggests the need for a certain amount of disaggregation of the

---

4. *Ibid.*, 162.

investment component of aggregate demand in "realistic" macroeconomic model building.

In the remaining chapters of Part II we will use the aggregate investment equation already introduced in this chapter

$$I = n_1 + n_2 r$$

where I is net investment (measured in billions of constant dollars) r is *the* rate of interest, and n_1 and n_2 are predetermined constants with $n_1 > 0$ and $n_2 < 0$. We should keep in mind, however, that this function holds *for a given state of expectations.*

After a discussion of money in Chapters 9 and 10, this equation will be used in the increasingly complete Keynesian models of Chapters 11 and 12. This equation will replace the previously used assumption that the prevailing level of investment in any time period is an exogenously given fact of life.

Money Supply
and Demand

In the simple Keynesian model presented in Chapters 5 and 7, net invest-ment was assumed to be exogenously determined. The investment function developed in Chapter 8,

$$I = n_1 + n_2 r$$

can now be used to replace the equation $I = \bar{I}$. Thus our simple Keynesian system can be written as

$$C = a_1 + a_2 Y_d \tag{9-1}$$

$$Y_d = Y - T \tag{9-2}$$

$$T = t_1 + t_2 Y \tag{9-3}$$

$$G = \bar{G} \tag{9-4}$$

$$I = n_1 + n_2 r \tag{9-5}$$

$$Y^* = C + I + G \tag{9-6}$$

The problem is that this system of equations cannot be solved simul-taneously to obtain equilibrium values for the endogenous variables. Given values for the predetermined parameters and variables—a_1, a_2, t_1, t_2, $\bar{G}$, n_1, and n_2—the system cannot be solved for specific equilibrium levels of C, Y_d, Y, T, G, I, and r. There are six equations but seven variables. The best we could do is reduce these equations to one equation.

The next step we will take in developing our static "Keynesian" model is to put Equations 9-1 to 9-6 aside for awhile and concentrate on adding a few more equations and variables to our model—equations depicting the supply of and the demand for money.

In this chapter we attempt to identify and explain the factors which determine the aggregate supply of and demand for money. The first objec-tive is to discuss the factors determining the *demand* for money. The de-mand for money is thought to be a function of the rate of interest and nominal income, that is, income expressed in current prices. The first part of the chapter is devoted to a discussion of the positive relationship between the transactions and precautionary demands for money and the level of nominal income. In the next section, the inverse relationship between the speculative demand for money and the rate of interest is discussed.

The second objective of the chapter is to discuss factors determining the *supply* of money. Our first assumption about the money supply is that the quantity of money that banks and monetary authorities want to supply is a predetermined variable. Although this practice is acceptable for many types of macroeconomic models, a more recent practice is to treat the supply of money as an endogenous variable, just like the quantity of money demanded. Hence, in Chapter 10, the supply of money is presented as a variable determined by economic forces brought explicitly into the model.

MONEY DEMAND

"Money" is generally defined as currency and demand deposits (checking accounts) held by the nonbank public. To determine the demand for money, Keynes employed the concept of liquidity preference—another behavioral concept in the same class as the propensity to consume and the inducement to invest. Why do households or business enterprises hold a portion of their wealth in money, a zero-yield asset, when positive-yield alternatives exist? There are, in fact, good reasons for holding money balances and foregoing interest earnings. These reasons may be conveniently categorized as transactions, precautionary, and speculative demands. Keep in mind that categorizing the demand for money is mainly for analytical convenience, since "money held for each of the three purposes forms, nevertheless, a single pool which the holder is under no necessity to segregate into three watertight compartments . . ."[1]

Transactions and Precautionary Demands for Money

One reason for holding money is that it is needed by households and businesses to bridge the gap between flows of revenues and expenditures. This "transactions demand" for money was emphasized in Chapter 4 in explaining the neoclassical theory of money and prices.

If all of one's wealth were in relatively nonliquid form, such as stocks, bonds, machinery, or rolls of copper wire, every time a purchase (either for consumption or investment) had to be made, some portion of these non-

1. J. M. Keynes, *The General Theory of Employment, Interest, and Money* (Harcourt Brace Jovanovich, 1936), 195.

liquid holdings would have to be converted into cash. This is both inconvenient and costly. Capital "conversions" are often very expensive. The magnitude of these cash holdings for households depends upon the time lag between receipts and expenditures, the availability of consumer credit, and the dollar volume of output; for businesses, their magnitude depends upon the availability of producers' credit and the amount and frequency of turnover of goods and services currently produced.

For example, the growing use of credit cards very likely will reduce households' transactions demand for *currency*. But because credit card accounts improve the ability of households to coordinate streams of spending and income, their transactions demand for *money* may also decline. A man could put his monthly paycheck in a *time* deposit, "charge" his monthly purchases and pay for them at the end of the month, without any direct service charge, by using his time deposit funds, which have been earning interest.

Since in the short run there is a fairly stable lag between receipts and expenditures, and since the availability of credit can reasonably be assumed to remain constant during the time period, we assume that the *average* amount of money which the nonbank public will want to hold due to the transactions motive depends upon the prevailing level of *nominal* income, that is, PY—the volume of final goods and services expressed in *current-period* prices. Think of a situation like the first two quarters of 1970 during which Y (net output valued using the prices which prevailed in some base period) remained just about constant. In terms of real output, the U.S. economy was in a stationary state. But the general price level was rising during these two quarters. Thus we can reasonably expect that the amount of money required to support transactions in 1970.2 was larger than 1970.1. Following this reasoning, economists view the quantity of money demanded for transactions as a function of nominal rather than real output.

The second motive for holding money is called "precautionary" demand. If all the revenues and expenditures of households and businesses were certain, even though a lag between revenues and expenditures occurs, there would be no reason for households and businesses to hold money for purely precautionary purposes, that is, as a reserve against unforeseen, but not totally unexpected, contingencies. Uncertainty does exist, however, for both receipts and expenditures. Uncertainty creates the need for cash balances to cover unexpected expenditures and make up for unexpectedly vanishing receipts. It seems reasonable to assume that the amount of money held as precautionary balances also depends upon nominal output.

Let us designate the amounts of money people wish to hold because of transactions and precautionary motives as L_1 and L_2, respectively. These amounts are expressed in current-period dollars; that is, they have not been divided by P, the general price index. We can now write

$$L_1 = \beta_1 PY \quad \text{and} \quad L_2 = \beta_2 PY$$

where β_1 and β_2 represent the proportion of nominal income required for transactions and precautionary money balances, respectively. In the short run both β_1 and β_2 are relatively stable; hence, L_1 and L_2 are determined when PY is known.

The above equations can be added:

$$L_1 + L_2 = \beta_1 PY + \beta_2 PY = (\beta_1 + \beta_2)PY$$

Hereafter, for simplicity, we will refer to $\beta_1 + \beta_2$ as b_3, so that our combined transaction and precautionary demand for money can be written as

$$L_1 + L_2 = b_3 PY$$

This relationship is shown in Figure 9-1. For a given value of b_3, the function gives the levels of $L_1 + L_2$ corresponding to various levels of PY. If $b_3 = 0.20$, for example, and $PY = 800$, $L_1 + L_2 = 160$.

Speculative Demand for Money

The third motive for holding money, "speculative" demand, is one o˜ Keynes' innovations. Keynes, himself a very successful speculator, wanted to incorporate into economic theory what he knew to be a fact of everyday life—wealth owners or wealth managers often hold cash, foregoing a virtually risk-free positive rate of return, which cannot be justified as being held for "transactions" or "precautionary" reasons. Also, to the extent that this portion of the quantity of money demanded can be separated from the total, and inspected in isolation, the quantity of money demanded for "speculation" varies inversely with the rate of interest.

The existence of a speculative demand for money itself, as well as the inverse relationship between this portion of the quantity of money demanded and the rate of interest, can be explained at many levels of complexity. There has been a great deal of controversy surrounding even Keynes' own explanation. We begin our discussion of these two points with a simple, rather intuitive explanation. A relatively formal explanation of the speculative demand for money follows the simple discussion.

Assume that it is March 1, 1974, and that the portfolio manager of a mutual fund has just sold at $1.00 per share 100,000 shares of common stock in a company he knows will be going bankrupt in a few months. Our manager, constantly in fear of having to go back into ladies ready-to-wear with his brother-in-law, is pondering what to do with his shareowners' $100,000. Assume that he *knows* that the price of Atomic Toy common stock has been falling, and that he *feels* it will "bottom out" at $10 a share in three weeks, on March 22. If our manager can buy about 10,000 shares of Atomic Toy at or near the bottom, he is going to look especially good in his first quarter report, because he is confident that even by March 31, Atomic Toy will be above $25 a share.

Figure 9-1

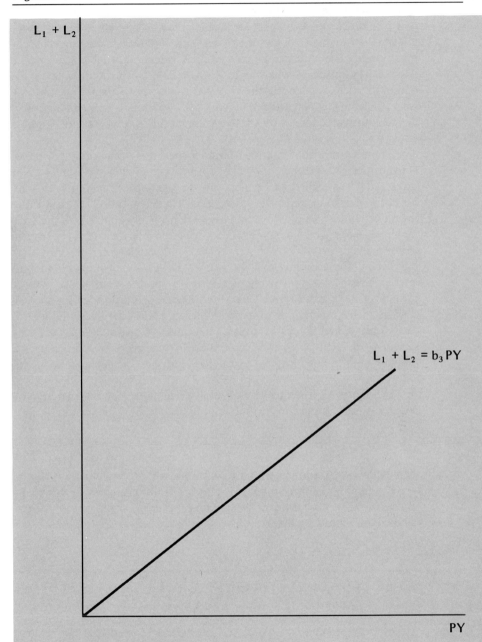

Now the question is what to do with the $100,000 between March 1 and whenever the Atomic Toy purchase is made—probably a few days before March 22, our manager's predicted price trough. One thing is absolutely clear: the manager can simply leave the $100,000 in his fund's checking account. The purchasing power will be instantly available to make the Atomic Toy purchase when he loses his nerve. But if he does leave the money in a demand deposit, the $100,000 is going to be idle for nearly three weeks. The savings entrusted to his care will be earning a *zero* rate of return, or even a negative rate of return to the extent that the general price level is rising during this three-week period.

There are a host of interest-bearing forms into which our manager can convert the $100,000. Yet all of these forms, such as the various public and private IOUs designed to be attractive to the short-run holder, involve *transactions costs* as well as *loss of liquidity*. These two "costs" of converting the money into an interest-bearing asset are probably quite small, but so is the three-weeks' worth of interest. The *higher* the interest rate, however, the *higher* is the probability that our manager, and people in similar situations throughout the economy, will be enticed to get out of money and into interest-bearing assets. The higher rates of interest swamp the wealth owners' or wealth managers' "costs" (both the monetary and nonmonetary costs of the transaction and the nonmonetary cost of the loss in liquidity). Therefore, we can expect an inverse relationship between "the" rate of interest (which is either an average of rates or some representative rate) and the volume of money held for speculative purposes, as depicted in Figure 9-2.

In Figure 9-2, the quantity of money demanded for speculative purposes (L_3) is an inverse linear function of the prevailing rate of interest (r):

$$L_3 = b_1 + b_2 r$$

where b_1 and b_2 are predetermined constants, with $b_1 > 0$ and $b_2 < 0$.

Combining the three money demands introduced earlier in this chapter, it is evident that the *total* demand for money $(L = L_1 + L_2 + L_3)$ depends upon r and PY; that is,

$$L_1 + L_2 + L_3 = \beta_1 PY + \beta_2 PY + b_1 + b_2 r$$

Or, since we have decided to refer to $\beta_1 + \beta_2$ as b_3, our demand for money function is written[2]

$$L = b_1 + b_2 r + b_3 PY$$

---

2. If this equation were obtained using "regression" techniques—i.e., if observations on L, r, and PY were "fitted" into this linear form and estimates of b_1, b_2, b_3 were obtained—b_1 would be a constant resulting from the levels of all three variables, not just the "speculative" demand for money and the rate of interest, as in the text.

Figure 9-2

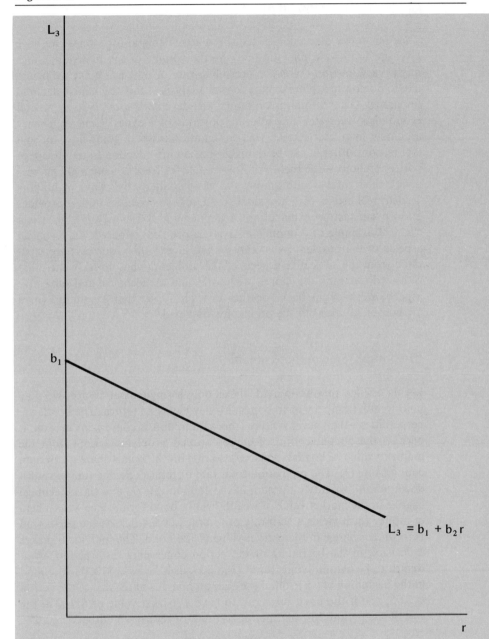

L_3

b_1

$L_3 = b_1 + b_2 r$

r

Portfolio Choice and
Speculative Demand for Money

Thus far in our discussion of the speculative demand for money, we have given an intuitive explanation of why the volume of speculative holdings might vary inversely with the prevailing rate of interest. What we would like to do now is explore a more formal analysis of this speculative demand for money. This formal presentation was developed *after* 1936 by several economists interested in exploring portions of Keynes' General Theory argument in greater detail.[3] This presentation is worth going into, for several reasons. First, it can be thought of as an introduction to the theory of portfolio choice—the theory of how people (at least "theoretical" people) divide their total wealth among the various alternative ways of holding wealth: real estate, common stock, cash, and so forth. Second, it provides a more satisfactory explanation of the demand for money. Third, it is a classical example of economic analysis: a problem is posed, the technical aspects of the problem (what can we get, given our resources?) are separated from the subjective aspects of the problem (what do we want—that is, how do we rank the choices we have?), and the technical and subjective aspects are brought back together in such a way that a solution (or a method of solution) to the problem is obtained.

"Technical" Side of the Problem

Let us assume that an individual has only a single asset choice. He may hold wealth in money or in bonds. Money yields no return. The bonds are perpetuities—they never mature (this assumption is convenient because it permits the circumvention of computational problems arising from the maturity value of bonds). Assume also that all the bonds share a common coupon rate (r). The per-period total rate of return (R), the rate of return *on all wealth*, would be the sum of the coupon rate (r) and the percentage change in the market value of wealth held in bond form, since wealth held in money form yields a zero rate of return. Let GA denote the per-period percentage change in the market value of the bond. The individual makes a decision in the beginning of the period concerning the fraction (a) of wealth to be held in bonds during the period. If he paid \$1000 for a bond in the beginning of a period, if the coupon rate due at the end of the period is 0.05, and if the bond turns out to have a market value of \$1100 at the end of the period, his total per-period rate of return would be

$$R = r + GA = 0.05 + 0.10 = 0.15$$

or 15% per period.

3. James Tobin, "Liquidity Preference as Behavior Towards Risk," *Review of Economic Studies*, Vol. 25 (February 1958), 65–68.

It would be possible to get a frequency distribution of the percentage gains and losses based on the performance of the bond during past time periods, as depicted in Figure 9-3. The distribution drawn in Figure 9-3 depicts the gains as being "normally" distributed in a nice bell-shaped curve which peaks at a zero level of GA. That is the "expected value" of changes in capital value (E_{GA}) during any given time period, from the point of view of the beginning of the time period, is zero.

A measure of dispersion of the distribution in Figure 9-3 is the "standard deviation" (s_{GA}):

$$s_{GA} = \sum_{i=1}^{n} (GA_i - \overline{GA})^2 / n$$

where GA_i is ith observed capital gain or loss, n is the number of observations, and $\overline{GA}$ is the arithmetic mean of the observed gains and losses.

It is customary to use the standard deviation of the capital gains distribution as an indicator of risk. The larger is s_{GA}, the more "spread out" or flatter is the distribution. Thus the larger is s_{GA}, the greater is the possibility that the price of this bond will change between the beginning and the end of the current time period. Note that s_{GA} is computed by using the *past performance* of the bond, while we are interested in how the price of the bond is going to behave during the *coming* period. Using s_{GA} as a measure of risk means that the past is assumed to be a reliable guide to the future— an assumption incompatible with "uncertainty," as defined in the Introduction to this part of the book.

We can summarize some of our above observations in a few equations:

$$R = a(r + GA) \tag{9-7}$$

In Equation 9-7, the *total* per-period rate of return (R) on a given amount of initial wealth is equal to the fraction of initial wealth held in bonds during the period (a) multiplied by the coupon rate (r) plus the actual percentage change in the market price of the bond (GA), which can be negative.

$$E_R = a(E_r + E_{GA}) \tag{9-8}$$

In Equation 9-8 the expected value of the *total* rate of return (E_R) is equal to a, multiplied by the sum of the expected value of the coupon rate, plus the expected value of the change in the market price of the bond. Since the coupon rate is a sure thing, $E_r = r$. Thus, given the assumption that $E_{GA} = 0$, Equation 9-8 can be written as

$$E_R = ar \tag{9-9}$$

The expected value of the total rate of return is then determined solely by the proportion of wealth held in bonds and by the coupon rate.

The risk of the return (s_R) is due solely to the risk of the capital gain, since r is fixed and known. Thus, the measure of risk is

Figure 9-3

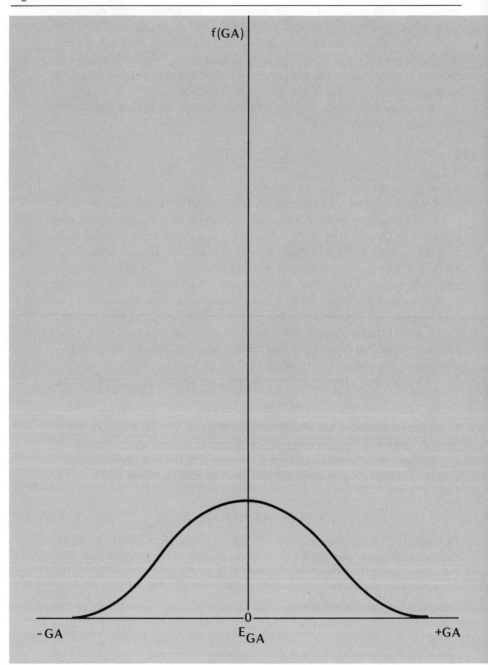

$$s_R = a s_{GA}$$

where s_{GA} is the standard deviation of the capital gain. Solving the equation above for a yields

$$a = \frac{s_R}{s_{GA}} \qquad (9\text{-}10)$$

which, when substituted into Equation 9-9, yields

$$E_R = \frac{r}{s_{GA}} s_R \qquad (9\text{-}11)$$

Equation 9-11 is an equation with two endogenous variables, E_R and s_R. The coupon rate (r) and the standard deviation of changes in the market value of bonds (s_{GA}) are exogenously determined. As far as we are concerned, they must be accepted as facts of life. Equation 9-11 is a linear equation with a slope of r/s_{GA}. If plotted, it would look as shown in Figure 9-4. This line is an "opportunity line" or a "line of attainable combinations," in the sense that it gives the combinations of expected total rate of return (E_R) and risk (s_R) which are attainable, given the prevailing values of r and s_{GA}. The higher is the expected rate of return, the higher is the risk which must be borne.

We have now isolated and discussed the "technical" side of the problem, using the word "technical" in the sense of "what is feasible, given present conditions?" We must now put aside this part of the problem for a while and discuss the preferences of the wealth holder or manager.

"Subjective" Side of the Problem

An "indifference curve" between expected rate of return and risk is a set of combinations of these two variables, among which the wealth holder is indifferent. Such indifference curves might be obtained from a "market survey," that is, by placing the wealth holder in an artificial environment. He might be told to imagine that he is attaining a given R—such as 10%— and bearing a certain risk—such as $s_R = 0.05$. The individual might then be asked what amount of R would be necessary if he had to bear an increased risk of, say, $s_R = 0.06$ and be just as happy as he was at the first combination. Repeated trials of this sort would produce one "indifference curve" between risk and expected rate of return.

It has been postulated that this particular type of preference map will have several major characteristics, corresponding to certain behavioral characteristics of wealth holders. First, a given "indifference curve" will always be upward-sloping. The line labeled U_0 in Figure 9-5 is a set of combinations of expected rate of return and risk among which the individual is indifferent; that is, they all yield the same level of satisfaction or "utility." This first "postulate" is that for the individual to be indifferent between points 1 and 2 in Figure 9-5, the higher risk (s_R) being borne at point 2

Figure 9-4

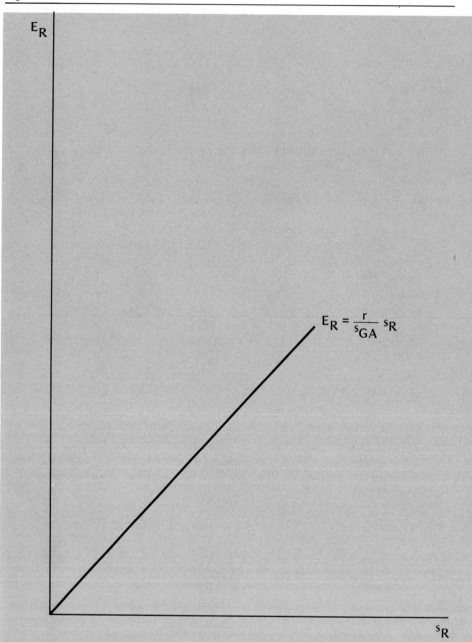

Figure 9-5

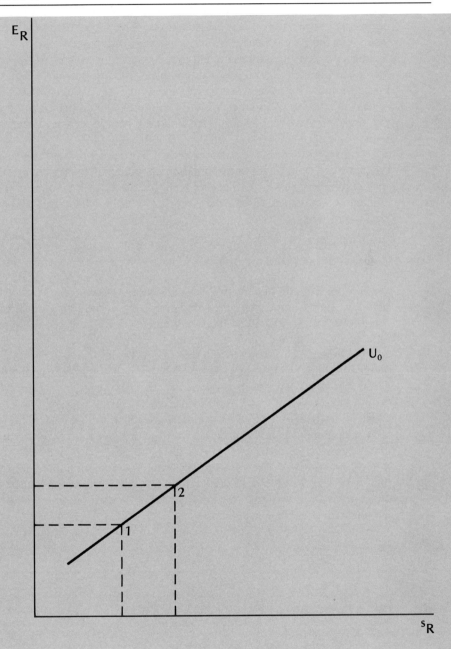

must be compensated with a higher expected rate of return (E_R). This makes sense for all people except those individuals who place a positive utility on bearing risk in the market itself. (For such "irrational" risk-lovers, the indifference curve would be *downward*-sloping.)

Second, a given indifference curve is postulated to be convex from below. U_0 in Figure 9-6 never becomes completely flat (that would violate the first postulate), but it increases at an increasing rate. An equal increment of risk (say the distances labeled 1 and 2) requires a larger increment in E_R, the higher is the initial level of risk. That is, there is an increasing "disutility" of risk.

One indifference curve has been drawn in Figure 9-6. But the space in the figure can be thought of as containing an indefinitely large number of such indifference curves, so that every point in the figure is a point on some indifference curve, none of which ever cross each other. This gives an "indifference map."

Solution of the Problem

We now combine the "subjective" side of our analysis with the "technical" side. Superimposing a preference map consisting of only two indifference curves over the "line of attainable combinations" of Figure 9-4 would produce a single diagram which might look like Figure 9-7.

We have drawn Figure 9-7 so that one of the indifference curves (U_0) just touches the line of attainable combinations. If we assume enough indifference curves have been generated so that the space in Figure 9-7 is "continuously dense" with indifference curves, there will be *one* curve which is tangent to our line of attainable combinations.

The point of tangency of Equation 9-7 with a given indifference curve, in our case U_0, gives the level of risk (s_{R*}) and the level of expected total rate of return (E_{R*}). They are the "optimal" combinations, in the sense that they yield the highest level of satisfaction (they are on the highest indifference curve) which is "technically" feasible—that is, which is along the line of attainable combinations.

This optimal level of risk (s_{R*}) can be substituted into Equation 9-10:

$$a^* = \frac{s_R^*}{s_{GA}}$$

Since s_{GA} is known, a^* (the *optimal* fraction of wealth to be held in bonds during the period) has been obtained.

Speculative Demand for Money

We must now work out what would have happened if the coupon rate (r)—which is *the* rate of interest in the present context—were higher during

Figure 9-6

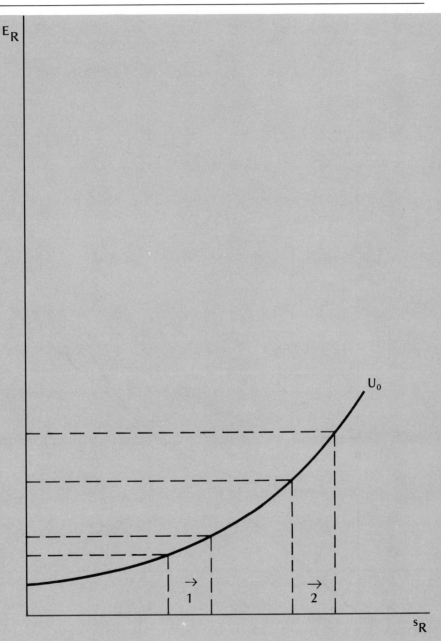

Figure 9-7

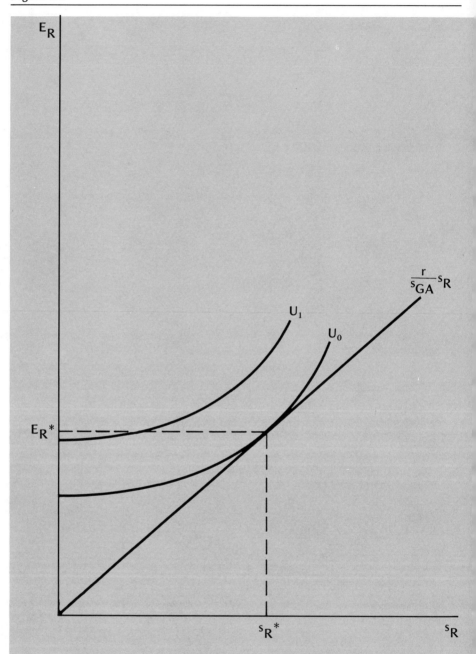

the current period. An increase in r will, all other exogenous terms remaining constant, cause the line of attainable combinations to rotate upward with the origin as a fixed point, as depicted in Figure 9-8.

As the line of attainable combinations rotates upward, it is now tangent to a higher indifference curve. This point of tangency occurs at a higher level of s_{R*}, as drawn in Figure 9-8. If a larger value of s_{R*} is substituted into Equation 9-10, the corresponding level of a^* will also be larger. That is, an increase in the coupon rate will, under these conditions, cause the individual wealth holder or manager to hold more of his wealth in the form of bonds.

This result is what we discussed in an intuitive fashion earlier in the chapter. As was mentioned, however, this analysis can be generalized to become a fairly complex (and useful) theory of portfolio choice.

MONEY SUPPLY

We have now shown that the quantity of money demanded by the nonbank public (L) depends on the prevailing level of nominal income (PY) and the rate of interest (r). What determines the quantity of money to be *supplied* by the central monetary authorities and the commercial banking system? In Chapter 10, we discuss the money stock (M) as an endogenous variable. But for now it will be taken as exogenously given:

$$M = \bar{M}$$

That is, the quantity of money the banking sector of the economy wants to supply on the average during some future time period is accepted as a fact of life.

MONETARY EQUILIBRIUM

The "money market" discussed in this chapter may be summarized algebraically as

$$L = b_1 + b_2 r + b_3 P Y \qquad (9\text{-}12)$$

$$M = \bar{M} \qquad (9\text{-}13)$$

$$L^* = M \qquad (9\text{-}14)$$

Equation 9-12 gives the quantity of money demanded by the nonbank public (L) as a function of the rate of interest (r) and level of nominal income (PY). Equation 9-13 denotes that the quantity of money supplied is assumed to be exogenously given, and Equation 9-14 is the relevant equilibrium condition. Equation 9-14 must be discussed in greater detail.

Equation 9-14, in conjunction with Equations 9-12 and 9-13, should

Figure 9-8

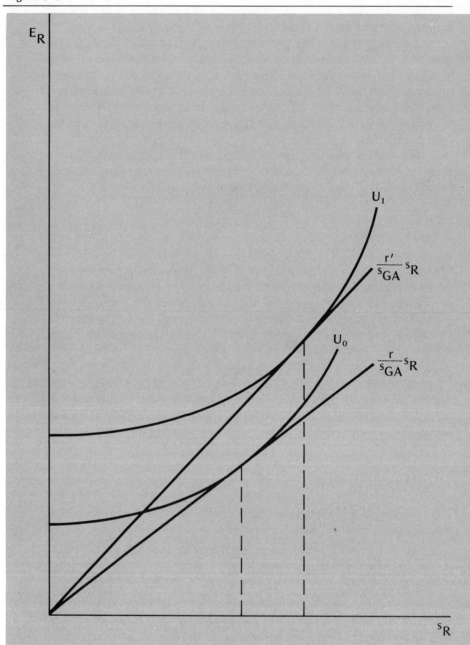

be thought of in the following way. The actual level of money holdings we would observe during the time period will turn out to be $\bar{M}$. Automatic market forces will cause r and PY to adjust so that the prevailing levels of these variables will correspond to a quantity of money demanded equal to the quantity of money the banking system wishes to supply.

To see how this equilibrium might come about, assume hypothetically that, at the end of some time period, the supply of and demand for money were equal; that is, $L^* = \bar{M}$, because the prevailing level of interest (r) and nominal income (PY) corresponded exactly to an L^* quantity of money demanded (which equaled the amount the monetary sector wanted to supply). Assume next that the monetary authorities wish $\bar{M}$ during the next period to be 5% greater than it was in this initial period. What market forces will cause L to increase commensurately with supply? We will assume that PY is relatively passive and focus on r as the equilibrating variable. This assumption follows economists conventional practice of focusing on interest rates as *the* important short-run money market variable.

One type of activity which will cause the money stock in the second period to be greater than it was in the initial period is for the central monetary authorities to make net purchases of IOUs from the non-bank public. They must entice the public to surrender these interest-bearing IOUs and accept the money the central monetary authorities want it to hold. To do this the central bank must offer prices which are attractive (that is, higher than those which have prevailed in the recent past).

The higher prices for the IOUs, however, will affect their yields. Think of the "yield" of an IOU as equivalent to the "rate of discount" introduced in Chapter 8. For example, if you wanted to obtain $100 today, you might be able to do this by selling a piece of paper to someone on which was printed the promise that you would repay the $100 plus 10% interest (that is, $110) a year from now. If you could find a buyer at $100, the "yield" on this IOU—that percentage which equates the future income stream to the present value (market price)—would be the same as its "coupon rate," the agreed-upon 10%:

$$100 = \frac{110}{1 + 0.10}$$

Now assume that someone, say a central bank, takes a sudden interest in acquiring this IOU and others like it. They could probably get this IOU by offering its current holder more than he paid for it, say $105. The coupon rate (10%), the time which must elapse before maturity (one year), and the face value ($100) are unaffected. But the yield is lowered:

$$105 = \frac{110}{1 + x}$$

where x turns out to be a little over 4.76%.

If you came along and wanted to sell a second piece of paper to raise still another $100, and the risk associated with your second IOU was the same as that associated with the first, you would not have to promise to pay back the $100 plus 10% interest in a year. Given the way the market was viewing your IOUs and others like it, you would not need to promise to pay more than $104.76 at the end of the year. In other words, the "coupon rate" on your IOUs would have fallen from 10% to 4.76%. In the same way, net purchases of U.S. Treasury IOUs by the Federal Reserve System often have a dampening effect on rates of interest. In fact, the average yield on government IOUs is often used by economists to denote *the* rate of interest.

The lowering of the rate of interest has the effect of raising L_3, the quantity of money demanded for speculative purposes. Or, since L_3 cannot really be separated from L, the decline in r (all else remaining constant) causes L, the total quantity of money demanded, to increase.

The foregoing type of adjustment process has been discussed by economists for *hundreds* of years. The relationships of the rate of interest, the price of debt instruments, the general price level, and the level of real output have been a rich and colorful topic in the history of economic thought. For now, however, we are simply interested in introducing you to our three "money-market" equations (9-12, 9-13, 9-14). Having discussed the money market, we are now ready to return to the simple Keynesian model introduced in Chapters 5 and 7, and summarized algebraically at the beginning of this chapter.

The Monetary Base and the Money Supply

10

In Chapter 9, we assumed that the supply of money is exogenously given—that the managers of the public and private banking system "decided" on the amount of currency and demand deposits they wanted to supply on the average during some future time period, and that these plans were realized. The prevailing level of this planned supply was thought of as depending on the profitability of various quantities of money supplied, from the point of view of commercial banks, and on some policy objectives, from the point of view of the central bank (in the United States, the Federal Reserve System).

In most simple "Keynesian" versions of a macroeconomy, the quantity of money supplied (M) is thought of as an important policy variable, assuming the central monetary authorities want to take advantage of it. If a prevailing level of M yields levels of output, unemployment, and/or inflation which are not "desirable," it is generally argued that the central monetary authorities can use the various "tools" legally available to them (which vary from country to country) to adjust M so that it is consistent—other parameters such as government spending remaining the same—with some desired combination of real GNP, inflation, unemployment, and other important macroeconomic variables.

Nevertheless, one major recent issue in monetary economics is whether or not the central bank can change the money stock with any degree of precision. Below, we present a representative money supply *function*. That is, an equation is developed in which the quantity of money supplied is an *endogenous* rather than an *exogenous* variable.[1]

---

1. Our presentation closely follows that of Jerry L. Jordan, "Elements of Money Stock Determination," *Federal Reserve Bank of St. Louis Review*, Vol. 51 (October 1969), 10–19.

COMPONENTS OF THE MODEL

Commercial banks are required to keep only a fraction of their total deposits on hand or on deposit at the central bank. The remaining amount can be loaned if customers are available. If the reserve requirement is 20% and someone deposits $1000 in a bank, the bank is permitted to loan *at most* $800 of this $1000. Assume that the full $800 *is* loaned and that *all* of the $800 is deposited in another bank. If the relevant minimum reserve requirement is still 20%, and if the second bank decides to become "loaned up," $640 of the new $800 deposit can be loaned. As this "frictionless" process continues, and if there is time for an indefinitely large number of these deposit-loan sequences to occur, the initial $1000 deposit will result in a total increase of $5000 in deposits.

This simple version of the monetary expansion resulting from fractional reserve banking rests on a number of assumptions: First, that all bank *deposits* are subject to the same reserve requirement. Second, that all *banks* are subject to the same regulations. Third, that banks are "loaned up" at all times; that is, they do not hold more reserves than the law requires. Fourth, that the *entire* amount of every loan is returned to the banking system; that is, there is no "currency drain." The public has a fixed, absolute amount of *currency* which it wants to hold, and this amount does not vary with the prevailing level of deposits.

In any actual economy, however, the above assumptions are quite unrealistic. In the following model we eliminate several of them. We assume that the amount of deposits *can* affect the amount of currency the public wants to hold, and that the total composition of private demand deposits, government demand deposits, and time deposits may change.

Let M denote the U.S. money stock, which consists of all the currency and commercial bank demand deposits *not* owned by the Treasury, the Federal Reserve banks, or commercial banks. That is, the money stock is the currency (CU) and demand deposits (DD) owned by the "nonbank public." Therefore

$$M = DD + CU \qquad (10\text{-}1)$$

One of the more important variables used in monetary analysis is the notion of the "monetary base" or "high-powered money."[2] The monetary base may be defined from the point of view of its "sources" or its "uses." The sources of the base are the liquid assets of the federal government (including the Federal Reserve), such as gold stock and Treasury cash holdings. U.S. securities held by the Federal Reserve are the dominant type of asset. The monetary base, from a "use" viewpoint, is the sum total of mem-

---

2. For an introduction, see Leonall C. Andersen and Jerry L. Jordan, "The Monetary Base— Explanation and Analytical Uses," *Federal Reserve Bank of St. Louis Review*, Vol. 50 (August 1968), 7–11.

ber bank deposits at the Federal Reserve and all currency in circulation (including the vault cash of member and nonmember banks).

We will emphasize here the "uses" approach to analyzing the monetary base (B). Hence, we will define it as the sum of the currency held by the nonbank public (CU) and the reserves (R) of all commercial banks, including the vault cash of nonmember banks:

$$B = R + CU \qquad (10\text{-}2)$$

There are three major types of deposits in commercial banks: private demand deposits (DD), Treasury deposits at commercial banks (TR), and time deposits (TI). The total amount of commercial bank reserves (R) can be thought of as a simple fraction (r_1) of total bank deposits:

$$R = r_1(DD + TI + TR) \qquad (10\text{-}3)$$

The prevailing level of r_1 depends on the existing institutional facts of life of commercial banking. It would be affected by the distribution of total deposits between banks which are, and banks which are not, members of the Federal Reserve System. It would also depend on how deposits are distributed among banks in different cities, since reserve requirements vary with city size. In addition, r_1 would depend upon the level of reserve requirements for demand deposits and time deposits, which are different. Hence, r_1 will also depend on how total deposits are distributed among these two types of deposits. Finally, r_1 would be affected by the amount of excess reserves commercial banks choose to hold.

The value of r_1 has steadily fallen over time in the United States from a level of approximately 0.14 in the early 1950s to about 0.09 in the early 1970s. One explanation of why r_1 has steadily fallen is that time deposits have grown more rapidly than demand deposits (perhaps because the nonbank public has been economizing on "money" during a period of relatively high interest rates) and time deposits are subject to much lower reserve requirements than demand deposits.

The simple model of credit expansion introduced earlier is based on the assumption that the public wants to hold a constant total *amount* of currency. If this were really true, all increases in the monetary base by the Federal Reserve would remain in the commercial banking system as reserves. Yet it is more realistic to assume that the public wants to hold a fixed *ratio* of currency to demand deposits:

$$CU = k_1(DD) \qquad (10\text{-}4)$$

Thus, for every dollar increase in demand deposits (DD), the public will want to increase their currency holdings by a certain amount.

One important influence on the prevailing level of k_1 is the extent of credit card use. As they are used for more and more purchases, we would expect the k_1 ratio to fall (although in actual fact it has been rising recently). Credit cards are *not* money, but rather a means of "settling up" at the end of a time period. Hence, as they are used more by more people, we can expect DD to be a little lower (people can now place a portion of what would previously have been idle balances in interest-bearing forms), but we can expect CU to be substantially lower. During the post-World War II years, k_1 drifted downward to a low of about 0.250 in the late 1950s and early 1960s, and up to about 0.29 in the early 1970s.

Most economists do not count time deposits as part of the nation's money stock. Yet banks must hold a portion of these deposits as reserves, although the fraction of reserves against time deposits is lower than the fraction applicable to demand deposits. Hence, a given change in bank reserves (part of the monetary base) will support a greater increase in time deposits than demand deposits. The relationship between time deposits (TI) and demand deposits (DD) can be expressed as

$$TI = k_2(DD) \tag{10-5}$$

The prevailing level of k_2 is influenced by the ceilings imposed on the interest rates for various classes of time deposits which can be paid by commercial banks. These ceilings, set by the Federal Reserve and the Federal Deposit Insurance Corporation, may be sufficiently low to deny commercial banks the opportunity to compete for their "traditional portion" of the nation's savings. The rate of return on alternative low-risk assets, such as savings and loan shares or commercial paper, may be higher than the ceilings, hence depressing the level of k_2. The value of k_2 has steadily drifted up from a level around 0.4 two decades ago to about 1.2 in the 1970s.

Treasury demand deposits with commercial banks (TR) are not included in the traditional definition of money. Nevertheless, banks are required to keep the same fraction of reserves against Treasury deposits as they do for private demand deposits. Thus changes in TR influence the amount of private demand and time deposits the commercial banking system can support with a given monetary base. So Treasury deposits can be expressed as a fraction of private demand deposits:

$$TR = h(DD) \tag{10-6}$$

The level of h is determined by the relationship between federal taxes and spending at any moment of time and the Treasury's decision to keep a portion of any current surplus in commercial banks rather than with the Federal Reserve. The value of h has fluctuated in tight cycles from a trough of 0.025 to a peak of about 0.06.

THE MONEY MULTIPLIER

It may be convenient at this point to repeat the six equations of this chapter:

$$M = DD + CU \tag{10-1}$$

$$B = R + CU \tag{10-2}$$

$$R = r_1(DD + TI + TR) \tag{10-3}$$

$$CU = k_1(DD) \tag{10-4}$$

$$TI = k_2(DD) \tag{10-5}$$

$$TR = h(DD) \tag{10-6}$$

These six equations can be condensed into one. Substituting Equations 10-5 and 10-6 into Equation 10-3 yields

$$R = r_1[DD + k_2(DD) + h(DD)]$$

Substituting the above equation and Equation 10-4 into Equation 10-2 gives

$$B = r_1[DD + k_2(DD) + h(DD)] + k_1(DD)$$

Factoring the DD term which appears in each element of the right-hand side gives

$$B = [r_1(1 + k_2 + h) + k_1]DD$$

The above equation can be solved for DD:

$$DD = \frac{1}{r_1(1 + k_2 + h) + k_1} B$$

According to Equation 10-4, $DD = CU/k_1$, so that the above equation may be expressed as

$$CU = \frac{k_1}{r_1(1 + k_2 + h) + k_1} B$$

Adding the above two equations together yields

$$DD + CU = \frac{1}{r_1(1 + k_2 + h) + k_1} B + \frac{k_1}{r_1(1 + k_2 + h) + k_1} B$$

According to Equation 10-1, $M = DD + CU$. Therefore, the equation above may be expressed as

$$M = \frac{1 + k_1}{r_1(1 + k_2 + h) + k_1} B \tag{10-7}$$

Equation 10-7 is a condensed version of Equations 10-1 through 10-6. The two variables are M (the money stock) and B (the money base). The two variables are connected by an expression which, if k_1, r_1, k_2, and h are relatively constant, is itself relatively constant:

$$\frac{1 + k_1}{r_1(1 + k_2 + h) + k_1}$$

This term is often referred to as the "money multiplier" (not to be confused with the Keynesian "multiplier" concepts introduced in Chapter 7). The money multiplier in the United States fluctuated between 2.65 and 2.75 in the 1950s and drifted down during the 1960s to about 2.5.

If the monetary authorities could predict the level of the money multiplier with complete accuracy, say if they knew it was going to be 2.5 during the second quarter of 1974, they would know that a $100,000 increase in the monetary base would result in a $250,000 increase in the money stock. The main policy activities of the Federal Reserve—open market operations, changes in minimum reserve requirements, and changes in the supply and cost of loans to member banks—directly influence the money base. But it can make predictable changes in the money stock only to the extent that it can predict the money multiplier.

CONCLUSION

A recent development in monetary macroeconomics was introduced in this chapter: the supply of money as an endogenous variable. But this topic is only a small part of recent developments. Economists have lately demonstrated a strong interest in monetary aspects of an economy. Some of these topics are beyond the traditional limits of macroeconomic analysis, being placed more properly in the categories of monetary theory, commercial and central banking, public finance, or international trade. Yet much of the debate about monetary aspects of a theoretical macroeconomy *is* important to macroeconomic analysis. One major issue—the old neoclassical question of whether or not a change in the quantity of money can alter any of the *real* aspects of an economy—is discussed in Chapter 11.

A Static Keynesian Model: Price Held Constant

EQUATIONS OF THE MODEL

It might be helpful to review the "Keynesian" equations we have developed so far. Consumer spending on current goods and services (C) is a linear function of disposable real income (Y_d):

$$C = a_1 + a_2 Y_d \quad \text{(with } a_1 > 0 \text{ and } 1 > a_2 > 0) \quad (11\text{-}1)$$

Disposable real income is equal, by definition, to real income (Y) less tax receipts (T):

$$Y_d = Y - T \quad (11\text{-}2)$$

Tax receipts are a linear function of real income:

$$T = t_1 + t_2 Y \quad \text{(with } t_1 > 0 \text{ and } 1 > t_2 > 0) \quad (11\text{-}3)$$

The level of spending by public authorities (G) is exogenously determined and known:

$$G = \bar{G} \quad (11\text{-}4)$$

Investment is a decreasing function of the "cost of investment"—the prevailing rate of interest (r):

$$I = n_1 + n_2 r \quad \text{(with } n_1 > 0 \text{ and } n_2 < 0) \quad (11\text{-}5)$$

Real national income (or equivalently, output) is, in equilibrium, sufficient to support the current spending plans of the three segments of the economy:

$$Y = C + I + G \quad (11\text{-}6)$$

The average stock of currency and demand deposits desired during the quarter (L) by the nonbank public is a linear function of the prevailing interest rate and the nominal or current-dollar value of income:

$$L = b_1 + b_2 r + b_3 PY \quad \text{(with } b_1 > 0, b_2 < 0, \text{ and } b_3 > 0) \quad (11\text{-}7)$$

The average stock of money supplied by public and private banking authorities during the quarter is exogenously fixed and known:

$$M = \bar{M} \qquad (11\text{-}8)$$

The supply of money and the demand for money are equal:

$$L = M \qquad (11\text{-}9)$$

Equations 11-1 through 11-9 contain ten "variables": C, Y_d, Y, T, G, I, r, L, P, and M. The fact that there are nine equations and ten variables means we have a small problem, similar to the one pointed out at the beginning of Chapter 9. The system of equations is "underdetermined"—that is, there are not enough equations to enable us to solve for the variables. This problem can be resolved by holding one of the variables constant at some arbitrarily chosen level. In our case, we will hold constant the general price level (P).

REDUCTION OF THE MODEL TO TWO EQUATIONS

We must now reduce Equations 11-1 through 11-9 to two equations, with only two variables, and then solve them simultaneously. Substituting 11-2 and 11-3 into 11-1 yields

$$C = a_1 + a_2(Y - t_1 - t_2 Y)$$

Multiplying a_2 through the parentheses gives

$$C = a_1 + a_2 Y - a_2 t_1 - a_2 t_2 Y$$

Further simplifying yields

$$C = a_1 - a_2 t_1 + a_2(Y - t_2 Y)$$

which finally may be written as

$$C = a_1 - a_2 t_1 + a_2(1 - t_2)Y \qquad (11\text{-}10)$$

Substituting 11-4, 11-5, and 11-10 into 11-6 yields

$$Y = a_1 - a_2 t_1 + a_2(1 - t_2)Y + n_1 + n_2 r + \bar{G}$$

The income and rate of interest terms in the above equation are equilibrium levels, but to avoid "messiness," the asterisks used in earlier chapters to denote equilibrium levels will be dropped. In this context, the word "equilibrium" is used in the sense that "all discrepancies between planned spending and planned real income are assumed to have been resolved."

Multiplying both sides of the above equation by (-1), and then transposing the $n_2 r$ term to the left-hand side and the Y term to the right-hand side, yields

$$n_2r = Y + a_2t_1 - a_1 - a_2(1 - t_2)Y - n_1 - \bar{G}$$

Factoring the Y term on the right-hand side yields

$$n_2r = a_2t_1 - a_1 - n_1 - \bar{G} + [1 - a_2(1 - t_2)] Y$$

which, after both sides are divided by n_2, becomes

$$r = \frac{a_2t_1 - a_1 - n_1 - \bar{G}}{n_2} + \frac{[1 - a_2(1 - t_2)] Y}{n_2} \qquad (11\text{-}11)$$

Equation 11-11 is a condensed form of Equations 11-1 through 11-6, taken together. It is a function with two unknowns, r and Y, and a number of predetermined variables and constants. Equation 11-11 is a set of combinations of real income (that is, current output valued in base-period prices) and the rate of interest for which spending plans by households, businesses, and government are satisfied.

Equation 11-11 is a linear equation. The constant term,

$$\frac{a_2t_1 - a_1 - n_1 - \bar{G}}{n_2}$$

will, for all realistic levels of the predetermined variables and constants in the numerator, be positive. Every term in the numerator, except a_2t_1, is preceded by a negative sign, and these negative terms will, taken together, swamp the one positive term (this is assured by virtue of $\bar{G}$ being, by far, the largest term in the numerator). The denominator is also negative, so that the constant term in Equation 10-11 will be positive. The slope of Equation 11-11

$$\frac{[1 - a_2(1 - t_2)]}{n_2}$$

is negative. Its numerator is positive because t_2 is a positive fraction so that $(1 - t_2)$ is a positive fraction, and since a_2 is a positive fraction, $a_2(1 - t_2)$ is a positive fraction. Thus, when $a_2(1 - t_2)$ is subtracted from unity, the result is *also* a positive fraction. Since the denominator of the slope of Equation 11-11 (n_2) is negative and the numerator is positive, the entire term is negative.

Hence, Equation 11-11 expresses an *inverse* relation between the rate of interest and the level of real income. This result is what we would expect from our equations. Of the three types of spending—C, I, and G—only I is affected by a change in the rate of interest. If r increases, I will decline. Thus, an increase in r will cause $C + I + G$ to decline and, for equilibrium to be maintained, Y must decline commensurately.

Putting aside Equation 11-11 for now, let us turn to the remainder of the model, Equations 11-7, 11-8, and 11-9. Substituting 11-7 and 11-8 into 11-9 yields

$$\bar{M} = b_1 + b_2r + b_3PY$$

The terms r and PY in the above equation are equilibrium levels: r is an "equilibrium" rate of interest, and PY is the "equilibrium" level of income, expressed in current-period prices. In this context, "equilibrium" is used in the sense of "all discrepancies between the anticipated quantity of money demanded and supplied are assumed to have been resolved."

The above equation may be written as

$$-b_2 r = -\bar{M} + b_1 + b_3 PY$$

or, after dividing both sides by $-b_2$,

$$r = \frac{\bar{M} - b_1}{b_2} - \frac{b_3}{b_2} PY \tag{11-12}$$

Equation 11-12 is a condensed form of Equations 11-7, 11-8, and 11-9. It is a function with three unknowns, r, P, and Y. Equation 11-12 is a set of combinations of nominal output (that is, current output valued in current-period prices) and the rate of interest, which equate the demand for money with the existing supply of money.

Equation 11-12 is also a linear equation. The constant term,

$$\frac{\bar{M} - b_1}{b_2}$$

is negative because the numerator will always be positive—the constant term (b_1) in the demand for money equation will never exceed the entire money stock—and the denominator is negative. The slope of Equation 11-12 $[-(b_3/b_2)]$ is positive because b_3 is positive and b_2 is negative.

Hence, Equation 11-12 expresses a *direct* relation between the rate of interest and the level of nominal income: other things equal, as nominal income increases, the quantity of money demanded increases (because of the transactions and precautionary motives). If the amount of money supplied by the banking system remains unchanged and if those supply plans continue to be realized, something has to give. The "speculative component" of the demand for money must decline. It will, if the rate of interest increases.

It may be helpful at this point to graph Equations 11-11 and 11-12. Equation 11-11 has two unknowns and can be graphed in two dimensions, using a Y scale and an r scale. Yet Equation 11-12 has three unknowns, so in order to graph it on the same diagram, the variable P must be held constant. Equation 11-11 and—for a particular value of the general price level (P'), where P' is equal to, say, 1.02—Equation 11-12 are graphed in Figure 11-1. The slope of Equation 11-12, when it is drawn in r–Y space (as in Figure 11-1), is $-[(b_3/b_2)P]$.

Corresponding to the given level of P and the prevailing levels of all predetermined variables and constants, there is an interest-rate/real-income combination which simultaneously satisfies both Equations 11-11 and 11-12. For this rate of interest (r'_{CM}) and this level of real income or output (Y'_{CM}) the "goods and services" or "commodity" side of the econ-

Figure 11-1

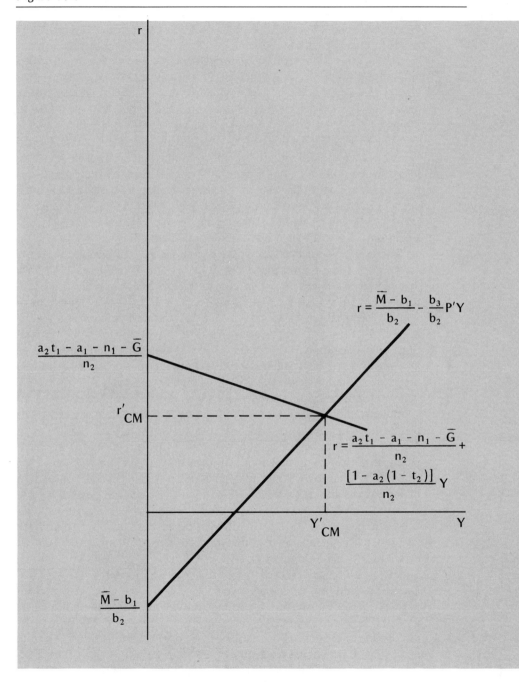

$$r = \frac{\overline{M} - b_1}{b_2} - \frac{b_3}{b_2} P'Y$$

$$\frac{a_2 t_1 - a_1 - n_1 - \overline{G}}{n_2}$$

$$r'_{CM}$$

$$r = \frac{a_2 t_1 - a_1 - n_1 - \overline{G}}{n_2} + \frac{[1 - a_2(1 - t_2)]}{n_2} Y$$

$$Y'_{CM}$$

$$Y$$

$$\frac{\overline{M} - b_1}{b_2}$$

omy is in equilibrium, that is, $Y = C + I + G$. The "monetary" side of the economy is also in equilibrium, that is, $L = M$. The CM subscript is used because r'_{CM} and Y'_{CM} do, taken together, satisfy both the "commodity" and the "money" sides of the economy. To make our diagram less cumbersome, Equation 11-11 can be identified as a "CE" or "commodity side equilibrium equation," and Equation 11-12 is an "ME" or "monetary side equilibrium equation." As a reminder, the fact that the ME schedule is drawn for a given level of P is denoted by subscripting ME with P', as in Figure 11-2.

We have so far in this chapter stressed the rather mechanical, *algebraic* determination of equilibrium. It would be good, however, to get an idea of why r'_{CM} and Y'_{CM} in Figure 11-2 are the levels of interest and real income toward which the economy is always tending and which we assume actually prevail during the time period. We can see how these levels will prevail by going "behind" the diagram to the original relationships—Equations 11-1 to 11-9—used to obtain the diagram.

Assume, hypothetically, that the prevailing levels of income and interest were for some reason the levels given at point D in Figure 11-2. This income-interest combination is compatible with "commodity" equilibrium—that is, at this level of Y and r, $Y = C + I + G$—but not with "money" equilibrium. The money "market" is in disequilibrium. At the level of Y given by point D, relatively little money is needed for transactions and precautionary purposes. Given M, therefore, a relatively large amount of money is available for speculative purposes. At the relatively high rate of interest corresponding to point D, however, the speculative demand for money is, like Y, also quite low. People have excess supplies of "speculative holdings of money." To get rid of these holdings, individuals might buy financial assets, such as the government IOUs discussed in Chapter 9. Again, as discussed in Chapter 9, this action by the nonbank public to get rid of money and into interest-bearing assets will cause the price of the latter to be bid up and, hence, their yields to decline. The action of individuals has caused the rate of interest to decline, toward r'_{CM} in Figure 11-2. As the rate of interest is forced down, the I component of aggregate demand $(C + I + G)$ will increase because investment has been stimulated. The greater level of investment will result in higher levels of Y, closer to Y'_{CM} in Figure 11-2.

Thus, automatic market forces would cause a movement from a disequilibrium interest-income point like D in Figure 11-2 to a point of equilibrium. These adjustments take time. But we are working with a fairly abstract, simple model in which time has been suppressed. We cannot determine the time tracks of our variables. We only determine the equilibrium levels toward which they are tending, and assume they get there. This analysis is a good first step, however. You should have a "feel" for the driving forces moving the economy toward equilibrium, even if our analysis does not permit the movements to be brought explicitly into the open.

Figure 11-2

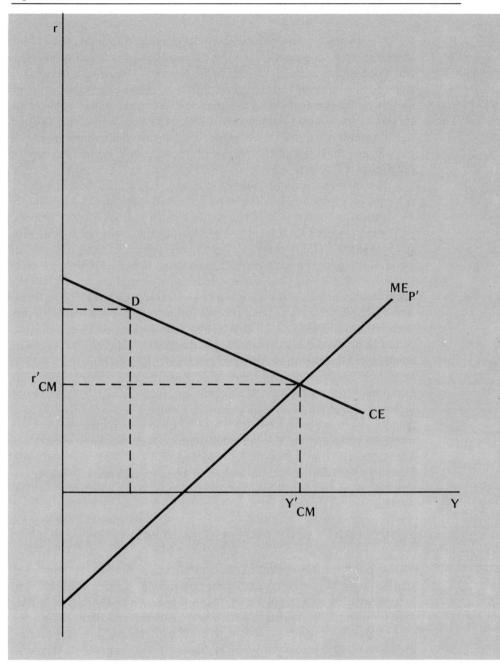

GRAPHICAL DERIVATION
OF THE CM FUNCTION

If, for some reason external to the model developed thus far, the general price level rose, Equation 11-11—the CE function—would not be affected. The slope of Equation 11-12—the ME_P' function—*would* be affected. The slope of this function varies directly with the general price level, although its vertical intercept would remain the same. An increase in P would cause the ME_P' function to rotate in such a way, as in Figure 11-3, that the new equilibrium level of real income would be less than the initial level of real income, and the new equilibrium rate of interest would be greater than the initial rate of interest.

The inverse relationship between P and Y_{CM} is made explicit in the three panels of Figure 11-4. The upper left panel in Figure 11-4 is meant to be identical to Figure 11-3. The lower left panel is simply a 45° "helping-line" diagram used to link the upper left with the lower right panel. The function labeled CM in the lower right panel is derived from the upper left panel. If the general price level is P', the corresponding equilibrium level of income is Y'_{CM}. This price-income combination produces point 1 in the lower right panel. Substitution of a higher general price level P'' into Equation 11-12 (the equation giving the $ME_{p'}$ function) yields a lower equilibrium level of income, Y''_{CM}. This second price-income combination is assumed to produce the point labeled 2 in the lower right panel. More points could be obtained by substituting other values for P into Equation 11-12. If enough points were obtained, we would begin to get an idea of the shape and slope of the prevailing CM function. In general, a CM function can be defined as a set of price and income combinations which must exist if equilibrium (equilibrium in both "sides" of the economy) is to be attained, given the prevailing values of the predetermined constants and variables in Equations 11-1 through 11-9. (A CM function could be obtained algebraically by solving Equations 11-11 and 11-12 simultaneously, taking advantage of the fact that they share a common left-hand side, r.)

PUBLIC POLICY AND THE CM FUNCTION

At this point it is convenient to discuss the impact on the CM function of changes in the prevailing levels of three predetermined parameters and variables associated with public policy. We will focus on the qualitative rather than the quantitative impact of a change in a particular constant or variable, everything else remaining constant. We will work through the first change, in the quantity of money supplied, fairly carefully, and present the other two more briefly.

An increase in $\bar{M}$ will have no effect on Equation 11-11, the CE function. The only effect will be on the constant term in Equation 11-12, or its

Figure 11-3

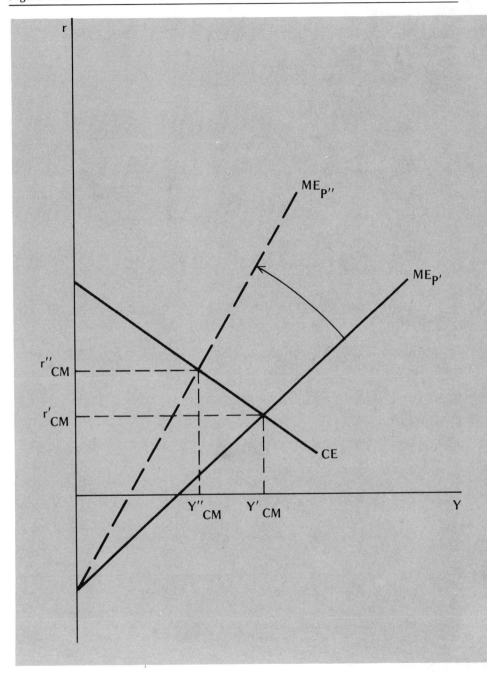

Figure 11-4

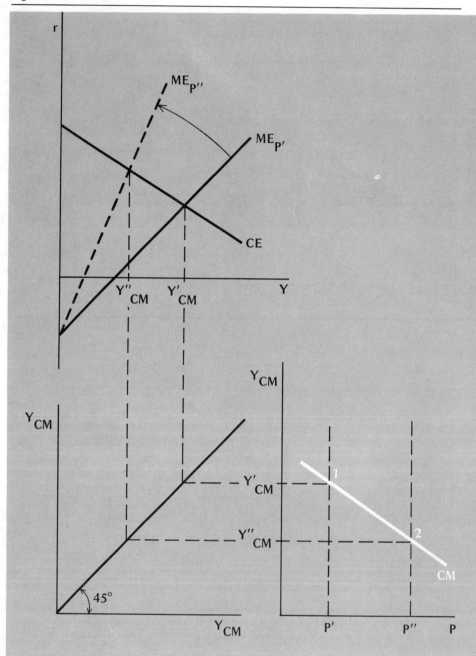

equivalent, the vertical intercept of the ME_p' function: $(\bar{M} - b_1)/b_2$. This intercept will always be negative because the numerator is positive—the constant term (b_1) in the demand for money equation will never exceed the entire money stock $(\bar{M})$—and the denominator (the coefficient attached to the r term in the money demand function) will be negative. An increase in $\bar{M}$ will cause the numerator to increase, and therefore will cause the entire term to become a larger negative number. Thus the vertical intercept of the ME_p' function will shift downward, as in Figure 11-5.

The solid and the dashed ME_P' functions in the upper left panel of Figure 11-5 are assumed to have been drawn using the same level of the general price index (P'). The dashed ME_{P}' function—the one corresponding to the increased money stock—intersects the CE function at a higher level of income than does the solid ME_P' function. Therefore, at any particular level of P, the level of Y_{CM} corresponding to the larger money stock exceeds the level of Y_{CM} corresponding to the smaller money stock. That is, an increase in the supply of money decreases the vertical intercept of the ME_P' function and causes the Y_{CM} function in the lower right panel of Figure 11-5 to shift upward. This impact is summarized in the first line of Table 11-1.

An increase in t_1 may be interpreted graphically as a shift up in the tax function. A larger flow of tax receipts would be obtained from a given level of Y. Such an increase would affect only the vertical intercept of the CE function, causing it to decline. The increase in t_1 reduces disposable real income, thereby reducing consumption and hence the level of Y at every possible rate of interest. The downward shift in CE would result in a downward shift in the CM function: at every possible price level, the level of Y would be less than it was before the increase in t_1.

An increase in $\bar{G}$, the exogenously given level of government spending, would cause the vertical intercept of the CE function to increase and cause the CM function to shift upward.

It should be noted that these effects of parametric changes are crude, "qualitative," or directional effects. The impact on the *shape* and *slope* of

Table 11-1

Initial Change	Effect on ME_P and CE Functions	Effect on CM Function
$\bar{M} \uparrow$	Vertical intercept of ME_P decreases	Moves upward
$t_1 \uparrow$	Vertical intercept of CE function decreases	Moves downward
$\bar{G} \uparrow$	Vertical intercept of CE function increases	Moves upward

Figure 11-5

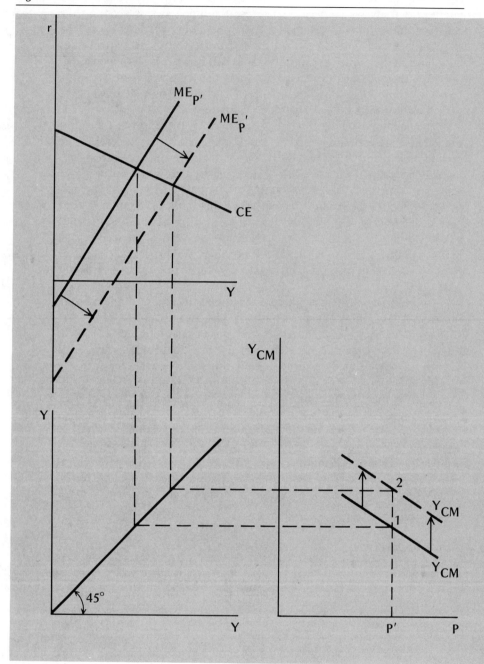

the CM function of some parametric change could best be determined by examining the original CM function itself, which we do not have, because we have not yet solved CE and $ME_{P'}$ functions simultaneously to get it. But directional changes are good enough for our purposes in Chapter 12.

Now we must put the CM function and its component parts aside for awhile and concentrate on expanding our basic equation system. We want to add equations so that the general price level (P) will become an endogenous variable. This is done in the next chapter.

A Complete Static
Keynesian Model

In Keynesian models of the type developed in our earlier chapters, the price level is held constant. This is one of the worst features of these models. Yet it *is* possible to expand the model we have been developing throughout Part II of this book. We will do this by introducing the "supply side" of our macroeconomy, that is, by introducing a production function and a labor market into the model. After developing the "complete" model, we give a numerical example, to show how the model works.

PRODUCTION, EMPLOYMENT, AND THE Π FUNCTION

The production or supply side of our complete Keynesian model is based on the same set of assumptions upon which the neoclassical model of Part I was based: (1) there are assumed to be n perfectly competitive firms, each producing one or more goods; (2) the managers of each of these n firms are responsible for producing different kinds of products by using "factors of production," or inputs; (3) all inputs are categorized as either labor (N) or capital (K); (4) both labor and capital are assumed to be homogeneous—it is impossible, for example, to distinguish among various units of labor.

We will expand the nine-equation model developed in the last chapter by reintroducing the concept of a "neoclassical" production function, presented in Chapter 3. National product (Y), equivalent to real income, is assumed to be functionally related to the aggregate quantity of labor employed (N), an important *endogenous* variable in this model, and the size of the capital stock ($\bar{K}$):

$$Y = AN^\alpha \bar{K}^{1-\alpha} \qquad \text{(with } A > 0 \text{ and } 1 > \alpha > 0\text{)} \qquad (12\text{-}1)$$

The capital stock is assumed to remain constant during the quarter. As was pointed out in Chapter 3, this latter feature is a characteristic of a short-run model. The period is sufficiently short to permit us to abstract from the changes in the nation's capital stock.

Although in the present static context the A term in the production function is a fixed coefficient, in a dynamic model it would be permitted to grow at some rate, such as

$$A_{t+1} = (A_t) (1.00625)$$

This feature would then incorporate technical progress into the model in the sense that the production function, independent of everything else, is shifting. In the time period $t + 1$, more output could be obtained from given levels of capital and manpower than is possible in period t. As was pointed out in Chapter 3, the fact that α is a positive fraction ensures that a given percentage increase in N will result in a less than proportional increase in Y. That is, the function exhibits diminishing marginal productivity of labor.[1]

One other use of Equation 12-1 can be noted here. If the labor force available at the beginning of the quarter (LF) is known, Equation 12-1 might be written as

$$Q = A(LF)^\alpha \bar{K}^{1-\alpha} \tag{12-2}$$

where Q is a specific level of output—introduced in Chapter 4 as "full capacity" output. It is the amount of output than can be obtained by employing everyone who currently wants to work (measured, say, by using the U.S. Bureau of the Census procedure).[2] We return to a discussion of this specific level of output shortly.

As discussed in Chapter 3, all the firms in an economy can be thought of as adjusting their number of employees so that the amount they must pay every worker is exactly equal to the value of the output produced by the last worker hired. That is, the "money wage rate" (W) will be equated to the value of marginal productivity $[P(dY/dN)]$ if firms are to maximize profits.

Given the production function

$$Y = AN^\alpha \bar{K}^{1-\alpha}$$

it follows that

$$\frac{dY}{dN} = \alpha A N^{\alpha-1} \bar{K}^{1-\alpha}$$

---

1. If the present model were cast in multiperiod form and K were permitted to change, as a result of this periodic net investment actually being added to K rather than being abstracted from it as in the present model, a given percentage change in K would also result in a lesser percentage change in Y.

2. In the United States, the Census Bureau estimates the work force, as well as the number of employed and unemployed individuals, by sampling roughly 33,000 households. This sample, the composition of which slowly changes ($\frac{1}{8}$ is new each month), is interviewed once each month, providing (by "blowing up" the sample findings) a monthly estimate of, among other things, the total work force. That is, an estimate is obtained of the number of individuals who are willing and able to work at their particular occupation at prevailing wage rates.

Thus we have Equation 12-3:

$$W = P\frac{dY}{dN} = P\,\alpha A N^{\alpha-1}\bar{K}^{1-\alpha} \tag{12-3}$$

Lastly, in this model it is assumed that the money wage (W) is exogenously given; that is, the amount paid to one worker for one quarter's work is the result of institutional factors beyond the scope of this model. Such institutional factors include minimum wage legislation and trade-union policies.

$$W = \bar{W} \tag{12-4}$$

For given values of A, α, and $\bar{K}$, Equation 12-1 can be plotted as shown in Figure 12-1. For every level of N—that is, for every "aggregate quantity of labor employed"—there is a specific level of Y, aggregate output (or equivalently, real income). Algebraically, the function increases at a decreasing rate because α is a positive fraction. This property incorporates the concept of diminishing marginal productivity of labor. The output-labor combination labeled Q and LF in Figure 12-1 is the combination given by Equation 12-2. It is the level of output (Q) attainable if everyone currently wanting to work (LF) is in fact employed. We return to this full-capacity concept later in this chapter.

Equations 12-3 and 12-4 cannot be plotted in the same space as Equation 12-1. In Equation 12-1 the dependent variable is aggregate output (measured in constant dollars, per time period); in Equations 12-3 and 12-4 the dependent variable is the money wage (measured in current dollars per man per time period). Another problem in trying to graph Equation 12-3 is that it contains three variables. W, P, and N. In order to get it into the W–N space, P must be held constant.

Equation 12-3—drawn for a particular level of the general price index (P'), where P' is equal to, say, 1.02—and Equation 12-4 are plotted in Figure 12-2. It should be stressed that current dollars per man per time period are measured along the vertical axis in Figure 12-2, but the horizontal axis is identical to that used in Figure 12-1. For a given level of P there is a given *value* of the labor marginal productivity function:

$$P\frac{dY}{dN} = P'\alpha\,AN^{\alpha-1}\,\bar{K}^{1-\alpha}$$

If the price level were to rise, the value of labor's marginal productivity would rise for any given level of N. Intuitively this occurs because, while real output does not change, the rise in the price level causes the money value of real output to rise. Similarly, a fall in the price level would reduce the value of labor's marginal productivity. In the lower panel of Figure 12-3 we have drawn three demand curves for labor, based on three price levels, P', P'', and P'''. If you draw a line from the vertical axis parallel to the horizontal axis, you see that labor's marginal productivity in real terms is

Figure 12-1

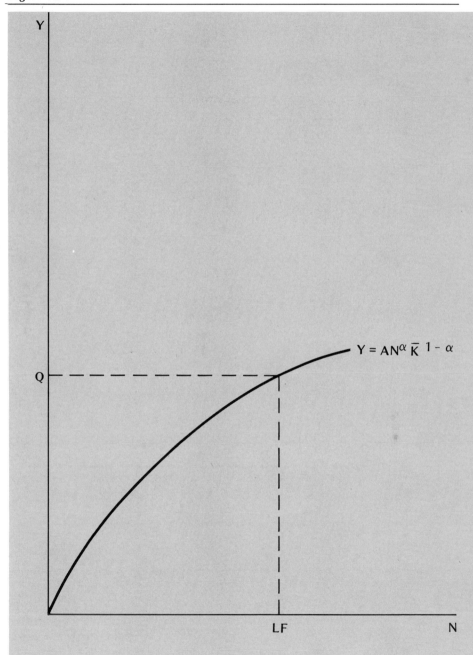

Figure 12-2

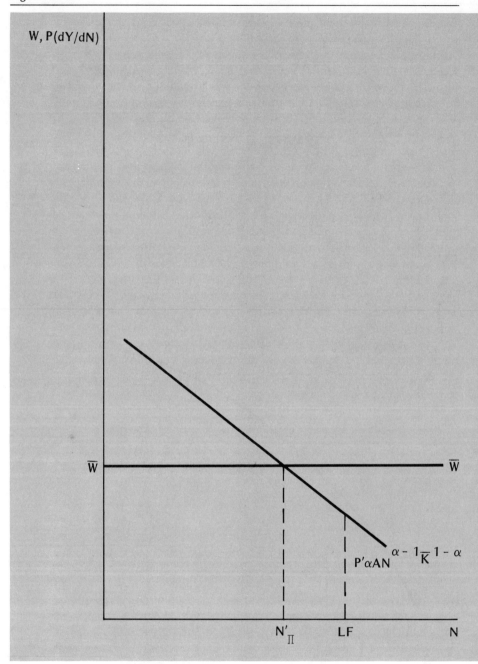

Figure 12-3

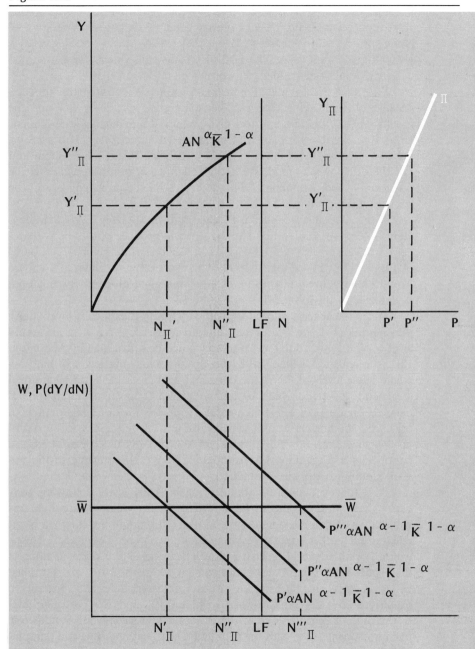

unchanged. But the demand for labor increases with successive increases in the price level. This is so because the horizontal line represents a constant money wage rate, W. The money value of the marginal product of labor goes up with increases in P, but the cost to firms of labor stays at a given money wage rate. The not surprising consequence is that firms' quantity of labor demanded, N, will increase.

$P(dY/dN)$ decreases as N increases because α is a positive fraction, i.e., because of diminishing returns. The point at which the $\bar{W}$ line and the $P'\alpha A N^{\alpha-1} \bar{K}^{1-\alpha}$ function intersect gives the profit-maximizing level of labor (N'_Π). The Π subscript is used to underscore the fact that this is a *profit-maximizing* quantity of labor. Given the fact that business hires labor and not the other way around, the actual quantity of labor employed is the quantity of labor demanded (N'_Π), regardless of the prevailing size of the available labor force (LF).

If the general price index is P', the profit-maximizing level of employment is N'_Π. An N'_Π level of employment will produce Y'_Π billions (base-period dollars) worth of final goods and services, as in the upper left panel of Figure 12-3. For a higher level of the general price index (P''), there would be an entirely new value of labor marginal productivity function, as depicted in the lower panel of Figure 12-3.

When the general price index is P'', the profit-maximizing level of employment is N''_Π. An N''_Π level of employment corresponds to an output level of Y''_Π. Many different levels of P could be substituted into Equation 12-3, the equation which yields the profit-maximizing levels of employment. These levels of P and the corresponding levels of Y can be graphed to generate a function such as the one labeled Π in the upper right-hand panel of Figure 12-3. This function (Π) represents a set of combinations of price and equilibrium output which must exist if business is to maximize profits, given the prevailing values of the predetermined variables and parameters in Equations 12-1 through 12-4. We are referring to the upward-sloping part of the Π function.

A Π function could be obtained algebraically in the following way: First solve both Equations 12-1 and 12-3 for N. The two resulting equations will share a common left-hand side, N. The right-hand sides can then be set equal to each other, and the resulting equation can be solved for Y. This Y will be Y_Π of Figure 12-3. That is, it will be the level of Y corresponding to the profit-maximizing level of employment where the latter is determined by (1) the prevailing levels of the predetermined variables and constants in Equations 12-1, 12-3, and 12-4—A, α, $\bar{K}$, and $\bar{W}$—and (2) a particular level of the independent variable in the equation, the general price index (P). For now we will work with the Π function as something obtained "graphically," as in Figure 12-3.

A disequilibrium in the labor market is possible if the price level is sufficiently high relative to the money wage level. In Figure 12-3, note the price level P''' in the lower left-hand panel. The amount of labor which firms wish to employ is N''', determined by the intersection of the value of the marginal productivity schedule, P''', and the given money wage rate, $\bar{W}$. However, the labor force is smaller than the amount of labor demanded by firms. This excess demand for labor is $(N''' - LF)$. Firms will hire as much labor as is available, LF. However, at LF, the value of marginal productivity is greater than the money wage rate, and we would expect that businesses would want to hire more workers. As a result, businesses will bid up the money wage rate in an attempt to increase their profits. When the money wage rate has risen sufficiently to eliminate the excess demand for labor, the labor market will be in equilibrium.

The Π function flattens out in Figures 12-3 and 12-4 because there is a ceiling on Y_Π, which is determined by the full employment capacity of the economy Q. On the horizontal segment of the Π function, firms are attempting but not succeeding in maximizing profits. What prevents them is the ceiling on the quantity of labor available.

EFFECT OF CHANGES IN WAGES, TECHNOLOGY, AND CAPITAL ON THE Π FUNCTION

In the preceding chapter we discussed the impact on the Y_{CM} function of changes in several of the relevant predetermined constants and variables. Now we should do the same for the Π function. The three changes in which we are interested are changes in $\bar{W}$, A, and $\bar{K}$. These changes can be discussed in terms of Figure 12-3.

For a given level of the money wage and a given level of the general price index, such as P' in the lower right panel of Figure 12-3, there is an equilibrium level of employment (N'_Π). If the money wage $(\bar{W})$ increases for some reason, the equilibrium level of employment corresponding to this given level of the general price index is lower than it was before. The change in $\bar{W}$ does not change the position of the production function in the upper left panel of Figure 12-3. Therefore, the decline in N_Π causes the economy to move down the given production function and Y_Π declines. Since a lower level of Y_Π is now associated with a given level of P, the Y_Π function will move to the right as a result of an increase in the money wage.

An increase in the A term in the production function can be thought of as an algebraic way of depicting technical progress. A higher level of A means that more output can be obtained from given amounts of labor and capital. The entire production function shifts upward. There is a value of labor marginal productivity function

$$P\frac{dY}{dN} = P'\,\alpha A N^{\alpha-1}\bar{K}^{1-\alpha}$$

for each value of A. If A increases, the function moves to the right, and the equilibrium level of employment increases. So the effect of an increase in A

Figure 12-4

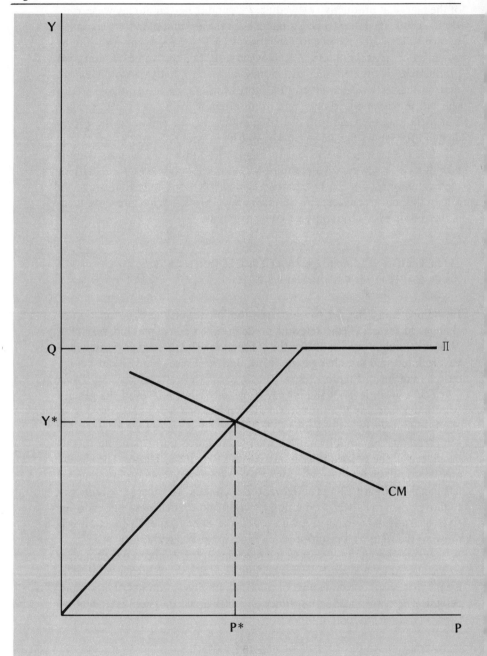

will be an increase in N_{Π}, which in itself would cause Y_{Π} to increase, but will have an even greater impact because of the upward movement of the production function. In short, an increase in A will cause the Π function to move to the left. A higher level of Y_{Π} will be associated with a given level of P.

An increase in $\bar{K}$, the capital stock, will have the same impact, qualitatively, as an increase in A. The Π function will move to the left.

MACROECONOMIC EQUILIBRIUM

The CM function obtained in the last chapter (the CM function represents equilibrium combinations of Y and P in the commodity market) and the Π function can be plotted in the same space because P is the independent variable and Y is the dependent variable in both functions. This is done in Figure 12-4.

The CM function in Figure 12-4 is drawn as a linear, inverse function because it appeared that way in the lower panel of Figure 12-4. The Π function in Figure 12-4 is drawn as a linear upward-sloping function. The function has a break at the point of full-capacity output. The portion of the production function past the $Q-LF$ combination of Figure 12-1 is irrelevant because it is (currently) unattainable. The equilibrium level of price and output are denoted by P^* and Y^* in Figure 12-4. These values are the solutions to Equations 11-1 to 11-9 and 12-1 to 12-4 taken together. If P^* and Y^* are known, every unknown in Equations 11-1 through 12-4 is also known. By combining the CM and Π functions, we have determined the equilibrium price level, P^*, and the equilibrium level of national income, Y^*. In Figure 12-4 this equilibrium falls short of that level of output which would generate full employment.

The main Keynesian conclusion is that the equilibrium level of output is quite independent of full-capacity output. The economy can be in equilibrium at less than full employment.

COMPARATIVE STATICS

The model which has been presented and solved in this chapter is a *static* model. We have abstracted from time in the sense that all adjustments are assumed to have had a chance to work themselves out. Logically, the next step is to trace out the impact on Y^* and P^* of changes in some of the more interesting predetermined variables and constants. Again the analysis abstracts from time. The changes are thought of in the following way: If one of the predetermined variables or constants were greater than it was when the original levels of Y^* and P^* were determined, would the new levels of Y^* and P^* be larger or smaller than the initial ones? This is a slightly dif-

ferent question than asking *how much* Y^* or P^* will change, given a specified change in one of the predetermined variables or constants.

The "multipliers" introduced in Chapter 7 were *quantitative* measurements. This model is sufficiently complex that expressions for "multipliers"
(exact equations used to determine the *amount* Y^* will change, given a certain change) would be relatively awkward algebraic expressions. To get
them, we would have to solve the *CM* function and the Π function simultaneously, express the result with Y^* as the sole dependent variable, and
determine the various partial changes in Y^* with respect to changes in each
of the predetermined variables and constants. In this section we will simply
trace through the *qualitative* changes in Y^* and P^* (that is, determine if they
increase or decrease) rather than the *quantitative* changes.

One change of special interest to Keynes was a *decrease* in the exogenously given money wage ($\bar{W}$). If the economy is in an underemployment
equilibrium in any given period, we can reasonably expect that there will be
downward pressures on the money wage during the next period. The bargaining strength of labor will have diminished relative to that of management. A decrease in $\bar{W}$ will only affect the Π function. As discussed earlier,
a *decline* in $\bar{W}$ will cause the Π function to move to the left, as in Figure
12-5. Note that at the full-capacity level of output, the new Π function corresponds with the old. The decrease in $\bar{W}$ will cause Y^* to increase and P^*
to decline, all other parameters remaining constant. The decrease in $\bar{W}$ will
result in a *decrease* in real output only if the *CM* function is *upward*-sloping
in the neighborhood of the shift. The decrease in $\bar{W}$ will be more defla-
tionary, the flatter is the *CM* function.

The effect on the equilibrium levels of *increases* in A and K will be the
same as a *decrease* in $\bar{W}$: the Π function moves to the left, Y^* increases, and
P^* declines.

From a policy point of view, the most interesting changes are in the
money supply ($\bar{M}$), government spending ($\bar{G}$), and the tax function (t_1, assuming we concentrate on the vertical intercept). All of these changes affect
only the *CM* function, as discussed in Chapter 11. An increase in $\bar{M}$ will
cause the *CM* function to move upward.

The effect of an increase in $\bar{M}$ on Y^* and P^* (everything else remaining
constant) will depend on the shape and slope of Π as well as the shapes and
slopes of the old and new *CM* functions. For example, assuming that these
functions look something like those drawn in Figure 12-6, an increase in $\bar{M}$
will be more inflationary and result in a smaller increase in output, the
flatter is the Π function.

An extreme case of this last point is depicted in Figure 12-7. As drawn
here, the initial *CM* function is already producing an equilibrium level of
output consistent with full capacity. In this case, an increase in the supply
of money would be purely inflationary.

An increase in $\bar{G}$ will affect only the *CM* function. An increase in $\bar{G}$ is
qualitatively the same as the effect of an increase in $\bar{M}$; that is, it will cause

Figure 12-5

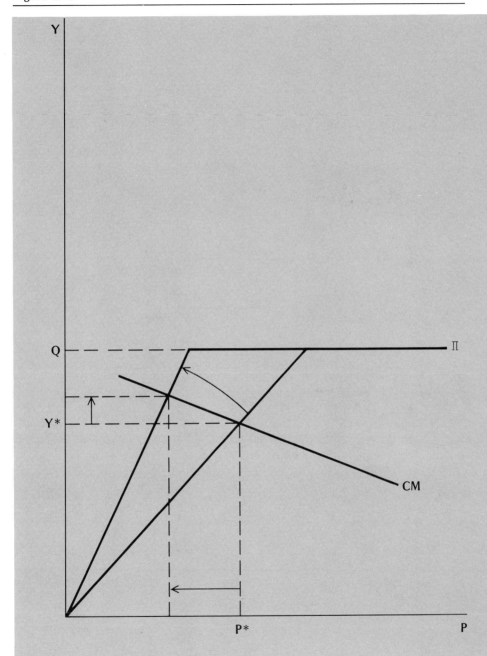

Figure 12-6

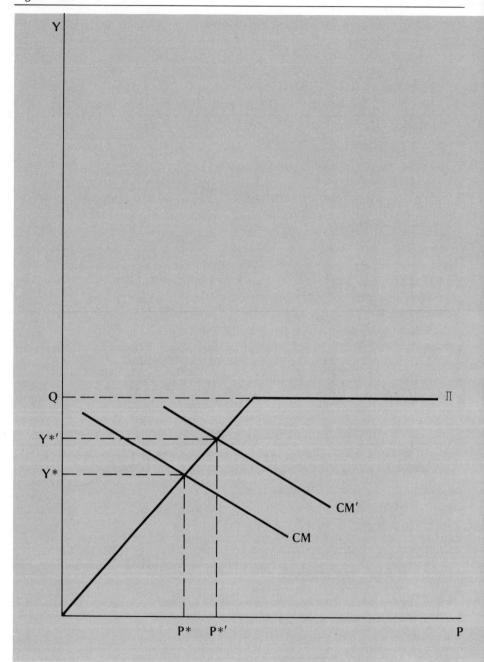

Figure 12-7

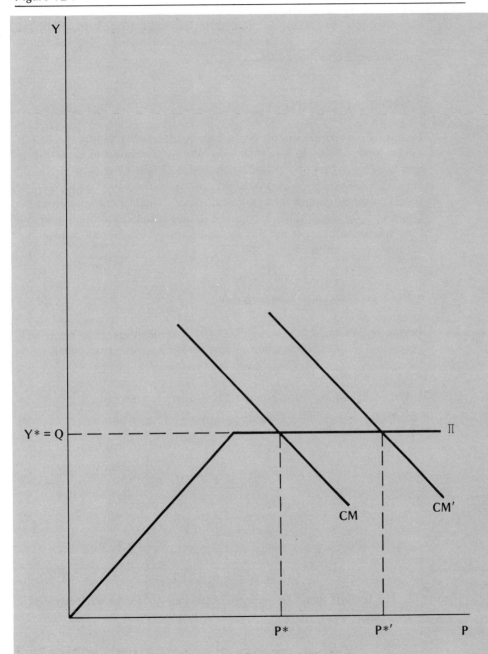

the CM function to move upward. Thus, the new equilibrium levels of price and output will be greater than the initial ones.

As discussed earlier, an increase in the vertical intercept of the tax function causes the CM function to move downward. This will cause equilibrium Y and P to decline.

NUMERICAL EXAMPLE

Perhaps a numerical example might help in understanding how the CM–Π model works. First, we repeat the equations of the model in general form and after each equation provide (relatively) arbitrarily chosen numerical values for the predetermined variables and constants in each equation. The necessary equations are then collapsed to obtain numerical versions of the CM and Π functions. The numerical CM and Π functions are plotted and then solved simultaneously. Finally, equilibrium values of all endogenous variables are computed.

Values for the Model's Parameters

Beginning in Chapter 5, we assumed that consumer spending on current goods and services (C) is a linear function of disposable real income (Y_d):

$$C = a_1 + a_2 Y_d \tag{12-5}$$

Let $a_1 = 20$ and $a_2 = 0.9$. Equation 12-5 then becomes

$$C = 20 + 0.9\, Y_d \tag{12-5'}$$

Disposable real income is equal, by definition, to real income (Y) less tax receipts (T):

$$Y_d = Y - T \tag{12-6}$$

Tax receipts are a linear function of real income:

$$T = t_1 + t_2 Y \tag{12-7}$$

Let $t_1 = 23.8$ and $t_2 = 0.22$. Equation 12-7 then becomes

$$T = 23.8 + 0.22\, Y \tag{12-7'}$$

The level of spending by public authorities (G) is exogenously determined and known:

$$G = \bar{G} \tag{12-8}$$

Let the prevailing level of government spending be \$185 billion, measured in constant or "base-year" prices:

$$G = 185 \tag{12-8'}$$

Net investment (I) varies inversely with the prevailing rate of interest (r):

$$I = n_1 + n_2 r \tag{12-9}$$

Let $n_1 = 45.38$ and $n_2 = -1.3$. Equation 12-9 then becomes

$$I = 45.38 - 1.3\,r \tag{12-9'}$$

Although the rate of interest on the right-hand side of Equations 12-9 and 12-9' is a percentage, we will follow the convention introduced earlier and enter it in this way: if $r = 10.5\%$, $r = 10.5$, and the prevailing level of investment consistent with Equation 12-9' would be \$31.73 billion (constant dollars).

National income (or equivalently, output) is, in equilibrium, sufficient to support current spending plans:

$$Y = C + I + G \tag{12-10}$$

Every item in the above equilibrium condition is expressed in "real" or "constant" billions of dollars.

The demand for money (L) depends on the prevailing interest rate (r) and on the nominal value of income:

$$L = b_1 + b_2 r + b_3 P Y \tag{12-11}$$

Let $b_1 = 75.9$, $b_2 = -7.3$, and $b_3 = 0.2$. Equation 12-11 then becomes

$$L = 75.9 - 7.3\,r + 0.2\,PY \tag{12-11'}$$

The supply of money is an exogenously given constant:

$$M = \bar{M} \tag{12-12}$$

Let the prevailing level of this predetermined variable be \$198.24 billion (current dollars). Unless the number is otherwise adjusted, it is by definition expressed in *current* dollars. Equation 12-12 then becomes

$$M = 198.24 \tag{12-12'}$$

The supply of money and the demand for money are assumed to be equal:

$$L = M \tag{12-13}$$

Both items in the above equilibrium condition are expressed in "nominal" or "current" billions of dollars.

National product (Y) is assumed to depend on the aggregate quantity of labor employed (N) and the size of the aggregate capital stock:

$$Y = A N^\alpha \bar{K}^{1-\alpha} \tag{12-14}$$

Let $A = 2.3$, $\alpha = \frac{1}{2}$, and $\bar{K} = 1444$. Equation 12-14 then becomes

$$Y = 2.3\,N^{1/2}(1444)^{1/2}$$

or

$$Y = 87.4\,N^{1/2} \tag{12-14'}$$

Full capacity output (Q) can be obtained by employing everyone who currently wants to work (LF):

$$Q = A(LF)^{\alpha}\,\bar{K}^{1-\alpha} \tag{12-15}$$

Again, let $A = 2.3$, $\alpha = \frac{1}{2}$, and $\bar{K} = 1444$ as in Equation 12-14. Also, let $LF = 81$. Equation 12-15 then becomes

$$Q = 2.3(81)^{1/2}(1444)^{1/2}$$

or

$$Q = 786.6 \tag{12-15'}$$

Y, K, and Q in the above equations are assumed to be expressed in billions of *constant* dollars. The variables N and LF denote "millions of workers."

All the firms in the economy can be thought of as adjusting their number of employees so that the amount they must pay every worker is exactly equal to the value of the output produced by the last worker hired. That is, the "money wage" (W) will be equated to the value of marginal productivity $[P(dY/dN)]$ if firms are to maximize profits:

$$W = P\frac{dY}{dN} = P\alpha\,AN^{\alpha-1}\bar{K}^{1-\alpha} \tag{12-16}$$

Given the values already assigned to α, A, and $\bar{K}$, Equation 12-16 becomes

$$W = P(\tfrac{1}{2})(2.3)(N)^{-1/2}(1444)^{1/2}$$

or

$$W = P\,43.7\,N^{-(1/2)} \tag{12-16'}$$

The money wage (W) is assumed to be a predetermined variable:

$$W = \bar{W} \tag{12-17}$$

Let the current money wage be

$$W = 5.1944 \tag{12-17'}$$

The money wage in the above equations is assumed to be expressed in thousands of current dollars, per man, per year.

A Numerical Version of the CM Function

The first step in finding a solution to this numerical example is to take advantage of the fact that Equations 12-15 through 12-10 have already been reduced to one equation in Chapter 11:

$$r = \frac{a_2 t_1 - a_1 - n_1 - \bar{G}}{n_2} + \frac{[1 - a_2(1 - t_2)]}{n_2}\,Y \tag{12-18}$$

Equation 12-18 yields the *CE* function used in Chapter 11.

Equations 12-11 through 12-13 have also already been reduced to one equation in Chapter 11:

$$r = \frac{\bar{M} - b_1}{b_2} - \frac{b_3}{b_2} PY \tag{12-19}$$

Equation 12-19 yields the $ME_{P'}$ function used in Chapter 11.

We are after something equivalent to the *CM* function used in Chapter 11 and this chapter. That is, we want a single function obtained by solving the *CE* and $ME_{P'}$ functions simultaneously. To get this function, we first need to substitute the numerical values assigned to our predetermined constants and variables into Equations 12-18 and 12-19:

$$r = \frac{(0.9)(23.8) - 20 - 45.38 - 185}{-1.3} + \frac{[1 - 0.9(1 - 0.22)]}{-1.3} Y$$

$$r = \frac{198.24 - 75.9}{-7.3} - \frac{0.2}{-7.3} PY$$

The above two equations reduce to

$$r = 176.123 - 0.22923 \ Y$$

$$r = -16.7589 + 0.027397 \ PY$$

Since the above equations share a common left-hand side, they may be solved simultaneously by setting their right-hand sides equal to each other:

$$176.123 - 0.22923 \ Y = -16.7589 + 0.027397 \ PY$$

Solving the above equation for Y yields

$$Y_{CM} = \frac{192.8819}{0.22923 + 0.027397 P} \tag{12-20}$$

A Numerical Version of the Π Function

Now that the first nine equations of our model have been collapsed into one equation, we can concentrate on the remaining equations. We need to obtain a Π function—a set of profit-maximizing combinations of Y and P—consistent with the numerical values of the predetermined variables and parameters in Equations 12-14', 12-16', and 12-17'.

Substituting the prevailing money wage, given by Equation 12-17', into Equation 12-16' yields

$$5.1944 = P \ 43.7 \ N^{-1/2}$$

The above equation can be solved for $N^{1/2}$:

$$N^{1/2} = \frac{P}{0.118865} \tag{12-21}$$

The equation for the production function, Equation 12-14', can now also be solved for $N^{1/2}$:

$$Y = 87.4 \, N^{1/2}$$

$$N^{1/2} = \frac{Y}{87.4}$$

The above equation and Equation 12-21 share a common left-hand side, $N^{1/2}$, so we can set their right-hand sides equal to each other:

$$\frac{P}{0.118865} = \frac{Y}{87.4}$$

or

$$Y_{\Pi} = 735.690 \, P \qquad (12\text{-}22)$$

Given Equation 12-20, the CM function,

$$Y_{CM} = \frac{192.8819}{0.22923 + 0.027397 \, P}$$

and the Π function,

$$Y_{\Pi} = 735.690 \, P$$

the values of Y_{CM} and Y_{Π} corresponding to values of P between ± 10 are given in Table 12-1. Although the negative range of P is not economically

Table 12-1

P	Y_{Π}	Y_{CM}
10	7356.900	383.310
9	6621.210	405.381
8	5885.520	430.152
7	5149.830	458.142
6	4414.140	490.030
5	3678.450	526.690
4	2942.760	569.279
3	2207.070	619.360
2	1471.380	679.104
1	735.690	751.604
0	0.0	841.434
1	−735.690	955.651
2	−1471.380	1105.746
3	−2207.070	1311.774
4	−2942.760	1612.159
5	−3678.450	2090.974
6	−4414.140	2971.904
7	−5149.830	5150.245
8	−5885.520	19184.593
9	−6621.210	−11121.599
10	−7356.900	−4311.173

relevant, it helps explain some of the algebraic peculiarities of our numerical example.

The values of Y_Π and Y_{CM} corresponding to the given values assigned to P in Table 12-1 are plotted in Figure 12-8. Of course the Y_Π function becomes a horizontal line at the full-capacity level of output (i.e., at $Y = 786.6$).

One peculiar characteristic of Figure 12-8 is the strange behavior of the CM function between $P = -8$ and $P = -9$. This discontinuity in Equation 12-19 results from the denominator becoming zero for (roughly) $P = -8.3669$. This causes Y_{CM} to become an "infinitely large" positive number as P approaches -8.3669 from zero, and to become an "infinitely large" negative number as P approaches -8.3669 from the other direction.

The two functions cross each other twice—roughly at $P = 1$, $Y = 800$, and at $P = -9.5$, $Y = -6500$. The last combination can be dismissed as being economically irrelevant. That is, it is a solution to the model which has no meaning from an economic point of view. But, fortunately, the other solution is perfectly reasonable. Incidentally, "unrealistic" solutions pop up periodically in relatively complex economic models.

Although we can obtain rough approximations of the "acceptable" equilibrium levels of Y and P from Figure 12-8, we can be more precise by "blowing up" the (relevant) shaded portion in the figure (which is equivalent to the area presented in earlier figures). To do so we solve the CM and Π functions simultaneously.

Solution

Equations 12-20 and 12-22 share a common left-hand side (Y). Using this fact, we can solve them simultaneously by setting their right-hand sides equal to each other:

$$\frac{192.88}{0.23 + 0.027\,P} = 735.690\,P$$

Multiplying both sides of this equation by the denominator of the left-hand side yields

$$192.88 = 735.69\,P\,(0.23 + 0.027\,P)$$

or

$$192.88 = 168.64\,P + 20.16\,P^2$$

Isolating all terms on the left-hand side gives

$$20.16\,P^2 + 168.64\,P - 192.88 = 0$$

This is a quadratic equation, algebraically straightforward though numerically awkward.

For any quadratic equation, such as

$$ax^2 + bx + c = 0$$

Figure 12-8

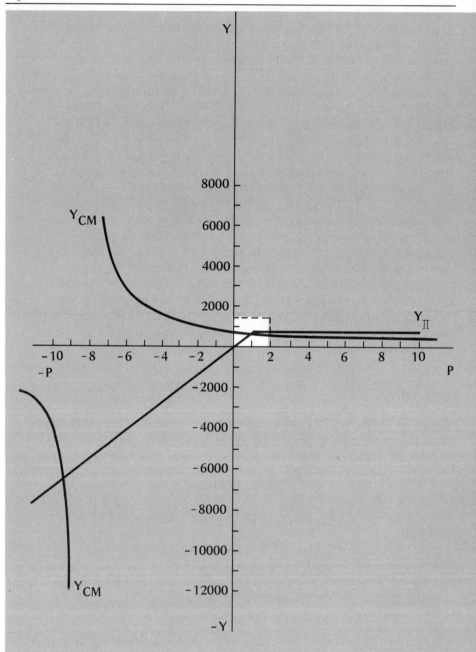

the (two) values of x which make the left-hand side zero (that is, the two "roots" of the equation) are given by

$$x = \frac{-b \pm \sqrt{b^2 - 4ac}}{2a}$$

In the above equation,

$$a = 20.16 \qquad b = 168.64 \qquad c = -192.88$$

Therefore, the equilibrium levels of P are given by

$$P = \frac{-168.64 \pm \sqrt{(168.64)^2 - 4(20.16)(-192.88)}}{2(20.16)}$$

Solving for P yields $P = 1.02$. The corresponding equilibrium levels of Y are 750 and -6902.149. These are the levels of P and Y at which the CM and Π functions cross each other in Figure 12-8.

Now that we know the equilibrium levels of price and real income, we can go back and solve for everything else. Given $Y^* = 750$, according to Equation 12-7', $T^* = 188.8$. Therefore, using Equation 12-6, $Y_d{}^* = 561.2$, and using Equation 12-5', $C^* = 525.08$. Since $L = M$, $\bar{M} = 198.24$, $P^* = 1.02$, and $Y^* = 750$, Equation 12-11' can be expressed as

$$198.24 = 75.9 - 7.3\,r + 0.2(1.02)(750)$$

Solving this equation for r yields an interest rate of $r^* = 4.2$ or 4.2% per year. Since $r^* = 4.2$, according to Equation 12-9', $I^* = 39.92$.

We can now check to see if Equation 12-10

$$Y = C + I + G$$

is satisfied; that is, if the equilibrium level of output is sufficient to support the prevailing amount of spending by households, businesses, and government. As a matter of fact, such is the case: $C^* = 525.08$, $I^* = 39.92$, and $\bar{G} = 185$. Thus, $C^* + I^* + G^* = 750$, which is Y^*.

Using Equation 12-14' and the fact that $Y^* = 750$, $N^* = 73.6164$. That is, although 81 million men want to work, only 73,616,400 men are demanded or employed by business. Therefore, the absolute level of unemployment, $LF - N$, is 7,383,600. The rate of unemployment, $(LF - N)/LF$ is about 9.1%.

All relevant variables can now be expressed in nominal or "money" terms by multiplying each "real" term by P^* or 1.02.

Extending the Example

The numerical example above emphasizes the Keynesian conclusion that the economy can be in equilibrium at less than full employment. Consistent with the equilibrium level of output in the example, $Y^* = 750$, is a relatively high rate of unemployment, 9.1%.

Although the algebra is somewhat cumbersome, the example can be expanded to show how appropriate changes in policy variables such as the money supply ($\overline{M}$), government spending ($\overline{G}$), and the tax function (t_1) can move the economy toward full employment. All of the necessary variables and constants for such an exercise are in the example. In addition, the magnitude of the multiplier effect of a change in a policy variable in this expanded model can be contrasted with the size of the multiplier effect in simple multiplier models.

It is important to remember that any policy decision that affects the CM function (everything else remaining constant) will affect the price level. Hence, policies designed to reduce the rate of unemployment by shifting CM upward will cause P^* to increase.

SUGGESTED READING

Consumption

James Tobin, "Consumption Function," in *International Encyclopedia of the Social Sciences* (Macmillan-Free Press, 1968), Vol. 3, 358–368. An excellent introduction to the "propensity to consume" and multiplier analysis. Pages 358–363 complement our Chapter 5, and pp. 363–368 complement our Chapter 6.

John Maynard Keynes, *The General Theory of Employment, Interest and Money* (Harcourt Brace Jovanovich, 1935). Keynes's pp. 61–65 and 74–85 on the relationship between saving and investment, and Chapters 8–10 on the consumption function, marginal propensity to consume, and the multiplier, are clear and particularly worthwhile.

Robert Ferber, *A Study of Aggregate Consumption Functions* (National Bureau of Economic Research, 1953). An excellent review of the literature on aggregate consumption functions, from the inception of the concept to the early 1950s. Studies surveyed by Ferber tended to verify Keynes's *absolute income hypothesis*.

———. "Research on Household Behavior," *American Economic Review*, Vol. 52 (March 1962), 19–63. In this article, Ferber reviews the most important empirical research from approximately the publication of Kuznets' data (1946) to the early 1960s. Although the emphasis is on empirical work, Ferber devotes space to important theoretical developments (for example, the *relative* and *permanent* income hypotheses) during the period. Although Ferber's stress is on consumer behavior at the microeconomic level, he does briefly analyze macroeconomic relations.

Simon Kuznets, *National Product Since 1869* (National Bureau of Economic Research, 1953); and "Proportion of Capital Formation to National Product," *American Economic Review*, Vol. 42 (May 1952), 507–526. Kuznets' estimates of savings in the United States from 1869 to 1929 contradicted the absolute income hypothesis and led to more comprehensive theories of consumer behavior.

Daniel B. Suits, "The Determinants of Consumer Expenditure: A Review of Present Knowledge," in *Impact of Monetary Policy* (Prentice-Hall, 1963), 1–57. Suits' study is an excellent review of the definition of consumption and the consumer unit, the history of the development of the concept, and the empirical literature on the subject.

Relative-Income Hypothesis

Dorothy S. Brady and Rose D. Friedman, "Savings and the Income Distribution," in *Studies in Income and Wealth*, Vol. 10 (National Bureau of Economic Research, 1947), 247–265. In this article, Brady and Friedman suggest that an individual's consumption is a function of the ratio of current income to average community income, thus introducing the *relative-income hypothesis*.

James Duesenberry, *Income, Saving and the Theory of Consumer Behavior* (Harvard University Press, 1949). See also James Duesenberry, "Income-Consumption Relations and Their Implications," in *Income, Employment and Public Policy* (1958), 54–81. Duesenberry's work is the major effort on the relative-income hypothesis and the previous-peak hypothesis. Duesenberry suggested that people strive for increasingly higher standards of living, and as these are achieved they are reluctant to return to lower standards when incomes fall. Accordingly, Duesenberry developed an aggregate consumption function that relates aggregate consumption to the ratio of current real income and an adjusted measure of the highest level of aggregate real income previously achieved.

Franco Modigliani, "Fluctuations in the Saving-Income Ratio: A Problem in Economic Forecasting," in *Studies in Income and Wealth* (National Bureau of Economic Research, 1949), 371–441. Modigliani suggested a consumption function similar to Duesenberry's, and he demonstrated that for aggregate data, the function produced a good statistical fit.

T. E. Davis, "The Consumption Function as a Tool for Prediction," *Review of Economics and Statistics*, Vol. 34 (August 1952), 270–277. A variation of the Duesenberry approach. Davis suggests that previous-peak consumption be substituted for previous-peak income in the Duesenberry consumption function. The reason for his suggestion is that individuals become adjusted to a certain level of consumption, not income, and that it is previous-peak *spending* that influences current consumption.

Permanent-Income Hypothesis

Milton Friedman, *A Theory of the Consumption Function* (National Bureau of Economic Research, 1957). In this book, Friedman sets forth a hypothesis on consumer behavior that has dominated research efforts since its publication. Labeled by Friedman the *permanent income hypothesis*, the central idea is that individuals base their consumption on their levels of average actual and expected real income over a number of periods rather than on the level of current real income.

Irwin Friend and Irving B. Kravis, "Consumption Patterns and Permanent Income," *American Economic Review*, Vol. 47 (May 1957), 536–555. In this article, Friend and Kravis attempt to refute Friedman's hypothesis.

Franco Modigliani and Richard E. Brumberg, "Utility Analysis and the Consumption Function: An Interpretation of Cross-Section Data," in *Post-Keynesian Economics*, ed. Kenneth K. Kurihara (Rutgers University Press, 1954), 383–436. In "The Life Cycle Hypothesis of Saving: Aggregate Implications and Tests" [*American Economic Review*, Vol. 53 (March 1963), 55–84] which investigates the validity of the Modigliani-Brumberg *life-cycle* hypothesis, Albert Ando and Modigliani summarize nicely this variation of the permanent income hypothesis: "The Modigliani-Brumberg model starts from the utility function of the individual consumer: his utility is assumed to be a function of his own aggregate consumption in current and future years. The individual is assumed to maximize his utility subject to the resources available to him, his resources being the sum of current and discounted future earnings over his lifetime and his current net worth. As a result of this maximization, the current consumption of the individual can be expressed as a function of his resources and the rate of return on capital with parameters depending on age. The individual consumption functions as obtained are aggregated to arrive at the aggregate consumption function for the community" (p. 56).

Michael J. Farrell, "The New Theories of the Consumption Function," *Economic Journal*, Vol. 69 (December 1959), 678–696. In a critical review of the "new" theories of the consumption function (notably, Friedman's and Modigliani-Brumberg's), Farrell broke the new theories down into three independent hypotheses: *the normal income hypothesis, the proportionality hypothesis, and the rate-of-growth hypothesis*. The normal income hypothesis states that "in any given period, an individual's current income . . . affects his current consumption . . . only through its effect on his normal income" (p. 79). Farrell found this hypothesis to be verified for U.S. farmers and businessmen, but he warned that it *might* not hold for other occupations in the United States or for those in other countries. The proportionality hypothesis states that "for any individual, the relationship between his consumption and his normal income is one of proportionality" (p. 80). This hypothesis, Farrell believed, is invalid. The rate-of-return hypothesis, which Farrell found to be substantially valid, is that the fraction of aggregate income saved is proportional to the rate of growth of aggregate real income.

Harold W. Guthrie, "An Empirical Evaluation of Theories of Saving," *Review of Economics and Statistics*, Vol. 45 (November 1963), 430–433. This is a modest empirical study that compares the hypotheses set forth by Keynes, Duesenberry, and Friedman and submits them to similar empirical tests using the same set of data.

Influence of Variables
Other than Income

James Tobin, "Relative Income, Absolute Incomes, and Saving," in *Money, Trade, and Economic Growth, Essays in Honor of John Henry Williams* (Macmillan, 1951), 135–156. Tobin suggests that the magnitude and composition of assets that households have accumulated may influence the level of real consumption.

Leslie G. Melville, "Consumption, Income, and Wealth," *Review of Economics and Statistics*, Vol. 36 (February 1954), 220–228. Melville concludes from his study that consumption depends mainly on the combined influence of income and accumulated wealth, and that the MPC is approximately equal to the APC, except when income is changing proportionately more rapidly than accumulated wealth.

Alan Spiro, "Wealth and the Consumption Function," *Journal of Political Economy*, Vol. 70 (August 1962), 339–354. Spiro's model of consumer behavior attempted to explain the observed relations among consumption, income, and wealth. Spiro's theory, in his words, "specifies that savings are the result of a discrepancy between the actual and the desired stock of wealth; when there is no discrepancy, savings equal zero. If income were to remain permanently constant, the desired stock of wealth would ultimately be accumulated and therefore consumption would equal net income. Positive savings would occur only if the secular trend of income is rising" (p. 339).

Harold Lubell, "Effects of Redistribution of Income on Consumers' Expenditures," *American Economic Review*, Vol. 37 (March 1947), 157–170; and his "Correction," *loc. cit.*, Vol. 37 (December 1947), 930. Lubell found that perfect equality in the distribution of income in 1941 would have produced a 5.82% increase in consumption. Using 1966 data, however, the authors of "Size and Composition of Consumer Savings" [*Federal Reserve Bulletin* (January 1967), 32–50] estimated that a 100% redistribution of income would cause only a 10% change in consumption, and that a 10% redistribution of income toward equality would increase consumption by less than 1%.

Keynesian Equilibrium
and Macroeconomic Policy

Alvin H. Hansen, "Note on Investment and Saving," in *Monetary Theory and Fiscal Policy* (McGraw-Hill, 1949), Appendix B. In this appendix, Hansen discusses fully the *ex post-ex ante* distinction, and the process of adjustment to equilibrium.

Thomas Dernburg, "Income and Employment Theory," in *International Encyclopedia of Social Sciences* (Macmillan-Free Press, 1968), Vol. 7, 122–131. Pages 122–126 offer an excellent discussion of Keynesian equilibrium, which is similar to our Chapter 5. The remainder of Dernburg's article extends the analysis in summary form.

Martin J. Bailey, *National Income and the Price Level*, 2nd ed. (McGraw-Hill, 1971). In Chapter 9 of his book, Bailey has a good discussion of the various multipliers.

Herbert Stein, "Fiscal Policy," in *International Encyclopedia of the Social Sciences* (Macmillan-Free Press, 1968), Vol. 5, 460–471. Stein presents an "overview" of fiscal policy, both pre and post-Keynesian.

Arthur Smithies, "Problem of Social Priorities," *American Economic Review*, Vol. 50 (May 1960), 301–309. In this article, Smithies discusses the balanced-budget controversy.

Investment

Barry N. Siegel, *Aggregate Economics and Public Policy*, 3rd ed. (Irwin, 1970), Chapters 8-9; and Edward Shapiro, *Macroeconomic Analysis*, 2nd ed. (Harcourt Brace Jovanovich, 1970), Chapters 11–13. Both of these textbooks have excellent discussions at the undergraduate level of investment demand analysis.

Robert Eisner, "The Aggregate Investment Function," in *International Encyclopedia of the Social Sciences*, (Macmillan-Free Press, 1968), Vol. 8, 185–194. A very good "introduction" to the topic, this article follows much of our presentation in Chapter 8.

William H. White, "Interest Inelasticity of Investment Demand—The Case from Business Attitude Surveys Reexamined," *American Economic Review*, Vol. 46 (September 1956), 565–587. In this paper, White examines the shortcomings of the various studies which have suggested that the investment-demand schedule is interest-inelastic.

In a later presentation, *Variability of Private Investment in Plant and Equipment*, Part II (Joint Economic Committee, 87th Congress, 2nd sess., Washington D.C., 1962), White set forth the factors which he believes corporations consider important in making investment decisions. This presentation is reprinted in Walter L. Johnson and David R. Kamerschen, eds., *Macroeconomics* (Houghton Mifflin, 1970), 95–115.

John W. Kendrick, "Some Theoretical Aspects of Capital Measurement," *American Economic Review: Papers and Proceedings*, Vol. 51 (May 1961), 102–111. This article has an interesting discussion of the conceptual problems involved in measuring the size of a nation's capital stock.

Robert Eisner, "Capacity, Investment, and Profits," *Quarterly Review of Economics and Business*, Vol. 4 (Autumn 1964), 7–12. Although the "acceleration principle" is not formally presented by us until Part III, Robert Eisner's nontechnical but nevertheless substantial paper presents a case for the acceleration principle as the major determinant of current business investment, a subject relevant to Chapter 8.

Money Supply and Demand

Lawrence S. Ritter, "The Role of Money in Keynesian Theory," *Banking and Monetary Studies*. ed. Dean Carson (Irwin 1963), 134–150. Ritter deals with the demand for money in general and the Keynesian innovation of the speculative demand. Ritter "brings money into" the simple Keynesian model (like ours in Chapter 7) much as we do beginning with Chapter 9.

Ronald L. Teigen, "The Demand and Supply of Money," *Readings in Money, National Income, and Stabilization Policy* (rev. ed.), ed. W. L. Smith and R. L. Teigen (Irwin, 1970), 74–112. For a clear and concise discussion of the demand for money, both classical and Keynesian views, see pp. 74–85 of this article.

Franco Modigliani, "Liquidity Preference," in *International Encyclopedia of the Social Sciences* (Macmillan-Free Press, 1968), Vol. 9, 394–408. Modigliani's treatment of the demand for money in Keynes' theory is particularly clear, and complements our Chapter 9.

James S. Duesenberry, "The Portfolio Approach to the Demand for Money and Other Assets," *Review of Economics and Statistics*, Vol. 45 (February 1963), 9–24. Duesenberry has an excellent section (pp. 16–23) on the motives that underlie consumer demand for money and other liquid assets.

Milton Friedman, ed., *Studies in the Quantity Theory of Money* (The University of Chicago Press, 1956). The first essay in this volume, Professor Friedman's "The Quantity Theory of Money—A Restatement," (pp. 3–21) is the major statement of Professor Friedman's model of the quantity theory of money as a demand function for money. This is an important part of the literature which has been neglected in our survey of macroeconomic analysis. A clear summary of this model is offered by

Joseph Aschheim and Ching-Yao Hsieh, *Macroeconomics: Income and Monetary Theory* (Merrill, 1969), 228–244.

Gardner Ackley, *Macroeconomic Theory* (Macmillan, 1961), 192–194, 384–385. This selection treats the so-called "liquidity trap," that is, a situation in which the demand for speculative balances may become very, very large. The reasons that the liquidity trap might exist are (1) if the interest rate is exceptionally low, the public will expect it *only* to rise, and (2) the low opportunity cost of liquidity.

E. Ray Canterbery, "A Note on Recent Money Supply Behavior," *Western Economic Journal*, Vol. 4 (Fall 1965), 91–98. Canterbery describes the behavior of the U.S. money supply during the early 1960s.

Thomas Mayer, *Monetary Policy in the United States* (Random House, 1968). Professor Mayer's relatively short book, written for undergraduate students, deals with (1) what monetary policy is and how it works, (2) advantages and disadvantages of monetary policy, and (3) the "best" monetary policy. See also Dwayne Wrightsman, *An Introduction to Monetary Theory and Policy* (The Free Press, 1971).

Lawrence S. Ritter and William L. Silber, *Money*, 1970. This book is a very readable account of the essentials of money and its relationship to the overall economy.

David L. Sills, ed., *International Encyclopedia of the Social Sciences* (Macmillan, 1968). The following entries would help acquaint the reader with those aspects of money which are normally not covered in books on macroeconomic *theory*, including this one: "International Monetary Economics," Vol. 8; "Monetary Policy," Vol. 10; and "Money: I. General and II. Quantity Theory," Vol. 10.

Ronald L. Teigen, "The Demand for and Supply of Money," in *Readings in Money, National Income and Stabilization Policy*, revised edition, ed. Warren L. Smith and Ronald L. Teigen (Irwin, 1970), 74–112. One of the most interesting topics in empirical macroeconomics has been the estimation of money demand functions such as that introduced in Chapter 9 and of money supply functions such as that introduced in Chapter 10. Professor Teigen reviews this empirical work as well as its theoretical underpinnings. His article reviews a body of literature which should not be ignored by the serious student of macroeconomic analysis.

One excellent contribution not referred to by Professor Teigen is Paul Zarembka, "Functional Form in the Demand for Money," *American Statistical Association Journal*, Vol. 63 (June 1968), 502–511.

A Static Keynesian
Model: Price Held Constant

John R. Hicks, "Mr. Keynes and the 'Classics,' A Suggested Interpretation," *Econometrica*, Vol. 5 (April 1937), 147–159. Our *CE–ME* model developed in Chapter 10 is based on this well-known article by Hicks. Hicks' *IS–LM* model was popularized by Alvin H. Hansen, *A Guide to Keynes* (McGraw-Hill, 1953), 126–153, and remains to this day the foundation on which all textbook Keynesian macroeconomic models have been constructed. An excellent textbook development of the *IS–LM* model (our *CE–ME* formulation) appears in Lester V. Chandler, *The Economics of Money and Banking*, 5th ed. (Harper & Row, 1969), Chapters 15 and 16. For an excellent mathematical treatment at an introductory level of *IS–LM* (our *CE–ME*), see K. C. Kogiku, *An Introduction to Macroeconomic Models* (McGraw-Hill, 1968), Chapter 4.

Dwayne Wrightsman, "IS, LM, and External Equilibrium: A Graphical Approach," *American Economic Review*, Vol. 60 (March 1970), 203–208. Wrightsman extends the *IS–LM* (our *CE–ME*) framework to include the foreign trade sector, thus superimposing an "external" equilibrium condition onto *IS–LM*.

A Complete Keynesian Model

Although the ingredients of our "complete" Keynesian model (*CM*–II) are well known, our development of the model is somewhat unique. A few easy-to-read, somewhat similar presentations, however, are Joseph P. McKenna, *Aggregate Economic Analysis*, rev. ed. (Holt, Rinehart and Winston, 1965), Chapter 13; George Heitman and Warren Robinson, "A Suggested Reformulation of the Basic Keynesian Model," *Quarterly Review of Economics and Business*, Vol. 9 (Autumn 1969), 51–55; Robert S. Holbrook, "The Interest Rate, The Price Level, and Aggregate Output," *Readings in Money, National Income, and Stabilization Policy* (rev. ed.), ed. W. L. Smith and R. L. Teigen (Irwin, 1970), 43–65; and R. J. Ball and R. G. Bodkin, "Income, the Price Level, and Generalized Multipliers in Keynesian Economics," *Metroeconomica*, Vol. 15 (1963), 59–81.

John M. Culbertson, *Macroeconomic Theory and Stabilization Policy* (McGraw-Hill, 1968), Chapter 20. In this chapter, Culbertson sets forth the meaning of fiscal policy and how to measure the effects of policy action, discusses alternative fiscal policies, and traces the record of U.S. fiscal policy.

Council of Economic Advisers, "The Effect of Tax Reduction on Output and Employment," *Annual Report of the Council of Economic Advisers* (1963), 45–51. Reprinted in *Readings in Money, National Income, and Stabilization Policy* (rev. ed.), ed. W. L. Smith and R. L. Teigen (Irwin, 1970), 339–345. The effect of tax reduction on output and employment is clearly set forth by the Council of Economic Advisers.

Lester V. Chandler, "Monetary Policy," in *International Encyclopedia of the Social Sciences* (Macmillan-Free Press, 1968), Vol. 10, 419–426. This brief article deals with the elements of monetary policy, the evolution and conflicts of objectives, and the effectiveness of monetary policy as a regulator of aggregate demand.

Milton Friedman, "The Role of Monetary Policy," *American Economic Review*, Vol. 58 (March 1968), 1–17; and "Some Issues of Monetary Policy," *The Annual Report of the Council of Economic Advisers* (January 1969), 85–93. Reprinted in *Readings in Money, National Income, and Stabilization Policy* (rev. ed.), ed. W. L. Smith and R. L. Teigen (Irwin, 1970), 495–502. Friedman suggests that the best guide to monetary policy is the supply of money, and that it should be increased at a steady rate. In the article by the Council, Friedman's suggestion is discussed.

Howard S. Ellis, "Limitations of Monetary Policy," in *United States Monetary Policy* (rev. ed.), ed. Neil H. Jacoby (Praeger, 1964), 195–214. Ellis presents the more traditional view of monetary policy.

James Tobin, "Money Wage Rates and Employment," in *The New Economics; Keynes' Influence on Theory and Public Policy*, ed. Seymour E. Harris. (Knopf, 1947), 572–587. Tobin discusses the effect of a general change in money wage rates on aggregate output and employment. This article relates well to our discussion of the same topic in Chapter 12.

G. B. Kaufman, "Current Issues in Monetary Economics and Policy," *The Bulletin* (New York University Graduate School of Business Administration, Institute of Finance), No. 57, May 1969. This is an useful current survey of the issues in monetary economics and policy, with an excellent bibliography.

Arthur M. Okun, *The Political Economy of Prosperity* (W. W. Norton, 1970). This short monograph, written by one of the Chairmen of the Council of Economic Advisers during the Johnson Administration, is devoted to a discussion of the acceptance of "Keynesian" economics and economists during the Kennedy-Johnson years. (See also E. Ray Canterbery, *Economics on a New Frontier*, Wadsworth, 1969).

The appendix to Okun's book, "Potential GNP: Its Measurement and Significance," is reprinted, with slight changes, from American Statistical Association, *Proceedings of the Business and Economic Statistics Section* (1962). The main point made in his paper is quite often referred to in discussions of macroeconomic policy.

RENEWAL OF NEOCLASSICAL
MACROECONOMICS: THE WEALTH EFFECTS

The following readings are devoted to the emergence of macroeconomic theories in which adjustments caused by changes in the general price level as well as in the rate of interest play a prominent role. Although these adjustment processes have many names, they are generally referred to as "wealth effects." These wealth effects are an important part of present-day "neoclassical" economists' arguments against Keynesian macroeconomics. To the extent that there has been an anti-Keynesian line of development since 1936, most of the literature devoted to these wealth effects is its written record.

Actually, there are two wealth effects—an interest-induced effect and a price-induced effect. Both were discussed and then ignored by Keynes, as well as by most of the economics profession. Both types of effect represent an attempt to make the neoclassical assumptions and results, presented in Part I, immune from Keynes' attack. Materials related to this attempt to shore up pre-Keynesian analysis are briefly surveyed following this discussion.

Price-Induced Wealth Effect

Assume, just for the sake of argument (not as implied recognition of the correctness of Keynes' work), that an economy is at a less-than-full-employment equilibrium during quarter 1. Secondly, assume that the real value of total private wealth is known, and that there is a certain fraction of this aggregate real wealth which households, producers of goods and services, and financial institutions in the economy want to hold in the form of real money balances. Third, assume that one consequence of the surplus capacity existing in quarter 1 is that businesses cut prices. At the set of prices which prevailed in quarter 1, business was unable to sell all the goods and services it could have produced; thus, price reductions occurred during quarter 2 as managers attempted to increase sales.

Note that this theory of price determination is not consistent with that presented in Part II, in which P was determined by the interaction between the CM and Π functions. If a less-than-full-employment equilibrium existed in that context, there was no *a priori* reason why, in the next period, prices *have to fall*. Nevertheless, following the post-Keynesian neoclassical reasoning: if there is surplus capacity, prices fall. Assuming that (1) the level of real money balances during quarter 1 was satisfactory, and (2) that the monetary authorities do not alter the nominal money supply during quarters 1 and 2, the decline in prices during quarter 2 causes the private sector to have excess real cash balances.

Individuals can attempt to get rid of these excess real balances in two ways: they may spend them on goods and services, or they may use them to buy securities. In the first case, direct action takes place to eliminate the existing excess capacity: money comes out of wallets, mattresses, and checking accounts and is directly spent on goods and services. In the second case, the fresh money coming into the markets for equities and bonds has the effect of increasing bond and equity prices (reducing yields) and hence reducing "the" rate of interest (whichever rate or average of rates has been selected as being representative). The lower rate of interest stimulates investment. The act of getting rid of the excess real balances increases one or a combination of two major components of aggregate demand, consumption and investment. Thus, in this way, the price-induced wealth effect may eliminate, or at least may begin the elimination of, the surplus capacity.

There is one major qualification which should be attached to this analysis. A portion of a nation's real money balances consists of demand deposits which are matched by loans to consumers as well as to businessmen. The principal and interest on these loans is expressed in current, nondeflated dollars. As the general price level declines, owners of the demand deposits are better off than before in real terms—but debtors are worse off. This symmetry of gains and losses may cause the debtors to react in such a way as to negate the effect of actions of the owners of demand deposits.

We are then left with the price-induced wealth effect being relevant only to coins, currency, and bank reserves. This portion of the money supply can be thought of as "public debt"—the IOUs of the central government (bank). But officials of the central government probably will not view this portion of the money supply as debt in the same way a private citizen would view his IOUs held by a neighborhood commercial bank. Furthermore, it is quite doubtful that the central government will be conscious of increases in the real value of this portion of its "debt." We can be especially certain of this in these days of fiat money—money the government does *not* have to convert into a metal, such as gold, at some fixed price if the holder wants to make such a conversion. Hence, the central bank probably has a "money illusion"—it is not concerned with changes in the real value of coins, currency, and bank reserves.

Only to the extent that *spending stimulation* resulting from the increase in the real value of coins, currency, and bank reserves is not offset by spending *retardation* resulting from the "loss" borne by the public as a whole, represented by the monetary authorities, will the price-induced wealth effect be a positive macroeconomic force.

Interest-Induced Wealth Effect

The interest-induced version of the wealth effect would complement the results of the price-induced wealth effect. Assume that a large fraction of private wealth is held in the form of fixed-interest-bearing negotiable IOUs. As discussed in Chapter 8, the "yield" on these securities is determined by their current market price, the income streams attached to them, and the time which must elapse before the maturity value will be paid.

The advocates of the interest-induced version of the wealth effect argue that a period of surplus capacity will probably also be a period of declining rates of interest. For many reasons, a recession or depression in aggregate economic activity will be accompanied by lower rates of return on physical assets as well as on money loans. For example, when discussing the price-induced wealth effect, we argued that when an economy is at a less-than-full-employment equilibrium, the general price level will fall. As individuals try to get rid of their now-excess money balances, some fresh money may find its way into bond and equity markets, causing yields, and hence the rate of interest, to fall.

The interest-induced wealth effect is based on taking this excess-capacity/declining-interest-rates argument one step further. The lower rate of interest would increase the market value of the IOUs, and the owners of wealth would be richer. An individual owner of securities may or may not actually realize his gain by selling securities, but he *is* richer. To the extent that this situation acts to stimulate spending by security owners, aggregate demand will be greater than it was before. Thus the interest-induced wealth effect may (help to) solve the initial problem of excess productive capacity. As in the case of the price-induced wealth effect, the economy is automatically headed for a full-employment equilibrium. In fact, aggregate equilibrium and full-employment equilibrium are again synonymous. Of course, the actual surge of aggregate demand brought about by either of the two wealth effects in a "real-life" economy is another question. What is logically correct in theory may be quantitatively insignificant in reality.

One of the main issues surrounding the two wealth effects has been to explain the theoretical framework required for them to be likely events if surplus capacity exists. Of course, neither effect can be rigorously developed as a "natural" or "intuitive" phenomenon within the context of the model developed in Part II, although Keynes was aware of both effects. A more complex abstraction of a macroeconomy is required.

After the wealth effects were accepted by many economists as a logically sound refutation of Keynes' argument that an economy might settle down to a less-than-full-employment equilibrium, Professor Lloyd A. Metzler of the University of Chicago noted a small problem.[1] One of Keynes' Cambridge colleagues, A. C. Pigou (a major advocate of using wealth effects as theoretical notions to take the sting out of *The General Theory*) had suggested that if the economy were at full employment, monetary policy would be totally helpless to alter anything expressed in real terms (that is, base-period dollars). The only effect of a 6% increase in the money supply would be a 6% increase in prices and things expressed in money terms (that is, current-period dollars).

According to Metzler, once the wealth effects were introduced—to rehabilitate neoclassical doctrine and immunize it against Keynesianism— they had the unattractive side effect of falsifying the traditional neoclassical doctrine concerning the effect of certain types of changes in the money supply during periods of *full employment*. According to Metzler, if wealth

1. Lloyd A. Metzler, "Wealth, Savings, and the Rate of Interest," *Journal of Political Economy*, Vol. 54 (April 1951), 93–116.

is introduced in the consumption function and if a portion of a nation's wealth is being held in interest-bearing debt, an increase in the money supply *through central bank open market operations* would lower the rate of interest—although an increase in the money supply in a manner *that does not affect the stock of government IOUs* will have no effect on the rate of interest. Hence, contrary to neoclassical thinking, an expansive monetary policy can achieve a redistribution of full-employment output away from consumption to investment.

"Wealth effects" are among the more interesting developments made in static macroeconomics since World War II. Their logic cannot really be disputed, once a compatible framework within which to present them has been agreed upon. They may be statistically trivial as a force for creating a capacity-reaching surge of aggregate demand, or for altering the allocation of full-capacity output between consumption (present enjoyment) and investment (future enjoyment), but they make sense in theory.

There has been a great deal of debate about the empirical significance of the two effects. First, it is not clear what forms of wealth should be included in the consumption function. Second, it is not clear how strong or quick the wealth effects really are. The first-round effects might be so small that by the time the wealth effect really started working, the economy would be wrapped up in an entirely different set of problems. Third, it is not clear to what extent various price changes, including changes in the different rates of interest, affect the real values of the various relevant forms of holding wealth.

William J. Baumol, *Economic Dynamics*, 3rd ed. (Macmillan, 1970). In Chapter 6, "Price Flexibility and the Equilibrium of the Economy," Professor Baumol discusses, in a very simple, straightforward way, the impact of a "fall in the price of a commodity in excess supply (for example, a fall in the wages of labor when there is unemployment)" when all other prices fall in the same proportion.

Gary S. Becker and William J. Baumol, "The Classical Monetary Theory: The Outcome of the Discussion," *Economics*, N.S., Vol. 19 (November 1952), 355–376. As noted at the beginning of this chapter, Keynes' *The General Theory* prompted a great deal of discusssion about the neoclassical dichotomy of value and monetary theories. Many economists believed that the predecessors of Keynes had invalidly "dichotomized" their theoretical macroeconomics. Professors Becker and Baumol have carefully reviewed the actual pre-Keynesian texts and find the charge to be unfair.

Robert W. Clower, ed., *Monetary Theory: Selected Readings* (Penguin Books, 1969). For the reader who would like to explore the recent developments in monetary theory in greater detail, this is an excellent set of advanced readings.

Gottfried Haberler, *Prosperity and Depression*, 3rd ed. (Harvard University Press, 1958; first edition, 1937). The price-induced wealth effect was first clearly stated by Professor Haberler (Chapter 8, Section 5, 233–247; and Chapter 13, Section 5, 491–503).

Harry G. Johnson, "The Keynesian Revolution and the Monetarist Counter-Revolution," *American Economic Review Papers and Proceedings*, Vol. 61 (May 1971), 1–14.

For another contribution along these lines, see Milton Friedman's *The Counter-Revolution in Monetary Theory* (Institute of Economic Affairs, 1970).

Robert Lekachman, ed., *Keynes' General Theory: Reports of Three Decades* (St. Martin's Press, 1964). Many of the selections in this book of essays are followed by retrospective views of the "Keynesian Revolution" by individuals who were intimately involved with it. One of the more interesting of these is a short essay by Paul A. Samuelson, "A Brief Survey of Post-Keynesian Developments" (pp. 331–347).

Lloyd A. Metzler, "Wealth, Saving, and the Rate of Interest," *Journal of Political Economy*, Vol. 54 (April 1951), 93–116. In this article Professor Metzler presented the original version of the wealth-effects model discussed above. The process of adjustment to equilibrium is examined in detail in the text of the article. The actual mechanics of the model are presented in an appendix.

Don Patinkin, *Money Interest and Prices*, 2nd ed. (Harper & Row, 1965). Professor Patinkin's book, along with Oscar Lange's *Price Flexibility and Employment* (Principia Press, 1944), are probably the most important contributions in the attempt to unite monetary theory and value theory. A more compact presentation of the core of Professor Patinkin's argument is his article, "Price Flexibility and Full Employment," originally published in the *American Economic Review* in 1948, and reprinted with corrections and modifications in *Readings in Monetary Theory*, ed. F. A. Lutz and L. W. Mints (Irwin, 1951), 252–283. The work of Patinkin and Lange has generated an enormous body of literature. One of the more important pieces is G. C. Archibald and R. G. Lipsey, "Monetary and Value Theory: A Critique of Lange and Patinkin," *Review of Economic Studies*, Vol. 26 (1958–1959), 1–22.

Textbook treatments of Patinkin's model are offered by Joseph Aschheim and Ching-Yao Hsieh, *Macroeconomics: Income and Monetary Theory* (Merrill, 1969), 96–100 and 209–210. See also David E. W. Laidler, *The Demand for Money: Theories and Evidence* (Intext, 1969), 3–35.

Boris P. Pesek and Thomas R. Saving, *Money, Wealth and Economic Theory* (Macmillan, 1967). Part I, "The Origins of the Wealth Effect" (pp. 1–

38), is devoted to introductions of both the price-induced and the interest-induced wealth effects. Professors Pesek and Saving emphasize the *paradoxical* nature of post-Keynesian macrostatics: *Both* versions of the wealth effect are in Keynes' *The General Theory*, yet the more zealous Keynesians viewed the wealth effect literature as a polemical *attack* on *The General Theory* itself. Furthermore, the wealth effects *themselves* strongly undermined the "money-is-only-a-veil" neoclassical argument discussed in Part I of our book.

For related surveys, see Don Patinkin, "Money and Wealth: A Review Article," *Journal of Economic Literature*, Vol. 7 (December 1969), 1140–1160; and Warren L. Smith, "On Some Current Issues in Monetary Economics: An Interpretation," *Journal of Economic Literature*, Vol. 8 (September 1970), 767–782.

A. C. Pigou, "The Classical Stationary State," *Economic Journal*, Vol. 53 (December 1943), 343–351. Professor Pigou, who was Professor of Political Economy at Cambridge during Keynes' lifetime, was named in *The General Theory* as arch villain. He was the flesh-and-blood straw man against whom Keynes leveled his attack. In his 1943 paper, Pigou counterattacked, using the wealth effect as a logical refutation of the "involuntary unemployment" argument of Keynes and his followers, especially the man who did more than anyone else to bring *The General Theory* to the United States, Alvin Hansen of Harvard University. By the time of Pigou's counterattack Keynes was busy with war matters, so Professor Hansen, whose own interpretation of Keynesianism was perhaps more Hansen than Keynes, was for some time the leading "Keynesian" economist, at least in the United States.

THE PLANNING APPROACH TO MACROECONOMIC UNDERSTANDING

PART III

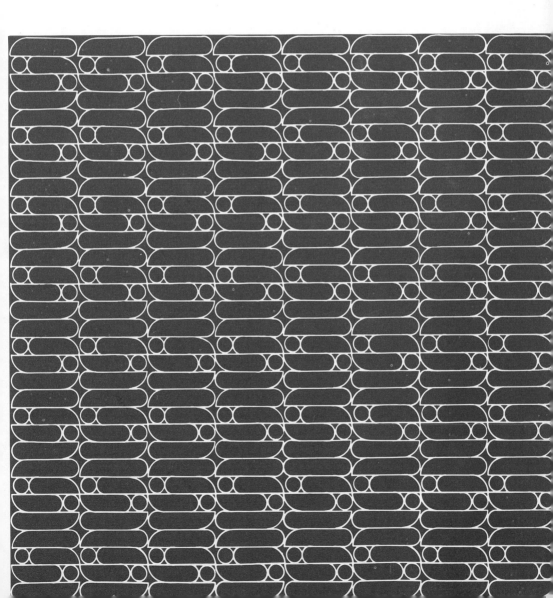

Only a few years ago it was possible to divide macroeconomics into two periods, before and after Keynes' *The General Theory*. Now it is becoming apparent that we are entering a third period, which, for want of a better term, we call the "planning period." This period is characterized by increasing involvement of the central government in economic decision making on the macro and microeconomic levels. Paul Samuelson, the Nobel prize economist, has said that the person who figures out a solution to the dilemma of simultaneous unemployment and inflation will deserve a Nobel prize. We would not risk predicting when this dilemma will be solved, but we do claim that the solution will entail a revolution in economic science. When it occurs, the theories and developments that are described in Part III, and which are now loose threads, will be neatly tied together.

We begin here with a review of where neoclassical and Keynesian macroeconomics has taken us in understanding national economic problems, and what these theories fail to provide. The connection between economic theory and political philosophy is made explicit. We then introduce the "loose threads" with which this part of the book is concerned, explaining the relationship between the economic problems raised and the potential contribution of government planning to the solution of these problems. For some of the problems the role of government is clearly pronounced; for others it is less so. We do not lay claim to certainty in this area, for we are dealing with the frontiers of theory and policy.

NEOCLASSICAL AND KEYNESIAN MACROECONOMICS AND PUBLIC POLICY

Neoclassical and Keynesian macroeconomic analyses are fundamentally alternative theories of the inner workings of an economy, and lead to different policy recommendations. For the neoclassical economists, inflation is the result of mismanagement of the supply of money. An excess supply of money leads directly to inflation. Unemployment is temporary, and a condition of disequilibrium. Public policies designed to stimulate aggregate demand are unnecessary and undesirable. They are unnecessary because proper manipulation of the money supply will bring about an equilibrium economy in which unemployment is minimized. They are undesirable because such policies result in increased intervention of the federal government in the workings of the economy. Economists persuaded of the theoretical superiority of the neoclassical model tend to believe in the desirability and workability of free markets. And they tend to downplay the role of fiscal policy as a proper tool of macroeconomic balance. Because neoclassically oriented economists look to the money market for explanations of the behavior of prices, they are colloquially called "monetarists."

Neoclassical economic theory and political philosophy are in harmony. The political philosophy maintains that government should not be involved in essentially private decisions, for to do so robs people of "economic freedom." The economic theory attempts to show that government involvement would not have a beneficial impact anyway. The permanent income hypothesis, which claims that consumption is a function of long-term expectations of income rather than disposable income in a given period, leads to the policy conclusion that a tax cut (or increase) will be ineffective in stimulating (or dampening) consumer spending. If consumers' spending habits are linked to their long-run expectations of income, a one-shot tax cut or tax increase will have little impact on their buying.

The Keynesian model shows that unemployment could persist forever in equilibrium. Fiscal policies, however, can nudge equilibrium toward full employment. By careful use of government spending and taxation, an equilibrium level of national income can be maintained which guarantees full employment of the labor force. Although Keynesians do not reject the use of monetary policy, their focus is on fiscal policies; hence they are known as "fiscalists."

It should be apparent by now that the theoretical differences between the neoclassical and Keynesian economists revolve around alternative assumptions regarding the structural relationships in the economy. The reason why this theoretical debate has not been "settled" by empirical analysis has to do with the difficulty of isolating unambiguous measurements of the variables.

During the 1960s, under Democratic administrations, decision makers were attuned to the advice of the fiscalists (even though monetary decisions are made by the independent Federal Reserve Bank). The economy responded to the 1964 tax cut with falling unemployment and increased growth rate, with the result that the stature of the fiscalists rose and their policy influence increased. Nevertheless, inflationary pressures also increased during the late 1960s. By the time the Republicans won the White House in 1968, severe strains in the economy were evident. After President Nixon took office, the rate of inflation *and* unemployment started turning upward. The problems of the economy seemed unyielding to the monetary and fiscal remedies that were applied. For the first half of the first Nixon administration, monetarists were given the opportunity to verify neo-classical theory. There is great controversy over whether or not it was a fair test (monetarists claim that their policies were not pursued long enough to show their effectiveness), but the course of the economy during the time that economic policy did follow the recommendations of monetarists is not in doubt. Inflation and unemployment continued to rise.

In a sense, we have reached the limits of *both* neoclassical and Keynesian analysis. Both modes of reasoning assume that *either* inflation *or* unemployment can be a problem at any given time, but not simultaneously. For the monetarist, the rate of inflation is quite independent of the rate of unemployment; for the fiscalist, there is a trade-off between the two. The trade-off is expressed in a theoretical construct called the "Phillips curve." While the neoclassical and Keynesian models have permitted us to formulate policies which keep unemployment and inflation within a range that seems narrow by comparison with the pre-World War II period, they have not eliminated these twin problems of modern economies. New theoretical work that goes beyond the earlier models has been done in the last several years which attempts to explain the relationship between unemployment and inflation. This work is the subject of Chapter 13.

UNEMPLOYMENT, INFLATION, AND GOVERNMENT PLANNING

In an effort to directly control inflation and stimulate employment, Western governments have turned to manpower planning and wage and price controls (known as "incomes policies"). In August, 1971, in a complete break with the ideological orientation of the Republican party, the Nixon administration inaugurated a policy to control key price and wage decisions, in an effort to reduce inflation and unemployment. A decade earlier, national labor-market policies had been initiated to reduce unemployment. Both wage-and-price and labor-market policies represent new directions for U.S. economic policy, although antecedents for these policies can be found in U.S. economic history. Nevertheless, they represent a substantial increase in the involvement of the central government in economic decisions that were previously considered to be private affairs.

Manpower planning in the United States has had essentially micro-economic functions. For example, the federal government has become involved in efforts to lower discriminatory barriers against minorities and women. During the 1960s, several programs were developed to remedy these and other labor-market problems. Such planning for the reduction of unemployment could be the basis of a national labor-market policy as an adjunct to monetary and fiscal policies. The analysis of unemployment and inflation in Chapter 13 is extended in Chapter 14 to show how manpower planning could reduce unemployment.

Incomes policies are much more familiar in Western European economies than they are in the United States. Such policies involve government economic intervention at the microeconomic level. For example, although collective bargaining has been the concern of national policy for some time, government intervention has been restricted to only the most vital industries, such as railroads and marine shipping. Under incomes policies, in contrast, the government is involved in any collective bargaining decisions that could have an impact on the rate of inflation. In Chapter 15 we review the theory of incomes policies and provide a description of their use both here and abroad.

FOREIGN ECONOMIC RELATIONS AND GOVERNMENT PLANNING

The relationship between the U.S. economy and the economies of the rest of the world has been virtually ignored in our development of the neoclassical and Keynesian models, primarily for the sake of clarity in exposition. However, the relationship is an important one, particularly as the U.S. government attempts to reconcile domestic policy objectives with balance-of-payments equilibrium. In Chapter 16 we introduce foreign economic relations into the macroeconomic model developed in Part II, and discuss the monetary aspects of world trade.

As it has been for most of the post-World War II period, the world's monetary arrangements are in flux. In order to facilitate trade after the war, the world's trading nations agreed upon a system of fixed rates of exchange among their currencies. In so doing they rejected the notion that a free market ought to determine these rates of exchange. They also took on the burden of insuring the stability of exchange rates. The world has witnessed increasing trade since 1945, but it has also undergone several monetary crises. As we enter the mid-1970s, the world monetary system is highly unsettled. In our discussion of this system, what emerges is the increasing role of governments in achieving equilibrium relationships among the economies of the world.

ECONOMIC GROWTH, ENVIRONMENTAL QUALITY, AND GOVERNMENT PLANNING

The macroeconomic problem of growth has been of central concern not only to advanced industrial economies but to underdeveloped economies for the past twenty-five years. During the 1950s and early 1960s, U.S. economic growth policy was often discussed in terms of competition with the

Soviet Union. Not only was growth deemed desirable for the increases in per capita income which resulted from it, it was considered vital in showing the rest of the world the superiority of American-style capitalism over Soviet-style communism. Recently, however, some environmentalists and economists have questioned the value of rapid growth in terms of the quality of life. We introduce our two chapters on economic growth with a discussion of the growth versus no-growth issue. In the United States, government agencies such as the Environmental Protection Agency have been established to consider the impact on the environment of such economic behavior as locating industrial plants. We are witnessing the emergence of government as a key decision maker in those areas which affect not only growth itself but the composition of growth as well.

The models of the economy developed in Parts I and II are static models—they are capable of determining equilibrium at a point in time, but not the rate of growth of GNP. In Chapters 17 and 18 we present dynamic models of the economy which are both Keynesian and neoclassical in nature—although these growth models are too rarified to yield clear policy prescriptions. Much of the work discussed is not yet sufficiently developed to permit policy inferences.

A TOOL FOR NATIONAL ECONOMIC PLANNING

Part III concludes with an introductory treatment of input-output analysis, one of the most widely used tools of economic planning. Input-output analysis permits us to uncover the structure of the economy by examining the interrelationships among the various sectors that contribute to GNP. The basic element of input-output analysis is the input-output table, which shows how the *output from* each industry is distributed among all the major industries and sectors of the economy. The table also shows the *inputs to* each industry from the other major industries and sectors.

Although input-output analysis is not extensively used in the United States, its use is growing, especially at the regional level. Full application of this tool would permit national economic planning to proceed on a more rational basis by making it possible, for example, to calculate the impact of a change in defense expenditures on employment and output.

It is appropriate to conclude Part III with a discussion of input-output, because it is of great potential value in coordinating decisions that are now being made centrally, and that appear to be increasingly made by government.

Unemployment
and
Inflation

Since the neoclassical and neoKeynesian models presented in Parts I and II both provide an analysis of unemployment and inflation, why do we devote a separate chapter in Part III to these macroeconomic phenomena? The answer is that theories to explain these related problems have been elaborated beyond the neoclassical and neoKeynesian frameworks. This chapter is devoted to explaining these theories, and to discussing the economic and political implications of policies designed to control inflation and unemployment. The two problems are interdependent, and an examination of one of them necessarily involves an examination of the other. The policy implication drawn from modern economic theory is that the choice of a particular rate of inflation is simultaneously a choice for a particular rate of unemployment. For this reason we have chosen to deal explicitly with inflation and unemployment together.

DEFINITION AND MEASUREMENT OF UNEMPLOYMENT

The U.S. Department of Labor's Bureau of Labor Statistics (BLS) computes employment and unemployment on the basis of a monthly survey of representative households, to discover

- who in the household was working during the week prior to the survey
- who among the employed in the household worked more and less than thirty-five hours during the week
- who in the household did not work and why
- who was looking for work and by what method
- the number of weeks those looking for work were engaged in the search for a job.

All persons 16 years old and over who were working or were temporarily absent during the survey week are counted as employed, regardless of the number of hours typically worked. All persons 16 years old and over who were not working, and were not ill, on vacation, involved in a labor dispute, or absent because of bad weather, and who *were actively looking for work* are counted as unemployed. The total of unemployed and employed by the above criteria are defined as the *labor force*.[1] The *unemployment rate* is the ratio of the unemployed to the total labor force.

Several problems immediately present themselves in interpreting the unemployment rate. Those who have become discouraged at the prospect of finding a job and have given up the search, believing perhaps that there are no openings for their skills, are not defined as unemployed. For the same reason, they are not part of the labor force. During periods of recession, when long-term unemployment rises, discouraged workers leave the labor force. Secondary workers, primarily women in households where there is a male wage earner, are particularly responsive to changes in employment opportunities. Studies of the labor force participation behavior of women have uncovered the fact that secondary workers enter the labor force during periods of expanding employment opportunities and leave it during contractionary periods.[2] Teen-agers and minority workers from ghetto areas also move in and out of the labor force during periods of job expansion and contraction. The consequence of these variations in labor-force participation is to understate the true extent of unemployment.

The unemployment rate fails to distinguish between those who work full time and those who work part time. If some of those who work part time would prefer to work full time but are unable to find full-time employment, it would be correct to say that they are partly unemployed, yet nowhere in the unemployment rate is this reflected. (Of course, there may also be some workers who would prefer part-time jobs but are obliged to work full time because employers have not structured their work to fit part-time labor. This is particularly true in the professions, although it is true for other kinds of work as well.) The BLS does collect data on part-time workers and indicates the reasons for their status. In 1971, for example, almost 2.7 million workers who worked part time, on average only 20 hours each week, would have preferred full-time employment.

A single unemployment rate does not reflect the composition of unemployment. For example, a 5% unemployment rate could represent, at one extreme, a situation in which 95% of the labor force was fully employed all the time and the remaining 5% of the labor force was perpetually unemployed. At the other extreme, a 5% unemployment rate could represent a situation in which 100% of the labor force is employed 95% of the time. In the first case, the burden of unemployment is visted exclusively on

1. See the U.S. Bureau of Labor Statistics, *Handbook of Labor Statistics* (U.S. Government Printing Office, 1971), 1–3.
2. See G. G. Cain, *Married Women in the Labor Force* (University of Chicago Press, 1966); and W. G. Bowen and T. A. Finegan, *The Economics of Labor Force Participation* (Princeton University Press, 1969).

5% of the labor force; in the second case the burden is shared by the entire labor force. While these figures were purposely chosen to illustrate extremes, they do make the point that unemployment is a problem partly because of the way it is distributed among various groups in the population. Teenagers, minorities, and women typically have higher unemployment rates than the national average. College-educated white males, in contrast, have had much lower than average unemployment rates during the post-World War II period. For example, in 1971, the aggregate unemployment rate was 5.9%—but the rate for females was 6.9%, for nonwhite workers 9.9%, and for nonwhite teenagers, 16 to 19 years of age, 31.7%.

ECONOMIC THEORIES TO EXPLAIN UNEMPLOYMENT

Neoclassical View

As was developed in Part I, the "neoclassical" view of how an economy works precludes equilibria at levels of employment other than those at which aggregate labor supply and demand are equal. In the neoclassical perfectly competitive framework, *involuntary* unemployment is logically impossible. Individuals can be unemployed, but only because they do not want to work, or because of *temporary* aberrations from the neoclassical theoretical frame of reference called perfect competition. Perfect competition is the fundamental neoclassical way of viewing an economy: In the long run, time will heal any blemishes. In the long run, full employment will prevail.

Unemployment is the result of temporary cyclical imbalances in the economy caused by shocks which could have their origin in several sources. Mismanagement of the money supply could result in cyclical imbalance. Balance-of-payments disequilibrium could cause a temporary decline in foreign and domestic demand for domestic goods. Technological changes could result in the decline of some industries, requiring the retraining of labor for different jobs in other industries.

Regardless of the cause, the neoclassical economist views unemployment as a temporary phenomenon. Given sufficient time, the economy will return to a full-employment position. There will be a certain amount of unemployment as the inevitable consequence of a dynamic economy. Individuals change jobs, geographical shifts in the location of industry occur, and there are people unemployed periodically because of the seasonal nature of their work (crop laborers, for example). But as long as the number of vacant jobs equals the number of those looking for employment, the economy is said to be at "full employment." During periods of cyclical unemployment, when the number of vacant jobs is less than the number of job seekers, the economy is considered to be in a state of temporary disequilibrium. Left to itself, however, natural forces will correct this imbalance and return the economy to its normal full-employment state.

The only unemployment during equilibrium periods that is consistent with neoclassical theory is "frictional" unemployment—that unemployment which is due to "frictions" in the labor market rather than to fluctuations in the level of economic activity. For example, a worker who has left one job to search for another is said to be "frictionally" unemployed during the period of job search. The departure can be the result of the worker's option (he is looking for a better job) or the firm's option (it is reducing its work force or looking for a better worker). The unemployment that results from this period of separation from work is the price paid for finding a more perfect match between employee and employer. Even during periods of very low unemployment, the rate has never dropped below 1%.

For neoclassical economists, therefore, the problem of unemployment is of marginal concern. Either it is cyclical and by definition temporary, or it is frictional, and a normal consequence of a dynamic economy.

NeoKeynesian View

The Keynesian challenge to the neoclassical view of unemployment was presented in *The General Theory* in 1936. Keynes showed how an economy could be simultaneously in equilibrium and have unemployed resources. This concept explained the world-wide depression that had lasted for all of the 1930s, and demonstrated that the economy was not self-correcting, as the neoclassical economists believed, but required increased purchasing to boost the demand for output, which in turn would lead to increased employment. Since the household and business sectors have no incentive to increase spending during a depression, it falls to the government to supply the necessary purchasing power. This can be accomplished directly by government spending, or indirectly by lowering taxes to encourage private spending.

The Keynesian prescription was difficult to accept for those who, for so long, had been taught that unbalanced central government budgets were unsustainable and reckless, and who held beliefs about the limited role of government which were incompatible with the requirements of substantial government intervention in the workings of the economy. After World War II, it was ridiculed in the popular press in the United States and rejected by policy makers as well as by many economists raised on classical doctrine.

Keynesian economics came late to the most prosperous of the Western economies. While European countries were enjoying unemployment rates of 2–3% during most of the postwar period, partly as a result of the application of Keynesian techniques, the unemployment rate in the United States rose to a peak of 6.7% in 1961 (it was 9.2% for blue collar workers in the same year). It was not until President John F. Kennedy's commencement address at Yale University in 1962 that the United States government *explicitly* adopted the principle of a planned budget deficit to stimulate employment and income. The reasons for this lag in the application of economic knowledge are undoubtedly complex. Perhaps the best explanation comes from Keynes, in his conclusion to *The General Theory:*

> I am sure that the power of vested interests is vastly exaggerated compared with the gradual encroachment of ideas. Not, indeed, immediately, but after a certain interval; for in the field of economic and political philosophy there are not many who are influenced by new theories after they are twenty-five or thirty years of age, so that the ideas which civil servants and politicians and even agitators apply to current events are not likely to be the newest. But, soon or late, it is ideas, not vested interests, which are dangerous for good or evil.

By the beginning of the decade of the 1960s, a full generation of professional economists had been schooled on Keynes and his American disciple, Alvin Hansen, and men turning thirty had had the new theory explained to them by Paul Samuelson, whose first edition of *Economics* appeared in 1948. Having spoken largely to one another during the Eisenhower era, Keynesian economists became President John F. Kennedy's chief economic advisors.

The first explicit application of Keynesian economics to the United States economy was the tax cut of 1964, promoted as a sure-fire method of stimulating the economy and reducing unemployment to under 4%.[3] Kennedy's support of the tax cut provided the new generation of Keynesians with an opportunity to put their theories into practice. With victory possible but not guaranteed in 1962–1963 (Congress still regarded deliberately unbalanced budgets as a sign of an unbalanced mind), the Keynesians were not prepared to concede that factors other than insufficient demand played any significant part in high unemployment rates.

Structuralist View

Keynesian economists expected the preKeynesians and those whose ideas were molded by them to be hostile to the use of planned budget deficits as a remedy for stimulating unemployment. However, opposition emerged from an unexpected quarter, when Charles Killingsworth and others claimed that aggregate demand analysis did not go far enough in explaining the continued existence of unemployment. They argued that the tax cut

---

3. For an analysis of the tax cut, see A. M. Okun, "Measuring the Impact of the 1964 Tax Reduction," in *Perspectives on Economic Growth* (Vintage Books, 1968), ed. Walter W. Heller.

would be inflationary and fail to reduce unemployment to acceptable levels. One claim made, which seemed powerful at the time but which has less force today, was that an affluent society had satiated itself with most major consumer demands. With the discovery of poverty in the 1960s, however, it became apparent that not everyone was buying their second electric toothbrush.

The second major claim of the structuralists was that labor could not be easily and quickly retrained to work in the growing service sector. In Congressional testimony, Killingsworth argued:

> We cannot safely accept the convenient assumption of economic theory that all labor is homogeneous, and the conclusions that only inertia or ignorance can impede the free flow of laborers from one industry to another as the patterns of consumer spending change. The displaced assembly-line worker may be readily adaptable to work in a filling station; he may be much less acceptable as a clerk in a department store; and without years of training, he cannot qualify as a teacher or a nurse.[4]

Killingsworth blamed the rise of unemployment on ever-increasing automation. According to this view, automation had reduced the demand for workers with little training and increased the demand for highly skilled and adaptable workers. Thus automation was viewed as being substantially different from technological change, which, the fiscalists pointed out, had always accompanied a dynamic economy. According to Killingsworth, the economy had undergone significant changes during the 1950s as a result of automation, and such changes could be expected at an even more accelerated pace in the future. The spectre of factories completely run by machines and needing little or no human labor was effectively and chillingly presented.

His arguments were based on figures comparing unemployment rates between 1950 and 1962 for workers of varying education. These figures showed an increase in the unemployment rate for all groups except those with more than a high school education. For those who completed college, the unemployment rate was 2.2% in 1950 and 1.4% in 1962, a 36.4% decrease. Killingsworth concluded that these figures confirmed his thesis that the demand for highly skilled workers was increasing very rapidly and that it would require equally rapid changes in the labor market to keep up. If workers could not upgrade their skills quickly enough, which he claimed was the case, unemployment would result even in the face of high aggregate demand.

Finally, he claimed that the labor-force participation rate was directly

4. Charles Killingsworth's testimony before the Subcommittee on Employment and Manpower of the U.S. Senate appears in *The Manpower Revolution* (Doubleday, 1965), ed. Garth Mangum.

related to the unemployment rate for any given subset of the labor force. As a result, the unemployment rates understated the true impact of unemployment, since those who might be seeking work when there was work to be had for their skill levels would give up the search when unemployment was high. Killingsworth concluded that "the labor-force participation-rate figures strongly suggest a large and growing 'reserve army'—which is not counted among the unemployed—at the lower educational levels, and that there is no evidence of any such reserve of college-trained men . . . long before we would get down to an overall unemployment rate as low as 4%, we would have a severe shortage of workers at the top of the educational ladder. This shortage would be a bottleneck to further expansion of employment." His analysis led him to advocate a massive investment in manpower retraining, as a permanent part of macroeconomic stabilization policy. In Chapter 14, the role of manpower planning is explored.

While some aspects of the structuralist view seem naive today, especially the concern with satiation and the fear of "workerless" factories, their concern with the retraining of the unskilled signaled a recognition of this useful approach to dealing with unemployment. There is, in fact, no inherent incompatability between the neoKeynesian and the structuralist views. Retraining would not be effective in the face of insufficient aggregate demand; raising aggregate demand would lead to inflation rather than increased employment *only if* the unemployed did not have the skills to fill the new job openings. It is now apparent that the two approaches are complementary. Thus, it may be difficult to understand the vehemence of the theoretical debate between the structuralists and Keynesians that dominated economic literature during the early 1960s.

An insight into the relationship between economics and politics provides the answer. The aggregate demand economists had not yet completely converted the policy makers to an understanding of Keynesian policies, and they were not prepared to admit that the stabilization tools they were fighting for were not going to do the job claimed for them. In addition, there was a fear that to emphasize the lack of skills of some workers (rather than the inadequacies of economic management) would lend credence to the Southern segregationists' contention that employment discrimination was the natural product of fundamental inequality rather than merely racial antipathy—all this during the period of intense struggle for civil rights.

Although the theoretical battle was heated, it was short-lived. As early as June 1963, Walter Heller, then Chairman of the Council of Economic Advisors, foresaw the need for a combined approach to solving unemployment problems:

> As unemployment melts away before expanding aggregate demand, we can expect problems of structural imbalances in particular labor markets to obstruct further expansion. If we are to succeed in re-

ducing unemployment below our interim goal of 4%, greater emphasis must be placed on structural policies designed to remove the obstacles of inadequate training and lack of mobility.[5]

DEFINITION AND MEASUREMENT OF INFLATION

Although intuitive definitions of economic phenomena are usually unreliable, the commonsense understanding of inflation is an exception—inflation is a rise in overall prices. "Overall prices" are measured by an index of prices of representative commodities. There are three major U.S. price indexes: the consumer price index (CPI), the wholesale price index (WPI), and the GNP deflator (also discussed and defined in Chapter 2).

The CPI measures the prices of goods and services bought by families of city wage earners and clerical workers. Price quotations for the index are obtained from a representative sample of stores where families of wage and salary workers make their purchases. In every period, prices of a typical bundle of goods and services are compared with the prices of the same goods and services in an arbitrarily chosen base period. The WPI shows the average prices of goods sold in the primary markets of the United States. A primary market is one in which the first important sale of a good takes place. Quotations used for calculating the WPI are the selling prices of representative producers. The GNP deflator is an index of the prices of *all* goods and services, including capital goods, entering into the GNP. It is prepared by the Department of Commerce as a byproduct of its estimate of GNP in current and constant dollars. Division of the current-dollar estimates by the constant-dollar estimates yields an implicit index of the overall rate of price change.[6]

All three of the price indexes have shown comparable increases since 1964, but this was not always true. We can see from the data in Table 13-1 that, for the period 1958–1964, for example, there was no inflation measured by the WPI, "creeping" or very mild inflation measured by the CPI, and slightly stronger inflation measured by the GNP deflator.

The GNP deflator has perhaps the broadest coverage and hence is closest to the general price level of final goods and services produced in the United States. Although most economists favor it as the best indicator of inflation, the GNP deflator is available only on a quarterly basis and only after a time lag. As a result, for purposes of policy making, observers of monthly prices rely on the CPI and the WPI.

Table 13-1 shows that since the end of World War II there have been

5. W. W. Heller, "The Administration's Fiscal Policy," in *Unemployment and the American Economy* (Wiley, 1964), 104.
6. An excellent discussion of the design and construction of price indexes appears in W. H. Wallace, *Measuring Price Changes: A Study of Price Indexes* (Federal Reserve Bank of Richmond, December 1970).

Table 13-1   Inflation, 1945–1972, as measured by the Consumer Price Index (CPI), the Wholesale Price Index (WPI), and the GNP Deflator

Year	CPI(1967 = 100)	WPI(1967 = 100)	GNP Deflator (1958 = 100)
1945	53.9	54.6	59.7
1946	58.5	62.3	66.7
1947	66.9	76.5	74.6
1948	72.1	82.8	79.6
1949	71.4	78.7	79.1
1950	72.1	81.8	80.2
1951	77.8	91.1	85.6
1952	79.5	88.6	87.5
1953	80.1	87.4	88.3
1954	80.5	87.6	89.6
1955	80.2	87.8	90.9
1956	81.4	90.7	94.0
1957	84.3	93.3	97.5
1958	86.6	94.6	100.0
1959	87.3	94.8	101.6
1960	88.7	94.9	103.3
1961	89.6	94.5	104.6
1962	90.6	94.8	105.8
1963	91.7	94.5	107.2
1964	92.9	94.7	108.9
1965	94.5	96.6	110.9
1966	97.1	99.8	113.9
1967	100.0	100.0	117.6
1968	104.1	102.5	122.3
1969	109.8	106.5	128.2
1970	116.3	110.4	135.2
1971	121.3	113.9	141.6
1972	125.3	119.1	145.9

Source: Economic Report of the President, *Council of Economic Advisors, January 1973.*

several waves of inflation, regardless of the index used to measure it. Price controls were lifted after the war, and the price level (whether measured by the CPI, WPI, or GNP deflator) increased approximately 34% from 1945 to 1948. Inflationary forces subsided during the recessionary period of 1948–1949, but were renewed at the outbreak of the Korean War. From mid-1950 to mid-1951, all three indexes rose substantially. From 1955 to 1958, a more moderate rise in the price level occurred.

From 1958–1964, as noted earlier, there was no inflation according to the WPI and only "creeping" inflation according to the other two indexes. The wave of inflation that began in 1965 with the escalation of the war in

Vietnam has continued to the present, although with the imposition of wage and price controls during the summer of 1971 the increase in the annual rate of inflation was halted at approximately 6%.

There are numerous sources of bias in all three major price indexes. A particularly important upward bias is that the indexes do not completely account for changes over time in the character of goods and services. For example, more and more foods are packaged ready to serve, so that food preparation time is reduced, thereby freeing leisure or work time for some or all members of the family. Another problem arises in introducing entirely new commodities into the index. An index compares this year's prices for certain goods with a base year's prices for the same goods. Periodically it is necessary to introduce new goods into the price index by constructing a new base period. This makes it difficult to compare prices *after* the base change with prices *before* the change.[7]

The CPI measures the wrong things, in part, if it is intended as a measure of inflation. For example, interest payments on mortgages are included, but interest is a factor payment rather than the price of a final consumption good. If the government raises interest rates to combat inflation, the change shows up as an increase in the CPI and therefore an *increase* in inflation.

The problems of comparability are less significant from year to year because it can be assumed that tastes do not substantially change on a yearly basis, and therefore the weights assigned various commodities in the price index will remain relatively constant. In the longer run, this assumption is questionable. The significance of our measures of inflation is that unions, firms, and government all make crucial decisions on the basis of published reports about price-level changes. If there is an upward bias which results in a 2% annual unwarranted increase in the measured price level, then misleading signals are being passed to key decision makers. One possible result is that anti-inflation policies may be set in motion unnecessarily, since 2% of the "observed" inflation is not really inflation at all but a result of inability to correct the price index.

CREEPING INFLATION AND HYPERINFLATION

It is sometimes useful to distinguish between an inflation rate which varies between, say, 3% and 8%, and one which regularly exceeds 20%. The former is called "creeping" inflation and calls for a set of policy responses different from the more dramatic inflation that occurred in Germany after World War I, which is called "hyperinflation." During the autumn of 1923,

7. A theoretical discussion of price-index construction and of overcoming the problems of changing tastes, quality, and technology can be found in F. M. Fisher and Karl Shell, *The Economic Theory of Price Indexes* (Academic Press, 1972); and see also Zvi Griliches, *Price Indexes and Quality Change* (Harvard University Press, 1971).

German prices doubled daily. Thrift institutions were destroyed, because there was no incentive to save. People eating in restaurants insisted on paying in advance, because the price of the meal rose while they were eating it. Creditors were paid in currency worth far less than when they had lent it out. Those on fixed incomes found themselves with almost valueless holdings. While it is not inevitable that hyperinflation will lead to the kind of social and political collapse that occurred in Germany, it is nevertheless an economic problem of the first magnitude.

It is frequently claimed that creeping inflation inevitably leads to galloping inflation, and therefore even mild inflation must be treated as a major economic problem. Historically this is not true, as an examination of the inflation rates for the United States and several other countries bears out.

ECONOMIC THEORIES TO EXPLAIN INFLATION

Neoclassical and Keynesian Theories

It is difficult to discuss inflation—*rising* prices— in the context of the single-period, static "neoclassical" and "Keynesian" models developed in Parts I and II. In each model, the prevailing general price *level* for a particular period is determined. We can, nevertheless, discuss what *would have* caused a difference in this level, or what might cause a difference in the price level of the next period if only one feature of the economy changed, all else being equal. In this fashion, price "changes" can be discussed.

In the neoclassical model, a dichotomy exists between the determination of "real" and "nominal" variables. Real variables are determined "first," by real forces, and then their monetary equivalents are determined by the interaction of the supply of and demand for money. The major determinant of the demand for money is the volume of economic activity it must support. Public and private monetary authorities determine the quantity of money to be supplied. In this context, inflation is basically a *monetary* phenomenon. The prevailing general price level this period or next period will be greater if more money is injected into the system.

As in the neoclassical model, the prevailing general price *level* for a particular *period* can be determined in the Keynesian model developed in Part II. But in this model, the general price level and the real level of output are determined *simultaneously*. There is no real–nominal dichotomy. Money is not brought into the picture after the real variables—the "important" ones—have already been determined. Monetary factors, taken together with the aggregate supply and demand for final goods and services, determine everything, including price. Inflation or price changes cannot be thought of as solely a monetary phenomenon or solely a production phenomenon or, in short, as the result of any single aspect of the economy.

"Keynesians" often *stress* rising prices as the result of increases in one or more of the four major components of aggregate *demand:* consumption; investment; government spending; or net exports. This stress is the result of the *empirical content* of the various extant versions of the model. Given the general (i.e., non-numerical) version of the model, there is no more an *a priori* reason to stress changes in aggregate demand than there is one to stress shifts in the production function as *the* cause of price changes. Nevertheless, it has become conventional to associate the neoKeynesian model with "demand-caused" or "demand-pull" inflation. That is, individuals whose main frame of reference is the Keynesian scheme of things view aggregate demand as the major *empirical* cause of price changes, perhaps because they view the major components of aggregate demand as volatile, and directly and sensitively linked to prices. As we see below, however, other economists have found it convenient to emphasize the supply side in their explanations of inflation.

Supply Theories

Supply theories of inflation claim that prices can rise because firms raise prices *even though there are no demand pressures.* Firms will raise prices either because labor costs have risen in excess of productivity increases, so that unit labor costs rise (the cost of labor that enters into a unit of output has gone up), or because they wish to increase profits. Firms can so operate because the markets in which they exist are highly imperfect. The two variants of the cost-push theory of inflation are administered prices and wage push.

Wage-push inflation results from the ability of organized labor to seek and obtain wage increases for its membership in excess of productivity gains. This can occur when the union is strong and when the industry with which it bargains has more to lose from a strike than it does from a settlement which results in temporarily reduced profits. If the industry anticipates that it can then raise its prices, it can pass the wage increase on to its customers, and its rate of profit will be unaffected in the long run. The kinds of industries in which this process can take place are the highly oligopolistic ones in which uniform prices predominate. Most primary and secondary output is produced in such industries, where price leadership is characteristic and competition is limited to nonprice factors.

Wage-push inflation can also result from union contracts which call for wage increases in the second and third year of the contract, regardless of the economic situation. As a result, wage increases may accrue to workers in an industry a few years after the contract was negotiated, during a period of recession. Note that rising wages in excess of productivity are not necessarily a sign of wage-push inflation. They could be the result of excess demand for labor, the result of high aggregate demand.

The second variant of cost-push inflation theory, *administered prices*, has enjoyed much less support among economists than the wage-push thesis, although it is a favorite explanation among union leaders. Administered prices occur in oligopolies and monopolies—they are prices which are partly controlled by the seller, in contrast to competitive markets where prices are "given" to individual firms and not subject to their control. "Profit push" results when firms in industries with administered prices raise their prices in excess of increases in costs in an effort to increase profits.

This explanation is questioned because firms are presumed to have already set their prices at the profit maximizing level (where marginal revenues equal marginal costs). Thus, there should be no reason to raise prices still higher if they were set correctly originally. This argument overlooks the fact that the firm may be raising its prices in anticipation of a rise in the cost of labor and is setting its price such that marginal revenue will equal marginal cost *after* a contract renewal is effected.[8]

Demand-pull and cost-push can exist simultaneously. Inflation may be initially caused by excess demand. The result is rising wages and prices. As employment increases and unemployment shrinks, cost-push elements from the wage and profit sides may enter the economy, resulting in additional upward impetus to prices and wages. Even after excess demand has been eliminated (by a tax increase, say) the cost-push elements may still make themselves felt. A two or three year labor contract may require increased wage payments even after the demand pressures have been reduced.

INFLATION AND UNEMPLOYMENT THEORY INTEGRATED: THE PHILLIPS CURVE

The theories of unemployment and inflation described have assumed that the economy either experiences inflation without unemployment or experiences unemployment without inflation. The structuralist view is an exception in that it offers an explanation of unemployment which is compatible with any rate of inflation. For the other theories described, output is perfectly elastic with respect to prices at less than full employment. In 1958, a British economist, A. W. Phillips, brought to light an empirical relationship between unemployment and the rate of change of money wage rates that has triggered a major effort to understand the relationship between inflation and unemployment. Phillips used data for the United Kingdom between 1861 and 1913 to generate a curve relating the rate of change of money wage rates to unemployment. The data for the period between the

8. The administered price thesis dates back to 1935, when Gardiner C. Means advanced it in a document for the U.S. Senate, *Industrial Prices and Their Relative Inflexibility*. The controversy over whether or not this thesis is substantiated is still alive, as can be found in Means' critique of recent studies of industrial price behavior, "The Administered-Price Thesis Reconfirmed," *American Economic Review*, Vol. 26 (1972), pp. 292–306.

two world wars and the post-World War II period fits the curve with re-markable accuracy.[9]

In Figure 13-1 the U.S. data on the percentage increase in average hourly earnings and the unemployment rates which corresponded to earn-ings increases for the years 1952 to 1971 have been plotted. A curve which roughly fits these points has been drawn in. This "Phillips"-type curve de-picts the case in which a 6.0% increase in wages coincides with approxi-mately a 3.3% rate of unemployment; a 3% increase in wages coincides with approximately a 5.9% rate of unemployment.

Although the Phillips curve in Figure 13-1 relates wages to unemploy-ment, we also call the relationship between inflation and unemployment a Phillips curve. The reason is that the rate of change in average wages, the rate of change in the general price level, and the unemployment rate are all tied together. From an inverse relationship between unemployment and the rate of change in money wages it is possible to generate an inverse rela-tionship between unemployment and inflation. It is necessary to make the assumption, an assumption borne out by historical experience, that wage and price changes move in the same direction. The reason that prices and wages move together is that unions and firms respond to each other's vic-tories. A union will press for wage increases if the firm has raised prices, claiming that to forego a wage increase would be to allow the gains from productivity to accrue only to the firm and owners of capital. A firm will raise prices if it has granted a wage increase in excess of productivity in-creases in order to retain its rate of profit. Thus we have a relationship among productivity gains, wage increases, and price increases:

Rate of Wage Increase = Rate of Productivity Gain + Rate of Price Increase

These three variables are related in Figure 13-2.

Notice that the right-hand wage change axis is scaled three percentage points higher than the left-hand price change axis (a 3% increase in wages corresponds to a 0% inflation rate, a 4% increase in wages corresponds to a 1% inflation rate, etc.). The rationale for this difference is an assump-tion that labor's productivity is rising at 3% per year, and an additional assumption that the relative shares of income accruing to capital and labor are constant. Both of these assumptions are based on empirical observa-tion.

Relative shares are constant if labor wages increase by their rate of pro-ductivity, because profits increase by the same rate as wages when prices are constant. A simple numerical example illustrates this point. In the first period, a worker produces 100 units of output which sell for $2.00 each, and he receives a wage of $100. The firm is left with $100. In the second period, as a result of new capital equipment and retraining, labor's pro-ductivity increases by 3%. Union leaders demand and obtain a 3% wage

9. A. W. Phillips, "The Relation Between Unemployment and the Rate of Change of Money Wage Rates in the United Kingdom, 1861–1957," *Economica*, Vol. 25 (1958), 293–299.

Figure 13-1   Unemployment and the rate of change in money-wage rates in the U.S., 1952–1972

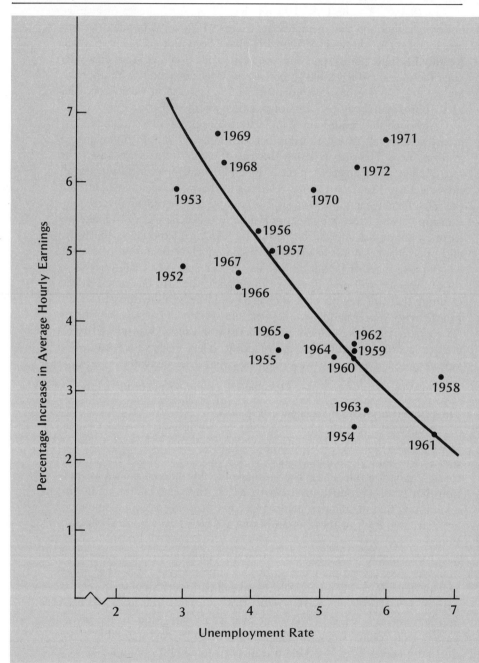

Figure 13-2   A Phillips-type curve relating inflation, unemployment, and
the rate of wage change

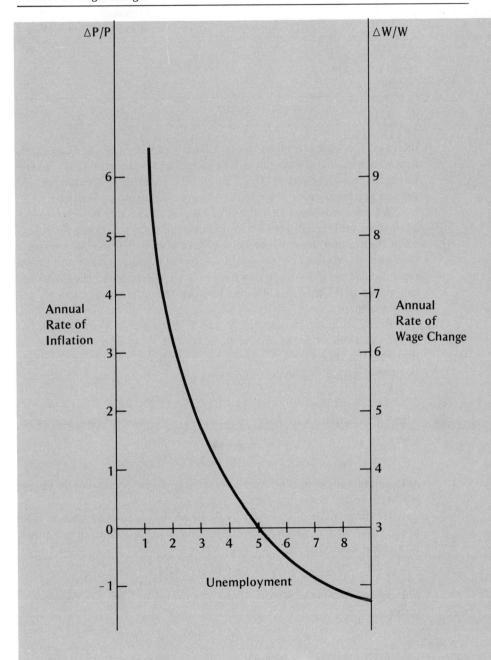

Table 13-2   The Distribution of Productivity Gains

	Wages	Physical Output	Price	Gross Revenue	Gross Revenue − Wages
Period 1	$100	100	$2	$200	$100
Period 2	$103	103	$2	$206	$103
Increase	3%	3%	0%	3%	3%

increase. The worker now produces 103 units of output. At $2.00 each, the firm now earns $206, pays out $103 in wages and is left with $103—income to capital has increased by 3%. Table 13-2 summarizes these changes. (A general algebraic proof is offered in Chapter 15, Incomes Policies.)

We have now seen that the Phillips plot of the rate of wage change against unemployment implies an inverse relationship between the rate of price change and unemployment. We have also seen that if wages rise in tandem with productivity, the relative shares of income to labor and capital need not change if prices do not rise. Now we will consider the theoretical rationale for Phillips' relationship between the rate of wage change and unemployment.

Recall from microeconomic theory that the firm's demand for labor, in the short run when the capital stock is fixed, is based on its production function, the price at which it can sell its output, and the money wage rate. Beginning with a production function,

$$Y = F(N, \bar{K})$$

where Y is output, N is labor input, and $\bar{K}$ is the fixed capital stock input, then

$$dY/dN = MPP_N$$

or the marginal physical product of labor is equal to the ratio of the change in output to the change in labor input.

The firm will hire labor up to the point where the last unit of labor brings to the firm as much extra revenue as the extra cost the firm incurs in hiring that unit; that is,

$$MR = MC$$

or marginal revenue is equal to marginal cost. Since, under perfect competition,

$$MR = P \quad \text{and} \quad MC = W/MPP_N$$

where P is price and W is the money wage rate, then

$$P = W/MPP_N$$

Thus, the firm's demand curve for labor is based on the price of its output, the cost of its labor input, and the production function which determines the marginal physical product of labor. We cannot simply sum up individual firms' demand for labor to arrive at aggregate demand for labor, because of the impact on price of wage changes in the labor market and output changes in the product market. We can, nevertheless, represent an aggregate-demand-for-labor curve as in Figure 13-3. At a given price level, the higher is the money wage, the lower is the demand for labor.

A supply curve for labor is drawn on the assumption that, at a given price level, more labor services will be offered the higher is the money wage. At W_e we have equilibrium in the labor market. But if the money wage were at W_0 we would clearly have excess demand for labor equal to $N_2 - N_1$. Wages will increase to eliminate this disequilibrium. Assume that the rate of increase in wages, $\Delta W/W$, depends on the amount of excess demand:

$$\Delta W/W = F(N_d - N_s)$$

or the rate of change in money wage rates is a function of the demand and supply functions for labor.

Statistically it is difficult to measure the labor demand and supply functions. However, the unemployment rate can serve as a proxy for excess supply of labor; the higher is the unemployment rate, the greater is the excess supply of labor. Since excess supply is the negative of excess demand

$$N_s - N_d = -(N_d - N_s)$$

we can rewrite the rate of wage change equation as

$$\Delta W/W = -F(U)$$

where U is the unemployment rate. The higher is the unemployment rate, the lower is the rate of change in money wage rates, and vice-versa, which is exactly what the Phillips curve shows.

EMPIRICAL ESTIMATES OF THE PHILLIPS CURVE FOR THE UNITED STATES

During the past several years, economists have attempted to estimate Phillips-type curves for several countries. Efforts have been made to find other variables which affect the rate of wage increases, and two have proved highly significant: the rate of price change and the rate of profitability. The net profit rate, R, has been defined as the ratio of net corporate profits to total corporate equity value.[10] It is this measure which unions look at in determining how far they can push for wage increases. The

10. G. L. Perry, *Unemployment, Money Wage Rates, and Inflation* (MIT Press, 1966).

Figure 13-3

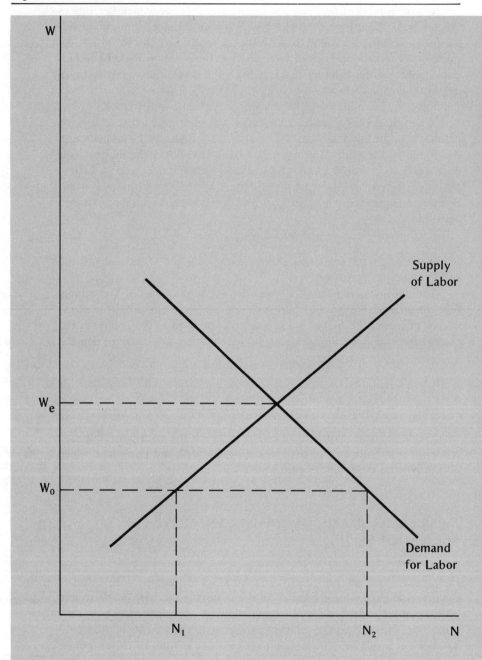

higher is R, the more room there is for negotiated wage increases. The lower is R, the more the corporation can claim inability to pay wage increases. The results of analysis confirm the expectation that R is positively related to $\Delta W/W$. In Figure 13-4 we have drawn three alternative Phillips curves, each based on a different R. The higher is R, the further out from the origin is the Phillips curve. At higher Rs, the trade-off between unemployment and inflation is more severe.

The Phillips relationship has two qualities which are particularly attractive to economists. The relationship was demonstrated to be extremely stable over time for U.K. data, and it permitted the integration of demand-pull and cost-push theories of inflation. The existence of a permanent Phillips curve is not accepted by all economists, however. Milton Friedman and others[11] have argued that in the long run there is no trade-off between inflation and unemployment. Friedman contends that there is a "natural" rate of unemployment in every economy which is dictated by structural relationships in that economy: minimum wage laws, skill levels of the labor force relative to existing technology, unionization, oligopolization, etc. It is only possible to reduce unemployment below the "natural" rate ("institutional minimum" would be a more descriptive term) temporarily, and then only at a cost of rising wages (as employers bid up the wages of scarce labor) and rising prices. The rising prices touch off new wage demands.

Friedman's critique of the Phillips curve claims that the relationship is based on a special case where the price level is constant. When the price level is constant, an increase in the money wage rate (used in the Phillips curve) is also an increase in the real wage rate. In Figure 13-5, a move to the left of point a represents an increase in the real wage; any point to the right of a represents a decrease in real wages—if the price level is constant. But if inflation takes place, a rise in the money wage is not necessarily a rise in the real wage. What happens during inflation?

For unemployment to be reduced, firms must be persuaded to hire more labor (assuming no change in the labor force, of course). But the only reason for firms to increase their labor employment is if the *real wage falls*, since the marginal physical product of labor will necessarily decline. This decline results from diminishing returns to labor, and because firms must turn to marginal, less productive workers if they are to expand employment. From our review of the theory of the demand for labor,

$$W = MPP_N \cdot P \qquad W/P = MPP_N$$

or the real wage must equal the marginal physical product of labor.

Since MPP_N falls as employment expands, and since the money wage W must rise if employment is to expand, firms must raise prices at a faster rate than wages are rising if the real wage is to fall. In the short run this

11. See Milton Friedman, "The Role of Monetary Policy," *American Economic Review*, Vol. 58 (1968), pp. 1–17.

Figure 13-4 Phillips curves under alternate assumptions about the ratio of net corporate profits to total corporate equity values

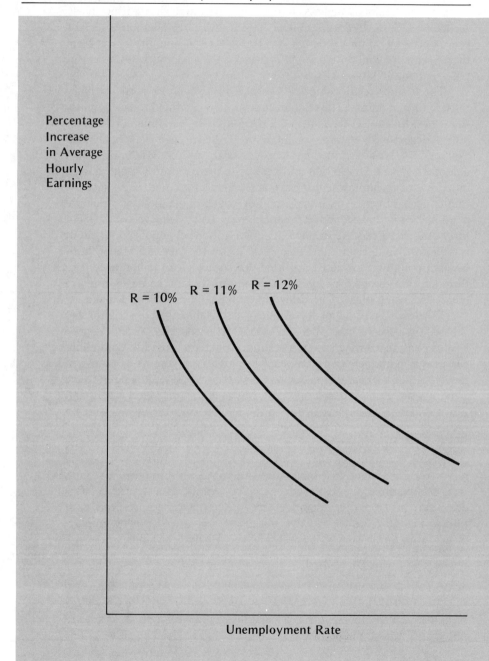

may be possible, and we may move to a lower level of unemployment with a higher rate of inflation. But, Friedman argues, soon workers will catch on to the fact that their real wages have fallen. Labor will bargain for a higher rate of wage increase than previously—higher by the amount of the price inflation they have come to expect. But then their real wage will have risen, and it will be inconsistent with a level of unemployment lower than *a* in Figure 13-5 (where *a* is the "natural" rate of unemployment). Firms will raise prices again.

What we are tracing here is a wage-price spiral, where wage increases are followed by price increases, which trigger, via a feedback process, yet higher wage increases. The likely outcome of this state of affairs is hyperinflation. But before that, of course, government will step in to control the inflation. The real wage will rise to its former level. As a result, the amount of labor employed will fall and unemployment will return to *a*, if not exceed it. So, Friedman concludes, the Phillips curve does not exist, except in the very short run. It is not possible to permanently reduce unemployment by trading off for more inflation.

Embodied in Friedman's theory is the testable proposition that labor cannot be persuaded to offer *more* of its services for a *lower* real wage. What do empirical studies reveal about the feedback from price increases to wage increases? George Perry, in estimating the impact of prices, profits, and unemployment on wages, found that

$$\dot{W_t} = -4.3 + 0.4\dot{P}_{t-1} + 14.7(1/u_t) + 0.4R_t + 0.8\Delta R_t$$

where $\dot{W_t}$ is the rate of change of wages, and $\dot{P}_{t-1}$ is the rate of change of prices lagged one period. If Friedman is right, the coefficient for prices should be unity, meaning that a 1% increase in prices is transmitted to a 1% increase in wages.

If those who believe the Phillips curve does provide us with a public policy guide are right, and money wages, not real wages, are all that workers look at in determining how much of their services to offer industry, then the coefficient should be zero. In fact, the coefficient is at 0.4. This means that a 1% increase in prices is associated with a 0.4% increase in wages. The real wage has fallen, thereby sustaining a lower level of unemployment at a higher price level. (Those familiar with calculus can differentiate $\dot{W_t}$ with respect to $\dot{P}_{t-1}$ and obtain 0.4—when wages change by 4, prices change by 10.)

If the Perry relationship is a stable one, then the Phillips curve does exist and it is possible to make the trade-off. The ultimate question is, over how long a time period can labor be persuaded to take a lower real wage? If it is long enough, it is possible to have lower unemployment than *a*, with a higher rate of inflation than 0, without leading to hyperinflation. And instead of long periods of unemployment and curtailed output (and the social problems associated with both) for the sake of a stable price level, we can have a full-employment economy producing at maximum output.

Figure 13-5 Rate of change of money-wage rates and excess supply of labor

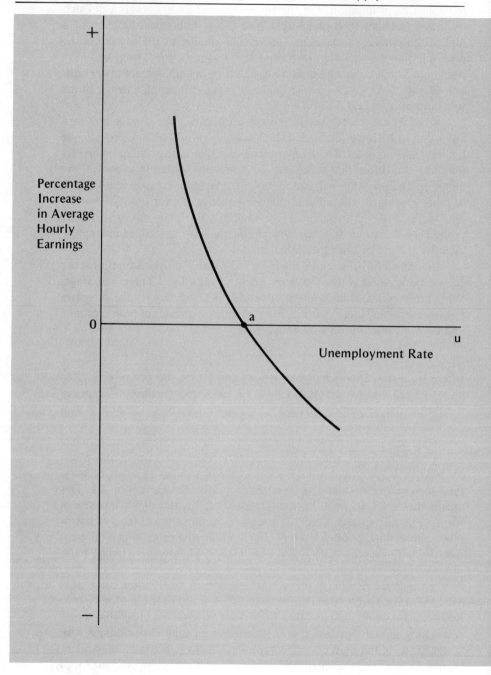

Evidence of some feedback from price increases to wage increases suggests that the Phillips curve becomes steeper over time. To the extent that workers can anticipate inflation, their wage demands reflect expected future price increases, and thereby become a self-fulfilling prediction. Public expectations about inflation are, therefore, crucial in determining the time period during which policymakers can reduce unemployment by permitting an increase in the rate of inflation. It may be several years, at the end of which time it may be necessary to force the public to revise its expectations of wage and price increases by such techniques as wage and price controls. In order to change expectations, however, it is necessary to know how they are formed and what influences them. Economists are currently focusing on how expectations are changed and on how the labor market works at the microeconomic level, in an effort to come to grips with the problems of inflation and unemployment.[12]

POLICY ON UNEMPLOYMENT AND INFLATION

If we accept the Phillips-curve finding of a trade-off between inflation and unemployment, then policymakers can only choose which unemployment-rate/inflation-rate mix they wish to adopt. The decision can be made in favor of greater price stability at the expense of higher unemployment, or the reverse. Recent experience in the United States suggests that a 4% unemployment rate can be achieved only at the price of inflation approaching 7%. This particular trade-off is the result of the structure of the American economy and reflects the following:

1. The existence of oligopolistic firms able to avoid price competition.
2. Well-organized unions that bargain collectively in an industry.
3. An unwillingness by firms to cut prices and workers to accept reduced money wages.
4. The speed and ease with which unemployed labor can be placed in existing vacancies.

It is possible that these structural relationships could be altered to bring about a more attractive trade-off between inflation and unemployment, but it would require several years to bring about structural changes affecting fundamental institutional relationships. While such changes are taking place, policymakers must decide where to locate the economy on the Phillips curve. It is an unfortunate but inescapable fact that a decision in favor of greater price stability is simultaneously a decision in favor of greater unemployment. (A newspaper cartoon appeared in 1972 in which an employee is being laid off by his boss with the encouraging remark: "Look

12. See E. S. Phelps et al., *Microeconomic Foundations of Employment and Inflation Theory* (Norton, 1970).

at it this way, Bixby—you're joining the front lines in the fight against inflation.")

The cost to individuals and to society-of unemployment are, perhaps, obvious. But what is the harm in inflation? We have already alluded to the spectre of hyperinflation, which can lead to major economic and political upheaval. Even eliminating the extreme case, constantly rising prices are believed to cause a reduction of confidence in the existing government and its economic arrangements. And inflation is psychologically unsettling— consumers are obliged to learn new sets of prices frequently and to alter their expectations about what they will have to pay for goods and services.

Are there real economic costs associated with inflation? The most frequent answer given is that inflation redistributes income unfairly, favoring debtors who owe fixed dollar sums which will be worth less when it is time for repayment, and penalizing creditors whose receipts will be eroded by declining purchasing power. The claim is also made that the poor and near-poor are harmed by inflation because they are least capable of hedging against a rising price level by owning common stocks and real property, assets that are presumed to rise in value with inflation. Small savers are also said to be victims of inflation because the interest they receive on savings is eroded by declining purchasing power. And finally, inflation is bad for a nation's balance of payments in a system where exchange rates are fixed between nations. In Chapter 16 we consider further the impact of foreign economic relations on the domestic economy. Here it is sufficient to point out that if a nation's price level is rising more rapidly than those of its major trading partners, its exports will decline and its imports will rise, adversely affecting its balance of payments. Note, however, that it is not the presence of inflation which harms the balance of payments; rather, it is a higher rate of inflation than those in competing trading nations. If inflation is creeping at the same rate in all nations, no one nation has a competitive advantage over the rest.

INFLATION, EMPLOYMENT, AND THE DISTRIBUTION OF INCOME

Only recently has much analysis been done to determine the impact of inflation on the distribution of income, either by size or function. The size distribution of income tells us what fraction of national income accrues to different groups of income earners. "The top 5% of income earners get 20% of the income" is a statement about the size distribution of income. The functional distribution of income refers to the shares of national income accruing to wage earners and providers of capital. It is a less informative indicator of inequality than the size distribution of income because wage earners who get paid $5000, $50,000 and $500,000 (a few business executives receive this much from salary alone) cannot be distinguished from one another. Similarly, the stock dividends for a family which earns $12,000 per year and owns a few shares of stock are not distinguished from the dividends paid to the $120,000 per year corporate executive.

It is difficult to evaluate the impact of inflation on the size distribution of income independently of the employment rate accompanying inflation. It is far better for a family to face rising prices when the head of the household (and perhaps the secondary income earner) is working, than to face stable prices with unemployment. Income distribution definitely changes during periods of inflation accompanied by rising employment. Wage differentials are narrowed, and secondary income earners enter the labor market. The poor and near-poor are better off during periods of inflationary expansion than they are during contraction. With recession, the reverse occurs. The last hired, the poor, are the first to be fired. If they are better off during inflationary full-employment periods, they are worse off during periods of stable prices and high unemployment. The impact of increasing aggregate demand on employment for the poor was estimated in 1965 in a study done for the Office of Economic Opportunity. C. E. Metcalf and J. D. Mooney estimated that a reduction from 5.4% to 3.5% in the national unemployment rate would increase full-time employment for the poor by 1,042,000 jobs, moving 1,811,000 persons above the poverty line.

Does a poor person's cost of living rise more or less rapidly than the CPI? Robinson Hollister and John Palmer of the University of Wisconsin's Institute for Research on Poverty have tried to answer this question by constructing a poor person's cost of living index and comparing it with the CPI during inflationary periods. Their conclusion is that the poor person's price index fluctuates less than the CPI. Inflation hurts the poor less than the nonpoor when measured by the prices paid for an average market basket of goods.

If periods of growing prosperity, accompanied by inflation, are good for the poor and the near-poor in terms of the employment-generating effect, what is happening to those whose income depends on welfare payments such as social security, aid for families with dependent children, or pensions? Do rising prices hurt this group? Edward C. Budd, in a study of the size distribution of income, has found that these transfer payments have increased more rapidly than the rate of inflation during the post-World War II period; but although real growth occurred during this period, the share of income accruing to transfer-payment recipients decreased.[13] Thus, the charge that inflation hurts the poor is untrue, at least in the aggregate. It is, of course, likely that individuals whose main source of income is private pensions or income from bonds fare badly. While the latter group is unlikely to include any but upper-income individuals, those dependent on private pensions include many middle and lower-income

13. E. C. Budd, "Postwar Changes in the Size Distribution of Income in the United States," *American Economic Review*, Vol. 55 (1970), pp. 247–260.

individuals. A society that wishes to minimize the impact of inflation on pensioners can provide direct compensation to such recipients, or insure that pension payments are tied to a cost-of-living index.

The charge that inflation hurts small savers is indisputable. Interest rates paid on deposits in commercial banks, savings and loan associations, and other lending institutions have risen with inflation, but the rise has been curtailed by ceilings imposed by federal financial regulatory agencies—the Federal Reserve Board and the Federal Home Loan Bank Board. This problem could be solved by eliminating ceilings on interest rates, a recommendation which has been made by a presidential commission on financial regulatory machinery.[14]

In making a given unemployment–inflation choice, policymakers ought to consider the benefits and costs associated with a given level of inflation and unemployment. Of course, the benefits and costs do not fall equally on all individuals, as politicians well know. But popular notions about the burden of inflation on the poor and near-poor are largely unfounded. The evidence that has emerged during the past few years, while admittedly sketchy, points to the conclusions that the differential size distribution of income is narrowed during periods of economic expansion and inflation, and that the ill effects of inflation on certain groups can be compensated with specific remedies. But cherished myths die hard. Perhaps after living with creeping and controlled inflation for a decade or two, it will seem no more frightening than a deliberately unbalanced budget or the existence of some unemployment in the economy.

STRUCTURAL REMEDIES FOR SHIFTING THE PHILLIPS CURVE

In the short run an economy may be confined to a given Phillips curve, but longer run measures can be taken to shift the curve leftward, thereby reducing the unemployment cost of inflation. The most obvious remedy follows directly from our analysis of the Phillips curve. Antitrust policy can be pursued vigorously against oligopolistic firms and monopolistic unions. By reducing pressures for wage increases and making it less likely that firms will accede to union demands for wage increases in excess of productivity increases, the cost-push pressures that lie behind the Phillips curve will be reduced. Although different administrations have pursued antitrust policies with more or less enthusiasm, no substantial effort has been made in the post-World War II period to break oligopolies into smaller, more competitive units or, except for the Taft-Hartley Act, to curtail union power.

Another structural remedy centers around an active labor-market

14. The President's Commission on Financial Structure and Regulation, *Report*, December 1971.

policy to reduce "down time" as workers search for jobs, and to improve the efficiency of matching workers with employers. Labor-market programs, including the use of the government as an employer, are the subject of Chapter 14.

Finally, governments can intervene directly in wage and price decisions in an attempt to control inflation. Such intervention is generally called "incomes policy" and has been resorted to by governments during wartime, when inflationary pressures are most severe, and occasionally during interwar periods. We discuss incomes policies in Chapter 15.

Manpower Planning in Macroeconomic Stabilization Policy

Neoclassical economists assumed that any disequilibrium in the supply and demand for workers with certain skills would be temporary, and remedied by the private sector. Insofar as training or retraining was required to remedy the disequilibrium, it would be provided by the employer, or sought independently by the employee. NeoKeynesian economists recognized that equilibrium in the labor market was not automatic, and that the government would have to play a role in stimulating aggregate demand to levels high enough to provide sufficient jobs for the available labor supply. However, during the late 1940s and 1950s, it was still believed that training was a private-sector function. By the 1960s, it became clear that certain groups within the economy—the technologically unemployed, minorities, teenagers—were unable to obtain training or retraining through the private market, and the federal government began developing a panoply of programs to deal with the special problems of the unemployed, and the underemployed. The aims of these programs were microeconomic in scope— they were intended to serve the needs of specific segments of the labor force rather than to provide a tool for economic stabilization.

We would not consider manpower analysis in a book on macroeconomics if the most recent theoretical developments in the field did not claim a macroeconomic role for manpower programs. This new theoretical analysis hypothesizes that manpower policy can be used to effect shifts in the Phillips curve, thus changing the trade-off between inflation and unemployment, and placing manpower programs alongside monetary and fiscal policy as a major tool in achieving economic stability. Application of manpower policy as a macroeconomic tool would require a significant expansion of manpower programs above their current levels, as well as a shift in focus from the disadvantaged to the entire labor force.

In this chapter, we consider briefly the development of current manpower programs, and then turn to a more detailed discussion of the potential macroeconomic implications of revised and expanded programs. Also discussed is the related issue of using direct public employment as a program to reduce aggregate unemployment. Finally, we consider the conflict between those who believe manpower programs should have a microeconomic orientation to the disadvantaged worker, and those who advocate an expanded macroeconomic role for such programs.

DISADVANTAGED-WORKER APPROACH TO LABOR-MARKET ANALYSIS

National programs to deal with unemployment date back to the New Deal, when a series of temporary measures were adopted which were the forerunners of modern manpower programs. The purpose of New Deal programs was to provide jobs, and through jobs, relief and self-respect. Training was only incidental. Although the programs were phased out as war production brought nearly full employment, they represented an important commitment on the part of the government to an active role in the economy, and in particular, to efforts in providing employment. This commitment was formalized in 1946 with the passing of the Employment Act, and the establishment of a Council of Economic Advisors. The Employment Act clearly indicated that the federal government had certain responsibilities in providing economic stability and "employment opportunities . . . for those able, willing and seeking to work . . . ." However, even the supporters of the bill had only vague, and often conflicting, ideas of what kind of government action would be permissible and desirable to achieve these goals.

In the fifteen years that followed passage of the Employment Act, doubts arose as to the ability of the private sector to train and employ all those looking for jobs, especially those who lived in economically depressed areas. The belief that such training ought to be a government responsibility emerged in the 1950s, when it became apparent that areas such as the coal mining sections of Appalachia would not be carried along with a rise in overall economic prosperity.

In 1961, Congress passed the Area Redevelopment Act, the first post-World War II program to retrain workers who had become unemployed because of outmoded skills or geographical shifts in industrial activity. It was aimed primarily at the Appalachian region, and was the first of a series of major manpower programs launched during the 1960s to deal with specific labor-market problems. Virtually all of the programs are supply-based programs, in that they focus on the skills of workers rather than the composition of the demand of labor. In 1962 Congress passed the Manpower Development and Training Act, a nationwide training program aimed at both the technologically displaced and the unskilled, and therefore at unemployable individuals in prosperous as well as depressed areas. MDTA training grew rapidly, doubling the number of enrolled trainees between 1963 and 1964, and again between 1964 and 1965. It became increasingly apparent during the middle 1960s that there was a group of the unemployed who lacked basic education and acceptable work habits, and who were not only unable to benefit from the general increase in economic prosperity, but who could not even qualify for training programs. To reach this group, fundamental changes in the philosophy and techniques of manpower training would have to be made. Amendments to the MDTA in 1963 expanded the act to include basic education and job counseling of trainees with low levels of education.

In the War on Poverty, manpower programs were expanded to include the Neighborhood Youth Corps and the Job Corps, both of which are aimed at youths, and provide special assistance in obtaining and keeping a job. Table 14-1 lists current federal manpower training programs with the average number of new enrollments for selected years. The purposes of these programs are to lower unemployment rates for minorities, women, and teenagers, and more generally, to try to equalize the skills of groups suffering higher than average unemployment rates with the skills of the average worker. This goal is, of course, not a macroeconomic goal. Manpower economists concerned with the special problems of the disadvantaged worker do not claim that the current manpower approach will affect the aggregate unemployment rate.

The following numerical example,[1] together with some assumptions based on empirical analysis of manpower programs, illustrates how little impact manpower training has on the overall unemployment rate. Consider a model of a labor market compartmentalized into a sector for average workers and a sector for disadvantaged workers. Assume that competitive pressures result in equal rates of wage increase in the two markets, and that this rate is 4% annually. We can define a Phillips curve for each market by relating wage change to the unemployment rate:

$$(\Delta W_1/W_1) = b_1/u_1 - a_1 \quad \text{and} \quad (\Delta W_2/W_2) = b_2/u_2 - a_2$$

If $a_1 = 8$ and $a_2 = 2$, and $b_1 = b_2 = 42$, then $u_1 = 3.5\%$ unemployment for average workers and $u_2 = 7\%$ unemployment for the disadvantaged. Assuming that 30% of the labor force are disadvantaged, the overall unemployment rate will be $30\%(0.07) + (70\%)(0.035) = 4.55\%$.

Given this simple two-sector model, what would be the impact on the overall unemployment rate of an extensive set of manpower programs which had the effect of reducing the disadvantaged labor force? A 10% figure is a generous estimate of such a reduction resulting from the last several years of manpower programs. The disadvantaged labor force, as a percent of the total labor force, would fall from 30% to 27%. The overall

1. This example is provided by R. E. Hall, "Prospects for Shifting the Phillips Curve Through Manpower Policy," *Brookings Papers on Economic Activity*, 1971, No. 3, 659–701, ed. A. M. Okun and G. L. Perry.

Table 14-1   New Enrollments[1] in Federally Assisted Work and Training Programs, Fiscal Years 1964 and 1970–1973 (Thousands)

				Fiscal Year	
Program	1964	1970	1971	1972 (esti- mated)	1973 (pro- jected)
Total	278	1,830	2,109	2,318	2,292
Institutional training under the MDTA	69	130	156	166	166
JOBS (federally financed) and other OJT[2]	9	177	184	136	131
Neighborhood Youth Corps:					
In-school and summer		436	562	583	567
Out-of-school		46	53	49	49
Operation Mainstream		12	22	22	22
Public Service Careers		4	45	32	29
Concentrated Employment Program		110	77	69	69
Job Corps		43	50	53	55
Work Incentive Program		93	96	112	133
Public Employment Program				160	92
Veterans programs	([3])	83	86	83	83
Vocational rehabilitation	179	411	468	517	558
Other programs[4]	21	285	311	335	339

1) Generally larger than the number of training or work opportunities programed because turnover of short-term training results in more than one individual in a given enrollment opportunity. Persons served by more than one program are counted only once.
2) Includes the MDTA-OJT program which ended with fiscal 1970 (except for national contracts) and the JOBS-Optional Program which began with fiscal 1971; also Apprenticeship Outreach, with 27,500 enrollees in fiscal 1971.
3) Included with "other programs."
4) Includes a wide variety of programs, some quite small—for example, Foster Grandparents and vocational training for Indians provided by the Department of the Interior. Data for some programs are estimated.
Note: *Detail may not add to totals because of rounding.*
Source: *Office of Management and Budget*, Special Analysis, Budget of the United States Government, Fiscal Year 1973, *pp. 140 and 142.*

unemployment rate would be $27\%(0.07) + (73\%)(0.035) = 4.45\%$. While a reduction in the overall rate of 0.1% is not trivial, it certainly does not indicate that current manpower programs aimed at the disadvantaged can play a major role in macroeconomic policy. However, this does not invalidate a manpower approach directed at the disadvantaged. To date, virtually all of the analyses of manpower programs have pointed to high economic returns from training.[2] Insofar as manpower programs upgrade the skills of disadvantaged workers, they have the effect of reducing the unemployment rate differentials between the average worker and the disadvantaged worker.

We turn now to a labor-market model of the Phillips curve developed primarily by Holt et al.[3] This work attempts to develop a theoretical basis for using manpower programs as a tool of macroeconomic policy. The Holt group analyzed a series of labor-market relationships and claims that the Phillips curve can be shifted to the left by the appropriate manipulation of manpower policy.

Recall that the Phillips relationship is a policymaker's dilemma. Either the nation must suffer from increasingly higher inflation as the unemployment rate is driven down, or the hardship of unemployment must be visited on increased numbers of citizens in an effort to slow the rate of price rise. It is an unenviable choice; however, if the Phillips curve could be shifted toward the left, the trade-off between inflation and unemployment would be less costly. Aggregate demand could be stimulated to reduce unemployment with little or no inflationary response. These possible effects are illustrated in Figure 14-1. Starting at A, with unemployment rate u_1 and inflation rate p_1, attempts at stimulating aggregate demand would result in a movement along Phillips curve I from A to B, with a consequent increase in inflation to p_2 and a decrease in unemployment to u_2. If, however, policies were available which could shift the Phillips curve to II, aggregate demand could be stimulated with no change in the price level, as shown by a movement from A to C. This desirable leftward shift in the Phillips curve might be accomplished through structural transformations in the labor market, effected by manpower planning.

It cannot be stated too emphatically that the macro approach to manpower planning is intended to supplement monetary and fiscal policy, not replace them. Its use assumes that aggregate demand pressures have been applied sufficiently to provide job opportunities. It is the aim of manpower planning to see that those opportunities are realized. It also needs to be emphasized that the role of manpower planning in macroeconomic stabilization is controversial. The theory presented below has been developed only recently, and the policy proposals are based on inferences from the models rather than on observations from experience. Indeed, some of those

2. The two major collections of benefit-cost studies of manpower programs are G. G. Somers, ed., *Retraining the Unemployed* (University of Wisconsin Press, 1968), and G. G. Somers and W. D. Wood, eds., *Cost-Benefit Analysis of Manpower Policies: Proceedings of a North American Conference* (Kingston, Ontario: Industrial Relations Centre, Queen's University, 1969).
3. This model can be found in several sources. C. C. Holt, C. D. MacRae, S. O. Schwertzer, and R. E. Smith, *The Unemployment-Inflation Dilemma: A Manpower Solution* (The Urban Institute, 1971); C. C. Holt et al., *Manpower Programs to Reduce Inflation and Unemployment: Manpower Lyrics for Macro Music* (The Urban Institute, 1971); C. C. Holt et al., "Manpower Proposals for Phase III," *Brookings Papers on Economic Activity*, 1971, No. 3; and C. C. Holt et al., "Manpower Policies to Reduce Inflation and Unemployment," in *Manpower Programs in the Policy Mix*, ed. L. Ulman (The Johns Hopkins Press, 1973).

Figure 14-1   Impact of shifting the Phillips curve on the inflation-unemployment tradeoff

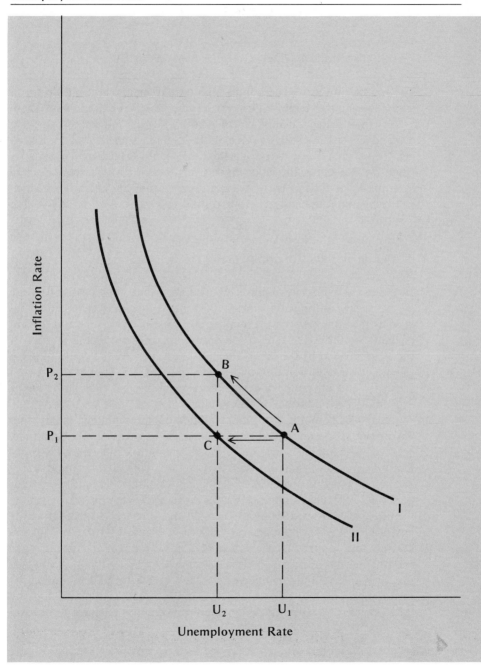

economists who have been most closely connected with the analysis of existing manpower programs are the most skeptical of the alleged promise of manpower policies in shifting the Phillips curve.

LABOR-MARKET MODEL OF THE PHILLIPS CURVE

The analysis of the macroeconomic approach to manpower policy rests on three labor-market relationships which lie behind the Phillips curve. These are (1) the vacancy-unemployment relation, (2) the impact of aggregate demand and size of the labor force on the level of vacancies and unemployment, and (3) the response of wages to the level of vacancies and unemployment. By explaining the labor-market relationships which determine the location of the Phillips curve, we can suggest labor-market policies which will bring about the desired leftward shift.

Job Vacancies and Unemployment

Several empirical analyses have revealed an inverse relationship between job vacancies and unemployment.[4] Just as the unemployment rate is defined as the ratio between the number of unemployed persons and the size of the labor force, the rate of job vacancies is defined as the number of vacancies divided by the labor force. In both cases, we are controlling for changes in the labor force, so that we can consider the relationship between vacancies and unemployment independent of the fact that both will be expanding if the labor force is expanding.

It should be pointed out that traditional microeconomic theory does not permit excess supply and excess demand to occur at the same time. Job vacancies are an indication of excess supply; unemployment is an indication of excess demand. Recall that excess supply, under simple supply and demand theory, results in a fall in the price of the commodity or factor until the market clears and excess supply is zero. This theory fails to explain the fact that both vacancies and unemployment have coexisted during the post-World War II period, as can be seen in Figure 14-2. Several factors are responsible for this phenomenon of job openings and unemployed people.

The skills of the unemployed may not match the skills required for vacant jobs. This may be true in fact, as in the case of a rural town looking for a doctor, or a corporation looking for a ceramics engineer to develop

4. J. C. R. Dow and L. A. Dicks-Mireaux, "The Excess Demand for Labour: A Study of Conditions in Great Britain, 1945–56," in *Oxford Economic Papers*, new series, Vol. 10 (February 1958), 1–33; C. Boschan, *Fluctuations in Job Vacancies—An Analysis of Available Measures* (National Bureau of Economic Research, 1969); J. G. Myers, *Job Vacancies in the Firm and the Labor Market* (The Conference Board, 1969).

Figure 14-2   Vacancies and unemployment, U.S. data: 1947-1969

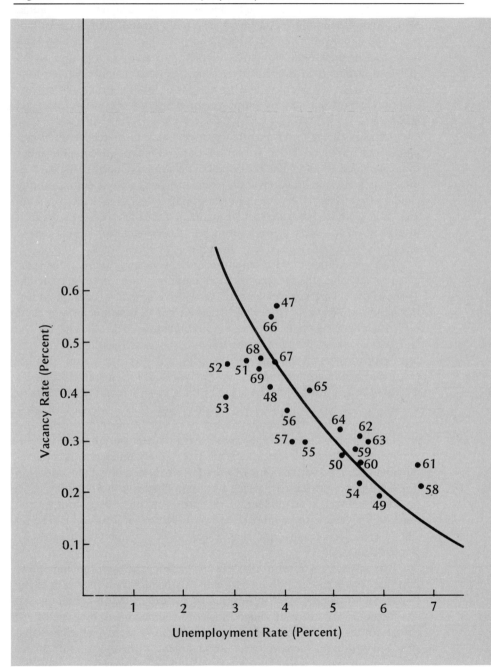

nose cones for missiles. Or it may be the result of a misconception of job qualifications, as in the case of a firm which requires a high school diploma for a job in the shipping department. There is a great deal of evidence that many job qualifications are arbitrary and not job-related. This is particularly true of educational standards adopted by employers during a period of labor surplus as a convenient screening device, but are retained long after the surplus evaporates. During periods of labor shortage, employers eventually drop unnecessary employment barriers in an effort to attract labor.

Another factor is the possibility of regional mismatch between employer and employee. There are substantial barriers to movement of labor to areas where employment is available, including financial costs, such as moving expenses, and psychic costs, such as leaving friends and uprooting children from schools. The Department of Labor defines each metropolitan area as a separate labor market, recognizing that there is a great deal of insulation of one market from another. This segmentation is reflected in unemployment rates, which vary among metropolitan areas.

Even when the potential employee and the vacant job are in the same geographical area, the two parties to an employment contract may be unaware of each other's existence. Anyone who has searched for employment through want ads or an employment service knows how much the process is characterized by chaos, frustration, and chance.[5] The efficiency of the search for jobs on the part of the unemployed, and the efficiency of the search for workers on the part of employers, will affect the relationship between vacancies and unemployment. To the extent that search efficiency is increased, there will be fewer vacancies for a given unemployment rate.

So far, we have explained why vacancies and unemployment can exist simultaneously. But why are they inversely related? If unemployment rates are higher than is customary, employees are reluctant to quit present employment; for the same reason, the unemployed are quicker to accept employment. During periods of lower than normal unemployment rates, job holders are in a strong bargaining position. They will more readily leave present employment, confident of the prospects of finding another job quickly. They can also be more selective of the type of job chosen. The result is a higher vacancy rate than usual when unemployment rates are lower than usual.

The inverse relationship between the vacancy rate and the unemployment rate is also based upon the assets of the unemployed, their borrowing power, and unemployment insurance. To the extent that the unemployed can finance expenditures during periods of unemployment, they can afford to wait for the most suitable job. If their expectations were to change so that they believed it was harder to find employment, if the duration of unemployment insurance were sharply reduced, and if merchants acted quickly

5. An excellent analysis of this process is provided by H. L. Sheppard and A. H. Belitsky, *The Job Hunt* (Johns Hopkins Press, 1966).

to curtail credit to the unemployed, the willingness of the unemployed to accept *any* job (thereby reducing the number of vacancies) would increase.

Thus, the vacancy-unemployment relationship is based on several factors:

1. Mismatch between the skills of the unemployed and the requirements of industry.
2. Mismatch between the location of the unemployed and the location of job vacancies.
3. The level of efficiency in employee search for a job and employer search for an employee.
4. The expectations of the unemployed regarding the availability of jobs.
5. The means to finance expenditures during unemployment.

The relative importance of these factors is not yet known, although research is underway.

What would cause the empirically observed vacancies-unemployment curve to shift to the left?: changes in the labor market that reduced mismatching; increased efficiencies; and lowered expectations. A set of labor-market programs could bring about these changes. These programs are the basis for the manpower approach to macroeconomic balance, and are described later in the chapter.

Aggregate Demand and the Vacancy-Unemployment Relationship

The vacancy-unemployment curve represents the possible combinations of vacancy rates and unemployment rates determined by the existing institutional structure of labor markets. Should this structure change, the position of the vacancy-unemployment curve would change. But what determines where, on this curve, an economy is located at any given time? The answer is the level of aggregate demand and the size of the labor force.[6]

Aggregate demand can be influenced by the government sector. In a short-run model, the labor force is treated as an exogenous variable. In the long run, the government can also have an impact on the size of the labor force through income-maintenance policies (consider the impact on labor-

---

6. The labor force is defined by the U.S. Department of Labor's Bureau of Labor Statistics as the sum of all individuals who are employed or unemployed. Employed persons comprise those who worked during the week the survey was made, and those who were not working but were temporarily absent. Unemployed persons comprise all persons who did not work during the survey week but were looking for work, or were laid off and waiting to be called back. See Chapter 13 for a discussion of the problems associated with measuring the labor force. See also the latest *Handbook of Labor Statistics* (U.S. Bureau of Labor Statistics). For a thorough discussion of labor force behavior, see Sar A. Levitan, Garth L. Mangum, and Ray Marshall, *Human Resources and Labor Markets* (Harper & Row, 1972), especially Part I, Labor Market Dynamics.

force size of lowering social-security eligibility from 62 to 55), anti-discrimination policies to lower barriers for women and minorities, and other long-run policies, such as free birth-control clinics.

In order to understand why aggregate demand and labor-force size determine the point on the vacancy-unemployment curve of an economy at any point in time, we need to recall the relationship between aggregate production and employment. The aggregate production function relates factor inputs to outputs (see Chapter 3). It is possible to estimate the level of output, in real terms, needed to sustain a given level of jobs if we have a measure of the productivity of labor and hold the capital stock constant. Put another way, we can estimate the needed increase in output to reduce unemployment by a given amount if we know the size of the labor force (e.g., a 1% reduction in unemployment of a labor force of 100 million requires 1 million more jobs). This increase in output needed to reduce unemployment is an estimate rather than a precise prediction. If government policy stimulates aggregate demand for output that requires labor-intensive production processes, then using the aggregate production function (which combines labor and capital intensive processes) to predict jobs created would lead to an underestimate.

Despite such problems, it is still possible to estimate the level of aggregate demand required (1) to sustain a given *level* of employment, and (2) to sustain a given *rate* of employment for a given size of labor force. At any point in time, the jobs generated by a given level of aggregate demand can be divided into those which are filled and those for which there are vacancies. This can be represented as

$$J = E + V \qquad (14\text{-}1)$$

where J is the stock of jobs, E is the number of employed persons, and V is the number of job vacancies. Divide both sides of the equation by the labor force (which is the sum of the employed and unemployed) to obtain

$$J/L = E/L + V/L \qquad (14\text{-}2)$$

J/L is the ratio of the stock of jobs to the labor force. E/L is the employment rate and V/L is the vacancy rate. Let U represent the number of unemployed. Then U/L is the unemployment rate. Since the sum of the employment rate (E/L) and the unemployment rate (U/L) must equal unity, we can rewrite Equation 14-2, substituting $1 - U/L$ for E/L:

$$\frac{J}{L} = \left(1 - \frac{U}{L}\right) + \frac{V}{L} \qquad (14\text{-}3)$$

Rearranging terms, we have

$$\frac{V}{L} = \frac{U}{L} + \left(\frac{J}{L} - 1\right) \qquad (14\text{-}4)$$

Equation 14-4 is the equation for a straight line with a slope of unity and an intercept of $J/L - 1$, and is drawn, together with the vacancy-unemployment curve, in Figure 14-3.

We can call the line represented by Equation 14-4 an "employment line." The significance of a slope of unity is that a given change in employment—holding the stock of jobs J and the size of the labor force L constant—is accompanied by an equal change, in the opposite direction, in the number of vacancies. If employment is increased by one person because someone who is unemployed finds a job (note that employment cannot be increased due to an increase in aggregate demand, for that would imply a shift in the employment line), vacancies are decreased by one unit.

In order for the employment line to go through the origin, the stock of jobs must equal the size of the labor force, in which case $J/L - 1$ would equal zero. $J/L - 1$ equals zero when $J = L$ and $V = U$. Over time the labor force is growing, and aggregate demand must be increased to augment the stock of jobs if the unemployment rate is to be kept from increasing above (U/L)—the intersection of the employment line with the vacancy-rate/unemployment-rate curve in Figure 14-3. If the stock of jobs is not augmented to keep pace with the growth in the labor force, $J/L - 1$ would be negative, the employment line would shift to the right, intersecting the vacancy-rate axis below the origin, and the unemployment rate would increase. Alternatively, if aggregate demand is stimulated to provide a greater stock of jobs than the size of the labor force, $J/L - 1$ would be greater than zero, the unemployment rate would decrease, and the employment line would shift to the left, intersecting the vacancy-rate axis above the origin. If this occurs, the stock of vacancies would exceed the number of the unemployed by $J - L$. Thus, for a given labor force and a given level of aggregate demand, we know the location of the employment line. The intersection of the employment line and the vacancy-unemployment relation determines the exact stocks of vacancies and unemployed persons that exist in the economy at any point in time.[7]

It may be useful, at this point, to restate the meaning of the vacancy-unemployment curve and the employment lines. The $V - U$ curve shows the set of possible vacancy rates and unemployment rates that can exist in an economy, based on the underlying institutional structure of the labor market. This institutional structure is based on expectations, efficiencies in search for jobs by employees and for hires by employers, and the degree of mismatching. Changes in the institutional structure would change this array of possible combinations of V/L and U/L; the $V - U$ curve can be shifted toward the origin or away from it. If we assume that the labor force

7. For simplicity, the interaction between aggregate demand and the size of the labor force is ignored in the above formulation. Actually, there is strong evidence that the labor force grows with increases in aggregate demand and shrinks with decreases. When demand for labor increases, additional workers enter the labor market, particularly women who are not the head of the household, and drop out of the labor market when demand decreases. For a thorough review of labor-force participation literature see H. S. Parnes, "Labor Force Participation and Labor Mobility," in *A Review of Industrial Relations Research*, Vol. 1 (Industrial Relations Research Association, 1970).

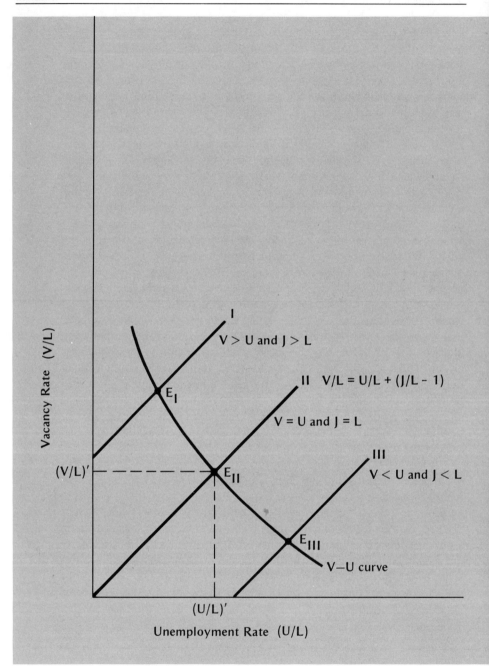

is held constant (in the short run this is a reasonable assumption), then the employment lines are determined by shifts in the stock of jobs that result from government policy affecting aggregate demand. The greater is the aggregate demand (again, holding L constant), the greater is the number of jobs demanded, and the higher is the intercept on the V/L axis of the employment line. If aggregate demand generated a stock of jobs such that $J = L$, the economy would be on employment line II in Figure 14-3. Along this line, vacancies are equal to the number of the unemployed.

Now let us remove the assumption of a constant labor force. Any given employment line is determined by the relationship between the level of aggregate demand, which determines the stock of jobs and the size of the labor force. Along employment line II, $J = L$, *regardless of the amount of J or size of L*. If the economy is at equilibrium point E_{II}, implying an unemployment rate of $(U/L)'$ and a vacancy rate of $(V/L)'$, an increase in aggregate demand relative to the size of the labor force (a measure taken to reduce unemployment) can be illustrated as a shift in the employment line upward, say from II to I. The new equilibrium point, E_I, is determined by the institutional constraints of the $V - U$ relationship. The increase in aggregate demand results in employers increasing the number of vacancies to meet the higher demand for output. The higher level of vacancies means that it is easier to find a job and the unemployment rate falls.

Government policy that affects aggregate demand affects the employment lines. Government policy that affects the labor market affects the position of the $V - U$ curve, although it cannot completely determine the $V - U$ curve. Individual preferences and expectations play a role in determining the $V - U$ curve. The combination of government, labor-market, and aggregate-demand policies will interact to determine the equilibrium V/L and U/L rates. It now remains to describe the third labor-market relation, which, in conjunction with the first two, is an explanation of the location of the Phillips curve.

Vacancies-Unemployment Relationship and Wage Changes

So far, we have explained the empirically observed relationship between vacancies and unemployment and indicated that a particular level of vacancies and unemployment is the result of the level of aggregate demand and the size of the labor force. The next element in this model to explain the Phillips curve is the relationship of vacancies to unemployment and the rate of wage change. If there is a low level of unemployment and a high level of job vacancies, employees are in a good position to demand higher wages or threaten to take a job elsewhere. Indeed, if there are few enough unemployed workers, the only way an employer can expand is to hire skilled employees from competitors by paying higher wages. Conversely, if unemployment is high and there are few job vacancies, the employee is in no position to demand wage increases—in fact, he may agree to take a voluntary cut in pay as a condition of retaining employment.

Of course these statements are subject to qualifications. Extensive two and three year union-negotiated contracts in major industries may result in wages increasing simultaneously with rising unemployment and falling vacancies. For any specific segment of the labor market, say the market for registered nurses, unemployment can be below and vacancies above the national average. Consequently, wages would have a tendency to rise in this market, even in the absence of such a tendency in the economy taken as a whole. Clearly, the relationship between wage change and vacancies-unemployment is a result of the relative bargaining power of employers and employees. As a general rule, however, we can say that the higher the ratio of vacancies to unemployment, the higher the rate of wage increase.

In Figure 14-4, alternative rates of wage change are drawn as radii from the origin; the steeper lines to the left represent higher rates of increase than the flatter lines to the right. $(\Delta W/W)_3$ intersects the vacancy-unemployment curve at a point which indicates a high-vacancy/low-unemployment level. $(\Delta W/W)_1$ intersects at a low-vacancy/high-unemployment level. The figure illustrates the positive relationship between V/U and $\Delta W/W$. Each radius represents a given rate of wage change, which is a function not of the absolute levels of V and U, but of the ratio between them. If the $V - U$ curve could be shifted, a given unemployment rate would be compatible with a set of wage-change rates.

SYNTHESIS OF THE LABOR-MARKET MODEL OF THE PHILLIPS CURVE

We now have the three labor-market relationships needed to explain the inflation-unemployment trade-off which lies at the heart of this model:

1. Vacancies and unemployment can exist simultaneously and are inversely related. This relationship is represented by the vacancy-unemployment curve in Figure 14-5a.

2. A given level of aggregate demand and a given size of labor force determine a specific combination of vacancies and unemployment rate, point S in Figure 14-5a.

3. The vacancy-unemployment combination elicits a rate of wage change, $(\Delta W/W)_S$.

We can move directly from these relationships in the labor market to the Phillips curve in Figure 14-5b.

Figure 14-4   Vacancy-unemployment curve and rates of wage change

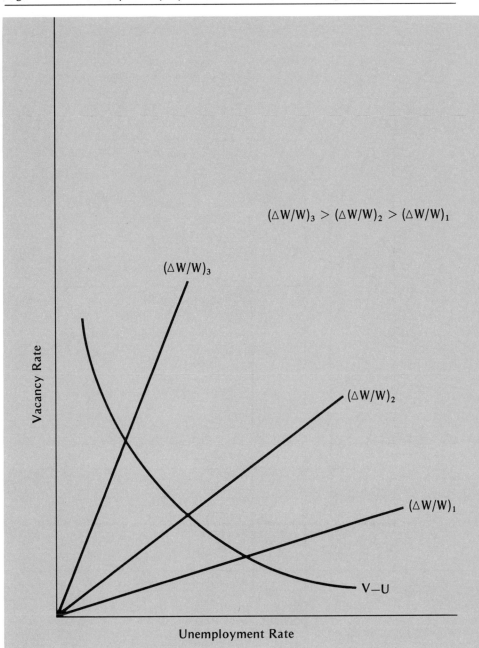

Figure 14-5   Phillips curve and the labor market

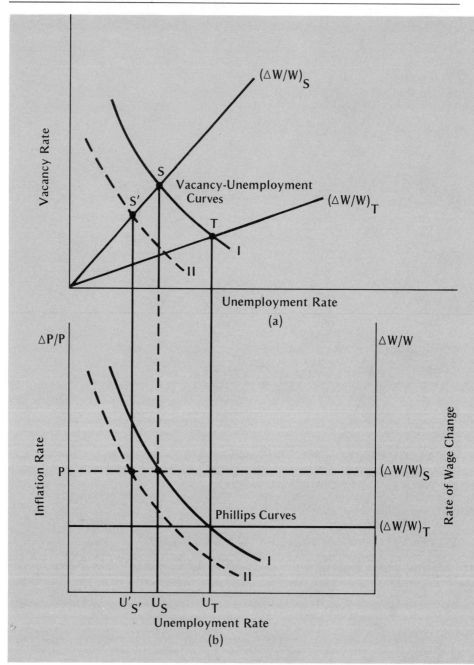

Assume that for a given size of labor force, aggregate demand policy locates the economy on the vacancy-unemployment curve at point S, which elicits a rate of wage change of $(\Delta W/W)_S$. This rate of wage change is associated with a specific rate of inflation for a given level of productivity (for an explanation of the relationship of productivity, the rate of wage change, and inflation, see Chapter 13). If, in an effort to reduce inflation, the government reduces aggregate-demand pressures, the economy will find itself with a higher unemployment rate and a lower vacancy rate—we move along the vacancy-unemployment curve toward the right. In Figure 14-5a this is illustrated by a movement from S to T, with the result that wage inflation is reduced from $(\Delta W/W)_S$ to $(\Delta W/W)_T$. A lower wage inflation is associated with a lower rate of price inflation. By varying aggregate demand and holding labor-force size constant, we can generate all the points along the Phillips curve. Thus, we have the Phillips curve inflation-unemployment trade-off explained by a set of labor-market relations.

The impact of an institutional change in the labor market, which causes the vacancy-unemployment curve to shift toward the origin, can be easily seen in Figure 14-5b. Shifting the vacancy-unemployment curve from I to II (holding aggregate demand and labor-force size constant) reduces the unemployment rate from U_S to $U'_{S'}$. If the rate of wage change remains at $(\Delta W/W)_S$, the rate of inflation will not change.[8] However, the inflation will now be associated with a lower unemployment rate. The Phillips curve will have shifted from I to II.

It should be evident that fiscal and monetary policy have no direct effect on the location of the Phillips curve. If aggregate demand is increased, the employment line shifts upward, the level of unemployment falls, the wage level increases, and prices increase. There is movement along the Phillips curve, but the curve itself does not shift. The only exception to this claim is the possibility that expectations of future inflation will encourage labor to hold out for wage increases, and will encourage oligopolistic employers to pay these increases in the expectation that they can pass the rising costs along to buyers.

It should be equally evident that there are two principal labor-market relationships which, if altered, could shift the Phillips curve. Shifting the vacancy-unemployment curve toward the origin results in a leftward shift in the Phillips curve. And if the wage response were to change so that there would be a lower rate of wage increase associated with a given vacancy-unemployment combination, the Phillips curve would again shift leftward. What specific policies would have the impact of influencing the vacancy-unemployment curve?

---

8. There is no reason why it should not change—the wage-response curve has been drawn as a straight line for illustrative purposes.

MANPOWER POLICIES TO SHIFT THE PHILLIPS CURVE

Information Programs

A program of labor-market information for employer and employee would reduce both vacancies and unemployment. Want ads are a major source of information about vacancies, but they are expensive for the employer, especially if the vacancy is not filled right away. A nationwide computerized job-information system would facilitate job search for the employee, and the employer could learn if potential employees are available for a given job. Inexpensive and instantaneous information would encourage the employer to choose production processes (where it is possible to choose among alternatives) on the basis of realistic estimates of how long it would take to fill positions. It might also inform job seekers of greater opportunities in alternative occupations.

Expanding labor-market information requires not only computerization of job information, but a method for disseminating information as rapidly as possible. A vastly expanded employment service would be needed to transmit job information to seeker and employer. There is a public employment service at present, but there is widespread agreement that it has been relatively unsuccessful in matching the unemployed with available jobs, especially for highly skilled and professional workers. The benefit of increasing labor-market information flow is that the duration of unemployment should be substantially reduced. If, however, the quality of placement is low and employee and employer find themselves mismatched, the turnover rate will be high. There is also the danger that a highly effective labor-market information system will itself increase turnover. If job availability is widely known, the inducement to quit present employment for more satisfying and lucrative alternative employment may be high. High employment turnover could lead to increases in the rate of wage change.[9] Thus, to reduce labor turnover, an employment service must focus on the quality of initial placement.

The net effect of an efficient information and placement program would be to reduce vacancies and unemployment. This, as we have discussed, would shift the vacancy-unemployment curve and the Phillips curve to the left.

Elimination of Specific Barriers

Efforts to overcome specific labor-market barriers can have an anti-inflationary impact. For example, recognizing that registered nurses are in

9. See C. C. Holt, "The Phillips Curve and Inflation and Unemployment," in *Microeconomic Foundations of Employment and Inflation Theory*, ed. E. S. Phelps (Norton, 1970), p. 251.

short supply (i.e., that vacancies exist), and that it takes an extended period of time to train nurses, the U.S. Department of Labor offers brief refresher courses in many metropolitan areas for RNs who have left the labor force, in the expectation that many nurses will return to the labor market and fill these jobs. While such a policy expands the labor force, it also reduces job vacancies. Assuming that those who are attracted back into the nursing profession by these refresher courses find employment, the net result is a reduction in both vacancies and unemployment (a leftward shift in the vacancy-unemployment curve).

Consider two other policies to eliminate labor-market barriers. Federal income-tax law permits, under certain conditions, employees to deduct the expense of moving costs when the move is necessitated by a change in job from one labor-market area to another. This lowers the barrier which exists among regional labor markets. Second, enforcement of equal employment-opportunity laws discourages the maintenance of color barriers which separate labor markets into "white only" and "black only" submarkets.

The principle in all three cases is the same: Policies aimed at reducing or eliminating labor-market barriers shift the unemployment-vacancy curve to the left, and therefore contribute to shifting the Phillips curve to the left.

Reducing Turnover

Policies that improve the match between employer and employee, and encourage employers to promote from within, will reduce labor turnover, thereby avoiding the unemployment and vacancies that result during the period of job search. A variety of programs can reduce labor turnover: establishing day-care facilities near centers of employment; improving job satisfaction; reducing worker layoffs with more accurate business planning; and providing extensive job counseling to match job and job seeker. These programs can minimize the time that workers are unemployed and looking for jobs.

Manpower Training

Training programs to endow unemployed workers with the skills necessary to fill job vacancies reduce both job vacancies and unemployment—if the program is successful in placing graduates in vacant jobs. Training therefore can shift the vacancy-unemployment curve leftward. But the effectiveness of manpower training in reducing inflation depends on the nature of the training. General training which equips workers to perform a variety of jobs would have a greater anti-inflationary impact than training which is specific to one job.[10] Training programs that emphasize the skills needed for jobs long vacant will encourage a reduction in the average duration of vacancies. In principle, training programs seek to reduce the mismatch between the job qualifications of employees and the job requirements of employers.

Wage inflation is highest in labor markets where the ratio of vacancies to unemployment is highest. Therefore, training programs should focus on occupations where there are shortages that can be remedied by teaching skills relevant to the occupation. Anticipating demand for specific types of labor so that workers can be trained in advance lessens the shortages, and therefore reduces the tendency to wage inflation.

Public Employment Programs

One obvious way of reducing unemployment is for the government to hire the unemployed. This was done during the Depression under such programs as the Works Progress Administration and the Civil Conservation Corps. The WPA employed over eight million people between 1935 and 1941 on construction and engineering projects, writers' and artists' projects, and vocational training for defense industries. The CCC employed young men to plant trees and do other conservation work. More than two and a quarter million young men were enrolled in this program for unskilled labor during the seven-year period 1933–1940. Despite this temporary foray into public employment, the federal government, particularly Congress, has resisted the idea that the government ought to provide jobs for those who cannot obtain employment in the private sector.

In 1971, with unemployment approaching the 6% level, Congress passed the Emergency Employment Act, a manpower program designed to provide employment directly for the unemployed and underemployed by giving funds to state and local governments, expressly for expanding public employment. The Public Employment Program (PEP) is automatically triggered by the unemployment rate, since expenditures are authorized when the national unemployment rate equals or exceeds 4.5% for three consecutive months. In addition, local areas with unemployment rates of 6% or more for three consecutive months are eligible for funds, regardless of the national unemployment rate. Ninety percent of the costs of the program, which are primarily salaries (the law requires that at least 85% of all funds be used for salaries), are paid for by the federal government, with local jurisdictions paying the balance. While special preference in hiring is given to Vietnam veterans, the PEP is also intended to serve the

---

10. For a discussion of general and specific training see Gary Becker, *Human Capital: A Theoretical and Empirical Analysis, with Specific References to Education* (National Bureau of Economic Research, 1964), Chapter 1.

disadvantaged, welfare recipients, workers unemployed as a result of cut-backs in government spending, and low-income groups.

While the expansion of local government is an aim of the PEP, the key objective is to reduce unemployment. As a result, funds cannot be used to provide jobs that would otherwise be funded by local jurisdictions or other federal programs. And the jobs created must be "transitional" jobs in the sense that they lead to permanent employment either in the public or private sectors. Congress authorized the expenditure of one billion dollars during the first year of PEP's operations, and it has been estimated that 145,000 jobs were created at an average annual salary of $7200. Since the labor force during 1971 reached almost 85 million, the jobs created represent a maximum possible reduction in the unemployment rate of 0.17%. Clearly, the program is too small to be considered a major weapon in dealing with unemployment. If it were expanded, however, would it effectively reduce unemployment without simultaneously creating inflationary pressures? To put the question more precisely, will the PEP shift the Phillips curve toward the left, or merely move the economy along the Phillips curve in the direction of less unemployment at the expense of higher inflation?

Although a thorough analysis of the employment effects of this program will necessarily await a few years' experience with it, *a priori* reasoning suggests that the program will not have a substantial job-creation impact, for it does not fundamentally change the demand for labor. The requirement that the program be set into motion only when the unemployment rate equals 4.5% or higher for three consecutive months, coupled with minimum restrictions on who must be hired under the program, means that those who obtain employment under PEP will be those who would have been hired by the private sector had aggregate demand been used to stimulate expansion. In this respect, the program is similar to any stimulation of aggregate demand, such as a tax cut.

It will be difficult to enforce the provision that those hired under the program be "additional" to what the state or local jurisdiction would have hired in the absence of the program, especially in the long run. For example, if a locality had planned to increase employment by 2%, but finds it can count on the PEP to pay for 90% of the costs of hiring, the temptation to abandon its initial plans and fill the planned 2% increase with those hired under the PEP will be difficult to resist.

Our conclusion that the current PEP does not shift the Phillips curve should not be interpreted to mean that no public employment program would be effective in reducing unemployment without inflationary consequences. If those hired by state and local governments would not have been hired, either in the public or private sectors, in the absence of a public employment program, the effect would be to reduce unemployment without reducing vacancies. Unemployment would be reduced directly by government hiring, but since the jobs created did not previously exist, vacancies are unaffected. The result is a leftward shift in the vacancy-unemployment curve and a consequent leftward shift in the Phillips curve. And to the extent that a public employment program provides non-transitional jobs and is accompanied by manpower programs of the kind discussed above, it can reduce labor turnover and can contribute to non-inflationary employment expansion.[11]

SUMMARY

The policies that flow from the labor-market analysis of the Phillips curve are aimed at both the supply of and demand for labor. If they are concerned with training workers to equip them with necessary job skills, they are equally concerned with restructuring jobs so they can be done by workers with existing skills. If they are concerned with computerizing employment services to aid the worker in finding a job faster, they are equally concerned with aiding the employer to find the worker faster. The focus is on the factors which affect quitting, hiring, and segmentation of the labor market. This focus differentiates the macroeconomic approach to manpower from the programs that marked the decade of the 1960s. Manpower programs during the 1960s were almost exclusively supply-based.

The examples given of methods to reduce the trade-off between inflation and unemployment are meant to be illustrative rather than exhaustive. They suggest that it is possible to deal with inflation through the use of manpower policies, in addition to traditional monetary and fiscal policies. Manpower planning in the United States is in its infancy. It is difficult to characterize efforts to deal with the labor force as "planning." Until recently, all manpower programs were aimed at specifically disadvantaged members of the labor force: coal miners in Appalachia who became unemployed because the coal industry declined; technologically displaced workers throughout the country; unskilled workers; teen-age workers. These programs have been essentially *ad hoc* responses to serious unemployment problems for groups within the labor force.

The programs outlined are the beginning of a manpower-planning policy which would complement monetary and fiscal policy. Serious manpower planning would require a much greater knowledge of labor-market relationships than we now have. And ultimately, it would require advance knowledge of the output decisions of the industrial sector. These output decisions could then be translated into manpower needs which could be anticipated. Only during wartime have Western economies attempted this

11. A discussion of public employment and job stability can be found in Bennett Harrison, *Public Employment and Urban Poverty* (The Urban Institute, June 1971).

kind of planning, although Sweden has made extensive progress in this area during the last several years.[12]

CRITIQUE OF THE LABOR-MARKET APPROACH TO MACROECONOMIC BALANCE

The labor-market model and policy prescriptions presented in this chapter have met with objections from manpower economists who have closely studied existing programs.[13] The objections they raise are based on an intimate knowledge of the operation and effectiveness of manpower programs. Without quarreling with the analysis of the three labor-market relationships underlying the Phillips curve, critics have claimed that the policy prescriptions are unworkable.

Manpower programs, in contrast with monetary and fiscal policies, are subject to exceedingly long lags. First there is a lag between the recognition time for needed program changes and the implementation time for such changes. Second, there is an even longer delay before the changing policy has an impact on the labor force. It takes time to obtain training facilities, hire instructors, recruit trainees, and place graduates in jobs. It would not be unreasonable to estimate a period of two and a half years as a minimum, from the start to the finish, for this cycle. Since business cycles have a shorter duration, it would be impossible to coordinate manpower programs with aggregate economic activity. Since the inception of manpower programs in 1961, extensive research has gone into analyzing the reasons for their success and failure. This research points to the extreme complexity of the problems of the disadvantaged worker and the long period of time needed to deal with these problems. Attempts to speed up the development of new training programs lead to a watering down of their contents and a reduction of their present effectiveness.

The manpower approach overestimates the ability of manpower programs to deal with problems created by institutional rigidities. For example, expanding the supply of labor in occupations with skill shortages should relieve inflationary pressures. However, many shortages exist because of institutional barriers that are created to develop shortages and thereby raise wages. This is characteristic of almost all occupations that involve licensing, occupations where unions limit membership, and professional jobs with degree requirements. Manpower programs that retrain workers for skills in such areas will not succeed in overcoming these institutional barriers. The manpower approach also ignores such factors as

12. See Eli Ginzberg, "Sweden's Manpower Policies: A Look at the Leader," *Manpower* (November 1970).
13. See Sar A. Levitan, "Manpower Programs for a Healthier Economy," in *Manpower Programs in the Policy Mix*, ed. Lloyd Ulman (Johns Hopkins University Press, 1973).

union contracts with escalator clauses, oligopolistic sellers, discrimination, and the vigilance (or lack of it) of antitrust law enforcement. All these factors contribute to the Phillips curve problem, yet labor-market analysis does not account for them.

Perhaps the most pointed criticism has less to do with the economics of manpower programs than it does with the politics of funding manpower programs. Present manpower programs are directed at the disadvantaged. If manpower programs are expanded to take on the labor-market roles outlined above, they will of necessity be less oriented towards specifically disadvantaged workers and more oriented towards the average worker. Their aim would be to reduce labor turnover. What would be the impact on the disadvantaged? Would their interests be ignored in the effort to reduce average turnover in the labor market? At present the average duration of employment is two years. Moreover, if expanded manpower programs failed to reduce the unemployment-inflation trade-off, would Congress become less inclined to fund these programs? This would result in even fewer training resources being devoted to the disadvantaged.

The debate on the proper role of manpower programs in aggregate economic policy is in its infancy. For that matter, our experience with manpower programs of any kind is relatively recent. Undoubtedly, as we continue to analyze efforts in the manpower area, our knowledge of both the function of labor markets and how to make them more efficient will improve.

Incomes
Policies

15

Chapter

In 301 A.D., the Emperor Diocletian issued an edict for the Roman Empire that fixed maximum prices for a range of goods and services including food, raw materials, textiles, transport, and placed a ceiling on wages. Its enforcement mechanism was the threat of death to violators.[1] This is an early example of an incomes policy. Incomes policies are efforts undertaken by governments to restrain inflation by actively participating in wage and price decisions. In modern times, they have been resorted to by Western countries when monetary and fiscal policies have appeared to be ineffective in achieving both low levels of unemployment and stable price levels. In Chapter 14, we discussed demand and supply theories of inflation, and the monetary and fiscal policies used to control inflation by lowering the level of aggregate demand. According to Phillips-curve analysis, the consequence of reducing inflation is increasing unemployment. Policy makers are thus faced with a difficult and politically unpopular choice: less inflation and more unemployment, or less unemployment and more inflation. They have turned to incomes policies in the hope of finding methods that will lower inflation while not increasing unemployment.

In this chapter, we explore some of the history of the application of incomes policies to the task of stabilizing a national economy. We are particularly concerned with the economic rationale for incomes policies, and the lessons to be learned from efforts to apply them. Since the Western European countries have engaged in extensive incomes policies during the post-World War II period, some attention will be paid their experiences. However, generalizations about the experiences in one country are not necessarily applicable to another. Much of the discussion, therefore, will focus on U.S. institutions. First, we discuss the experience of selected Euro-

1. For a fascinating history of monetary inflation during the reign of the Roman emperor Diocletian, see H. Mitchell, "The Edict of Diocletian," *Canadian Journal of Economics and Political Science*, Vol. 13 (1947), pp. 1–12.

pean countries, and then turn to an examination of incomes policies in the United States. Toward that end, we will consider the institutions that are developed to create and enforce controls, and the criteria for wage and price changes.

Although the criteria for granting wage increases have varied with different incomes policies, they have all had to consider the mathematical relationships among unit-labor costs, the productivity of labor, and wages. The unit-labor cost is the cost of labor entering into one unit of output. If one worker earns $2.00 per hour, and produces 20 units of output in an hour, the unit-labor cost is $.10. By productivity we mean the average productivity of labor, or, alternatively, the number of units of output per worker-hour. The average productivity of the worker in our example is 20 units per hour. We can define the average productivity of labor for every industry. In addition, we can define the average productivity of labor for the economy as a whole as the total number of units of output per worker-hour. The average productivity for all economies is rising over time because of new inventions, augmentation of the capital stock relative to the labor force, and increased education of the labor force. If an economy is experiencing an increase in average productivity, wages can be raised by the same percentage without raising unit-labor costs: a conclusion illustrated in Chapter 13 (see Table 13-2).

EUROPEAN INCOMES POLICIES

European countries have been much less reluctant than the United States to use incomes policies as part of their arsenal of macroeconomic stabilization tools. In some countries, efforts to control wages have been institutionalized in specifically created boards and councils; in others, the government has indirectly attempted to influence wage and price changes. It is difficult to make generalizations about European experience because each country has had somewhat different objectives. Even within a country, objectives sought from incomes policies have changed over time and have included controlling inflation, improving balance-of-payments positions, and redistributing income. To illustrate the variations in objectives and problems with incomes policies, we present sketches of experiences with those policies in the United Kingdom, France, and Germany.

United Kingdom

In Britain, since the end of World War II, incomes policies have been used to deal with a series of balance-of-payment crises and with an unsatisfactory rate of growth in output. Low levels of labor productivity, high unit-labor costs, and strong unionism have made it difficult to keep wages from rising, even in the face of rising unemployment, and has led the government, especially during the 1960s, to rely on incomes policies to stimulate output and reduce domestic inflation.

British policy makers have considered devaluation to be an alternative to incomes policies because it would increase the demand for British exports and reduce the level of imports. An incomes policy would, if effective, keep unit-labor costs from rising and make British exports more competitive in the world market. Devaluation was vigorously resisted, especially by the Labour government, which came to power in October 1964, because of the blow it would strike to British prestige, and because it would initially raise the cost of living. (Since many consumer goods are imported, a devaluation would raise the domestic prices of these goods). The limited success of the incomes-policy effort is reflected by the devaluation that the government was eventually forced to accept in November 1967.

Before 1965, to combat inflation, incomes policies were invoked several times to meet balance-of-payments crises. After the October 1964 elections, incomes policies were used more broadly and vigorously, with enforcement techniques passing through several stages. First, the government tried to get voluntary compliance based on the good relationship that was expected to exist between a Labour government and the unions. When the average rate of hourly earnings increased by 7.6% in 1968, a statutory freeze was imposed, with a goal of zero increase. This effectively reduced the average hourly earnings rate increase to 1.7%, but as soon as the freeze was relaxed, average hourly earnings increased by 8.8% per year. The labor unions, initially well disposed to incomes policies, had become openly hostile by 1969. Their opposition, combined with the approach of a general election, led the government to weaken the policy when it came up for reconsideration. Although it was not dropped entirely, the incomes policy was put in a deep freeze. Prospects for a revival of incomes policies decreased after June 1970 when a Conservative government was elected, because the Conservatives had been ideologically and politically opposed to the Labour government's incomes policies.

Evaluations of the success of the policies of the 1960s have varied. The Price and Incomes Board, which was charged with operating the incomes policy, has claimed that it was successful in restraining wage increases and in inspiring a larger than expected aggregate output increase, but other economic studies dispute this conclusion. It appears that incomes policies were more effective when (1) voluntary compliance was backed by strong government compulsion, (2) when the freeze on wages was absolute (what the British have called a "nil norm"), and (3) when the country was facing a currency crisis. Even these conditions were not enough to insure success for more than a temporary period, as illustrated by the need for devaluation, and the increased hostility of the Labour government to controls.

Although incomes policies are now out of favor with the Biritsh government, it is not impossible that a future balance-of-payments crisis or continued wage increases would lead to a revival, although one would expect that such a revival would have more limited goals than those accompanying earlier policies.[2]

France

In contrast to the incomes policies of other European nations in the post-World War II period, France has relied almost entirely on price control as a means of dealing with rising wages and inflation. Control of prices rather than wages reflects the belief in France that inflation is caused more by excess demand elements—factors that cause the *CM* function to shift—than by collective bargaining pressures from unions. Trade unionism in France, in contrast to Britain, has been organizationally weak, and opposition to collective bargaining among employers has remained strong.

Price control in France enables the government to set prices in the nationalized industries of coal, gas, and electricity. Most of France's industries have participated in government "planning contracts" that permit some flexibility in pricing, in return for which the industries agree to allocate productivity gains among wages, dividends, investment, and development research. In addition, the industries are subject to a compulsory review of price increases. The planning contracts are part of the French system of national planning known as "indicative planning," which is a unique combination of government coercion and industry cooperation. The government planning board provides industries with a set of demand projections (based on an input-output table for the economy), and makes recommendations for achieving the plan's targets. A combination of subsidies offered to firms following the plan's guidelines, plus education of industry leaders regarding the plan's benefits, encourages fulfillment of the plan's requirements.[3]

The political and economic disruption that occurred during 1968 led to devaluation, a temporary price freeze, and renewed efforts to administer planning contracts. Although the price-control policy was not completely discredited by the events of 1968 (consumer prices rose more slowly than increases in wages in 1968), the political and economic limitations of price

2. Two recent evaluations of European incomes policies are: Lloyd Ulman and R. J. Flanagan, *Wage Restraint: A Study of Incomes Policies in Western Europe* (University of California Press, 1971); and Walter Galenon, ed., *Incomes Policy: What Can We Learn from Europe?* (New York State School of Industrial and Labor Relations, 1973). For a discussion of Britain's National Board for Prices and Incomes, and its operations between 1965 and 1970, see J. F. Pickering, "The Prices and Incomes Board and Private Sector Prices: A Survey," *The Economic Journal*, June 1971. A two-equation quarterly model of wage and price inflation and restraint policies in the United Kingdom is provided by R. G. Lipsey and J. M. Parkin, "Incomes Policy: A Reappraisal," *Economica*, Vol. 37 (1970), 115–138; and J. M. Parkin, "Incomes Policy: Some Further Results on the Determination of the Rate of Change of Money Wages," *Economica*, Vol. 37 (1970), 386–401.
3. An excellent description and analysis of French planning is provided by S. S. Cohen, *Modern Capitalist Planning: The French Model* (Harvard University Press, 1969).

restraint were obvious. The effect of price controls on wages was not great enough to achieve balance-of-payments equilibrium.

Since 1968, the government has tried to restrain wage increases through the use of employee profit-sharing plans and contracts that link pay to labor productivity while still avoiding direct wage controls. The success of these new attempts is uncertain so far, but they have not been greeted enthusiastically by workers or the labor movement. Had the price controls been successful, holding the line on the prices of consumer goods would have led to substantially moderated wage increases nationwide, which would have abated cost-push pressures on goods that enter the export market. The consequence would have been greater exports and amelioration of balance-of-payments disequilibrium.

West Germany

Prior to the 1960s, inflationary pressures in West Germany were the result of excess demand from rightward shifts in the *CM* curve. Unions had exhibited great restraint in avoiding inflationary bargaining. Strong employer resistance and the memories of the devastating unemployment and inflation prior to World War II had combined to make German unions unusually reluctant to push for wage settlements that might contribute to inflation.

During the 1960s, however, unit-labor costs increased more rapidly than did productivity. As a result, the average cost of producing the nation's output increased, and out of a fear that demand-induced inflation would lead to a wage inflation, followed by still greater domestic price increases, economists and politicians recommended incomes policies focusing on wage controls. The first attempt to control wages occurred in 1960, when the President of the Bundesbank called for a wage guidepost pegged at 4%, the assumed annual average rate of increase in productivity. When the rise in average productivity proved to be 6.4% in 1961, unions severely criticized the prediction, and have remained doubtful about the reliability of government guidelines.

By the mid-1960s, a seven-man Council of Economic Experts was established to make politically neutral recommendations for noninflationary wage increases. The council issues annual reports indicating the rate of wage increase consistent with economic stability. It meets with unions and management leaders and attempts to persuade them to accept wage agreements that are linked to average productivity increases. Enforcement has been voluntary, and the council has urged the government not to intervene if employers or labor violate the wage standards.

So far, the West German incomes policies and voluntary cooperation have not been put to the test. However, a new militancy among younger West German workers surfaced in 1969, and it is increasingly less likely that voluntary bargaining institutions can continue to be as effective as in the past. In actuality, West German incomes policies have amounted to semi-official "jaw-boning" and have depended on the self-restraint of the West German worker.

U.S. INCOMES POLICY DURING TWO WORLD WARS

There is nothing so effective as a war to give governments license to alter the rules of the economic game. During peacetime, there are many obstacles to central direction and coordination of economic institutions. During wartime, these obstacles are easily overcome. This seems to hold true in other crises situations, suggesting that incomes policies show the greatest promise for realizing short-run objectives, but cannot be expected to serve as well in the long run.

World War I

Seven months before the United States entered World War I, Congress authorized a Council of National Defense to coordinate industries and resources for a possible war effort. President Wilson appointed an Advisory Commission, consisting of representatives from industry and labor, which quickly reorganized itself into several specific agencies once the war broke out. One of them, the General Munitions Board, became concerned with the prices government paid for its purchases—a price-control effort in a small sphere. A Committee on Supplies was charged with securing the production of needed raw materials. Within a year after the initial establishment of the Council of National Defense, it became apparent that more comprehensive industry control was necessary, and the council created for that purpose the War Industries Board. The War Industries Board created a Price Fixing Committee that provided advice on prices of raw materials. Additionally, Congress created Food and Fuel Administrations to regulate prices and stimulate production in these industries.

   These *ad hoc* agencies (and they by no means exhaust the list) had to stimulate production of war-related commodities while restraining rising prices occasioned by new government demand. Food prices were rising during the war, owing to the needs of the Allies for wheat, which the United States was supplying. Consumers had begun hoarding essential foods to avoid being caught by a shortage. The government was faced with need to increase food-supply production, which was accomplished by encouraging greater agricultural efficiency, and by making direct payments to farmers and processors of beef, pork, fluid milk, and butter.[4]

4. The U.S. Department of Agriculture's Economic Report No. 223, *Price Control Program 1917–1971*, April 1972, provides a review of government efforts to deal with food prices, as well as an excellent bibliography.

There was no wage control during World War I. Government efforts were centered around prices, with the expectation that controlling the cost of living would mitigate labor's demand for wage increases.

Fuel shortages led to a series of measures to stimulate production while curtailing consumption. National campaigns were launched, including "heatless Mondays," and for the first few months of 1918, non-defense plants (with some exceptions) were ordered to cease burning fuel on Mondays.

In summary, the U.S. foray into an incomes policy during World War I was limited. The objectives were simply to expand production of key outputs and keep prices from rising rapidly. The response to these needs was the creation of *ad hoc* agencies that secured cooperation from industry and labor. At the war's end, the machinery was dismantled.[5]

World War II

The chief difference between the efforts taken during the World Wars was the extent of control. During World War I, controls were selective and limited. During World War II, control of prices became the rule, to which exceptions were granted. Selective price control was established in early 1941. An Office of Price Administration (OPA) was created by Executive Order, and charged with developing and administering a program of price control for the duration of the war. In April 1942, the OPA issued a General Maximum Price Regulation that froze all prices at their March 1942 levels.

Initially food was exempted from the freeze, but by 1943 the OPA extended the freeze to food as well. Consumer rationing was instituted for such essentials as meat and vegetables, gasoline, tires, and other goods. The black market that arose was only minimal, due to vigorous enforcement and popular support for the war. The OPA instituted 280,000 enforcement orders against violators, winning 95% of its cases.

Since the nation's output of nonwar goods and services was insufficient to meet demand at existing prices, there was tremendous upward pressure on prices. Some of this pressure was alleviated, however, by the government's massive campaigns to persuade individuals to save by buying bonds. Part of the success of the price-control program is attributed to the willingness of many people to defer consumption until after the war, in full expectation that their savings could be used to buy consumer goods unavailable during the war.

Controls did not last long after the war was over. Food rationing was terminated by mid-1945; the excess-profits tax was repealed by the end of that year; and although the OPA continued to exist into 1947, its effective-

5. A detailed account of price control during World War I is provided by G. P. Adams, Jr., *Wartime Price Control* (American Council on Public Affairs, 1942).

ness was over with the war, and with it, the shaky stabilization agreement also came to an end.

The control system worked effectively during World War II for several reasons:

1. The major interest groups in the economy agreed to cooperate for the war effort.
2. Unions agreed not to strike, and to accept a wage freeze in return for price freezes on most consumer goods.
3. Business agreed to controls and to an excess-profits tax in return for labor cooperation.
4. Farm interests accepted controls on food prices in return for subsidies and favorable farm prices.

The economists administering the price-control program found the controls to be effective and not nearly as difficult to administer as many had anticipated before the war.[6] John K. Galbraith, one of the key administrators of the OPA, has observed that price controls were most effective (and most easily enforced) for goods produced by imperfect competitors. The nearer the market approached the economist's model of pure competition, the more difficult it was to control prices. The greatest difficulties were encountered in controlling food and clothing prices, and even with rationing, it was difficult to counteract the black market in these commodities.

Galbraith offers several explanations. In imperfectly competitive industries, prices are relatively inflexible, and once announced by firms in an industry, tend to hold for several months at a time. The initiative for price changes generally is taken by the seller, rather than the buyer. In making these observations, Galbraith wrote: "I am tempted to frame a theorem that is all too evident in this discussion: it is relatively easy to fix prices that are already fixed."[7]

WAGE-PRICE GUIDEPOSTS

The first peacetime efforts at control were the wage and price guideposts adopted by the Kennedy administration in 1962 as a means of restraining cost-push inflation. The guideposts attempted to limit average wage increases to the extent of average increases in productivity. Key wage and price decisions were monitored by the Council of Economic Advisers, and pressure was put on union leaders and industry managers to keep increases

6. S. E. Harris, *Price and Related Controls in the United States* (McGraw-Hill, 1945); see also J. K. Galbraith, *A Theory of Price Control* (Harvard University Press, 1952).
7. Galbraith, *A Theory of Price Control*, p. 17.

within limits recommended by the Council. However, in 1967, the guideposts were abandoned.

If the guideposts and the philosophy that lay behind them were merely a chapter in American economic history they would warrant no more than a footnote here. But they are of more than historical significance; the guideposts provide a model for macroeconomic control which may become increasingly appealing in the United States, especially after experience with the more pervasive wage-price controls.

GUIDELINES FOR THE GUIDEPOSTS

Both Presidents Truman and Eisenhower used the office of the presidency to influence key wage and price decisions, but it was not until 1962, in the Annual Report of the Council of Economic Advisers, that the text for guideline policy was laid out. In six brief pages, the council answered the question: "How is the public to judge whether a particular wage-price decision is in the national interest?"[8]

The council made a judgment that the functional distribution of income—that is, the distribution of income between wage earners and capital earners—had to remain unchanged as a condition for obtaining even minimal cooperation from union leaders and firm managers. While labor and capital would each prefer to take a larger share of the income pie (at the expense of the other) if they could get away with it, both can be persuaded to strike an uneasy bargain of stabilizing the current distribution. In the absence of such an agreement, cost-push inflation would be inevitable, as unions try to push up their members' wages, driving down profits, while firms try to combat unions' successes by raising prices to increase profits.

The basis of price and wage decisions, the council claimed, should be the average productivity increase for the economy. If average wage increases equal the national average productivity increase prices need not change for relative income shares to remain constant. A simple arithmetical example illustrates this proposition. Assume that the sales from one worker's work for one year is $10,000. If his or her wages are $7500, then the remainder of $2500 goes to owners of other factors of production, primarily capital. Now apply a productivity increase of 3.5%. Sales from the worker's work for the next year will be $10,350—if prices do not change. Allowing the worker's wages to rise with the productivity increase brings them up to $7762.50. The difference between the value of the worker's output and wages is now $2587.50, an increase of 3.5%. The pre-wage-increase and post-wage-increase income distribution is unchanged:

8. *Economic Report of the President Together with the Annual Report of the Council of Economic Advisers* (U.S. Government Printing Office, 1962), 185–190.

$$\text{Capital/Labor} = \$2500/\$7500 = \$2587.50/\$7762.0 = 1/3$$

The proposition that relative shares remain constant when wages increase at the same rate that average productivity increases, can also be proved algebraically, assuming that the general price level is unchanged. Let W = an index of wages, P = an index of prices, Y = physical output, N = quantity of labor; and let subscripts 1 and 2 refer to periods 1 and 2. If prices do not change, $P_1 = P_2 = P$. We begin with the premise that the increase in wages equals the increase in average productivity:

$$\frac{W_2 - W_1}{W_1} = \frac{Y_2/N_2 - Y_1/N_1}{Y_1/N_1}$$

Multiply both sides by Y_1/N_1:

$$\frac{W_2 Y_1}{W_1 N_1} - \frac{Y_1}{N_1} = \frac{Y_2}{N_2} - \frac{Y_1}{N_1}$$

Multiply both sides by $PN_1 N_2 W_1$:

$$PN_2 W_2 Y_1 = PN_1 W_1 Y_2$$

Divide both sides by $W_1 N_1 W_2 N_2$:

$$\frac{PN_2 W_2 Y_1}{W_1 N_1 W_2 N_2} = \frac{PN_1 W_1 Y_2}{W_1 N_1 W_2 N_2} = \frac{PY_1}{W_1 N_1} = \frac{PY_2}{W_2 N_2}$$

Subtract one from both sides

$$\frac{PY_1}{W_1 N_1} - \frac{W_1 N_1}{W_1 N_1} = \frac{PY_2}{W_2 N_2} - \frac{W_2 N_2}{W_2 N_2}$$

Since $PY = WN +$ Profits, then

$$\frac{\text{Profits}}{W_1 N_1} = \frac{\text{Profits}}{W_2 N_2}$$

Therefore, the distribution of income between capital and labor is unchanged.

Assuming the constancy of income distribution between labor and capital, the council established the principle that average wage increases should equal average productivity gains. In industries where productivity gains are equal to the national average, prices will be constant. In industries where productivity exceeds the national average, prices will fall. And where productivity gains are below the national average (or zero), prices will rise. From this, the price and wage guideposts were formulated. Wages would increase in all industries at the average rate productivity increased for the economy as a whole. The rationale for the wage guidepost was that competition in the labor market results in a tendency toward equality of wages for similar jobs, regardless of the productivity in a specific industry. The price guidepost called for prices to decrease, remain constant, or increase with respect to similar changes in industrial productivity as measured against the national average.

If wages are supposed to serve the function of regulating labor input among industries, and prices are supposed to serve the function of allocating output among buyers, would not these regulatory mechanisms be destroyed under the guideposts? The council, anticipating these and related problems, provided for wage and price changes that deviated from the guideposts under certain conditions. They are:

(1) Wage-rate increases would exceed the general rate in an industry which would otherwise be unable to attract sufficient labor; or in which wage rates are exceptionally low compared with the range of wages earned elsewhere by similar labor, because the bargaining position of workers has been weak in particular local labor markets.

(2) Wage-rate increases would fall short of the general guide rate in an industry which could not provide jobs for its entire labor force, even in times of generally full employment; or in which wage rates are exceptionally high compared with the range of wages earned elsewhere by similar labor, because the bargaining position of workers has been especially strong.

(3) Prices would rise more rapidly, or fall more slowly, than indicated by the general guide rate in an industry in which the level of profits was insufficient to attract the capital required to finance a needed expansion in capacity; or in which costs other than labor costs had risen.

(4) Prices would rise more slowly, or fall more rapidly, than indicated by the general guide in an industry in which the relation of productive capacity to full-employment demand shows the desirability of an outflow of capital from the industry; or in which costs other than labor costs have fallen; or in which excessive market power has resulted in rates of profit substantially higher than those earned elsewhere on investments of comparable risk.[9]

The reasons the council offered for permitting deviations from the guideposts in wage and price decisions are sufficient to suggest the complexity of administering them. The determination of "level of profits," or "exceptionally high wage rates," or "needed expansion in capital," is rarely clear cut.

In the 1962 report, the council also called attention to the conceptual problems that had to be faced to arrive at an average productivity measure. How long a period should be used to measure productivity trends? Yearly changes are too erratic as a guide to wage changes. Longer periods could bias the productivity measure downward if productivity is rising. For example, the average annual percentage change in output per man-hour, measured from 1909 to 1960, was 2.4%, but the period from 1947 to 1960

9. Ibid., p. 189.

witnessed a 3% rate. The council eventually settled on a 3.2% rate as a measure of productivity gains. For shorter periods, say five years, it is necessary to isolate the productivity trend from changes in productivity that are the result of temporary swings in capital investment. Another difficulty arises from alternative ways of measuring output and labor input, which could result in different measures of labor productivity.

Contrary to what is popularly believed, the guideline program was not voluntary. It is true that there was no explicit legal authority, but in fact the administration had several weapons at its disposal. The personal power of the president could be invoked to urge compliance from key firms and unions, with specific price and wage changes that the CEA judged to be noninflationary. The antitrust division of the Justice Department could be assigned the task of investigating a given industry for possible violations in restraint of trade. The threat of investigation, either implied or explicit, was often sufficient to gain "voluntary" cooperation. For some industries, the existence of huge government stockpiles of the industry's commodity posed an economic threat. If the industry raised prices, the government could unload surpluses at lower prices, thereby making any announced price increase short-lived. Although it was never used, this tactic was threatened when aluminum companies announced a price rate increase during early 1966. The threat proved sufficient.

The weapons against unions were weaker. Primarily, unions were talked into restraining their wage demands by a promise from the administration that price increases would be limited by the government. The issue of income distribution between labor and capital does not present itself as forcefully in the United States as it does in Western Europe. This is because labor's share, the fraction of national income which is "compensation of employees," has remained within the narrow range of 65% to 71% during the post-World War II period. In several Western European countries, the share of national income going to labor has been increasing, with the result that European unions are reluctant to agree to an existing distribution.

U.S. INCOMES POLICIES DURING THE 1970s

On August 15, 1971, President Richard M. Nixon announced a "New Economic Program," under which all wages and prices were frozen for a ninety-day period. A Cost of Living Council, composed of key government officials, was established to monitor the freeze and to provide a framework for an incomes policy to commence at the end of the ninety-day period. Prior to the announcement of his new program, President Nixon had taken the advice of monetarist economists, and followed an "economic game plan" that relied primarily on monetary policy and only secondarily on fiscal policy. Several of the president's close economic advisers had spoken out against incomes policies, and it was clear, prior to the announcement, that wage and price controls represented an incursion into private markets, to which the administration had a strong ideological aversion.

President Nixon had often commented unfavorably on the bureaucracy needed to control prices and wages during World War II, on the basis of his experience as a lawyer with the OPA. What explains, then, the adoption of an incomes policy? When Nixon took office in January 1969, unemployment was 3.5%; by August 1971, it had risen to 6.1%. The rise in unemployment resulted from efforts to reduce inflation by moving down and to the right along the Phillips curve. However, the wholesale price index, which was rising at the rate of 4.8% in 1969, increased during the first half of 1971 to 5.2%. Disappointment with the input of monetary and fiscal policies in reducing the rate of inflation, concern with the high rate of unemployment and underutilization of plant capacity, the emergence of a balance-of-trade deficit for the first time in the post-World War II period, and the anticipation of a presidential election in 1972, all played a part in bringing about an incomes policy.

In addition to the freeze, the Nixon program called for the elimination of a federal excise tax on automobiles and the establishment of a 10% surcharge on all dutiable imports. These measures represented an attempt to affect the composition of aggregate demand. The elimination of the excise tax on automobiles was intended to stimulate demand in an industry which had excess capacity. The import surcharge was intended to stimulate domestic production of those goods that competed with imports, especially in such industries as steel, automobiles, textiles, and electronics. The effort to stimulate auto production recalled a campaign during the Eisenhower administration that exhorted consumers to purchase cars with the slogan: "You auto buy now!" Although the effort to affect the composition of consumer demand was not continued as the Nixon program was expanded, it did suggest that government could, via selective tax policy, attempt to funnel consumer demand toward depressed industries.

In the weeks following the freeze announcement, while economists, journalists, and legislators discussed the implications for future economic control, plans were laid for the second phase of the Nixon program. The Cost of Living Council established two decision-making agencies: a Price Commission with seven members representing the public; and a fifteen-member Pay Board, with five labor representatives, five business representatives, and five public members. Although there was initial reluctance, labor agreed to serve on the Pay Board (within six months, four of the five labor representatives quit the Pay Board, and it was then reconstituted with seven members, all representing the public). The Cost of Living Council established a three-level classification scheme for price and pay increases: large firms ($100 million in sales and 5000 employees) had to obtain advance clearance for wage and price changes; intermediate-size firms ($50–100 million in sales and 1000–5000 employees) had to report changes as they were effected (by 1972, intermediate-size firms no longer were required to report changes); and small firms, while not required to report changes, were asked to maintain records and keep within the guidelines established.

The Price Commission set 2.5% as a maximum permissible increase in prices, while the Pay Board adopted a 5.5% standard for wage increases. Both standards were based on an assumed long-term average productivity trend of 3% increase per year (a wage standard of 5.5% coupled with an average productivity trend of 3% implies a rise in unit labor costs of 2.5%).

Several wage settlements that exceeded the 5.5% standard were agreed upon by the Pay Board. According to Arnold Weber, an economist at the University of Chicago and former public member of the Pay Board, wage increases that exceeded the standard were approved in certain key industries (e.g., coal, railroads) out of fear of strikes.[10] Large wage increases prompted the firms affected to petition the Price Commission for price increases larger than 2.5%. The Price Commission sometimes refused to grant increases sufficient to cover the higher unit-labor costs. The result was complaints from industry about shrinking profits. Some coordination was provided through the Cost of Living Council, but problems that arose from the separation of the pay and price administrations were never eliminated.

No large-scale bureaucracy was required. Although wage and price standards were established, the allowable increases were not automatically granted. Firms had to petition the Pay Board or Price Commission and present evidence to justify their request. As a consequence, the administrative burdens of controls rested principally with individual firms. During 1972, about 4000 persons (of which 3000 were in the Internal Revenue Service) were directly involved in the stabilization program, in contrast to 60,000 during World War II, and 15,000 during the Korean War.

The most important exemption from the control procedure was farm prices, although controls were placed on processing and distribution activities. Since the price of fresh produce is affected by seasonal variation and weather conditions, it would have been extremely difficult to arrive at a base price from which increases could be granted. In addition, these prices are determined in competitive markets, and price fluctuations equilibrate supply and demand. The theory of the controls was that rising prices in the manufacturing sector were not the result of excess demand but of labor costs rising in excess of productivity. Thus, the prices of manufactured goods could be suppressed without shortages resulting. It was feared that controls on farm prices would result in shortages, as well as curtailment of supplies. To control rising foods prices, the administration resorted to measures intended to increase supplies. Limitations on the import of meat were suspended, government-controlled stocks of meat and grains were

10. Arnold Weber, "Making Controls Work," *The Public Interest*, no. 30, Winter 1973.

sold, export subsidies for wheat and rice were reduced, and limits on planting several commodities were eased.

On January 11, 1973, the president terminated mandatory wage and price controls over most of the economy, retaining controls on the food distribution and processing industry, the health care industry, and the construction industry. These three areas were considered to be particularly susceptible to wage and price increases. The Pay Board and Price Commission were abolished, and the Cost of Living Council, now under the leadership of Harvard economist John T. Dunlop, was given the task of monitoring the voluntary controls.

At the same time that the Pay Board and Price Commission were abolished, an advisory group to the Cost of Living Council was created. Consisting of ten members representing labor and management, the Labor-Management Advisory Committee's function was to recommend changes in the general wage standards formerly established by the Pay Board.

The Cost of Living Council continued to monitor key wage and price decisions. It was charged with the authority to issue a binding order for adjusting wage and price decisions that it considered excessive. In effect, the administration was telling major collective bargaining units that wage and price decisions considered excessive under Phase II would continue to be restrained under Phase III, with the major difference being that the Cost of Living Council would be "looking over business and labor's shoulder" rather than being directly involved in approving individual requests. However, in establishing Phase III, the administration gave little indication regarding how frequently and swiftly the Cost of Living Council would act to remedy excessive wage and price decisions.

What was the experience with the rate of increase on wages and prices before and during Phase II? In Table 15-1 several measures of prices and wages are presented for the pre-freeze periods, the ninety-day freeze, the first three months of Phase II, and the next nine months before the end of Phase II and the beginning of Phase III. With the exception of food, the figures show a decline in inflation during the freeze, a rise during the period after the freeze was lifted, and a decline thereafter to below pre-freeze rates. The statistics on wage increases parallel the sequence exhibited with prices. Average hourly earnings, which had risen at the rate of 6.9% before the freeze, dropped to a rate of 3.1% during the freeze. During the first three months after the freeze, they jumped to an annual rate of 9.5% and then fell to a rate of 5.6%.

With respect to Phase III, there was uneasiness from business, labor, and foreign sources regarding the willingness of the Nixon administration to act forcefully against inflationary wage and price decisions. The administration justified its decision to pare down the machinery of controls on the grounds that inflationary expectations had been halted, and that as the economy approached full employment, the distortions in resource allocation caused by controls would become severe. Evaluation of Phase III

Table 15-1   Changes in price measures, 1968 to 1972, and changes in wage measures, 1969 to 1972 (percent; seasonally adjusted annual rates)

	Pre-freeze		Freeze Phase I	Phase II	
Price Measure	Dec. 1968 to Dec. 1969	Dec. 1969 to Dec. 1970	Dec. 1970 to Aug. 1971	Aug. 1971 to Nov. 1971	Nov. 1971 to Feb. 1972	Feb. 1972 to Dec. 1972
Consumer price index:						
All items	6.1	5.5	3.8	1.9	4.8	3.0
Food	7.2	2.2	5.0	1.7	9.7	3.6
All items less food	5.7	6.5	3.4	2.3	2.9	3.0
Commodities less food	4.5	4.8	2.9	.0	2.4	2.5
Services[1]	7.4	8.2	4.5	3.1	4.7	3.3
Wholesale price index:						
All commodities	4.8	2.2	5.2	−.2	6.9	6.5
Farm products and processed foods and feeds	7.5	−1.4	6.5	1.1	14.7	14.7
Industrial commodities	3.9	3.6	4.7	−.5	4.0	3.4
	1968 IV to 1969 IV	1969 IV to 1970 IV	1970 IV to 1971 II	1971 II to 1971 IV	1971 IV to 1972 I	1972 I to 1971 IV[2]
Fixed weight GNP price deflators:						
Total GNP	5.4	5.1	5.9	3.0	6.1	3.2
Gross private product	5.1	4.5	5.0	2.6	4.5	2.9
Personal consumption expenditures	5.0	4.3	4.5	2.4	3.6	2.8
Implicit GNP price deflators:						
Total GNP	5.3	5.3	5.1	2.2	5.1[3]	2.3
Total U.S. purchases[4]	5.3	5.5	5.0	2.3	5.3[3]	2.6

Private business
GNP:

Nonfarm	4.7	5.1	4.3	1.2	3.6	1.5
Farm	10.4	−7.3	12.1	16.3	20.1	21.5

1) Based on unadjusted indexes as these prices have little seasonal movement.
2) Preliminary.
3) Increase in pay of Federal Government employees accounted for about 1¼ percentage points of the total increase.
4) Total GNP less net exports of goods and services.
Sources: *Department of Commerce, Bureau of Economic Analysis, and Department of Labor, Bureau of Labor Statistics.*

	Pre-freeze		Freeze Phase I	Phase II	
Wage Measure	Aug. 1969 to Aug. 1970	Aug. 1970 to Aug. 1971	Aug. 1971 to Nov. 1971	Nov. 1971 to Feb. 1972	Feb 1972 to Dec. 1972[1]
Average hourly earnings, private nonfarm economy[2]	6.9	6.9	3.1	9.5	5.6
	1969 II to 1970 II	1970 II to 1971 II	1971 II to 1971 IV	1971 IV to 1972 I	1972 I to 1972 IV[1]
Average hourly compensation, all employees:					
Total private economy	7.2	7.6	5.2	8.9	5.7
Nonfarm	7.1	7.6	5.1	8.9	5.9
Average hourly earnings, private nonfarm economy[2]	6.5	7.4	5.7	8.0	6.0

1) Preliminary.
2) Adjusted for overtime (in manufacturing only) and interindustry employment shifts.
Source: *Department of Labor, Bureau of Labor Statistics.*

would be premature; but it is possible to begin to weigh the impact of Phase II and other European and U.S. attempts at controlling inflation with incomes policies.

EVALUATING INCOMES POLICIES

In the course of describing incomes policies in Europe and the United States, we have touched on the issue of their effectiveness in achieving macroeconomic balance. Here we turn explicitly to the question of what incomes policies actually accomplish. We are not concerned only with whether inflation is slowed or stopped. What is crucial is that *inflation be slower than it would have been in the absence of controls*. It is perfectly possible that the onset of an incomes policy coincides with a reduction in inflation that is not directly a result of the policy. We cannot, therefore, merely compare the inflation rates before and after the policy to find an easy answer. An even more difficult question to answer is what is the long-run effect of incomes policies? If the policy is lifted, are inflationary forces that have been kept at bay unleashed? That is, does the policy merely buy time?

Several studies have attempted to determine if the Phillips curve has shifted to the left as a result of the policy. (For a description of the Phillips curve, see Chapter 13.) These studies estimate the relationship between unemployment and the rate of increase in wages that prevail with and without an incomes policy—and the difference is attributed to the policy.

Figure 15-1 shows a linear Phillips curve. The rate of increase in wages, $\Delta W/W$, is measured on the vertical axis, and the unemployment rate, U/L (the number of unemployed divided by the labor force), is measured on the horizontal axis. The equation for this simplified Phillips relationship is

$$\frac{\Delta W}{W} = a_1 - a_2\left(\frac{U}{L}\right)$$

The constant term, a_1, is the percentage increase in wages if the unemployment rate were zero; the negative slope, a_2, is an estimate of how much a given reduction in U/L, the unemployment rate, is associated with a given increase in $\Delta W/W$, the percentage increase in wages.

In order to determine the impact of an incomes policy on shifting this wage-rate/unemployment-rate relationship, the equation above can be modified to include a dummy variable, D. The dummy variable is assigned a value of one for those observations made during the period when the policy is in effect, and a value of zero for those observations made when there is no incomes policy. The new equation is

$$\frac{\Delta W}{W} = a_1 - a_2\left(\frac{U}{L}\right) + a_3 D$$

Notice that when there is no incomes policy, or $D = 0$, the two equations are identical. When the policy is in effect, however, and $D = 1$, the intercept on the vertical axis of the curve is $a_1 + a_3$. If the policy is effective, the Phillips curve should shift toward the origin—a given unemployment rate should now be associated with a lower rate of wage increase. An effective incomes policy, therefore, is one for which a_3 is negative, so that $a_1 + a_3$ is less than a_1. Thus, the intercept on the vertical axis is reduced by a_3. If the policy has no effect, a_3 will be zero.

The method described for estimating the impact of incomes policies is

Figure 15-1 A linear Phillips curve

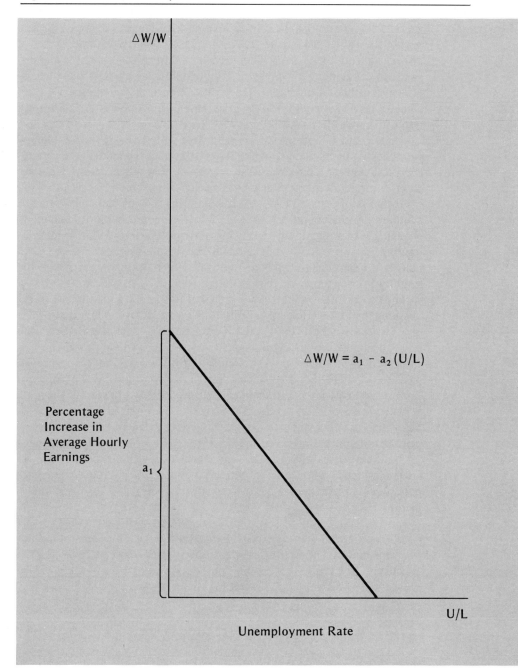

$\triangle W/W$

$\triangle W/W = a_1 - a_2\,(U/L)$

Percentage
Increase in
Average Hourly
Earnings

a_1

U/L

Unemployment Rate

a simplified version of ones actually used to statistically estimate their effectiveness. Several of these tests have been made of the U.S. wage-price guideposts, and most appear to show a positive impact on wage restraint during the 1962–1966 period. For example, a study by George L. Perry, projecting from the 1947–1960 relationship between wage changes and unemployment (among other factors) estimated what changes would have occurred in manufacturing wages in the absence of guideposts. He concluded that wages could have been expected to increase at a significantly faster rate than they actually did.[11]

While this and other studies point to a leftward shift in the Phillips curve during the guidepost period (suggesting that the guideposts were responsible for restraining wages), it is possible that other factors might account for the movement. Black and Kelejian, for example, suggest that the composition of demand had been stable during the guidepost period when compared to the period before 1962. When the composition of demand is changing, expanding industries increase wages to attract labor, while contracting industries do not reduce wages. As a result, wages were rising more rapidly prior to the guidepost period rather than during it, because of the stability in the composition of demand. According to this study, when a variable to account for the composition of demand is added to the wage-unemployment equation, the effects of the guideposts are eliminated.[12]

Several studies of the United Kingdom have concluded that the rate of wage change was largely unresponsive to the presence or absence of incomes policies. Under certain circumstances, incomes policies can even have an adverse effect. One study suggests that during periods of high unemployment, the impact of incomes policies is to encourage a higher rate of wage increase than would prevail without an official wage standard. Since high unemployment is associated with low demand for labor, it imposes automatic restraint on wage increases. However, the wage standard set by the incomes policy creates an expectation of appropriate wage increases, which is reflected in collective bargaining. As a result, the incomes policy raises the rate of wage increase during periods of high unemployment.[13]

Evaluation of Phase II of the Nixon administration's incomes policy is still in its beginning stages. Two early studies illustrate different evaluation approaches, and reach somewhat opposing conclusions regarding the effectiveness of Phase II. They are, no doubt, forerunners of the vigorous debate which will take place regarding the impact of controls.

11. See George L. Perry, "Wages and the Guideposts," *American Economic Review*, Vol. 57 (1967), pp. 897–904.
12. Stanley W. Black and Harry H. Kelejian, "A Macro Model of the U.S. Labor Market," *Econometrica*, Vol. 38 (1970), pp. 712–741.
13. See R. G. Lipsey and J. M. Parkin, "Incomes Policy: A Reappraisal," *op. cit., n.* 2; see also J. M. Parkin, "The Phillips Curve: A Historical Perspective, Lessons from Recent Empirical Studies and Alternative Policy Choices," in *The Current Inflation*, ed. H. G. Johnson and A. R. Nobay (London: Macmillan, 1971).

Barry Bosworth, of the Brookings Institution, compared the rates of inflation, wage change, and unemployment for the period just prior to the initiation of the Nixon freeze with the rates for the first three quarters[14] after the freeze, and found that controls slowed down all three variables. Even though specific wage and price decisions by the Pay Board and Price Commission exceeded the standards, a general climate of restraint was induced by the controls program. Bosworth observes that the wage restraint program was more effective than price restraint.

Robert J. Gordon, of the National Bureau of Economic Research and the University of Chicago, performed a statistical analysis of the impact of Phase II wage and price controls.[15] Gordon projected what wages and prices would have been in the absence of controls, and found that inflation was almost two percentage points below his prediction. This finding is in agreement with Bosworth's estimations that prices were restrained. The rate of wage advance predicted in the absence of controls, 0.5%, was only slightly above what occurred under controls. If indeed prices were restrained while wages were not, the distribution of income shifted in favor of labor.

CONCLUSION

It is difficult to find a clear-cut relationship between incomes policies and wage and price stability except for the favorable effect that they have had in the very short run.[16] Despite inconclusive evidence, incomes policies will continue to be part of macroeconomic stabilization efforts because they are politically popular during times of greater than average inflation. No doubt, the duration of controls will depend on their perceived effectiveness and the social cost incurred on their behalf. Even where the controls involve a small bureaucracy and therefore a low direct administrative cost, the society must bear the indirect cost to firms of reporting to the bureaucracy and maintaining records on productivity.

Controls replace, to some extent, the marketplace with a conference table. Key decisions on expansion and capital allocation are ultimately made by the controlling agencies instead of by firms.[17] Government neces-

14. Barry Bosworth, "Phase II: The U.S. Experiment with an Income Policy," *Brookings Papers on Economic Activity*, 1972, No. 2.
15. R. J. Gordon, "Wage-Price Controls and the Shifting Phillips Curve," in *Brookings Papers on Economic Activity*, no. 2, ed. A. M. Okun and G. L. Perry (The Brookings Institution, 1972).
16. This conclusion is drawn by Ulman and Flanagan, *Wage Restraint: A Study of Incomes Policies in Western Europe, op. cit., n 2*; and A. M. Ross, "Guideline Policy—Where We Are Now and How We Got There," in *Guidelines, Informal Controls, and the Market Place*, ed. G. P. Shultz and R. Z. Aliber (University of Chicago Press, 1966).
17. For a discussion of the inefficiencies associated with controls, see William Poole "Thoughts on the Wage-Price Freeze," *Brookings Papers on Economic Activity*, 1971, No. 2.

sarily becomes more directly involved in collective bargaining than it is in the absence of controls.

A major question mark regarding the use of controls is their duration. If a government is going to apply and release controls as the economy becomes inflationary and then stable, that in itself will fuel inflationary expectations, as participants rush to make sure that their interests are not being hurt when a freeze is applied. The union leader who negotiates a sizable increase in wages and fringe benefits just before a freeze will look smart to his rank-and-file; the corporate executive who raises prices just before the freeze will show a superior profit statement at the end of the year. The process is analogous to children playing musical chairs—when the music stops someone is left standing and looking foolish.[18] As a result, lifting controls may have to be a gradual process, with governments standing ready to reassert authority upon evidence of wage and price decisions that are in excess of previously established standards.

Despite the problem of timing, and the possible inefficiencies introduced by controls, incomes policies have many attractive features. As we have seen, the Keynesian prescription for inflation—reduction of aggregate demand—leads to an increase in unemployment. It may be that the level of unemployment necessary to reduce inflation to an acceptable level is politically intolerable. If so, no government will risk allowing unemployment to rise to the extent necessary to control inflation. At the same time, however, it is difficult for a government not to take action against rising inflation. Wage and price controls often present themselves as a politically palatable alternative.

18. On August 23, 1971, the *Wall Street Journal* carried a story with the banner "Many Firms Anticipating Controls, Raised Prices, and Reviewed Wages Before Freeze." The article points out that numerous concerns raised list prices and discounts in the hopes that a higher list price would be advantageous if a freeze came about. Many companies revised their salary structures to be prepared to claim, in the event of controls, that their plans predated the freeze.

Foreign Economic Relations

16
Chapter

The economic relations between the United States and the rest of the world have been virtually ignored in the macroeconomic models presented so far, because macroeconomic theory can be explained with greater clarity in the context of a "closed" model (one which is divorced from foreign relations) than an "open" model. For most economies of the world, the omission of the foreign sector in a macroeconomic model would render the model useless. But in discussing the U.S. economy, foreign trade is of far less significance than for most other nations. Exports of goods and services have averaged only 5% to 6% of the U.S. GNP during the post-World War II period. Of the approximately 80 million jobs in the United States, only about 750,000 are in the foreign-trade sector. These figures suggest that a closed model of the U.S. economy is not unrealistic.

Yet, although U.S. foreign trade is relatively small, it has become an important consideration to national policymakers. Often the government's desire to balance international accounts has led to policies that yield results opposite those needed in the domestic economy. In the early 1960s, for example, the desire to alleviate the U.S. balance-of-payments problem was probably responsible for the government's failure to pursue an expansionary policy to reduce the unemployment rate.

This chapter shows how our closed macroeconomic models can be expanded to include foreign economic relations. Consideration is given to the trade of goods and services (and the consequences that trade has for output and employment), and the means of international payment (and the consequences for domestic monetary policy of the world's monetary arrangements).

IMPORT AND EXPORT FUNCTIONS

The foreign-trade sector consists of exports (Ex), which are goods and services produced domestically and sold to foreigners, and imports (Im), which are goods and services produced abroad but consumed by United States citizens. The production of exports creates real income and employment domestically. The demand for exports, therefore, has a stimulating impact on domestic production, as does government, investment, or consumer-sector demand. If the demand for exports should increase, the national product will rise, assuming slack in the economy. If the economy is fully employed, the impact of the rise in foreign demand for U.S. output would be inflationary, much as it would be if fiscal policy continued to stimulate the economy after the slack had been taken up.

Imports have just the opposite effect on the national product Purchasing power flows away from the domestic economy; imports represent a leakage from aggregate demand for domestic output. An increase in imports—owing to a change in tastes, for example—has a contractionary impact on the economy, much as a reduction in government spending would have. It should be apparent that we can expand our closed-economy model by redefining the equilibrium condition for the national product as

$$Y = C + I + G + (\text{Ex} - \text{Im})$$

Exports are part of the demand for output (on the right side of the equation), and represent part of domestic national product (on the left side of the equation). Since consumption, investment, and government include expenditures on imports, imports must be subtracted from the sum of these expenditures to determine a measure of the output attributable to the domestic economy.

The difference between exports and imports (Ex − Im) is referred to as the "balance of trade." For the United States, the merchandise balance of trade (the difference between exports and imports of goods) was positive for every year from 1945 to 1970. In 1971, it was negative in excess of two billion dollars. The reasons for this reversal are discussed below.

Exports are typically treated as an exogenous variable in macroeconomic models. This is done partly because foreign demand for output is a function of foreign incomes and tastes, and partly for analytical convenience. Changes in domestic productivity and the domestic price level influence foreign demand; yet, owing to the difficulties of including these variables in an explanatory model of export change, they are omitted from consideration.

Imports, on the other hand, are intimately related to the level of domestic income. Since imports to the United States are exports from the rest of the world, imports to some extent depend on price differentials. For example, if domestic prices should rise (all else being equal), foreign goods and services might be substituted for more expensive domestic goods. At the same time that the volume of imports increases, exports decrease, as foreign importers shift their purchases to countries that offer goods at relatively lower prices. An obvious implication is that domestic inflation, other things being equal, tends to further unbalance trade.

If we assume a level of imports that will take place regardless of the national income level, and a component that is related to national income, we can write an import function:

$$\text{Im} = m_1 + m_2 Y$$

Figure 16-1 shows this simple import function. Autonomous imports are equal to m_1. This represents imports that would take place regardless of changes in the national income level. Some amount of certain goods, such as coffee beans, will be imported regardless of national-income fluctuations. This function assumes that the remainder of annual imports will vary with national income. The marginal propensity to import, m_2, relates changes in imports to changes in national income in the same way that the marginal propensity to consume relates changes in consumption to changes in national income. This simplified function treats imports as an aggregate variable. In complex models, separate equations are specified for imports of services and goods.

Although this simplified import function ignores changes in tastes and relative price levels between U.S. goods and services and foreign goods and services, it is not altogether unrealistic. There is a close correlation between yearly changes in imports and yearly changes in GNP for the United States.

INCORPORATION OF TRADE INTO A MACROECONOMIC MODEL

With the introduction of the foreign-trade sector, the closed model introduced in Chapter 5 can be expanded. By augmenting our model to handle relations with the rest of the world, a greater degree of realism is obtained. Starting with the equilibrium condition in an open-economy model, and assuming that investment, government expenditure, and exports are exogenous, we have

$$Y = C + \bar{I} + \bar{G} + \overline{\text{Ex}} - \text{Im}$$

Defining consumption and import functions gives

$$C = a_1 + a_2 Y$$

$$\text{Im} = m_1 + m_2 Y$$

Solving for Y yields

$$Y = \frac{1}{1 - (a_2 - m_2)} (a_1 + \bar{I} + \bar{G} + \overline{\text{Ex}} - m_1)$$

This reduced-form equation should be compared with that obtained from closed-economy models. Figure 16-2 permits a ready graphic comparison. Note the equilibrium obtained for national income with a closed model

Figure 16-1   A simple import function

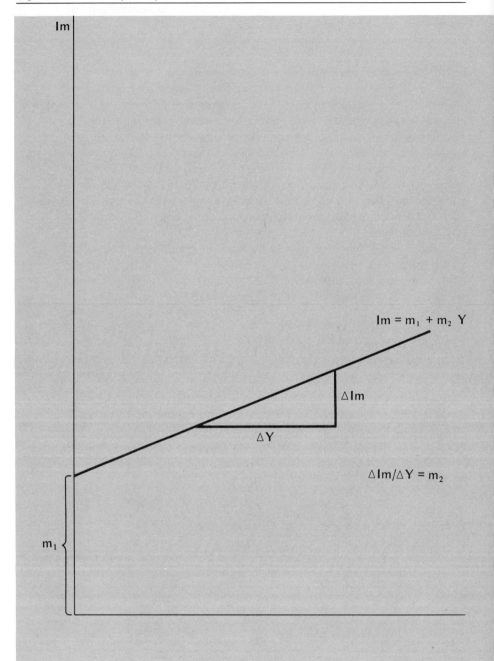

Figure 16-2 Comparison of closed and open models of national income

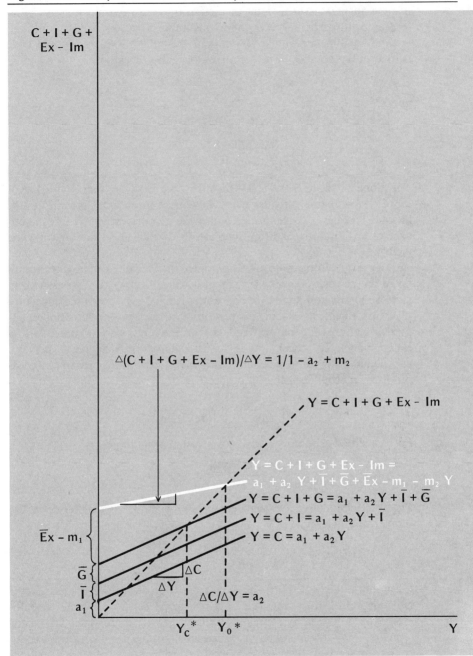

$(Y_c{}^*)$ and with an open model $(Y_o{}^*)$. Although our graph shows national income augmented as a result of foreign trade, it need not necessarily be increased. In particular, if autonomous imports exceed exports, national-income equilibrium will be lower than the equilibrium that would have existed in the absence of a foreign sector. Why? Because

$$Y' = C' + I' + G'$$

and

$$Y' = \frac{C' + I' + G' + (\overline{\text{Ex}} - m_1)}{(1 - m_2)}$$

$$Y'' < Y' \quad \text{if} \quad (\overline{\text{Ex}} - m_1) < 0$$

The slope of the $C + I + G + \text{Ex} - \text{Im}$ line is flatter than the slope of the $C + I + G$ line, because every increment in national income results in some leakage of expenditures out of the country, which damps the impact of an initial expenditure increase (or decrease) on national income increase (or decrease).

The expenditure multipliers computed in Chapter 7 can now be recomputed on the basis of an expanded national-income model. If we assume an increase in any component of aggregate demand—autonomous consumption, investment, government expenditure, or exports—the multiplied impact on national income will be less than the multiplier computed with a closed model. To repeat, this is due to leakages from aggregate demand into demand for foreign goods. Using investment as an example, the expenditure multiplier in the open model is

$$\frac{\Delta Y_o}{\Delta I} = \frac{1}{1 - (a_2 - m_2)}$$

For the closed-economy model, the investment multiplier is

$$\frac{\Delta Y_c}{\Delta I} = \frac{1}{1 - a_2}$$

The multiplier based on the open-economy model is smaller than the simpler multiplier:

$$\frac{1}{1 - (a_2 - m_2)} < \frac{1}{1 - a_2}$$

It is important to note that with the introduction of the foreign-trade sector into our model, a_2 is now the marginal propensity to consume *both* domestically produced and foreign-produced goods and services. Hence the term $a_2 - m_2$ is the marginal propensity to consume *domestically* produced goods and services. By itself, a_2 is expected to be greater than m_2; a rise in Y would be accompanied by less in additional imports than in additional consumption. Of course, in the unlikely case where $a_2 = m_2$, the foreign-trade multiplier equals one, and all of the additional income generated by an autonomous injection of spending into the economy would be spent on imports.

The equilibrium conditions in the open-economy model may not be sustainable for more than several quarters if imports exceed exports. Assume that in a closed-economy model, investment exceeds savings by an amount equal to the excess of tax collections over government expenditures. There is no inherent reason, in this closed economy, why the government sector cannot continue to run a surplus and sustain the excess of investments over savings. But if we maintain all the conditions assumed for the closed-economy model and then open the model, imports must exceed exports to the extent that investment plus government expenditures exceeds savings plus taxes. (You should be able to prove to yourself that Savings + Taxes + Imports = Investment + Government Expenditure + Exports.)

Two consequences follow. The first is that a nation's ability to continue importing more than it exports may be curtailed if the rest of the world refuses to continue extending credit to finance net importing. (Or the nation's foreign reserves will be depleted). The second consequence is that a reduction in imports (which would reduce the leakage from aggregate demand) will have a stimulating effect on the nation's economy. If the economy's initial equilibrium is at full employment, then inflation will be the result, rather than expanded output.

More generally, domestic monetary and fiscal policy have constraints on them that originate in the economy's foreign economic relations. Efforts to encourage domestic expansion will be hampered to the extent that leakage into demand for imports takes place. To the extent that increasing national income stimulates increased imports without a matching increase in exports, a foreign-trade deficit may result that is not sustainable in world money markets.

EXPORTS IN THE 1970s

In 1971, for the first time since 1945, merchandise imports exceeded merchandise exports in the United States. The possibility that the United States would cease to be a leading net exporter caused great concern to government, business, and labor leaders. It was their view that the trade deficit reflected weaknesses in the American economy that would affect employment and continued growth of trade.

To reverse the situation, the government exhorted business and labor to become more competitive. Domestically, congressmen urged passage of a bill establishing quotas on imports of goods for which domestic competitors existed. Internationally, the United States vigorously pressured its trading partners to take steps to lower barriers to American goods. The most potent measure taken by the United States, in grudging cooperation with its trading partners, was a devaluation of the dollar relative to foreign currencies, averaging approximately 10% in December 1971, and a further devaluation of 10% in February 1973. The monetary aspects of these devaluations will be discussed below.

Despite efforts to stimulate exports, some economists believe that the trade deficit is likely to continue for at least the next decade, but that it will not pose a serious problem for the economy. As our national income rises, Americans are demanding a greater ratio of services to goods. These services, especially transportation, education, and government, are not, with some exceptions, exportable. In addition, due to higher labor costs in the U.S., American firms have found it increasingly more profitable to set up subsidiaries abroad than to produce goods in this country for export. As a result, labor leaders have accused American business of fleeing the country to exploit cheap foreign labor, while business leaders have accused labor of demanding an uncompetitively high wage rate.

Both union and management assume that the loss of export markets is undesirable. Some economists, in contrast, see this as the inevitable development of a mature creditor economy.[1] In their view, while the trade deficit will continue, it will be offset by payments from abroad on American investments. This net investment income will increase with continuing business investment abroad. The impact on labor in those industries suffering in international markets can be mitigated by programs that facilitate a shift of workers to industries with increasing employment. In any event, the number of workers affected is a relatively small fraction of the labor force. These economists are arguing that with the exception of agriculture, which will continue to remain dependent on foreign markets and where efforts to increase U.S. competitive posture will pay off, it just does not pay to devote too much time and effort on commercial trade policy. A primary concern should be U.S. earnings from previous investments abroad and increased service exports, including management and technology.

Underlying these conflicting views on the seriousness of the trade deficit are differences on how to solve the fundamental problems posed by the means of international settlement. Traditionally, the United States has run a trade and net-investment surplus which has paid for our substantial outflows for travel, transportation, unilateral transfers, and military expenditures. But the net-investment income alone is not sufficient to cover the items that have been in deficit during the 1960s plus the newly developed trade deficit. In 1971, for example, the net investment-income surplus was $7.5 billion; the merchandise trade deficit amounted to $1.7 billion, and the deficit on all other fundamental items was $16 billion. The total was a net deficit of $10.2 billion (the balance on current account and long-term capital flows). Periodic exchange-rate adjustments may permit the United States to run overall deficits. But if the United States is to achieve balance-

1. See Lawrence B. Krause, "Why Exports are Becoming Irrelevant," *Foreign Policy*, Summer, 1971; and "Trade Policy for the Seventies," *Columbia Journal of World Business*, Vol. 6, No. 1, January-February 1971.

of-payments equilibrium, then some of the debit items will have to be reduced or some of the credit items augmented, or both. Which items are focused on is only partly dictated by economic considerations. Ultimately it becomes a political judgment as to whether the United States pursues policies of expanding export-producing industries to reduce a trade deficit, or cuts back on military expenditures and foreign aid.

MONETARY ASPECTS OF INTERNATIONAL TRADE

Unless nations are prepared to barter, international trade requires some means of international payment. For American importers intending to purchase French wines, it is necessary to buy a supply of francs. For French importers who wish to purchase American computers, it is necessary to buy a supply of U.S. dollars. For short periods of time it is, of course, possible that foreigners will be willing to accept dollars for our imports; similarly it is possible that we will accept foreign currencies for our exports. This is especially true when it is anticipated that the foreign currency will soon be needed to make purchases. In fact, there are inventories of the currencies of the major trading nations available in most countries. These inventories are held by dealers in foreign currencies and central banks. The size of the inventory depends on the volume of trade between the countries involved. The larger the volume of trade, the greater the inventory. These inventories comprise, in large part, international transactions balances.

The rate at which one currency is exchanged for another is the exchange rate. In principle (and sometimes in practice), this rate could be set by the marketplace and permitted to fluctuate as speculators and firms doing business abroad bought and sold foreign currencies. Greater and lesser amounts of domestic currency could be offered as demand for foreign currency increased and decreased. Occasionally a country's government will allow its currency to exchange with foreign currencies at a rate set by the marketplace. Canada has allowed the Canadian dollar to fluctuate freely during several years since 1945. The West German, Japanese, and British governments all allowed their economies to "float" after the world balance-of-payments crisis of early 1973. In general, however, most of the Western nations have fixed the rates of exchange among currencies by international agreement.

These rates are fixed within narrow bands. The marketplace causes fluctuations in the daily exchange rates; central banks enter the marketplace and buy or sell currencies to keep the exchange rate within the band internationally agreed upon. When a government is unable or unwilling to maintain the agreed-upon exchange rate, an international monetary crisis occurs. These crises are characterized by great uncertainty and temporary disruption of trade, as some exporters and importers defer sales and purchases until the new exchange rates are settled. There have been several such international monetary crises since the Western nations agreed to a fixed-exchange system at Bretton Woods, New Hampshire, in 1944. A fixed-exchange system, while it may provide temporary stability among foreign currencies, also carries with it the danger of periodic collapse. So far the world's trade relations have recovered in the wake of each crisis. To comprehend the causes of these crises, it is necessary to first understand what is meant by a balance-of-payments surplus or deficit. For that we turn to Table 16-1, the U.S. balance of payments, 1972.

THE BALANCE OF PAYMENTS

The balance of payments is a summary of the transactions between a country and the rest of the world that result in money flowing out of the country (payments) and money flowing into the country (receipts). The summary of transactions is broken down into a current account, which records flows of goods and services; a capital account, which records flows of securities and real investments; and a reserve account, which records changes in monetary reserves.

The current account summarizes imports and exports of goods and services. Although merchandise has been of greatest importance in world trade, services are becoming increasingly significant in the U.S. balance of payments. Of special interest is income on investments—interest, royalties, dividends. This income represents the return on past investments abroad. In the wake of World War II and the destruction of Europe's industrial capacity, there was a strong demand for U.S. goods. As a result, the U.S. balance of trade (merchandise exports-merchandise imports) was in such substantial surplus that the United States could carry on military and reconstruction aid programs (which result in an outflow of dollars) and still run surpluses on current account. In 1950, the U.S. ran its first current-account deficit.

Accompanying U.S. surpluses was a dollar shortage in the rest of the world. Not having the dollars to pay for U.S. exports, the rest of the world paid in gold and securities. By the early 1960s, the dollar shortage had turned into a dollar glut, as a result of increasing self-sufficiency in Europe (which eased the demand for U.S. output), U.S. investments abroad (which led to dollars flowing out of the country), military expenditures abroad (NATO, Vietnam), and growing U.S. tourism (not offset by foreigners visiting the United States).

The sum of payments and receipts on current account is known as the "net balance on current account." The sum is exactly offset by the net balance on capital account plus changes in U.S. official reserve assets.

The capital account is divided into long-term and short-term capital

Table 16-1   U.S. Balance of Payments, 1972 (millions of dollars)

	Credit (+)	Debit (−)	Net
Current Account			
Private			
Merchandise	48,769	−55,681	−6,912
Services			
Travel expenditures	7,027	−9,880	−2,853
Income on investments	13,130	−3,379	+9,751
Other	2,158	−1,924	+234
Current private balance			+220
Government			
Export of military goods and services (+)	4,200		
Military aid (−)		4,200	0
Other military transactions	1,166	4,724	−3,558
Other grants and payments		2,174	−2,174
Miscellaneous governmental transactions	1,211	4,054	−2,843
Current government balance			−8,575
Net balance on current account			−8,353
Capital Account			
Long-term loans (−) and borrowings (+)			
Private		−151	
Government		−1,339	
Net long-term foreign investments			−1,490
Net balance on current accounts and long-term investment			−9,843
Short-term loans (−) and borrowings (+)			
Private		+1,905	
Purchase of equities		+10,119	
Government		+189	
Net short-term foreign investments			12,213
Reserve Account			
Gold		+547	
Foreign currency reserves		−515	
Net changes in gold and foreign currency reserves		+32	
Allocation of special drawing rights		+710	
Errors and omissions		−3,112	
Offset to "basic deficit"			+9,843

Source: Survey of Current Business, *Vol. 53 (June 1973), p. 28.*

flows. Long-term capital flows are usually thought to be "basic" or "fundamental" items in the balance of payments, reflecting "real" investment opportunities, as contrasted with speculative or portfolio investments. During the 1950s, private American capital began flowing to Europe to take advantage of growing profit opportunities. As these investments pay off, the income appears as investment credits in the current account. In addition to private capital outflows, the U.S. government, directly and via international agencies, has contributed to capital outflows by loans for economic development and military equipment. Since many of these loans are made on the condition that they be used to purchase U.S. produced goods and services, the outflow is a hidden subsidy for American exporters.

The net balance on current account and the long-term capital account is referred to as the "basic" balance. Changes in the current and long-term capital account are considered "basic" in the sense that they are the result of "real" (as contrasted with monetary) market opportunities. A change in tastes stimulates American demand for Chinese food, resulting in importation of canned lychee and dried mushrooms. A U.S. corporation sees an opportunity to manufacture light machinery in Spain, resulting in a long-term capital outflow. Both of these actions are responses to "real" market conditions. An outflow of dollars to the London capital market in search of higher interest rates is a monetary phenomenon, and is therefore excluded from the "basic" balance.

The remainder of the items in the balance of payments—short-term capital flows, and changes in the gold and other reserve assets account—are "balancing items." They represent monetary flows made in connection with the activity underlying the basic balance. For example, assume that an importer in the United States does not pay for some merchandise with the currency of the country from which he is importing, but, instead, owes the money to the seller in the foreign country. What that seller is doing is "lending" the amount to the importer, which means there is a capital outflow from abroad and a capital inflow into the United States. This shows up as a credit in the U.S. short-term capital account.

When we speak of a balance-of-payments deficit or surplus, we are referring to the balance of a selected set of items in the balance of payments. The balance of payments is always in "balance" in the sense that the sum of receipts must exactly equal the sum of payments. There are several definitions of balance-of-payments deficits or surpluses in addition to the "basic" balance already defined. The "liquidity" balance is made up of the net balance on current account, plus net long-term capital outflow (which is the basic balance), plus short-term U.S. capital outflow. The reason for this definition is that U.S. short-term capital movements (in contrast to foreign short-term capital movements) are not volatile during periods of monetary crisis, and should, therefore, be counted with other items in the account that have long-term stability. The "official reserve transactions" balance is made up of the net balance on current account, plus net long-term capital outflow, plus net short-term private capital outflow. These items reflect private transactions that require offsetting by central banks.

ECONOMIC CONSEQUENCES OF BALANCE-OF-PAYMENTS DISEQUILIBRIUM

The "fundamental" items in the balance of payments need not add up to zero in each calendar year. Even if the exchange rates were properly chosen to minimize deficits and surpluses, random variations alone could cause deficits in some years and surpluses in others. Over some long-run period, however, these deficits and surpluses must cancel out. If they do not, as they have not for the United States during the past twenty years, the currency is said to be in "fundamental disequilibrium" with those of the rest of the world. The United States has run deficits partly by persuading other countries to absorb the net outflow of its currency, and partly by exporting gold (which is a credit item since it results in a flow of dollars into the country). Between 1946 and 1971, the U.S. gold stock fell from 20.7 billion dollars to 10.2 billion dollars.

Until recently, the United States would exchange gold for dollars held abroad at the rate of 35 dollars per ounce. In March 1968, The Group of Ten[2] (the central banks of ten leading trading and banking nations) agreed to cease trading gold in the free market by freezing all gold reserves already within the central banks of the trading nations. All private persons who held gold could sell the metal on the free market at whatever price the market determined. A two-tier gold system developed, with an official price and a free-market price. At times, the free-market price has been almost twice that of the official price.

On August 15, 1971, the rules of the game were changed again, this time unilaterally by the United States in completely suspending U.S. trading in gold. The refusal to convert dollars for gold was a step towards the demonetization of a metal whose market value would be, in the absence of its monetary role, something under $20 an ounce. Symbolically, however, the United States is still tied to gold. In 1971 the United States agreed to devalue the dollar from $35 to $38 per ounce as part of a general agreement to reduce the value of the dollar *vis-à-vis* other currencies by approximately 10%, on the average. In 1973 the dollar was further devalued to $42.22 per ounce.

2. The Group of Ten includes the United States, the United Kingdom, Belgium, France, Italy, Netherlands, West Germany, Canada, Japan, and Sweden. Switzerland participates in the Group of Ten as an observer (since it is not a member of the International Monetary Fund).

ECONOMIC MEANING OF DEVALUATION

In the long run, a country running a deficit has other alternatives to exporting gold or increasing its currency held abroad. It can take steps to encourage domestic exports and inhibit imports by initiating tariffs; by giving subsidies to export industries; by exhorting management and labor to increase its competitive position; or, more drastically, by raising the ratio at which its currency is swapped for other currencies on the world market. An increase in the ratio is a devaluation, and serves to stimulate exports (the devaluing country's goods become cheaper abroad) and discourage imports (foreign goods become more expensive).

A simple numerical example illustrates this proposition. Assume a pre-devaluation exchange rate of one dollar for five francs, and a post-devaluation exchange rate of one dollar for four francs. An article that costs 100 francs in France (and whose price does not change after devaluation) costs (ignoring shipping and other costs) $20 in the United States before, and $25 after, devaluation. It costs more to buy foreign goods in terms of domestic currency and less to buy domestic goods in terms of foreign currency.

This general statement, and the simple example offered, does not mean that there is a simple relationship between the percentage of devaluation and changes in prices. That the domestic price of an article does not change after a foreign devaluation is an assumption which may not be warranted. For example, if foreign demand for the good in question represents a substantial percentage of total demand (defined to be domestic demand plus foreign demand), the devaluation may have the effect of raising the domestic price: the demand curve shifts to the right as a result of increased foreign demand.

The impact of devaluation on the internal price level of the devaluing country is also uncertain. How much foreign input goes into domestically produced output? If it is substantial (as it is *not* for the United States), devaluation adds to the cost of producing domestic goods. How much of the devaluation will sellers of imported goods absorb? A fall in the price of the imported good could cushion the full impact of the devaluation. The upshot of these possibilities is that the impact of exchange-rate readjustments on trade flows is not a simple one. What must be computed are the elasticities of demand for imports with respect to price increases, and the elasticities of foreign demand for exports with respect to price decreases. From these elasticities we can estimate the impact of devaluation on trade flows.

While elasticities have been computed for major categories of goods, they have not been calculated for services. What will be the effect of a devaluation on shipping, or on private remittances? Since the trade balance consists of the net imports of services and goods, the answers to these questions are critically important if we are to predict the impact of devaluation on the balance of current account.

POLICY IMPLICATIONS OF DEVALUATION

When an economy is underemployed and running a balance of payments deficit, strong political pressures are generated to solve both problems simultaneously by restricting trade, usually with tariffs and quotas. If restrictions are potent enough, imports can be reduced to the extent that domestic substitutes exist. Devaluation is another mechanism for shifting domestic demand from the goods of other countries to the goods of the devaluing country. It is often claimed, on behalf of both trade restriction measures and devaluation, that employment will be stimulated. It cannot be sufficiently emphasized, however, that while this is possible for one or more nations, it is not possible for all nations to simultaneously increase exports and decrease imports. Efforts to shift demand in this way ("beggar-thy-neighbor" policies) seek to increase domestic demand at the expense of demand for foreign output.

Paradoxically, while a country running a deficit is generally thought to be in a disadvantaged position, especially when compared with countries enjoying surpluses, it is at the same time benefiting from greater real income than it would have without a deficit. This extra real income is being financed by the rest of the world's willingness to sell to the deficit country on credit, either by holding its currency or accepting IOUs. Thus, when an exchange-rate adjustment is made to eliminate continuing deficits in a country's balance of payments, its real income is reduced. The significance of this for the United States is minor because the foreign trade sector as a fraction of GNP is so small. But for a country that imports 20% or more of its GNP, such as Great Britain, a devaluation represents a substantial reduction in real income. This reduction will affect the mix between consumption of domestic and foreign goods, independently of a change in their relative prices.[3]

Nothing has yet been said about the economic consequences of a balance-of-payment surplus. In one sense, there are no direct and immediate consequences of running surpluses indefinitely. A country will simply accumulate foreign currencies and gold while its exports exceed its imports. The country is not forced to take any domestic action to deal with its surplus since the surplus poses no direct problem (in the way that a deficit threatens to exhaust a country's gold reserves).

In another sense, the surplus is costing the economy real income. Because a surplus country's currency is undervalued relative to the rest of the world's currencies, its exports are attractively priced abroad, and imports are unattractive alongside domestically produced substitutes. As a consequence, the country has fewer goods than it would have if its currency were revalued. In 1969, the West German Deutschemark was revalued by 9.3%, partly to slow the rapid accumulation of gold and

---

3. For the student who is familiar with indifference-curve analysis, the various outcomes of a reduction in real income and a change in the relative prices of domestic and foreign goods can be easily demonstrated.

foreign currencies, and partly to aid in the domestic anti-inflation effort. Again during early 1971, the West German central bank considered the mark undervalued. This time the value of the mark was allowed to be determined by market forces, and it appreciated by about 5% relative to the dollar.

THE SPECIAL ROLE OF THE DOLLAR IN INTERNATIONAL MONETARY RELATIONS

It has already been explained that nations need inventories of foreign currencies to facilitate trade. These inventories, along with gold and Special Drawing Rights (SDRs), an international money to be discussed below, are what is known as "international liquidity." The principal currencies held as reserves are the British pound, the French franc, the West German Deutschemark, the Swiss franc, and pre-eminently, the United States dollar.

There are several reasons why the dollar is of keystone importance. Although exports as a fraction of U.S. GNP are relatively small, in absolute amounts they are large. Consequently, the dollar is a useful currency to hold because so much of a country's transactions will involve trade with the United States. The dollar, until recently, has not depreciated, internally, as rapidly as the currencies of other major trading nations. Even in the last few years, inflation in the United States has been less than in Japan, France, the Netherlands, and the United Kingdom. The relative stability of the dollar makes it attractive as an international reserve.

The demand for international reserves rises with a rise in world income and world trade. Seven percent is a conservative estimate of the annual growth rate in world trade. International reserves must rise to facilitate this trade increase. Gold production has been rising at the rate of 2% a year, of which part goes into industrial and cosmetic use. The remainder of the growth in world reserves comes from the deficits run by key currency countries, such as the United States. Thus, the United States is in the following quandary: When it takes steps to cut its deficit, it threatens world trade by choking off a source of international liquidity; and when it does not take steps to cut its deficit, it runs the risk of speculative attempts to force devaluation. In addition, the accumulation of dollars abroad is uneven. The central banks of surplus producing countries, such as West Germany, find themselves accumulating more dollars than they would like to have, while less developed countries that import in excess of exports find themselves with insufficient dollar reserves.

There is something remote and mysterious about "speculative runs on the dollar," but actually the principle of speculation is not complicated. If it is anticipated that the dollar will be devalued (or that one or more foreign currencies will be revalued), speculators, import-export firms, and banks will find it advantageous to sell dollars for the currency that is going to gain in value relative to the dollar after devaluation. If the speculators are correct, they can buy back more dollars than they sold, paying with the revalued currency. Say one dollar exchanges for four marks before devaluation. The speculator sells dollars and obtains marks. After devaluation, assume the exchange rate is one dollar for three marks. The speculator buys back one dollar for three marks and has one mark left over. (There are some transactions costs.) One consequence of a speculative rush against the dollar (or any other currency) is that the heavy wave of selling depresses the dollar price. If the exchange rates agreed upon are to be maintained, the United States must buy these dollars, paying with foreign currencies and running down its reserves. The central banks of other nations must also agree to buy dollars when offered by speculators in search of safer currencies.

In 1968, speculators anticipated a U.S. devaluation relative to gold and engaged in massive selling of the dollar. The Group of Ten, except France, adopted a two-tier gold system. No country would sell gold to any purchaser except a central bank. This was the first step in demonetizing gold. Gold was free to be priced in the marketplace. In the wake of the May student and labor demonstrations, France joined the agreement later that year, which caused a run on France's gold stock. The second step in demonetizing gold took place on August 15, 1971, when the United States announced that it would not sell gold; the dollar was allowed to float, which caused a devaluation. On December 18, 1971, a new set of exchange rates were negotiated among the major trading partners.

SPECIAL DRAWING RIGHTS

In addition to currencies of the major trading nations and gold, Special Drawing Rights (SDRs) were created by international agreement in 1970 to supplement international liquidity needs. SDRs are created by the members of the International Monetary Fund, an institution created after World War II to facilitate balance-of-payments equilibrium among the trading nations of the world. SDRs are an international money guaranteed by the willingness of nations to accept them as they would gold or a nation's currency in payments for goods and services. SDRs are called "paper gold" because they satisfy all of the monetary functions fulfilled by gold. Annually, the members of the IMF determine how much in SDRs is to be created. This amount is then distributed to members according to their quotas in the fund. SDRs are now the fastest growing component of international reserves. If they continue to grow at their present rate, they should represent the largest component of liquidity within ten to fifteen years. So far, the SDRs have gained acceptance, suggesting both the possibility of the IMF acting as a world central bank, and the ultimate total demonetization of gold, leaving South Africa to market its metal to jewelers and dentists.

Economic
Growth (I)

WASHINGTON, Dec. 15, 1970—President Nixon celebrated today a
landmark economic statistic that has been achieved, in part, by the
inflation that he has spent two years trying to control. The statistic
was $1 trillion—the level, according to the Commerce Department,
at which the nation is now producing the goods and services that
make up the gross national product. To mark the growth of the
economy to a $1 trillion annual rate, the Commerce Department
invited the President to the departmental auditorium to watch its
new "GNP clock"—a large board full of lights and numbers—flash
the statistic at noon. When it became clear that Mr. Nixon would not
arrive on time, departmental technicians worked madly to turn the
machine back. But it seemed to develop a life of its own, flashing
the trillion-dollar figure at 12:02, and when the President arrived at
12:07, $2.3 million more had been added to the total. *The New York
Times*, December 16, 1970.

The neoclassical and Keynesian models presented in Parts I and II are
essentially static, constructed to determine equilibrium at a point in time
and to explain how equilibrium is reached. When we turn our attention to
economic growth, we necessarily leave behind the static approach and
turn to dynamic models of the economy.[1] The central questions here are:

---

1. One of the major characteristics of economic analysis since the appearance of Keynes'
The General Theory has been a remarkable increase in the quantity as well as the level of
sophistication of mathematics used by economists. This increase is due in part to economists'
growing desire to analyze certain *dynamic* processes in more formal, rigorous terms than
earlier generations of economists had been able to do. Even though we have tried to hold a
tight rein on the use of mathematics in this book, there is more in this and the next chapter
than in other parts of the book, a natural consequence of the dynamic nature of economic
growth theory. Where necessary, we have explained the basis of the mathematics for those
unfamiliar with elementary calculus.

1. What factors determine the rate of growth of an economy?
2. How can our models be expanded to explain the equilibrium time paths of key macroeconomic variables?
3. Should economic growth be encouraged through public policies?

In this chapter, we first turn to a discussion of the new debate that challenges the notion of growth as a "good thing." Then we take up the growth theory that emerged along Keynesian lines during the immediate post-World War II period. We will explore the power—and limitations—of this theory.

In Chapter 18, we consider what is called "neoclassical growth theory," a subject that has occupied the scholarly attentions of economists for the past twenty years.

GROWTH AND DEVELOPMENT

Measurement and explanation of the economic maturation process in relatively less developed countries is a topic that economists separate from the theory of economic growth. Growth theory is often thought to be part of macroeconomics, while development economics—a mixture of micro theory, macro theory, industrial organization, demography, and foreign trade and finance theory—is a separate subject, deserving to stand by itself.

Even limited in this way, most economists would probably agree that the theory of economic growth has attracted an enormous share of the profession's attention since World War II. Amartya Sen, who has made substantial contributions in this area, observed that economists have simply been reacting to world conditions:

> Interest in growth revived at first slowly and then by leaps and bounds. This was to a considerable extent the result of an immense practical concern with growth after the Second World War. The war-damaged economies were trying hard to reconstruct fast, the underdeveloped countries were attempting to initiate economic development, the advanced capitalist countries being relatively free from periodic slumps were trying to concentrate on raising the long-run rate of growth, and the socialist countries were determined to overtake the richer capitalist economies by fast economic expansion. Growth was everybody's concern and it is no wonder that in such a milieu growth theory was pampered by the attention of economists.[2]

More recently, economic growth has become the key issue for economists concerned with the ecological implications of continuing increases in per

2. Amartya Sen, "Editor's Introduction," *Growth Economics* (Penguin, 1970), p. 9.

capita—and even absolute—output. The British economist E. J. Mishan, for example, has argued that economic growth and technological innovation have been harmful to affluent societies because they have been accompanied by intolerable deterioration in the quality of life. Reflecting this changing interest in economic growth, a recent introductory economics textbook contains a chapter on "Economic Growth and Ecology."

Since growth is one of the major areas of policy that governments have been concerned with, it is appropriate to ask: What policy implications of the theory will be developed? While growth models appear to be quite complicated, they are in fact too simple to support clear policy inferences. The economist Robert Solow describes these models as "reconnaissance exercises." If we discover that the models have promise for a broader understanding of the growth process, we will have to start doing on a large scale the difficult and tedious work that will render the models useful for policy. Right now we are still in the stage of setting up simple analytical models.

GROWTH AND GOVERNMENT POLICY

In an effort to isolate the contributions of the various inputs to economic growth, Edward Denison compared output to inputs over time in a now-historic study for the Committee for Economic Development, *The Sources of Economic Growth in the United States*. We would expect output to grow merely because inputs have grown. To the extent, however, that output growth exceeds input growth, we can attribute it to changes in the quality of inputs. In Table 17-1 (which comes from a more recent study[3] by Denison), more than half of the average annual growth rate in the United States between 1955 and 1962 is accounted for by increases in labor and capital resources. The remaining growth of 2.67% per year is explained by increases in output per unit of input. This growth is largely due to technological improvements, education, and increased efficiency.

By identifying the sources of growth, it is possible to suggest what policies would be helpful in its stimulation. The maintenance of full employment by macroeconomic stabilization techniques is clearly essential. An economy that permits under-utilization of its labor and capital resources forfeits not only current output, but future output, to the extent that forgone output consists of investment goods. Educational investment is another highly critical factor affecting our economic growth. In Table 17-1, increases in education of the labor force accounted for 20% of the national income growth rate; research and development accounted for 29% of the growth rate.

Based on his analysis, Denison presents an array of government

3. Edward F. Denison, *Why Growth Rates Differ* (Washington, D.C.: The Brookings Institution, 1967).

Table 17-1   Sources of Growth in Total National Income in the United States, 1955–1962

Source of Growth	Contribution to Growth Rate in Percentage Points	Percent of the Growth Rate Accounted for by Each Source
Average annual national income growth rate	2.67	100
Growth due to increase in amount of resources	1.70	64
Changes in labor	0.97	36
Increases in employment	0.73	27
Reduction in hours of work	−0.20	−08
Changes in age-sex composition	−0.08	−03
Increases in education	0.52	20
Changes in capital	0.73	27
Increases in residential housing	0.25	09
Increases in international assets	0.06	02
Increases in nonresidential structures and equipment	0.35	13
Increases in inventories	0.07	03
Growth due to increases in productivity of resources	0.97	36
Advances of knowledge	0.76	29
Improved allocation of resources	0.25	09
Economies of large-scale production	0.30	11
Effects of irregularities in growth of total effective demand and in agricultural output and effects of deflation procedures	−0.34	−13

policies that can affect the growth rate. However, even those choices with maximum impact have a relatively low effect on growth. Thus, while his analysis suggests a number of growth-affecting policies, the impact of such policies, with the exception of aggregate demand policies, is likely to be small.

GROWTH VERSUS NO GROWTH

So far we have raised the question of how government can affect the growth rate. We have yet to deal with the problem of what growth rate is desirable, or even of encouraging a policy of no growth. During the past several years, the issue of whether any economic growth is desirable has emerged as consciousness of environmental problems has been raised. For the first time in this century, economists have seriously considered the possibility that economic growth might be undesirable. Some have argued that the ultimate consequence of not arresting economic growth will be to put the human species in jeopardy, since we are continuing to deplete our natural (and irreplaceable) resources at an accelerated rate.

The economists Kenneth Boulding and Barbara Ward have coined the expression "spaceship earth" to suggest that the world is a closed system in which all resources are limited. Until recently, humankind could view the earth as an inexhaustible supply of the prerequisites to life. But due to the total population expansion in the past one hundred years, we have rapidly approached the limits of our resources. In consequence, we must begin to develop the technology to recycle our resources and limit our population; we must live on the earth as we would in a spaceship.

There is no single approach to no growth. There is, instead, a range of opinions involving social, political, and economic judgments. Ezra J. Mishan, a distinguished British welfare economist, focuses on one of the weakest points in current economic analysis—the treatment of externalities.

Externalities are the costs that society bears by the actions of firms, individuals, and governments not reflected in prices. For example, a firm that discharges pollution into a river is throwing off a cost onto society— the cost of a polluted river. The firm does not bear the cost, and the prices of its products are lower than they would be if the firm were obliged to install devices to avoid this pollution. When such externalities are paid for by the firm, they are internalized. While economists have long recognized the concept of externalities (it appears in virtually every introductory text), they have tended to dismiss them as either unimportant or incalculable.

Mishan and many other no-growth economists argue that externalities may be the most important part of the social cost of production, and that leaving them out results in an inflated GNP. Consequently, when we pursue policies to increase growth in GNP, we may not be increasing real output— we are merely increasing our externalities. The results may not be felt immediately, but they cannot be ignored in the long run. Mishan has put it this way:

> As the carpet of "increased choice" is being unrolled before us by the foot, it is simultaneously being rolled up behind us by the yard. . . . In all that contributes in trivial ways to his ultimate satisfaction, the things at which modern business excels, new models of cars and transistors, prepared foodstuffs and plastic objets d'art, man has ample choice. In all that destroys his enjoyment of life, he has none.[4]

Mishan recommends that we develop measures that more adequately reflect our economic well-being. By developing measures of "true" production of goods and services (those goods and services that add to our well-being), revised national income measures could then be used to reflect

4. E. J. Mishan, *Technology and Growth: The Price We Pay* (Praeger, 1969).

increases in social welfare. Mishan and others agree that the development of such measures lies ten to twenty years in the future. In the interim, Mishan suggests a variety of plans to improve the quality of life. These include "people preserves"—residential areas in which motorized vehicles would be banned—and a "bill of amenity rights," which would add to the traditional rights of liberty and property, the rights of privacy, quiet, clean air and water. Violators of these rights would have either to cease infringing on them or to purchase from the affected individuals permission to continue doing so. Thus, an airline could install completely effective anti-noise devices or buy the permission of those inconvenienced. Mishan claims he is not against growth or technological advance—he is simply in favor of noting the undesirable aspects of growth and change so that as we grow, our welfare is increased.

Although Mishan appeared heretical when he first started propounding his ideas on economic growth (some called his ideas Mishanic), his views now appear to be moderate alongside those of a group of MIT management engineers. Their study, contained in a report receiving wide attention, has a simple message: Either growth must stop or civilization will![5] The report describes a computer simulation model of the entire world that incorporates a series of alternative projections for economic growth, and predicts "if the present growth trends . . . continue unchanged, the limits of growth on this planet will be reached sometime within the next hundred years." Five basic factors were incorporated in the model: population increase; agricultural production; nonrenewable resource depletion; industrial output; and pollution generation.

A computer simulation permits us to begin with a set of initial conditions and hypotheses of relationships among critical variables, and, utilizing the high speed of the computer, "play out" the future. The conclusions reached in *The Limits to Growth* are not tentative. Unqualified disaster is predicted if growth is not halted in the very near future. In contrast with Mishan, the MIT group claims that pollution and world malnutrition cannot be solved directly but must be attacked by achieving a cessation of growth. The conditions necessary for achieving equilibrium are a freeze on the population and capital stock.

Opposition to the no-growth idea is varied. At one extreme are economists who argue that technological advances will keep ahead of exhaustion of natural resources, providing new sources of energy (such as solar power) as we use up old ones (such as coal or petroleum). Their faith in technological change stems from Thomas Malthus' claim of a stationary state (a no-growth economy) over a century ago, on the grounds that agricultural output would limit population growth. For over a generation, economists have explained that the Malthusian trap resulted from the erroneous assumption that productivity would not increase.

5. D. H. Meadows et al., *The Limits to Growth, A Report for the Club of Rome's Project on the Predicament of Mankind* (Universe, 1972).

A growing number of economists have conceded that growth brings costs as well as benefits, and have urged that growth be curbed. However, they point out that limitations on growth will create a new series of problems. As even Kenneth Boulding, a proponent of no growth, says:

> In the stationary state, if the poor are to get richer, then the rich must get poorer, and what is even more frightening, if the rich are to get richer, they can do so only by increasing their exploitation of the poor. And since the rich may be the most powerful, they may have strong incentive to do so. . . . The dialectical processes to which a stationary state would be exposed would thereby become much more acute and might easily destroy the state's precarious equilibrium, the decay of all legitimacies, and a Hobbesian nightmare of retro-gression in the war of all against all.[6]

Thus, no-growth policies intensify the conflict between rich and poor, not only within a country, but between the rich and poor countries of the world. It is difficult to expect other nations to greet with enthusiasm the message emanating from the wealthiest country in the world that they must not aspire to the wealth we already enjoy. The social consequences of the stationary state have also been commented on by the economist Walter W. Heller. He fears that no-growth policies will limit social mobility and arrest the possibilities for change and innovation.

One alternative to no growth is to incorporate the costs of pollution into the prices paid for goods, thus utilizing the market mechanism. A recent study[7] by William Nordhaus and James Tobin (discussed in Chapter 2) concludes that the market can deal with increasing scarcity of fuel (which has been predicted) since prices will rise and, as a result, there will be a powerful incentive for more efficient use of these fuels and the develop-ment of substitute materials. Nordhaus and Tobin consider the abuse of "free" public goods such as air and water as far more serious. But this abuse stems from the absence of an adequate pricing system—if govern-mental policy were directed toward charging users (taxing polluters), the problem would be manageable. If, in other words, the market mechanism were developed for public as well as private goods, resource allocation would be consistent with eliminating (or sharply reducing) negative exter-nalities and continuing real economic growth. Thus, with respect to both private and public resources, we may be very far from seeing them ex-hausted, if the market mechanism can be expected to ration them.

In a sense this conclusion is in harmony with Mishan's message: pay attention to externalities so that we are sure that increases in production lead to increases in welfare rather than to increases in "illfare." The differ-

6. Kenneth Boulding, "New Goals for Society?" in *Energy, Economic Growth, and the Environment*, ed. S. H. Shurr (Johns Hopkins University Press, 1972).
7. William Nordhaus and James Tobin, "Is Growth Obsolete?" in *Economic Research: Retrospect and Prospect*, Vol. 5 (National Bureau of Economic Research, 1972).

ence between Nordhaus and Tobin on the one hand, and Mishan on the other, is that Mishan believes if these externalities were truly counted, including the cost of cleaning up past pollution, the result would be a stationary state. Nordhaus and Tobin believe that including all costs would still produce increases in real economic growth.

To summarize, there are at least four issues involved in the growth or no-growth controversy, only some of which are economic ones:

1) What factors improve the quality of life and add to the well-being and happiness of people? Mishan, for example, shows a marked preference for the amenities of life that characterized upper middle class Victorian England, and an abhorrence of anything associated with automobiles and airplanes. Whether or not one shares Mishan's utility function, it must be recognized that the quality-of-life issue is a social one, not an economic one.

2) What does the GNP measure? To the extent that the creation of pollution is counted as output in the national income accounts, we are not properly measuring production that adds to economic welfare. We must therefore face the difficult task of redefining these accounts or, alternatively, cease to rely on them as an index of economic well-being.

3) There is the empirical issue of the earth's limited resources and the capacity of humankind to develop new technology that is adjustable to changing resources. We no longer blindly believe that increased technology will save us. But we should not ignore the possible benefits of future techno-logical developments. One of the major criticisms of *The Limits to Growth* is that its simulation model does not adequately consider the possibility of technological advances. The empirical problems we are faced with are better measurements of current resources, and extrapolations about future technological change from past trends.

4) Methods must be explored by which the market mechanism can be harnessed to take into account presently ignored externalities.

When we develop the analytical tools and empirical data referred to above, we will be in a better position to determine if a policy of no growth is or is not necessary. It is even possible that we will discover negative growth to be necessary—that we must produce *less* over time, rather than the same or more, to be in equilibrium with the earth. At present, however, what emerges from the anti-growth/pro-growth debate is as much moral philosophy as it is economic science.

KEYNESIAN GROWTH THEORY

Soon after the appearance of Keynes' *The General Theory*, many of the same economists who were writing about its politically interesting short-run aspects were attracted by the possibility of using the core of Keynesian eco-nomics to further an understanding of the *growth* of a macroeconomy—

that is, the *movement* of a developed, industrialized economy through time, as opposed to its maturation. *The General Theory* became the foundation for contemporary growth theory. Interestingly enough, through time, many of Keynes' propositions and assumptions have become more important than his results in long-run macroeconomics. For example, the Keynesian notion of a relatively stable relationship between consumption and disposable income became a foundation for dynamic macroeconomics, just as it had for static macroeconomics. And after a brief, truly Keynesian period in growth theory when less than full employment was assumed, economists began *assuming* that resources were fully utilized at all times.

The "Domar" Model: Focus on Investment

Beginning in 1946, Evsey Domar of MIT developed a model of economic growth along Keynesian lines which concentrated on the rate of growth of net investment.[8] Domar first focused on the link between net investment and changes in a nation's productive capacity. He then explored the conditions required for a change in productive capacity resulting from an act of investment matched by an equal change in aggregate demand.

Assuming away this capacity-creating aspect of net investment—that is, the connection between net investment, capital stock, and output—is a common feature of short-run "Keynesian" models, such as the one presented in Part II. In developing the *CM*-II model in Chapters 9 and 10, aggregate net investment was assumed to occur at the same time that the level of capital stock in the production function remained constant. This apparent inconsistency was required to bring the supply side of the economy into the model without making the model unnecessarily complex.

Domar chose to give the capacity-creating aspect of net investment a prominent role in his model of the process of economic growth. The Domar model is usually presented within the context of a completely closed private economy; that is, foreign trade and government are ignored. Thus, consumption and net investment, both measured in base-period dollars, are the only sources of demand for real national output.

Our exposition of Domar's model will begin with the way he linked net investment and changes in productive capacity. Assume that $5 worth of additional capital stock would *make it possible* for a nation to increase its net output by $1 per time period, and that this five-to-one relationship holds for all levels of investment. Letting ΔQ denote the change in the maximum feasible output, and I denote the prevailing level of net invest-

8. Evsey Domar, "Capital, Expansion, Rate of Growth, and Employment," *Econometrica*, Vol. 14 (April 1946), 137–147; "Expansion and Employment," *American Economic Review*, Vol. 37 (March 1947), 34–55; "The Problem of Capital Accumulation," *American Economic Review*, Vol. 38 (December 1948), 777–794. All these essays are reprinted in Domar's *Essays in the Theory of Economic Growth* (Oxford University Press, 1957).

ment, the above relationship can be expressed as

$$\Delta Q = g_1 I \tag{17-1}$$

where g_1 is the change-in-potential-output/investment ratio, or "capital coefficient." This "capital coefficient" is a technical fact of life. Economists might be able to measure it, but it is *determined* by engineering capabilities.

This addition to *potential* output is solely a "supply-side" notion. For this potential addition to become a *realized* addition, there must be a corresponding increase in the *demand* for goods and services.

Following Kuznets' empirical results introduced in Chapter 6, current consumption (C) over long periods of time can be thought of as a constant fraction of real income (Y). This "long-run" version of the consumption function is one in which the average and marginal propensities to consume are equal. Thus, current saving ($Y - C$) can be expressed as a simple fraction of the current level of Y:

$$S = sY \tag{17-2}$$

where the marginal (and average) propensity to save is denoted by s.

Assume that the prevailing level of investment is exogenously given ($I = \bar{I}$). Macroeconomic equilibrium requires that $S = I$. Real income must be such that the volume of saving corresponding to this particular income level matches the exogenously given level of investment:

$$S = sY$$
$$S = sY = \bar{I}$$
$$Y = \frac{1}{s}\bar{I} \tag{17-3}$$

Equation 17-3 embodies a simple relationship between equilibrium income and the prevailing level of investment. The two variables are linked by $1/s$, the inverse of the marginal propensity to save, which is the simple investment multiplier developed in Chapter 6.

It follows from the above equation that a *change* in the exogenously given level of net investment $\Delta \bar{I}$ will create $\Delta \bar{I}/s$ base-period dollars of demand:

$$\Delta Y = \frac{1}{s}\Delta \bar{I} \tag{17-4}$$

Assume that, initially, before the capacity-creating increment in investment occurred, aggregate demand (Y) and potential aggregate output (Q) were equal. Thus, the fresh act of investment took place in an environment characterized by full-capacity macroeconomic equilibrium. After the change in the nation's capital stock, full-capacity equilibrium will again prevail if the resulting change in potential output (ΔQ) is matched by the resulting change in aggregate demand (ΔY). The conditions that must prevail for ΔQ to equal ΔY can be found by setting the right-hand sides of

Equations 17-1 and 17-4 equal to each other:

$$\frac{1}{s}\Delta \bar{I} = g_1 \bar{I}$$

which may be written as

$$\frac{\Delta \bar{I}}{\bar{I}} = g_1 s \tag{17-5}$$

The left-hand side of Equation 17-5 is the percentage change in *net investment* (*not* in the capital stock itself), and the right-hand side is the product of the capital coefficient and the marginal (and average) propensity to save. This product is the "required" investment growth rate if full-capacity equilibrium ($Y = Q$) is to prevail. Larger values of g_1 and/or s would, of course, increase this required growth rate. For example, if g_1 were equal to 0.20—that is, if $5 worth of additional capital would make it possible for a nation to increase its output by $1 per time period—and s were equal to 0.10—that is, if society would save $0.10 of this $1 increase in Y—the equilibrium condition (Equation 17-5) requires that net investment increase by 0.02 or 2% per time period. Remember that $g_1 s$ is an *equilibrium* rate (at which $\Delta Q = \Delta Y$), not necessarily the actual rate prevailing at any particular moment.

Schematically, the "Domar view" of the economic growth process can be seen in terms of Figure 17-1. The view begins with the concept of investment, as on the left-hand side of Figure 17-1. Investment is linked to aggregate demand through the "multiplier" concept and to potential output through the capital coefficient. The equilibrium condition is $Y = Q$ or $\Delta Y = \Delta Q$, so that the equilibrating process focuses on the concepts of aggregate demand and potential output. The variable which is "solved for"—that is, the variable for which we directly obtain an equilibrium rate of growth—is net investment, the variable with which we began.

The "Harrod" Model: Focus on Income

Three years after the publication of Keynes' *The General Theory*, R. F. Harrod developed a model of economic growth which was also a dynamic version of the Keynesian view of a macroeconomy.[9] Harrod's model was published before Domar's, and they are, as we will see, quite similar. Nevertheless, the development of macroeconomic theory was stunted during World War II, and Harrod's work (1939), and Domar's work (beginning in 1946) are now thought worthy of dual recognition for their part in orienting macroeconomics in the direction of growth theory.

While Domar's model focused on net investment, Harrod's model

9. Roy Harrod, "An Essay in Dynamic Theory," *Economic Journal*, Vol. 49 (March 1939), 14–33; *Towards a Dynamic Economics* (Macmillan, 1948), 63–100.

Figure 17-1   The Domar view of economic growth

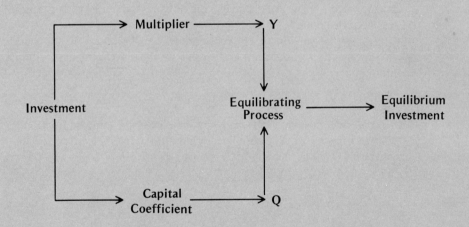

focused on aggregate real income or output. Harrod attempts to determine the rate at which national income must grow to satisfy both the saving plans of households and the investment plans of businesses. Short-run models of Keynesian economics stress the rate of interest as the key variable determining the prevailing level of net investment. It is assumed in Part II, for example, that net investment is inversely related to the interest rate. In our presentation of the Domar model above, we abstract from the factors that *determine* the prevailing level of net investment; we simply take it as a predetermined variable.

Harrod, on the other hand, assumes that the current level of net investment depends on the change in the level of aggregate economic activity (ΔY) taking place during the current time period. For Harrod, current investment is given by

$$I = g_2 \Delta Y \qquad (17\text{-}6)$$

The term g_2 refers to an "accelerator coefficient," and Equation 17-6 itself is said to embody the "accelerator principle." The current level of investment is assumed to be given by a constant (g_2) times the change in the level of aggregate real income. For any investment to take place *at all*, ΔY must be positive. For net investment to grow—that is, for net investment in this period to exceed net investment in the previous period—ΔY of this period must exceed the level of ΔY in the previous period—if g_2 is constant, or at least not declining.

A simple version of Harrod's model can be based on the standard saving function (Equation 17-2) used in the development of Domar's model:

$$S = sY$$

That is, current saving (S) is again assumed to be a constant fraction (s) of current output (Y). The equilibrium condition ($I = S$) leads to the following result

$$I = g_2 \Delta Y = S = sY$$

or

$$\frac{\Delta Y}{Y} = \frac{s}{g_2} \qquad (17\text{-}7)$$

The left-hand side of Equation 17-7 is the percentage change in output "required" if the volume of saving is to be consistent with the volume of net investment. The right-hand side is the marginal (and average) propensity to save divided by the accelerator coefficient. Harrod refers to this percentage as the "warranted" rate of growth. Remember that s/g_2, just like sg_1 in Domar's model, is an *equilibrium* rate (at which $S = I$), not necessarily the actual rate prevailing at any particular moment. Harrod's warranted rate of growth, s/g_2, is the percentage change in Y which satisfies the condition $S = I$.

The key aspects of Harrod's abstraction of the growth process are presented in Figure 17-2. Harrod's view begins with the concept of output, as on the left-hand side of Figure 17-2. Output is linked to saving through the "consumption function" and to net investment through the "accelerator principle." The equilibrium condition is $S = I$, so that the "equilibrating process" focuses on the concepts of saving and net investment. The variable which is "solved for"—that is, the variable for which we directly obtain an equilibrium rate of growth—is output, the variable with which we began.

A HARROD DIFFERENCE EQUATION MODEL

In economic *statics* it is assumed that the interaction among variables occurs during a given period of time, such as a quarter of a year. For example, we argue in Part II that current saving depends on current income, and that current investment depends on the current interest rate. In such a context, the equation $S = I$ embodies the assumption that the time period (say a quarter of a year) is sufficient for the required interest-rate/income-adjustments to occur, so that the volume of saving and investment being done during the period are, in fact, equal. The analysis is really timeless because time has been submerged; it is only implicit in the analysis. We simply take a given stretch of time and assume that things work themselves out during this period.

Both the Harrod and the Domar views of economic growth have been presented so far in this chapter as if they were really *static* models. This enabled us to introduce their economic core without having to bother with a careful treatment of time.

Now we want to develop one of these models, Harrod's, in such a way that time is explicitly taken into account. There are two approaches to time in economic analysis. Time can be thought of as something discrete—something that can be chopped up into periods of a given length, such as 91-day quarters—or as something continuous. In the following model, time is thought of in discrete terms; in Chapter 18 it is thought of as something continuous.

Difference equations are an important tool in modern macroeconomic analysis. They are used where variables at different points appear in the same equation. For example, the saving function used in the foregoing Domar and Harrod models relates current-period saving to current-period income. Using the subscript t to "date" the variable as the prevailing level of that variable during the current period, the Domar-Harrod saving function can be expressed as

Figure 17-2 The Harrod view of economic growth

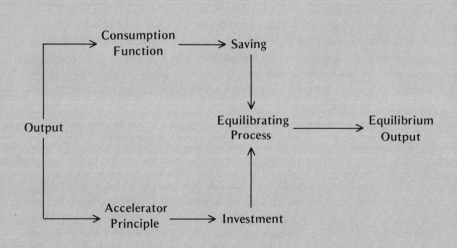

$$S_t = sY_t$$

It is quite possible, however, that this period's level of saving is determined by *last period's* output (Y_{t-1}). If so, the saving function would become

$$S_t = sY_{t-1} \tag{17-8}$$

To get an actual saving function of this type, we could fit a line through the points obtained by plotting the level of S prevailing in one period against the level of Y prevailing in the previous period.

Assume that the version of the accelerator principle used in discussing Harrod's model (see Equation 17-6) is the relevant one:

$$I_t = g_2(Y_t - Y_{t-1}) \tag{17-9}$$

The equilibrium condition is $S_t = I_t$. Therefore, we must set the right-hand sides of Equations 17-8 and 17-9 equal to each other:

$$sY_{t-1} = g_2(Y_t - Y_{t-1})$$

so that

$$\frac{Y_t - Y_{t-1}}{Y_{t-1}} = \frac{s}{g_2} \tag{17-10}$$

Equation 17-10 should be familiar by now. It is the Harrod result that equilibrium requires national output to grow at a rate of s/g_2.

Now we need to express this growth relationship in a slightly different fashion. The left-hand side of Equation 17-10 may be written as

$$\frac{Y_t - Y_{t-1}}{Y_{t-1}} = \frac{Y_t}{Y_{t-1}} - \frac{Y_{t-1}}{Y_{t-1}} = \frac{Y_t}{Y_{t-1}} - 1$$

Therefore Equation 17-10 itself may be expressed as

$$\frac{Y_t}{Y_{t-1}} - 1 = \frac{s}{g_2}$$

or
$$Y_t = (1 + s/g_2)Y_{t-1}$$

That is, if income in the previous period (Y_{t-1}) is known, income in the current period (Y_t) has to be $(1 + s/g_2)Y_{t-1}$ if equilibrium ($S_t = I_t$) is to prevail.

In Figure 17-3, previous-period output (Y_{t-1}) is measured along the horizontal axis, and current-period output (Y_t) is measured along the vertical axis. Assuming we know the prevailing levels of s and g_2, the equation above (which gives equilibrium output) can be drawn in Figure 17-3 as a straight line with a zero intercept and a slope of $(1 + s/g_2)$. Assume further that we know the level of output in the initial period, which we will refer to as period zero. Equilibrium output in period 1, given by the line drawn in Figure 17-3, is the amount Y_1 marked off on the vertical axis. This amount (Y_1) can be brought down to the horizontal axis by using the 45°

Figure 17-3

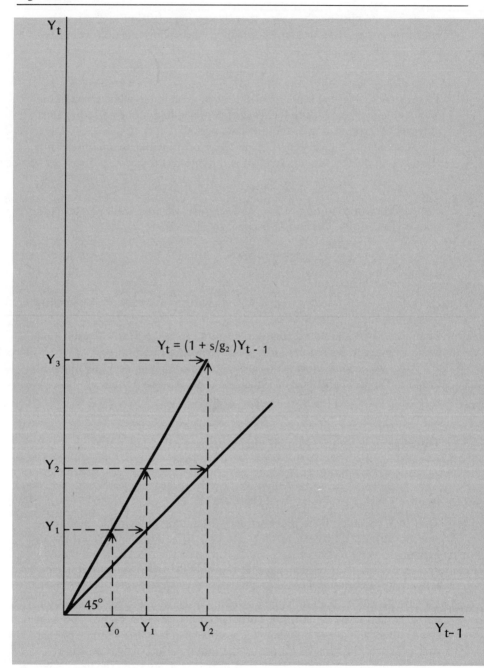

line. Income in period 1 is now the relevant level of Y_{t-1}. Income in period 2 is given by Y_2 in Figure 17-3.

The diagram in Figure 17-3 permits us to trace the level of equilibrium output in period t if we know

1. s and g_2
2. the prevailing level of output in some initial period (Y_0)
3. the number of time periods separating the current period (period t) and the initial period (period 0)
4. that s and g_2 do not change between period 0 and period t
5. that the relevant equilibrium output prevails in every time period between period 0 and period t.

Tracing through all these steps to find Y_t diagrammatically would be a tedious chore. It can be done more directly by using algebra. The basic relationship between current and previous period output is

$$Y_t = (1 + s/g_2)Y_{t-1}$$

If period $t - 1$ is period 0 (the "initial" period), and period t is period 1, the above equation may be written as

$$Y_1 = (1 + s/g_2)Y_0$$

If period t is now period 2, and period $t - 1$ is therefore period 1, the basic relationship between current-period and previous-period output is

$$Y_2 = (1 + s/g_2)Y_1$$

The term Y_1 appears in both the above equations. Substituting the entire right-hand side of the first equation into the right-hand side of the second yields

$$Y_2 = (1 + s/g_2)(1 + s/g_2)Y_0$$

or
$$Y_2 = (1 + s/g_2)^2 Y_0$$

In general, we can assert that

$$Y_t = (1 + s/g_2)^t Y_0$$

The above equation is a *solution* to the difference equation model. It is the current level of output *if and only if* we can be sure that the five conditions discussed above are satisfied.

This simple dynamic view of how an economy grows has been further developed by many economists working in several countries. Harrod's growth model has been a popular base for increasingly complex theories of economic growth.

NUMERICAL EXAMPLE OF THE HARROD MODEL

The usual way of explaining growth equilibrium in economic dynamics is to let the planned level of one component in an "equilibrium condition" (such as $S_t = I_t$) be realized. For example, we could assume that current saving plans are always realized, so that planned saving is equal to realized saving and realized saving is equal to realized investment. (This is because saving plans are the mirror image of consumption plans, and business has inventories that households can buy, even though business may not expect them to be sold during the current period.)

To make this point clearer, let us re-examine the Harrod equations for planned saving (Equation 17-8) and investment (Equation 17-9):

$$S_t = s Y_{t-1}$$

$$I_t = g_2(Y_t - Y_{t-1})$$

Assume that the propensity to save is 0.2, so that if last period's income were 100 ($100 billion in base-period dollars), current saving plans would be 20. Assume further that $g_2 = 4$, and that business managers *expect* the current level of Y to be 110. Under these conditions, planned net investment would be 40. That is,

$$I_t = g_2(Y_t - Y_{t-1})$$

$$40 = 4(110 - 100)$$

If *saving* plans are assumed to be realized—that is, if the level of saving is going to turn out to be 20—and if the $S_t = I_t$ condition is to prevail, the level of investment must also be 20. Y_t will be 105, rather than the 110 expected by business managers when they planned for I_t to be 40. The equilibrium condition can be thought of as being brought about by business experiencing an undesired (and unexpected) inventory disinvestment of the full 20 ($20 billion).

THE HARROD-DOMAR TECHNOLOGY

A Fixed-Coefficients Production Function

Both the Harrod and the Domar models of economic growth are either implicitly or explicitly based on a particular view of the production process that has not yet been discussed. This view can be put under the general heading of "fixed-coefficients" production functions, which is one important way economists view the process of creating outputs from inputs. This view of technology focuses on a *fixed* relationship between the minimum capital and the minimum labor required to produce a unit of output. A simple example of this kind of fixed relationship is combining the services of one man with a shovel. In such a case, *substitution* between labor and capital is out of the question; they must always be used in a strict one-to-one proportion.

Throughout this book, labor (N) has been measured in millions of full-time workers (so that $N = 1$ refers to 1 million full-time workers), while capital (K) and output (Y) were measured in billions of base-period dollars (so that $K = 1$ or $Y = 1$ refers to \$1 billion worth of goods and services, measured in base-period prices). In the context of an economy as a whole, a fixed-coefficients approach to the production of goods and services can be thought of in the following way.

Assume that at least one tenth of a labor unit (that is, one tenth of a million full-time workers, or 100,000 full-time workers) and at least two units of capital (\$2 billion worth of capital goods measured in base-period prices) are required to produce one unit of aggregate output. Assume also that *the above numerical relationship between capital and labor is applicable no matter what the level of aggregate output happens to be.* If the economy is to enjoy \$500 billion worth of aggregate final output (that is, if $Y = 500$), *at least* 1000 units of capital and 50 units of labor must be available.

The point labeled 1 in Figure 17-4 denotes the minimum amount of capital $(K = 1000)$, and the minimum amount of labor $(N = 50)$ required to produce \$500 billion worth of output $(Y = 500)$. If more labor, say $N = 75$, but no more capital is available, the level of output would still be 500, and 25 units of labor would be redundant. If $N = 50$ and $K = 2000$, the level of Y would still be 500, and 1000 units of K would be redundant. The dotted line forming an L with point 1 as its corner can be thought of as a set of combinations for N and K that yield an output level of 500, although only the corner combination is "efficient" in the sense that no resources will be idle if exactly this combination is available. The point labeled 2 in Figure 17-4 denotes the minimum level of capital $(K = 2000)$ and the minimum level of labor $(N = 100)$ required to produce \$1000 billion worth of output $(Y = 1000)$.

There are several ways in which this aggregate fixed-coefficients function can be used to help us better understand the process of economic growth. We will again use t and $t - 1$ as subscripts to denote the level of variables prevailing in period t and period $t - 1$. One special "growth implication" of our fixed-coefficients framework should be introduced at this time. Assume that K_{t-1} and N_{t-1} were such that Y_{t-1} was produced efficiently. With reference to Figure 17-4, we were at a "corner" in period $t - 1$. Therefore, output in period $t - 1$ can be expressed in both of the following ways:

$$K_{t-1} = v_1 Y_{t-1} \qquad\qquad (17\text{-}11)$$

$$N_{t-1} = v_2 Y_{t-1} \qquad\qquad (17\text{-}12)$$

Figure 17-4

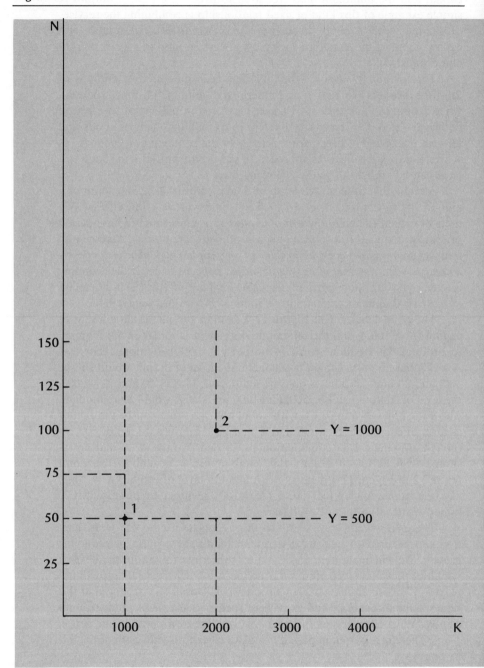

where v_1 and v_2 are the minimum amounts of capital and labor, respectively, required to produce one unit of output. If we are *also* to be in an efficient position (that is, at a "corner") in period t, capital and labor in period t must be such that

$$K_t = v_1 Y_t \qquad\qquad (17\text{-}13)$$

$$N_t = v_2 Y_t \qquad\qquad (17\text{-}14)$$

By subtracting Equation 17-11 from 17-13, and 17-12 from 17-14, we see that

$$K_t - K_{t-1} = v_1 Y_t - v_1 Y_{t-1}$$

and $\qquad\qquad N_t - N_{t-1} = v_2 Y_t - v_2 Y_{t-1}$

Thus it is apparent that

$$\frac{K_t - K_{t-1}}{K_{t-1}} = \frac{v_1 Y_t - v_1 Y_{t-1}}{v_1 Y_{t-1}} = \frac{Y_t - Y_{t-1}}{Y_{t-1}}$$

and

$$\frac{N_t - N_{t-1}}{N_{t-1}} = \frac{v_2 Y_t - v_2 Y_{t-1}}{v_2 Y_{t-1}} = \frac{Y_t - Y_{t-1}}{Y_{t-1}}$$

That is, full-factor employment in any two consecutive time periods requires equiproportional changes in capital, labor, and output:

$$\frac{K_t - K_{t-1}}{K_{t-1}} = \frac{N_t - N_{t-1}}{N_{t-1}} = \frac{Y_t - Y_{t-1}}{Y_{t-1}}$$

No matter what type of production function is being used, the above equations are referred to as a "balanced-growth" condition. In the context of a fixed-coefficients model, the balanced-growth condition is also required if two successive periods are to be "efficient" periods.

Fixed Coefficients and the Accelerator Principle

The fixed-coefficients production function can be used to discusss the process of economic growth in a context where emphasis is placed on the supply side of aggregate economic activity. If Y_t is thought of as the current-period level of output planned by business, the capital coefficient in our production function can be used to obtain a demand function for capital:

$$K_t = v_1 Y_t$$

If the production plans of business are assumed to be realized in each period, so that Y_t and Y_{t-1} denote planned *and* actual aggregate output, the corresponding levels of K_t and K_{t-1} can be thought of as the actual capital stocks held, on the average, during the various periods. Therefore, we can write

$$K_t - K_{t-1} = I_t = v_1 Y_t - v_1 Y_{t-1} = v_1(Y_t - Y_{t-1})$$

that is,
$$I_t = v_1(Y_t - Y_{t-1})$$

The above equation is an algebraic version of Harrod's "accelerator principle." The constant (v_1) is the accelerator coefficient (g_2) used earlier in this chapter. In the version of the accelerator principle introduced here, stress is placed on the accelerator coefficient as a *technical* parameter. This particular use of the fixed-coefficients production function is based on a "supply-side" approach to macroeconomic theory. Business plans for the production of goods and services are focused upon *and* assumed to be realized.

In our earlier discussions of the Harrod model, we viewed the accelerator (g_2) as a *behavioral* parameter. We emphasized that it was how business managers reacted to the spread between Y_t and Y_{t-1} when formulating their current investment plans. A "demand-side" approach to aggregate economic activity was taken. We assumed that households expect a certain level of income to prevail, out of which they plan a given volume of saving. Assuming these plans are realized, for equilibrium to prevail, this volume of saving "warrants" an equal volume of investment.

THE HARROD MODEL AND LABOR FORCE GROWTH

It is convenient at this point to put the technological aspects of growth theory aside, and concentrate on the labor force. For many decades, economists stressed the *circular* connection between population and the productive capacity of the economy. Emphasis on this inexorable cycle, with population affecting output and output affecting population, was most pronounced in the "Malthusian" content of "classical" economics. Since the 1870s, however, economists have become convinced that earlier theories about the second link between output and population were too crude. The determinants of the size and health of a nation's population at any moment in time were considered to be outside the province of economics. They were accepted as facts of life.

As suggested in Part I, *neoclassical* economists used "utility analysis" to determine the *supply of labor* that would be forthcoming out of any *exogenously given population*. The real wage was the key independent variable determining the quantity of labor supplied. But the neoclassical supply of labor function was a *short-run* function, giving the varying quantities of labor to be supplied (as the real wage varied) *out of a given population*. (The Keynesian short-run model developed in Part II was based on an exogenously given work force—the supply of labor was not viewed as being determined within the confines of the model.)

The theory of economic growth, on the other hand, deals with the progression of an economy through time; that is, it deals with economies where the size and quality of the population itself are probably changing. Most contemporary growth theory is based on the assumption that the labor force simply grows at some exogenously given percentage.

Let us assume that the labor force grows at some rate n (where n is some percentage per period, such as 2%), so that the current labor force (N_t) may be expressed as

$$N_t = (1 + n)N_{t-1}$$

The term n is assumed to be determined by physiological, psychological, and biological factors beyond the scope of the traditional boundaries of economics. The size of n must be known, but once known, it is accepted as a fact of life. The above equation may now be used to stress one of the main results of the Harrod view of economic growth.

Assume that (by some fortuitous accident) period $t - 1$ is a full-employment position. That is, K_{t-1} and N_{t-1} are such that Y_{t-1} is produced efficiently. As discussed earlier in this chapter, if period t is also to be a period of "efficiency," with no redundant labor or capital, balanced growth must prevail:

$$\frac{K_t - K_{t-1}}{K_{t-1}} = \frac{N_t - N_{t-1}}{N_{t-1}} = \frac{Y_t - Y_{t-1}}{Y_{t-1}}$$

Now the growth rate of labor is going to be n, no matter what else happens. The "warranted rate of growth" (s/g_2) is the percentage change in Y that satisfies the condition of $S = I$. It is reasonable for us to expect free-market forces to bring this growth rate. But there is no reason to expect this warranted growth rate (s/g_2) to exactly match the growth rate of labor (n). Since s, g_2, and n are all determined independently, there is no reason to expect that $s/g_2 = n$. One very important result in Harrod's theory of growth is that redundancies in factors of production, such as labor, are likely to occur. It is for this reason that *Harrod's model is viewed as a dynamic extension of Keynes' work.*

CONCLUSION

While the Harrod-Domar approach to economic growth *does* answer the question "What is the equilibrium growth path?" it does so in a highly unsatisfactory way. The answer depends on capital and labor staying in a fixed relationship to each other, so that both factors of production can be used. The unwarranted and natural rates of growth must equal each other as well. If these conditions are *not* met—and there is little reason why they should be in the real world—the Harrod-Domar model predicts unemployment of labor and capital, with no mechanism in the economy to return to full employment. As a result of its instability, the model is referred to as having a "razor edge." In the following chapter we will consider a model of growth that avoids the problems associated with the Harrod-Domar approach. Before turning to this work, we suggest you read this chapter's two appendices on *continuous versus discrete time* and *differentiation rules*.

APPENDIX A: CONTINUOUS VERSUS DISCRETE TIME

In discrete-time models such as those previously presented, the main function of time was to "date" or subscript variables. Difference equations are the basic tool of dynamic analysis in a discrete-time context. The prevailing levels of variables during different time *intervals* are related in equations such as the following one (a basic equation in our discussion of Harrod's theory of growth):

$$Y_t = (1 + s/g_2)Y_{t-1}$$

In macroeconomics, flow variables are usually expressed at annual rates. In a discrete-time context—in which time is cut up into periods, such as 91-day quarters—flow variables are period totals expressed at annual rates. If we choose to divide time into monthly units, flow variables would be *monthly* totals at *annual* rates. Flow variables in a discrete-time context present no major difficulties; we simply measure the volume of flow during whatever time period we choose to use—a day, month, quarter, or whatever—and convert the number to an annual rate. *Stock* variables in discrete-time analysis *are* troublesome, because we have to decide whether to measure the stock at the beginning, the middle, or the end of the time period, or compute an average for the period.

In a *continuous*-time context, time has *two* important functions. First, as in a discrete-time context, time is a reference point, such as 3 p.m., January 3, 1974. We are capable of explicitly identifying any specific *point* in time; we are no longer limited to intervals. If time is continuous, it can also be used to denote the change in a variable over time, not during a *period*, but at an *instant*.

Stock variables, in the context of continuous time, present some serious difficulties from a quantitative point of view (who would make all the calculations or estimates?). From a theoretical point of view, however, the notion of continuous, up-to-the-minute measurements of stock variables presents no problems. However, *flow* variables, such as Y, require more careful handling. In earlier chapters, Y was a quarterly total expressed at an annual rate. In a continuous time context, Y is an instantaneous total expressed at an annual rate. Y at any moment in time can be thought of as though obtained by taking a picture of the flow of final goods and services at that moment—if exactly this flow is maintained for 365 days, the total volume of the flow for the year will be Y. A good example of an instantaneous total expressed at an annual rate was the United States

Department of Commerce's "GNP Clock," a "device" used to "indicate" the instant when the U.S. economy became a "trillionaire."

Generally, discrete time is used for economic convenience, while continuous time is used for mathematical convenience. Viewing flows as *quarterly* totals expressed at annual rates is better for injecting realism into theory and applying theory to reality. But viewing flows as *instantaneous* totals expressed at annual rates is better for using mathematics to develop theory. Although this dynamic, continuous approach to economic analysis has resulted in a highly mathematical literature, only a few techniques need to be introduced now to help you follow the arguments in the next chapter.

APPENDIX B: THREE DIFFERENTIATION RULES

Earlier in this book we explained that the "slope" or "first derivative" of any continuous function having only one independent variable, such as $y = f(x)$, is expressed as dy/dx. This expression should be read "the change in y resulting from a small change in x."

1) The general rule for finding the "first derivative" of the function

$$y = ax^m + b$$

is

$$\frac{dy}{dx} = amx^{m-1}$$

2) In the case of multiple independent variables, such as with the function $y = f(x, z)$, the first derivative is expressed as $\partial y/\partial x$. This expression, $\partial y/\partial x$ should be read "the change in y resulting from a change in x alone"—that is, the variation in y resulting from a change in x with the level of z remaining constant. For any specific function, such as $y = ax^m z^n$ where a, m, and n are constants, the change in y resulting from a change in x alone is $\partial y/\partial x = amx^{m-1}z^n$.

3) Finally, assume we again have a function with, say, three variables, but that each variable, as well as a, varies with a fourth variable, such as t, so that

$$y(t) = a(t)x(t)z(t)$$

Here y is dependent on the level of t as well as on the levels of a, x, and z; each of which is also dependent upon t in its own way. It can (but will not) be shown that the change in y with respect to a change in t, dy/dt, for the above equation is given by

$$\frac{dy}{dt} = \frac{\partial y(t)}{\partial a(t)}\frac{da}{dt} + \frac{\partial y(t)}{\partial x(t)}\frac{dx}{dt} + \frac{\partial y(t)}{\partial z(t)}\frac{dz}{dt}$$

Economic
Growth (II)

THE "NEOCLASSICAL" PRODUCTION
FUNCTION: GENERAL PROPERTIES

The main source of rigidity or inflexibility in the model introduced in
Chapter 17 is the notion of a fixed-coefficients production function. To a
great extent, the results of the model are attributable to the fixed relationship assumed to exist between the minimum amounts of labor and capital
required to produce one unit of output. This formulation rules out the
possibility of substitution between labor and capital, a very *realistic* possibility which needs to be incorporated into many classes of models. In the
mid-1950s economists interested in economic growth seized on the idea of
developing the "neoclassical" technology in a growth context. While the
Harrod-Domar technology permitted only fixed-factor proportions, the
neoclassical technology (so-called because it was developed by J. B. Clark
and others between the 1870s and 1930s) permitted variable factor proportions.

Although neoclassical production functions have been developed in
several different forms, four characteristics are common to all of them.
We have discussed and even used some of these characteristics in earlier
chapters, but it is useful to spell them out in an orderly fashion at this time.

1) Both stock and flow variables in a neoclassical production function, as the concept is used in this chapter, are thought of in terms of continuous rather than discrete time. The maximum output of consumer products and new net investment goods a nation can produce at any given time,
$Y(t)$, is a function of available labor, $N(t)$, and capital, $K(t)$, as well as the
prevailing level of technology, $A(t)$. Note, however, that flow variables
(such as income) and stock variables (such as capital) are now expressed
as $Y(t)$ and $K(t)$, instead of Y_t and K_t. In Chapter 17, t was a subscript that

denoted the prevailing level of the variable during period t. Now the variables are themselves functions of time. It should be pointed out, however, that discrete-time versions of the neoclassical production function could be developed, as could continuous-time versions of the fixed-coefficients production function.

2) In the neoclassical technology, capital and labor are continuously substitutable for each other. In the upper panel of Figure 18-1, depicting a fixed-coefficients technology, there are an infinite number of capital-labor combinations which will provide a given $\bar{Y}$ level of output, but only one is "efficient"—the "corner" combination. All neoclassical production functions, in contrast, are such that there are an indefinitely large number of capital-labor combinations which will yield a given level of output, such as $\bar{Y}$ in the lower panel of Figure 18-1. None of these combinations is in any sense more "efficient" than any other. It should be clear from the lower panel of Figure 18-1 that neither capital nor labor can ever be "redundant" in a neoclassical framework. The functions in both panels are referred to as "equal product curves" or "isoquants." The isoquant in the lower panel has no corner, so the notion of factor redundancy is not relevant.

3) The "law" of diminishing returns is applicable in the neoclassical framework. It is usually expressed in the following way: For a given technology, the addition of equal amounts of a variable factor of production to fixed factors of production will eventually result in successively smaller additions to output. This relationship can also be put in percentage terms. If the variable input increases by x percent, output increases by less than x percent.

4) A "neoclassical" production function is characterized by "constant returns to scale," a property we explore in greater detail later in this chapter. For now, simply note that constant returns to scale means that if *all* inputs increase by some common percentage, output increases by the same percentage.

THE COBB-DOUGLAS PRODUCTION FUNCTION

In earlier chapters, we used a fairly popular version of the neoclassical production function:

$$Y = AN^{\alpha}K^{1-\alpha}$$

This production function was introduced by Charles W. Cobb and Paul H. Douglas (economist and former Illinois Senator) in 1928.

Economists usually try to apply general functions whenever possible so that their analyses cover a wide range of cases. Later in this chapter we employ a general neoclassical production function. For now it is convenient to work with one of the explicit versions—the Cobb-Douglas version. Earlier, we discussed four basic properties of neoclassical production

Figure 18-1

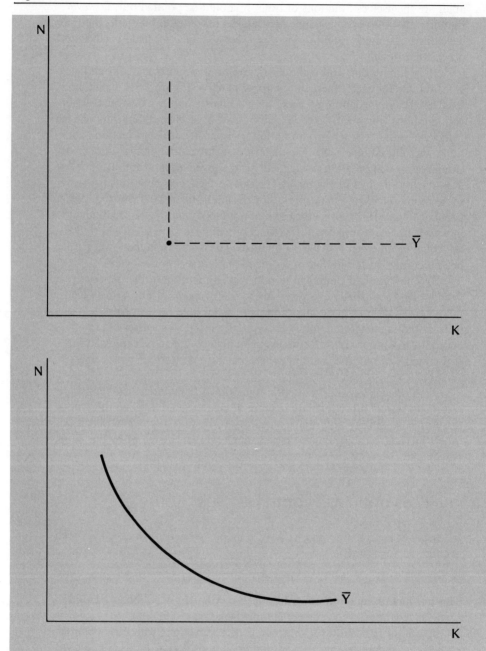

functions. Now let us confirm that these properties are present in our Cobb-Douglas function:

$$Y(t) = A(t)[N(t)]^\alpha[K(t)]^{1-\alpha}$$

The first property, that the variables are continuous functions of time, *is* explicitly incorporated in the above function. But attaching a t term to every variable makes manipulation of the function awkward. Therefore, we will drop the t notation but continue to think of all these variables as the levels prevailing at any given instant in time, with the flows expressed at annual rates.

The second property of neoclassical production functions is that there is an indefinitely large number of capital-labor combinations which can produce a given level of output. Let $\bar{Y}$ be some specific level of aggregate output. Substitute this level into our Cobb-Douglas function:

$$\bar{Y} = AN^\alpha K^{1-\alpha}$$

Given values of α, A, and $\bar{Y}$, the above equation has only two unknowns, N and K. The combinations of N and K that satisfy the above equation could be plotted against each other. The general shape of the curve would depend on the values of α, A, and $\bar{Y}$, but we do know that it would be a continuous inverse function; that is, as K increased, N would decline. This function gives the infinite number of combinations of N and K which, if available, would yield a $\bar{Y}$ level of output. In a Cobb-Douglas context it should be clear that neither labor nor capital can be "redundant," in the fixed-coefficients sense of the word.

The third property of neoclassical production functions is diminishing returns. If α is assumed to be a positive fraction, varying one of the inputs in the above equation while holding the other constant will cause Y to increase, but the percentage increase in Y will be less than the percentage increase in the one input. For example, assume that $A = 2$, $\alpha = \frac{1}{2}$, and $K = 100$. If

$$N = 100, 120, 144, 173$$

$$Y = 200, 220, 240, 260$$

and the percentage increases in the two variables are

$$N: +20\%, +20\%, +20\%$$

$$Y: +10\%, +9\%, +8\%$$

then equal percentage increases in the variable input, labor, results in decreasing additions to output.

The fourth property of neoclassical production functions, constant returns to scale, can be demonstrated to hold for the Cobb-Douglas case. Assume that both factors of production increase by λ. The new level of income (Y) can be expressed as

$$Y' = A(\lambda N)^\alpha(\lambda K)^{1-\alpha} = A\lambda^\alpha N^\alpha \lambda^{1-\alpha}K^{1-\alpha} = \lambda^{\alpha+1-\alpha}AN^\alpha K^{1-\alpha} = \lambda AN^\alpha K^{1-\alpha}$$

That is, $Y' = \lambda Y$. For example, if $\lambda = 1.02$, both factors as well as the level of output will have increased by 2%.

A NEOCLASSICAL FACTOR-PRICE FRONTIER

The Cobb-Douglas production function can be shown to lead to certain very specific propositions concerning the distribution of aggregate income characteristic of neoclassical production functions in general. Efficient use of factors of production requires that the marginal productivity of labor ($\partial Y/\partial N$) and of capital ($\partial Y/\partial K$) be equal to the cost of labor (W/P) and the rate of interest (r). That is,

$$\frac{W}{P} = \frac{\partial Y}{\partial N}$$

$$r = \frac{\partial Y}{\partial K}$$

Given the production function

$$Y = AN^\alpha K^{1-\alpha}$$

and using the second differentiation rule given in Appendix B to Chapter 17, the two marginal productivities can be expressed as

$$\frac{\partial Y}{\partial N} = \alpha A\left(\frac{K}{N}\right)^{1-\alpha} \tag{18-1}$$

$$\frac{\partial Y}{\partial K} = (1-\alpha)A\left(\frac{K}{N}\right)^{-\alpha} \tag{18-2}$$

Introducing the letter k to denote the capital-labor ratio (K/N), and assuming that both factors are used efficiently, we have the factor-price/marginal-productivity equations:

$$\frac{W}{P} = \frac{\partial Y}{\partial N} = \alpha Ak^{1-\alpha} \tag{18-3}$$

$$r = \frac{\partial Y}{\partial K} = (1-\alpha)Ak^{-\alpha} \tag{18-4}$$

Since α is a positive fraction, as k increases (that is, as "capital deepening" occurs) $\partial Y/\partial N$ and hence W/P increase, and $\partial Y/\partial K$ and hence r decline.

By plotting positive, increasing levels of k along the left-hand as well as the lower axes of Figure 18-2, the above two equations may be graphed in the northwest and southeast quadrants. For any value of the capital/labor ratio, such as k', there are corresponding levels of the real wage ($W/P)'$ and the rate of interest (r'). A "factor-price frontier" can be derived geometrically in the northeast quadrant of Figure 18-2 by plotting many of these real-wage/interest-rate combinations. The "frontier" could also be obtained by solving each of the two factor-price/marginal-productivity equations above for k, setting the resulting right-hand sides equal, and solving for W/P.

We will demonstrate that the constant-returns technology of the Cobb-Douglas production function is such that the two factor payments "exhaust" the entire net national product; that is,

$$Y = (W/P)N + rK$$

By "exhaust" the entire net national product, we mean that the total physical product will be exactly enough to pay each input, labor and capital, an amount of physical product equal to its marginal product. It is this proposition that marks the Cobb-Douglas production function as "neoclassical." Another point about the distribution of income that can be easily made in the Cobb-Douglas context relates not to the *absolute* shares of net output going to those who supply labor and capital services, but rather to the *relative* shares.

In order to make this point, it is necessary to differentiate Equations 18-3 and 18-4 with respect to k (which is the K/N ratio):

$$\frac{d(W/P)}{dk} = \alpha(1 - \alpha)Ak^{-\alpha}$$

$$\frac{dr}{dk} = -\alpha(1 - \alpha)Ak^{-\alpha-1}$$

and divide the former equation by the latter:

$$\frac{d(W/P)/dk}{dr/dk} = \frac{d(W/P)}{dr} = \frac{\alpha(1 - \alpha)Ak^{-\alpha}}{-\alpha(1 - \alpha)Ak^{-\alpha-1}}$$

$$\frac{d(W/P)}{dr} = -k$$

If we multiply both sides of the above equation by $r/(W/P)$ and substitute K/N for k, we have

$$\frac{d(W/P)}{dr} \frac{r}{W/P} = -\frac{rK}{(W/P)N}$$

This equation gives us an indication of the responsiveness of a change in the real wage to a change in the interest rate. That is, the "elasticity" or responsiveness of the factor-price frontier is the ratio of the income shares.

At any given level of r (such as r') in Figure 18-2, the "elasticity" of the frontier at that point is the proportional rate of change in W/P with respect to a very small change in r, in the neighborhood of r'. If this elasticity is unity, for example, total real wages and total interest are each one half the total net national product. As capital deepening occurs—that is, as K/N increases—there is a shift up the factor-price frontier from the

Figure 18-2

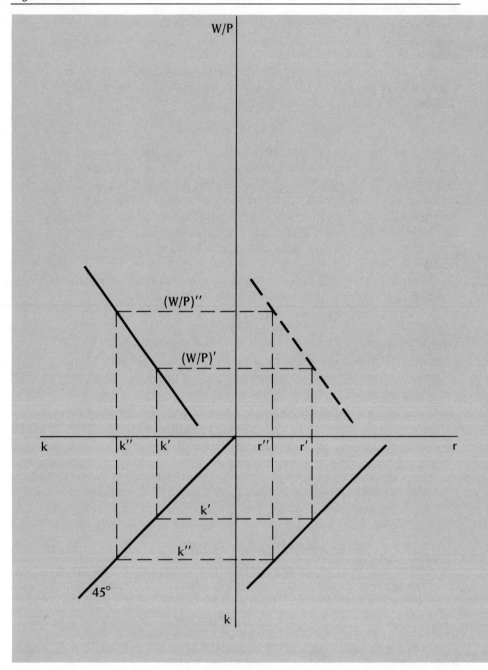

r' ... $(W/P)'$ combination to the r'' ... $(W/P)''$ combination (with reference to Figure 18-2). As this shift occurs, the relative share of capital will increase, remain the same, or decrease if the elasticity becomes a larger negative, remains the same, or becomes a smaller negative number.

TECHNOLOGICAL CHANGE

In recent years economists have been interested in measuring technological change. Not all the economic growth that has occurred in recent decades can be explained by growth in labor and capital inputs alone. The skill with which labor and capital are used to produce goods and services *has* improved, and economists would like to be able to say precise things about the rate of this improvement.

There are several alternative ways of viewing technological progress, even within the "neoclassical" framework. In this section we are concerned with the method attributable to Robert M. Solow.[1] In measuring technological change, Solow attempted to separate the sources of economic growth, using the Cobb-Douglas version of the neoclassical production function previously introduced:

$$Y(t) = A(t)[N(t)]^{\alpha}[K(t)]^{1-\alpha}$$

We know that, given the above production function,

$$\frac{dY}{dt} = \frac{\partial Y(t)}{\partial A(t)}\frac{dA}{dt} + \frac{\partial Y(t)}{\partial N(t)}\frac{dN}{dt} + \frac{\partial Y(t)}{\partial K(t)}\frac{dK}{dt} \qquad (18\text{-}5)$$

Using the two expressions for the marginal productivities obtained in the previous section, Equations 18-1 and 18-2, and the fact that

$$\frac{\partial Y(t)}{\partial A(t)} = [N(t)]^{\alpha}[K(t)]^{1-\alpha}$$

we have expressions for three of the terms on the right side of Equation 18-5.

The notion of a "time derivative"—such as dY/dt—should be thought of as the change in a variable with respect to a very small change in time, at a given point in time.[2] To be exact, we should "date" our time derivatives with a subscript, such as

$$\left(\frac{dY}{dt}\right)_t$$

1. Robert M. Solow, "Technical Change and the Aggregate Production Function," *The Review of Economics and Statistics*, Vol. 39 (August 1957), 312–313.
2. With reference to the Department of Commerce's "GNP clock," the change in GNP with respect to a change in time (d(GNP)/dt) would be the amount GNP was changing, at 12:02 p.m., December 15, 1970, expressed at an annual rate, i.e., if this particular rate of change were to continue for 365 days.

But this practice makes the equations more cumbersome than they need to be, so simply keep in mind that all the time derivatives (dY/dt, dA/dt, dN/dt, and dK/dt) are themselves functions of time, just as are Y, A, N, and K.

Therefore, making the proper substitutions for $\partial Y/\partial A$, $\partial Y/\partial N$, and $\partial Y/\partial K$ in Equation 18-5, we have

$$\frac{1}{Y}\frac{dY}{dt} = \frac{1}{A}\frac{dA}{dt} + \frac{\alpha 1}{N}\frac{dN}{dt} + (1-\alpha)\frac{1}{K}\frac{dK}{dt} \tag{18-6}$$

Let G_Y denote the rate of growth of income, G_A the rate of growth of A (the amount the production function is "shifting" per time period), n the rate of growth of labor, and G_K the rate of growth of capital. The above equation can then be expressed as

$$G_Y = G_A + \alpha n + (1-\alpha)G_K$$

or

$$G_A = G_Y - \alpha n - (1-\alpha)G_K \tag{18-7}$$

The dependent variable on the left-hand side of Equation 18-7 is, in our neoclassical context, the measure of technological progress. Data on the past performance as well as estimates of future performance of three of the four independent variables on the right-hand side of Equation 18-7 are relatively easy to obtain. The past and future performance of G_Y, n, and G_K present no really challenging measurement problems. But where can we get past observations and future estimates for α? The answer to this question lies at the core of neoclassical theory itself.

One of the nice features of neoclassical economic theory is the way in which interrelationships between production and distribution can be developed. While α would be difficult to measure if we focused on production and nothing else, α also denotes a distributional concept which is relatively easy to measure. As will now be shown, α is total wage income divided by total output, or the "relative income share of labor."

We know from earlier discussions that the efficient use of labor requires that the marginal productivity of labor be equated to the real wage:

$$\frac{W}{P} = \frac{\partial Y}{\partial N}$$

Given the Cobb-Douglas version of the neoclassical production function, we also know that

$$\frac{\partial Y}{\partial N} = \alpha A N^{\alpha-1} K^{1-\alpha}$$

Labor's "relative share" of aggregate output can be expressed as

$$\frac{(W/P)N}{Y}$$

or
$$\frac{\alpha A N^{\alpha-1} K^{1-\alpha} N}{A N^{\alpha} K^{1-\alpha}} = \alpha$$

Therefore, if we have data on the past performance of labor's share of aggregate output, we also have data for α in Equation 18-7.

For example, if output last year increased by 6%, the quantity of labor employed increased by 2%, the rate of growth of capital was 5%, and labor's share of aggregate output was 70%, we can easily use Equation 18-7 to determine last year's rate of technological progress:

$$G_A = G_Y - \alpha n - (1 - \alpha)G_K$$

$$G_A = 0.06 - (0.7)(0.02) - (1 - 0.7)(0.05)$$

$$G_A = 0.031$$

That is, according to this formulation, the A term in the production function increased by 3.1% last year.

On the basis of calculations of this type, Solow found that the rate of technological change averaged approximately 1.5% annually during the period 1909–1949. He found that only 14% of the increase in output per worker during this period could be accounted for by increased capital per worker. Hence, on the basis of this model, it appears that technological advance has been far more important than physical investment as a source of economic growth.

The policy implication that follows from Solow's analysis is apparent: government policies should encourage "technological change." But what is this mysterious factor of production? It includes everything that might give rise to a shift in the production function; it includes such activities as research and invention, and improvements in the education and health, as well as possible changes in the location, of the labor force.

NEOCLASSICAL GROWTH: EQUILIBRIUM AND STABILITY

The neoclassical growth model is, of course, a model of *growth*, and we now should work through some of its growth properties. Recall Equation 18-6:

$$\frac{1}{Y}\frac{dY}{dt} = \frac{1}{A}\frac{dA}{dt} + \alpha\frac{1}{N}\frac{dN}{dt} + (1 - \alpha)\frac{1}{K}\frac{dK}{dt}$$

Equation 18-6 shows that the growth rate of output is the weighted sum of the growth rates of A, N, and K.

The growth implications of Equation 18-6 can be explored by adding three more traditional neoclassical assumptions. First, we assume that the growth rate of A is constant. The "shift factor" A in the production function is assumed to increase exponentially, so that the state of technology—

what can be obtained from given amounts of labor and capital—is improving at a *constant* percentage rate, G_A:

$$G_A = \frac{1}{A}\frac{dA}{dt} \tag{18-8}$$

Second, we assume that the growth rate of labor is constant. We are simply asserting that the growth rate of the labor force is an exogenously given variable. The quantity of labor supplied at the prevailing real wage is growing at every moment in time at a per period rate of n. In the context of continuous time, the labor available at instant t may be expressed as

$$N_t = N_0 e^{nt}$$

N_0 is the labor force at some initial period, and e is the "base e," that is, approximately 2.71828. The time derivative[3] of the above expression is

$$\frac{dN}{dt} = nN_0 e^{nt}$$

Dividing both sides of the above equation by N yields

$$\frac{1}{N}\frac{dN}{dt} = \frac{nN_0 e^{nt}}{N_0 e^{nt}} = n \tag{18-9}$$

Third, as in the Harrod-Domar context, saving is assumed to be a *constant* fraction of Y, and saving and investment are equal, at every moment in time. The instantaneous change in the capital stock, which is expressed at an annual rate (dK/dt), is the instantaneous level of investment. Thus, the condition $I = S$ may be written as

$$\frac{dK}{dt} = sY$$

Dividing both sides of the above equation by K yields

$$\frac{1}{K}\frac{dK}{dt} = s\frac{Y}{K} \tag{18-10}$$

Substituting G_A from Equation 18-8 (for the rate of change in technology), n from Equation 18-9 (for the growth rate of labor), and the right-hand side of Equation 18-10 (for growth rate of capital) into Equation 18-6 yields

$$\frac{1}{Y}\frac{dY}{dt} = G_A + \alpha n + (1 - \alpha)s\frac{Y}{K} \tag{18-11}$$

In Equation 18-11 the growth rate of income is a function of only one

---

3. The standard form for the derivative of an exponential function such as $y = ae^{bx}$ is

$$\frac{dy}{dx} = bae^{bx}$$

variable, the output-capital ratio Y/K. Everything else in Equation 18-11 is constant.

Equations 18-10 and 18-11 share a common independent variable (Y/K), and their dependent variables have the same time dimension, percentage per time period. Therefore they can be plotted in the same diagram, as in Figure 18-3. The slope of Equation 18-10 is s, the marginal (and average) propensity to save. Since α is a positive fraction, the slope of Equation 18-11, $(1 - \alpha)s$, is less than that of Equation 18-10. Also, the line representing Equation 18-10 goes through the origin, while the line representing Equation 18-11 has a positive vertical intercept, $G_A + \alpha n$.

The equilibrium growth rate of output is defined as that level of $(1/Y)(dY/dt)$ which if already attained will be permanently sustained, and if not already attained, will be attained as time goes by. The rate of growth of output corresponding to the intersection of the lines representing Equations 18-10 and 18-11—that is, the growth rate of output corresponding to $(Y/K)^*$ in Figure 18-3—is the "equilibrium" growth rate of Y in the present context.

To see why this is true, select some specific level of the output-capital ratio, say $(Y/K)'$ in Figure 18-3. At this level, the growth rate of output exceeds the growth rate of capital, and the Y/K ratio will increase. If the Y/K ratio were greater than $(Y/K)^*$, the growth rate of output would be exceeded by the growth rate of capital, and the Y/K ratio would decline. Thus, in this sense, the output-capital ratio labeled $(Y/K)^*$ in Figure 18-3 is the "equilibrium" level. If this level does not prevail, automatic forces will move the economy toward it, and if it does prevail, it will not change unless one or more of the constants in Equations 18-10 or 18-11 changes.

To obtain an expression for the equilibrium growth rate of output, put the left-hand side of Equation 18-10 back into the right-hand side of Equation 18-11, to solve them simultaneously:

$$\frac{1}{Y}\frac{dY}{dt} = G_A + \alpha n + (1 - \alpha)\frac{1}{K}\frac{dK}{dt}$$

Remember that any given level of the output-capital ratio, such as $(Y/K)^*$, will be perpetuated if

$$\frac{1}{Y}\frac{dY}{dt} = \frac{1}{K}\frac{dK}{dt}$$

Therefore the equilibrium growth rate of output may be expressed as

$$\left(\frac{1}{Y}\frac{dY}{dt}\right)^* = G_A + \alpha n + (1 - \alpha)\left(\frac{1}{Y}\frac{dY}{dt}\right)^*$$

$$\left(\frac{1}{Y}\frac{dY}{dt}\right)^* - \left(\frac{1}{Y}\frac{dY}{dt}\right)^* + \alpha\left(\frac{1}{Y}\frac{dY}{dt}\right)^* = G_A + \alpha n$$

$$\left(\frac{1}{Y}\frac{dY}{dt}\right)^* = \frac{G_A + \alpha n}{\alpha} \tag{18-12}$$

Figure 18-3

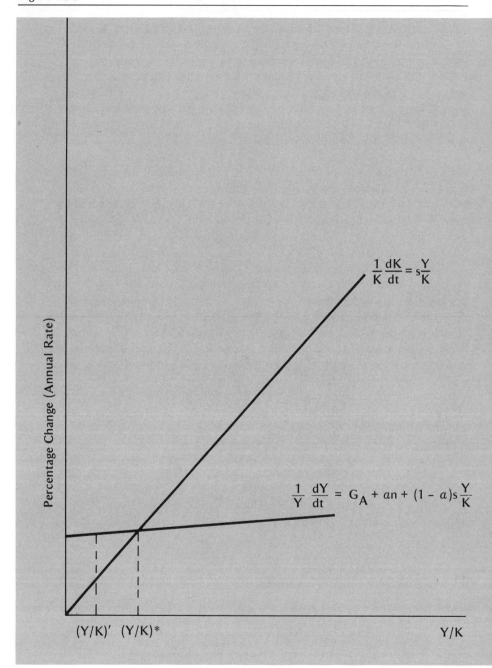

$$\frac{1}{K}\frac{dK}{dt} = s\frac{Y}{K}$$

$$\frac{1}{Y}\frac{dY}{dt} = G_A + an + (1-a)s\frac{Y}{K}$$

Percentage Change (Annual Rate)

$(Y/K)'$ $(Y/K)^*$

Y/K

In Equation 18-12, the equilibrium growth rate of output is shown to be dependent upon G_A, α, and n. Note that the equilibrium growth rate of output does *not* depend on the marginal (and average) propensity to save. *In this neoclassical model, the proportion of income which society saves and invests has no effect on the equilibrium growth rate.*

An increase in α means that the labor exponent in the production function increases at the direct expense of the capital exponent in the production function $(1 - \alpha)$. Because α and n are positive fractions, *an increase in α increases the numerator of the above equation by less than the denominator is increased, and the equilibrium growth rate of income declines.* Increases in G_A and n both clearly cause the equilibrium level of income to increase.

If $G_A = 0$, that is, if there is no technological progress, Equation 18-12 reduces to

$$\left(\frac{1}{Y}\frac{dY}{dt}\right)^* = n$$

The equilibrium growth rate of income equals the exogenously given growth rate of labor. Output and labor would grow at the same rate, so that Y/N—output per worker, a good indicator of the average standard of living—would remain constant.

AN OPTIMAL RATE OF GROWTH

In this section, some normative content is added to the Cobb-Douglas version of the neoclassical model. We go about finding the conditions necessary for per capita consumption to be at a maximum. Assuming again that $S = I = dK/dt$, consumption at any moment in time can be expressed as

$$C = Y - \frac{dK}{dt}$$

Dividing both sides by N gives

$$\frac{C}{N} = \frac{Y}{N} - \frac{dK}{dt}\frac{1}{N}$$

or

$$\frac{C}{N} = \frac{Y}{N} - \frac{1}{K}\frac{dK}{dt}\frac{K}{N}$$

Consumption per Worker

The left-hand side of the above equation is per worker consumption. If we assume that there is a relatively constant relationship between the labor force and the population, consumption per worker can be associated with consumption per head. If "balanced growth" prevails, capital and labor are growing at the same rate; that is

$$\frac{1}{N}\frac{dN}{dt} = n = \frac{1}{K}\frac{dK}{dt}$$

During balanced growth, therefore, the equation for per-worker consumption may be written as

$$\frac{C}{N} = \frac{Y}{N} - \frac{1}{N}\frac{dN}{dt}\frac{K}{N}$$

or

$$\frac{C}{N} = \frac{Y}{N} - n\frac{K}{N} \tag{18-13}$$

In the Cobb-Douglas context, output per head (Y/N) can be expressed as

$$\frac{Y}{N} = \frac{AN^\alpha K^{1-\alpha}}{N} = AN^{\alpha-1}K^{1-\alpha} = A\left(\frac{K}{N}\right)^{1-\alpha}$$

The far right-hand side of the above equation can be substituted into Equation 18-13 in place of Y/N:

$$\frac{C}{N} = A\left(\frac{K}{N}\right)^{1-\alpha} - n\frac{K}{N} \tag{18-14}$$

The capital-labor ratio is the only variable in either of the two components on the right-hand side of Equation 18-14, so they can be plotted in the same space, as in Figure 18-4. In Figure 18-4, nK/N is a straight line because its slope n, the rate of growth of labor, is assumed to be constant. Y/N continuously increases, but at a decreasing rate, because the exponent $1 - \alpha$ is a positive fraction.

For any level of the capital-labor ratio, such as $(K/N)'$ in Figure 18-4, the vertical distance *between* the two functions is consumption per worker, such as $(C/N)'$. Note that this is true only for balanced growth situations; that is, as long as any *specific* level of K/N is sustained, this vertical distance gives the corresponding consumption per worker.

Now, the really *normative* question is—which balanced growth situation yields the highest sustainable level of consumption per worker? To maximize C/N, Equation 18-14 should be differentiated with respect to K/N and the result set equal to zero:

$$\frac{d(C/N)}{d(K/N)} = (1 - \alpha)A\left(\frac{K}{N}\right)^{1-\alpha-1} - n = 0$$

$$n = (1 - \alpha)A\left(\frac{K}{N}\right)^{-\alpha} \tag{18-15}$$

The left-hand side of Equation 18-15, the condition necessary for C/N to

Figure 18-4

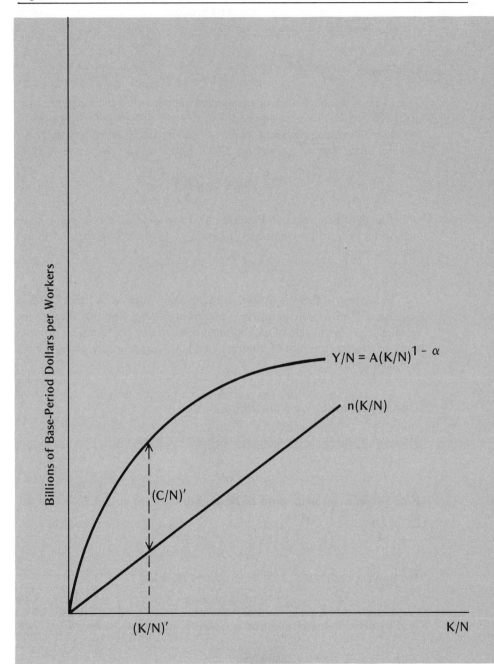

be as large as possible, is the growth rate of labor. We now need to show that the right-hand side is the marginal productivity of capital or, if capital is used efficiently, the rate of interest.

Optimality

The efficient use of factors of production requires that the marginal productivity of each factor be equated with the corresponding factor price. In the case of capital, efficiency requires that its marginal productivity be equated to the rate of interest (r). From Equation 18-4, where $k = K/N$, we have

$$r = (1 - \alpha)A\left(\frac{K}{N}\right)^{-\alpha} \tag{18-16}$$

The right-hand side of Equation 18-16 is identical to the right-hand side of our optimality condition, Equation 18-15. Therefore their left-hand sides are equal:

$$r = n$$

In summary, there is a single capital-labor ratio (K/N) that yields a maximum level of consumption per worker (C/N). For this level to be reached, the growth rate of capital must be such that the marginal productivity of capital (the rate of interest) equals the exogenously given growth rate of labor.

Optimality and Income Distribution

We have found that, for any balanced-growth situation,

$$\frac{C}{N} = \frac{Y}{N} - n\frac{K}{N}$$

If per worker consumption is to be as high as possible, $n = r$, so that the above equation becomes

$$\frac{C}{N} = \frac{Y}{N} - r\frac{K}{N}$$

Multiplying both sides of the equation by N yields

$$C = Y - rK$$

But, by definition, consumption is equal to income less saving:

$$C = Y - S$$

It follows from the above two equations that

$$S = rK$$

That is, for a balanced growth situation to be such that consumption per worker is maximized, saving must equal the income from capital.

If technology is unchanging, and constant returns to scale exist in the aggregate for firms in the economy, we are now able to show a distributional peculiarity of our neoclassical production function—payments to the factors of production exhaust aggregate output.

Total payments to the factors of production exhaust real output if we show that the following equation is true:

$$Y = \left(\frac{W}{P}\right)N + rK$$

Since efficient utilization of resources requires that

$$\frac{\partial Y}{\partial N} = \frac{W}{P} \quad \text{and} \quad \frac{\partial Y}{\partial K} = r$$

we have

$$Y = \frac{\partial Y}{\partial N}N + \frac{\partial Y}{\partial K}K \tag{18-17}$$

Given the Cobb-Douglas production function

$$Y = AN^\alpha K^{1-\alpha}$$

the marginal productivities of labor and capital can be expressed as

$$\frac{\partial Y}{\partial N} = \alpha AN^{\alpha-1}K^{1-\alpha}$$

$$\frac{\partial Y}{\partial K} = (1-\alpha)AN^\alpha K^{-\alpha}$$

Substituting the right-hand sides of these two equations into Equation 18-17 for $\partial Y/\partial N$ and $\partial Y/\partial K$ yields

$$Y = (\alpha AN^{\alpha-1}K^{1-\alpha})N + [(1-\alpha)AN^\alpha K^{-\alpha}]K$$

$$Y = \alpha AN^\alpha K^{1-\alpha} + (1-\alpha)AN^\alpha K^{1-\alpha}$$

$$Y = AN^\alpha K^{1-\alpha}$$

Thus, the two factor payments *do* exhaust the entire aggregate output. We have shown that this result holds in the Cobb-Douglas context, but it can be proven to hold always for all "neoclassical" production functions.

We have just demonstrated a distributional peculiarity, product exhaustion, of neoclassical production functions:

$$Y = (W/P)N + rK$$

But, in optimal growth, we know that $rK = S$, so that

$$Y = (W/P)N + S$$

$$Y - S = (W/P)N = C$$

Thus, total consumption must equal the labor share of total product.

The results obtained so far cannot be interpreted to denote, however, that workers must consume and capitalists must save all their respective income. What is required for the economy to stay on the optimal growth path is that aggregate savings from both workers and capitalists equal the share of total product distributed to owners of capital.

SUMMARY

The fundamental assumption employed in neoclassical growth analysis is the existence of an aggregate production function. The relationships among output, technology, and the factors of production involve four characteristics: (1) stock and flow variables are expressed in continuous time; (2) capital and labor are continuously substitutable for each other; (3) for a given technology, the addition of equal amounts of a variable factor of production to fixed factors of production eventually results in successively smaller additions to output; (4) if all inputs increase by some common percentage, output increases by the same percentage. Within this framework, maximum per-worker consumption will prevail at any point in time if the marginal propensity to save is such that saving is equal to the income from capital, and consumption is equal to the labor share of total product.

Input-Output Analysis as a Planning Tool

19

The national income and product accounts introduced in Chapter 2 are a method of measuring the value of a nation's output, or the aggregate income generated in its production. The flows of output from one industry to another are passed over, however, since only sales to final buyers are made explicit. Inter-industry economic activity is submerged because intermediate production is not included in the national income accounts (to avoid double counting). While the income and product accounts are deliberately designed to isolate economic variables, they can be powerfully augmented by data which traces the supply and demand relationships among the various sectors contributing to the GNP.

To study the output of the separate economic sectors, rather than the aggregate output, it is necessary to disaggregate GNP into a number of different producing industries or sectors. An *input-output table* is a framework for organizing such disaggregated data. In addition, and more importantly, it provides a basis for analyzing the relationships between final demand for output and the intermediate output that must be forthcoming to meet this final demand.

This view of the economy as a network of producing sectors, each of which provides output for itself and other sectors, permits us to answer some fundamental questions about the impact of changes in the economy *before those changes take place*. It therefore enables us to make plans for such changes. For example, what will be the impact on employment of a reduction in the defense component of the government sector? If we can project the growth in state and local government spending during the next ten years, what will be the impact of those government purchases on employment? on outlays for new and existing structures? on the computer industry? If residential home construction were to increase by 5% annually, and mobile home construction by 15% annually, during the next three years, what might be the impact on suppliers of the construction industry?

Input-output analysis was invented by Wassily W. Leontief during the early 1930s. Leontief's original table was for the year 1919. The economy was divided into 41 major sectors. More elaborate versions were developed for 1929 and 1939, and by 1952 an official U.S. government table was available for the year 1947. While the data for the 1947 table was assembled for 500 detailed sectors, the published version was compressed into a more manageable table consisting of 200 sectors.

Official U.S. government interest in input-output analysis waned during the mid-1950s, as conservative critics raised fears that detailed knowledge of the structure of the economy would jeopardize personal freedom. However, by the end of the 1950s, the Department of Commerce was given responsibility for constructing periodic input-output tables that could be integrated with the national income accounts.[1] In 1964, the Department published an input-output table for the year 1958 in which the economy was divided into 86 sectors.[2] This was followed in 1969 by a more thorough set of tables for the U.S. economy in 1963.

In this chapter we develop a simplified input-output model and use it to illustrate the impact of a change in government expenditure.

AN INPUT-OUTPUT TABLE

Table 19-1 is a very simple input-output table in which an economy has been divided into three productive sectors: agriculture, manufacturing, and services. It allows us to see the relationships among these productive sectors, the contributions of each to final demand, their levels of gross output, and the way that each uses inputs of labor, capital, and imports.

It is important to note that neither final demand nor gross output is the same as GNP. GNP is defined as the current market value of all final goods and services produced during a given time period. *Final total* output is GNP plus imports, and *gross* output includes the value of intermediate goods as well as final goods. Since the input-output table measures all *transactions* in the market for goods and services, double-counting is deliberate.

The data in the *rows* labeled 1), 2), and 3) shows how the value of gross output in each sector is delivered to the three producing sectors as intermediate goods, and to the four components of final demand: consumption; government; gross investment; and exports. A sector's gross output is the value (in current dollars) of total output produced by the sector, including the portion consumed by the industry itself. Reading across the first row (agriculture), for example, we see that, of the value of gross output of agricultural goods (300), 69 are used in the production

1. William I. Abraham, *National Income and Economic Accounting* (Prentice-Hall, 1969), 150.
2. Preliminary results were published in U.S. Department of Commerce, Office of Business Economics, *Survey of Current Business*, November 1964. Revised tables appeared in the September 1965 issue.

Table 19-1   Hypothetical Input-Output Table

	1	2	3	4	5	6	7	8	9	10
Outputs										
Inputs	Agriculture	Manufacturing	Services	Total Intermediate Output	Consumption	Government	Gross Investment	Exports	Final Total Output (Demand)	Gross Total Output
1) Agriculture	69	136	—	205	25	—	10	60	95	300
2) Manufacturing	51	612	237	900	475	40	105	180	800	1700
3) Services	30	255	110	395	300	150	135	20	605	1000
4) Factor payments:										
a) Wages	40	340	370	—	—	—	—	—	—	750
b) Profits	90	40	120	—	—	—	—	—	—	250
5) Indirect business tax and nontax liability	6	85	39	—	—	—	—	—	—	130
6) Capital consumption	8	79	38	—	—	—	—	—	—	125
7) Imports	6	153	86	—	—	—	—	—	—	245
8) Total (gross) purchases	300	1700	1000	1500	800	190	250	260	1500	—

processes of agriculture itself, and 136 are sold to manufacturing. Hence, "intermediate" agricultural products are valued at 205, leaving 95 available to be sold as final goods. Of this value, 25 were purchased by households, 10 were acquired by all productive sectors as gross investment, and 60 more were sold abroad.

Below the double line, the rows labeled 4) a) and b) show the factor incomes generated in producing the nation's final output. These incomes are divided into 750 for wages, and 250 for profits. Looking at wages, for example, we see that agriculture was responsible for wages of 40, manufacturing for wages of 340, and services for 370. The remaining rows in Table 19-1 show how indirect business tax and nontax liabilities (row 5), capital consumption allowances (row 6), and imports (row 7) figure among each productive sector's inputs.

The first three columns indicate the origin of all inputs in the nation's production processes. Reading down the first column (agriculture), for example, we see that to produce gross output valued at 300, the agricultural sector had to use 69 of its own output, and purchase materials of 51 and 30 from manufacturing and services, respectively. Note that the manufacturing sector makes the largest contribution to final output (800); it must purchase 136 from agriculture and 255 from services to be used as inputs, as well as 612 of its own output.

There are numerous advantages to organizing aggregate data in an input-output table. The table shows the gross output, including intermediate goods, for each productive sector. It shows the contribution each sector makes to final demand. It shows, reading down the columns, the cost structure of each sector. It shows the productive sectors' demands for labor, entrepreneurial services, capital (as reflected by depreciation allowances), and imports. It shows clearly the relationships of productive sectors to the major components of final total demand.

We can see from Table 19-1 that gross output of the three productive sectors (column 10, rows 1–3) equals total purchases, or inputs (columns 1–3, row 8). The total of all rows in the production sector (rows 1–3) must equal the total of all columns in the purchases sector (columns 1–3) for the same reason that GNP from the product side must equal GNP computed from the factor payments (including non-income charges). Note also that the sum of rows 4–7 in column 10—factor payments plus non-income charges and imports—equals the total of column 9, which is final total demand (GNP plus imports).

INPUT-OUTPUT ANALYSIS*

It is possible to use a hypothetical input-output table (Table 19-1) for a theoretical model, which given some assumptions discussed below, explains (or predicts) the effect of any change in final demand on the output of the productive sector.

Symbols and Relationships

To begin the development of the theoretical model, we need the following symbols and relationships:

r = any given one of n sectors.
Y_r = the value of the *gross* output of sector r.
y_{rc} = the value of intermediate goods sold by sector r to sector c.
y_r = the value of *final* output sold by sector r.

* In this section, our treatment borrows heavily from C. G. F. Simkin, *Economics at Large* (Weidenfeld and Nicolson, 1968).

P_r = the price of the output of sector r.
X_r = *gross* production in sector r ($X_r = X_c$).
x_{rc} = the quantity of intermediate goods sold by sector r to sector c.
x_r = the quantity of *final* output sold by sector r.

$$Y_r = y_{rc_1} + y_{rc_2} + \ldots + y_{rcn} + y_r$$

where n is the number of sectors. An alternative notation is

$$Y_r = \sum_{c=1}^{n} y_{rc} + y_r$$

where $\sum_{c=1}^{n}$ means the sum of ($y_{rc_1} + y_{rc_2} + \ldots + y_{rcn}$) $\hspace{2cm}$ (19-1)

and

$$Y_r = P_r X_r \hspace{4cm} (19\text{-}2)$$

where

$$X_r = \sum_{c=1}^{n} x_{rc} + x_r \hspace{3cm} (19\text{-}3)$$

In Equation 19-1 the value of gross output equals the value of all intermediate goods plus the value of final output. If we apply this equation to our hypothetical input-output of Table 19-1, we have:

$$Y_1 = y_{11} + y_{12} + y_{13} + y_1 = 69 + 136 + 0 + 95 = 300$$

$$Y_2 = y_{21} + y_{22} + y_{23} + y_2 = 51 + 612 + 237 + 800 = 1700$$

$$Y_3 = y_{31} + y_{32} + y_{33} + y_3 = 30 + 225 + 110 + 605 = 1000$$

In Equation 19-2, the value of gross output is the product of the price of the units of output sold and the number of units. In Equation 19-3, gross physical output equals the output of intermediate goods plus final output.

Assumptions

To simplify the analysis, we assume that all prices are constant and equal to unity; that is, $P_r = 1$. This assumption allows us to equate value to quantity (for example, $Y_r = X_r$). This assumption is not entirely unrealistic. It enables us to "normalize"—for example, if ground beef is $0.80 a pound this period, we associate this price with 1.00. If next period the price is $1.20 a pound (an increase of 50 percent), we refer to the new price as 1.50. Thus, at least in the current period, we can abstract from prices and associate Y_r with X_r.

Another assumption crucial to the analysis is that inputs are used in *fixed proportions* to produce a given unit of output. If prices are constant, and if fixed proportions between inputs and output exist, we can determine the technical coefficients of production by dividing the totals for columns

Table 19-2

	Agriculture	Manufacturing	Services
1) Agriculture	0.230	0.080	
2) Manufacturing	0.170	0.360	0.237
3) Services	0.100	0.150	0.110
4) Factor Payments			
a) Wages	0.133	0.200	0.370
b) Profits	0.300	0.024	0.120
5) Indirect business taxes, etc.	0.020	0.050	0.039
6) Capital consumption	0.027	0.046	0.038
7) Imports	0.020	0.090	0.086
	1.000	1.000	1.000

1–3 in Table 19-1 into the purchases of inputs that enter the particular column. For example, to produce one unit of output, the agricultural sector needs 0.230 of that unit from itself, 0.170 from manufacturing, 0.100 from services, and so on. By dividing the totals (row 8) of columns 1–3 into the purchases of inputs, we obtain Table 19-2.

Let a_{rc} represent the technical coefficient that measures the amount of input from sector r needed by sector c in order to produce one unit of output. Hence the coefficients relate to production requirements; that is,

$$a_{rc} = \frac{x_{rc}}{X_r} \tag{19-4}$$

A Simple Input-Output Model

The simplest form of an input-output model can be developed by rewriting Equation 19-4:

$$x_{rc} = a_{rc}X_c$$

Substituting the right-hand side of this equation into Equation 19-3 in place of x_{rc} yields

$$X_r = \sum_{c=1}^{n} a_{rc}X_c + \bar{x}_r$$

or

$$X_r - \sum_{c=1}^{n} a_{rc}X_c = \bar{x}_r \tag{19-5}$$

The bar over the x_r term denotes that the prevailing levels of the final demands are taken as being exogenously given. Equation 19-5 is actually a system of n linear equations. They are sufficient to determine the n outputs X_c, and thus the n inputs x_{rc}.[3]

By applying the technical coefficients from our hypothetical input-output table to Equation 19-5, we obtain

$$X_1 - 0.230\,X_1 - 0.080\,X_2 \qquad\qquad = x_1 = \quad 95$$

$$X_2 - 0.170\,X_1 - 0.360\,X_2 - 0.237\,X_3 = x_2 = 800$$

$$X_3 - 0.100\,X_1 - 0.150\,X_2 - 0.110\,X_3 = x_3 = 605$$

or

$$0.770\,X_1 - 0.080\,X_2 \qquad\qquad = x_1 = \quad 95$$

$$-0.170\,X_1 + 0.640\,X_2 - 0.237\,X_3 = x_2 = 800$$

$$-0.100\,X_1 - 0.150\,X_2 + 0.890\,X_3 = x_3 = 605$$

We now have three levels of gross output to obtain (X_1, X_2, and X_3), and three linear equations with which to solve for them. Solving by the usual methods, we obtain:

$$X_1 = 1.34451x_1 + 0.17925x_2 + 0.04777x_3 = \quad 300$$

$$X_2 = 0.44091x_1 + 1.72528x_2 + 0.45979x_3 = 1700 \qquad (19\text{-}6)$$

$$X_3 = 0.22533x_1 + 0.31095x_2 + 1.20640x_3 = 1000$$

From Equation 19-4 we can now find the various levels of intermediate inputs required to produce the three levels of gross output:

$$x_{11} = a_{11}X_1 = 0.230\,X_1 = \quad 69$$

$$x_{21} = a_{21}X_1 = 0.170\,X_1 = \quad 51$$

$$x_{31} = a_{31}X_1 = 0.100\,X_1 = \quad 30$$

$$x_{12} = a_{12}X_2 = 0.080\,X_2 = 136$$

$$x_{22} = a_{22}X_2 = 0.360\,X_2 = 612$$

$$x_{32} = a_{32}X_2 = 0.150\,X_2 = 255$$

$$x_{13} = a_{13}X_3 = 0.000\,X_3 = \quad 0$$

3. In applying the model in cases where there are many productive sectors, it is necessary to use matrix algebra. Let A be an n-by-n matrix of technical coefficients which applies to productive sectors; let $\bar{x}$ be an n-by-1 matrix of final demand. If X is an n-by-1 matrix of gross output, then

$$AX + \bar{x} = X$$

Since A and $\bar{x}$ are known, we can solve for X:

$$\bar{x} = X - AX = (I - A)X$$

$$X = (I - A)^{-1}\bar{x}$$

The symbol I denotes the identity matrix.

$$x_{23} = a_{23}X_3 = 0.237\,X_3 = 237$$

$$x_{33} = a_{33}X_3 = 0.110\,X_3 = 110$$

Changes in Final Demand

Up to this point, we have assumed that the level of final demand in each productive sector is fixed and known. The model, however, is useful in estimating the effects of changes in one or more components of the final demand. Assume a situation where the government wants to more than double government spending and maintain final total output at its current level. It must decrease consumption, investment, and exports. The new structure of final demand is given in columns 5–9 in Table 19-3. This new structure is the government's *policy objective*. Now, of course, the question is: What change in the composition of output is required to fulfill the objective?[4] To answer this question, it is necessary to derive the remainder of the new matrix.

First, insert the new productive sectors' final demands into Equation 19-6 to estimate sector gross output:

$$X_1 = 1.34451(75) + 0.17925(775) + 0.04777(650) = 271$$

$$X_2 = 0.44901(75) + 1.72528(775) + 0.45979(650) = 1669$$

$$X_3 = 0.22533(75) + 0.31095(775) + 1.20640(650) = 1042$$

Second, multiply the technical coefficients in Table 19-2 by the corresponding sector gross output (Column 10) to obtain the output column for that sector (Columns 1–3).

If we investigate Table 19-3, we see that the stabilization policy was in fact effective. Although government spending more than doubled (column 6, row 8), final output remained constant (column 9, row 8).

ROLES OF INPUT-OUTPUT ANALYSIS

As we have seen, input-output analysis is a flexible new tool for economic analysis. It has been used, both here and abroad, for many kinds of forecasting, planning, and intersectoral analysis. The usefulness of input-output analysis rests on its ability to uncover the relationships among sectors. Without this tool, it would be impossible to trace all of the intricate relationships among industries and/or productive sectors in the economy.

Although it may be relatively easy to derive from national product accounts the direct requirements (labor, imports, intermediate materials,

---

4. It is important to bear in mind that total output cannot exceed the limits imposed on it by the supply of inputs.

Table 19-3

Inputs	1 Agriculture	2 Manufacturing	3 Services	4 Total Intermediate Output	5 Consumption	6 Government	7 Gross Investment	8 Exports	9 Final Total Output (Demand)	10 Gross Total Output
Outputs										
1) Agriculture	62	134	—	196	20	—	5	50	75	271
2) Manufacturing	46	601	247	894	450	100	95	130	775	1669
3) Services	27	250	115	392	230	300	100	20	650	1042
4) Factor payments										
a) Wages	36	334	385	—	—	—	—	—	—	755
b) Profits	82	39	124	—	—	—	—	—	—	245
5) Indirect business tax and nontax liability	5	84	41	—	—	—	—	—	—	130
6) Capital consumption	7	77	40	—	—	—	—	—	—	124
7) Imports	6	150	90	—	—	—	—	—	—	246
8) Total (gross) purchases	271	1669	1042	1482	700	400	200	200	1500	

etc.) to produce a given level of national output, the *indirect* input requirements would be impossible to deduce (owing to the necessity of following requirements through the endless chain of inputs successively more remote from the beginning point). However, to determine what is required to produce a given level of output, national planners need to know the indirect as well as the direct input requirements. Input-output analysis has been applied in command as well as capitalist economies, and in most underdeveloped countries.

United States

The U.S. Department of Labor's Bureau of Labor Statistics has been preparing a series of reports on the employment impact of U.S. economic growth.[5] These reports predict the number of employees that will be required, under varying assumptions regarding the rate of growth, in 82 industrial sectors. Although the level of detail is not as great as had been anticipated when plans were drawn up during the early 1960s to increase the sophistication of input-output analysis, efforts are now underway to advance understanding of the sources of economic growth by making estimates of capital and labor input requirements on an industry-by-industry basis. The value of these reports, not only to government, but to industry as well, should be apparent. By anticipating the consequences of economic growth for employment, the Department of Labor could plan manpower programs *in advance* of their being needed so that the shift of labor from one industry to another would be facilitated. A firm can utilize input-output tables in planning its own expansion on the basis of future-demand estimates that are more realistic than "seat-of-the-pants" techniques.

France

France's "indicative" planning, to which we made reference in Chapter 15 (incomes policies) uses input-output analyses as well as other analytical tools to make five- to ten-year projections of final demands. Forecasts are made by a General Commission on the plan with the aid of other government agencies. These forecasts are submitted to committees made up primarily of business leaders. The purpose of these reviews is to "educate" key decision makers in the economy about the production goals of the various sectors. The plan is sent to parliament and is then published. Uncertainty regarding output goals of industries is reduced considerably (which may help explain the high rate of growth in France). While various demographic and foreign-trade projections are a necessary input to the plan, input-output tables are the critical elements. While the plan is non-coercive and does not imply government sanction for the projected outputs, the expectation is that increased information will lead to greater efficiency, making explicit government planning unnecessary.

Soviet Union

Although one might expect a centrally planned economy to welcome a technique that promises coherence in national planning, the Soviet Union was initially hostile to input-output analysis. Much of the suspicion was due to its highly mathematical nature, which was considered bourgeois, and that it was developed in America. When, in the mid-1950s, economists

5. See the Bureau of Labor Statistics' Bulletin No. 1536, "Projections, 1970: Interindustry Relationships, Potential Demand, Employment," (1966); Bulletin No. 1672, "Patterns of U.S. Economic Growth: 1980 Projections of Final Demand, Interindustry Relationships, Output, Productivity, and Employment," (1970); and Bulletin 1733, "Projections of the Post-Vietnam Economy, 1975," (1972).

in the Soviet Union began to urge that input-output analysis be utilized, the fact that its inventor was Russian-born was used to render it respectable.

Soviet planning begins with the transmission of the state's economic goals set by the political leaders of the Gosplan, the central planning board. Gosplan translates these goals into the production goals issued to enterprises. Having received its production goals, the enterprise informs Gosplan what inputs it will need to have them realized. After a complex process of negotiation between the enterprise and Gosplan, final production and material input figures are arrived at. Gosplan has the task of insuring that supplies and demands will be in balance. The value of input-output analysis comes from the speed at which the planning task can be accomplished.[6]

Regional Planning

Not only does input-output analysis have application for macroeconomic planning, it has also proved to be a very useful tool in regional planning.[7] Regional input-output analysis can be used to predict the consequences for local industries of national economic changes. While most regional input-output studies focus on the impact of change on existing industries, some try to measure the impact of the location of a new industry in the area. For example, what will be the employment and sales effects of these potential changes? The major difference between national and regional input-output studies, especially when the national economy is highly insulated from foreign trade (as is the U.S. economy), is that a regional area has a high export-import level which must be incorporated into the model. For example, a major attempt has been made to apply input-output analysis to the Philadelphia SMSA (standard metropolitan statistical area) which considered the impact of Vietnam war expenditures on the metro economy.

Among the latest contributions to the literature on the applications of input-output analysis is Leontief's approach to dealing with pollution.[8] He suggests that existing input-output tables can be modified by the addition of rows and columns representing pollutants as inputs and outputs. Pollutants are an input in the production process because they are a necessary concomitant of the inputs that go into production. In addition, they are an output because they accompany the final product. Once we arrive at some estimate of pollutant outputs, we can determine the consequences of reducing pollutants in terms of reduced outputs of final products.

6. See Herbert S. Levine, "Input-Output Analysis and Soviet Planning," *American Economic Review*, Vol. 52, May 1962.
7. See Charles M. Tiebout, "Regional and Interregional Input-Output Models: An Appraisal," *The Southern Economic Journal*, Vol. 24 (October 1957); Walter Isard and Thomas W. Langford, *Regional Input-Output Study: Recollections, Reflections, and Diverse Notes on the Philadelphia Experience* (MIT Press, 1971).
8. Wassily Leontief, "Environmental Repercussions and the Economic Structure: An Input-Output Approach," *The Review of Economics and Statistics*, Vol. 52, No. 3, August 1970.

LIMITATIONS OF INPUT-OUTPUT ANALYSIS

Although input-output analysis is a useful tool for economic policymakers, its usefulness is diminished somewhat by two of the basic assumptions of the analysis, namely that there can be no substitution among inputs in the production of a given commodity, and that total output is simply the sum total of sector (or industry) outputs. The former assumption precludes changing the input mix (the technical coefficients) in response to changes in technology and/or changes in relative input prices.

While there is no direct way around this limitation, it is of course possible to update the data on a frequent basis. However, frequent updates are not only costly, but difficult to bring about, due to the massive data requirements. While input-output analysis has proven useful in making limited predictions about the future, its full potential for comprehensive national planning has yet to be realized.

SUGGESTED READING

Unemployment and Inflation

M. Bronfenbrenner and F. D. Holzman, "A Survey of Inflation Theory," *American Economic Review* (September 1963). Somewhat dated, this survey article provides a thorough review of the "state of the art" as it existed at the beginning of the 1960s.

R. G. Lipsey, "The Relation Between Unemployment and the Rate of Change of Money Wage Rates in the United Kingdom, 1862–1957: A Further Analysis," *Economica* (February 1960). This important article provides a revision of Phillips original work.

G. L. Perry, *Unemployment, Money Wage Rates, and Inflation* (MIT Press, 1966). The "Phillips" relationship is demonstrated for U.S. data in this early study of the relationship between unemployment and inflation.

E. S. Phelps, et al., *Microeconomic Foundations of Employment and Inflation Theory* (Norton, 1970). This collection of over a dozen essays deals with labor market relationships which may determine the location of the Phillips curve.

————, *Inflation Policy and Unemployment Theory* (Norton, 1972). Phelps describes a theory of optimal inflation and unemployment. In addition, he shows how social expenditures to reduce inflation can be evaluated for their efficiency.

Albert Rees, "The Phillips Curve as a Menu for Policy Choice," *Economica*

(August 1971). This clearly written article provides a review of what is known about the location of the Phillips curve.

Milton Friedman, "The Role of Monetary Policy," *American Economic Review* (March 1968). Milton Friedman's presidential address before the American Economic Association. As with most of Friedman's writing, it is a model of clarity. See especially his discussion of short-run and long-run Phillips curves.

James Tobin, "Inflation and Unemployment," *American Economic Review* (March 1972). James Tobin's presidential address before the American Economic Association. His address reviews what is known about inflation and unemployment as inseparable phenomena, and considers policy implications.

Manpower Planning in Macroeconomic Stabilization Policy

Robert E. Hall, "Prospects for Shifting the Phillips Curve through Manpower Policy," *Brookings Papers on Economic Activity*, No. 3 (The Brookings Institution, 1971). Considers the potential quantitative impact of manpower programs on reducing aggregate unemployment without raising inflation, and concludes that they are of marginal significance at best.

Charles C. Holt, C. Duncan MacRae, Stuart O. Schweitzer, and Ralph E. Smith, "Manpower Proposals for Phase III," *Brookings Papers on Economic Activity*, No. 3 (The Brookings Institution, 1971). In contrast to the paper by Hall, Holt et al. explain how manpower programs could be effective. See also their *Manpower Programs to Reduce Inflation and Unemployment: Manpower Lyrics for Macro Music* (The Urban Institute, 1971).

Sar A. Levitan, Garth L. Mangum, and Ray Marshall, *Human Resources and Labor Markets: Labor and Manpower in the American Economy* (Harper & Row, 1972). A textbook in labor economics. Part VI is concerned with manpower and economic policy.

Edmund S. Phelps et al., *Microeconomic Foundations of Employment and Inflation Theory* (Norton, 1970). This collection of over a dozen essays deals with the labor-market relationships which may determine the location of the Phillips curve.

Lloyd Ulman, ed., *Manpower Programs in the Policy Mix* (Johns Hopkins University Press, 1973). See especially the essay by R. A. Gordon, "Some Macroeconomic Aspects of Manpower Policy."

Incomes Policies

Stephen S. Cohen, *Modern Capitalist Planning: The French Model* (Harvard University Press, 1969). The relationship between French planning and control of wages and prices is described. This is the definitive work on the French planning process.

John Kenneth Galbraith, *A Theory of Price Control* (Harvard University Press, 1952). Galbraith reviews his experiences with the World War II price and wage stabilization machinery and suggests lessons to be learned from that experience.

Seymour E. Harris, *Price and Related Controls in the United States* (McGraw Hill Book Company, 1945). A highly detailed accounting of World War II controls.

Randall Hinshaw, ed., *Inflation as a Global Problem* (Johns Hopkins University Press, 1972). A series of papers and comments made at a conference in the spring of 1971. Although most of the contents are devoted to international monetary relations, there is a discussion on the usefulness of incomes policies.

H. G. Johnson and A. R. Nobay, eds., *The Current Inflation* (London: Macmillan, 1971). The result of a conference at the London School of Economics held during early 1971. Several papers are devoted to measuring the effectiveness of incomes policies.

D. C. Smith, *Incomes and Wage-Price Policies: Some Issues and Approaches* (Kingston, Ontario: Industrial Relations Centre of Queen's University, 1967). Smith makes the case for the utility of incomes policies and describes how such policies are devised.

Lloyd Ulman and Robert J. Flanagan, *Wage Restraint: A Study of Incomes Policies in Western Europe* (University of California Press, 1971). The postwar experiences of over half a dozen European countries are described.

Foreign Economic Relations

Peter L. Bernstein, *A Primer on Money, Banking, and Gold* (Random House, 1965). An exceptionally lucid book aimed at the intelligent layman, Bernstein explains the relationship between the Federal Reserve System, the money supply, and gold. Although events have outdated some of his discussion on international economic relations, much of the work is still useful.

Milton Friedman, "The Case for Flexible Exchange Rates," in *Essays in Positive Economics* (University of Chicago Press, 1953). In this persuasive and important essay, Friedman argues for the determination of exchange rates in the world's money markets.

H. G. Grubel, *World Monetary Reform, Plans and Issues* (Stanford University Press, 1963). A compendium of plans for dealing with the international monetary system. Authors include bankers and government officials, as well as economists.

Charles Kindleberger, *International Economics* (Irwin, 1963). One of the most widely used and respected textbooks in the field of trade and balance of payments.

Anne O. Krueger, "Balance-of-Payments Theory," *Journal of Economic Literature* (March 1969). A review of the theory underlying international monetary relations, combined with a thorough bibliography of the literature.

Guide to Foreign Trade Statistics: 1971 (U.S. Government Printing Office). A specialist's reference work on domestic and foreign trade reports; contains a thorough description of the foreign trade statistics program. *Not* a book of statistics.

Robert Triffin, *Our International Monetary System: Yesterday, Today and Tomorrow* (Random House, 1968). A convenient source for learning about Triffin's plan to reform international monetary arrangements.

Economic Growth

William J. Baumol, *Economic Dynamics*, 3rd ed. (Macmillan, 1970). This outstanding book includes a thorough presentation of Harrod's model, as well as of more recent growth models. In Chapters 9 and 10, Baumol presents a clear discussion of the meaning and solution of difference equations. See also A. Kooros, *Elements of Mathematical Economics* (Houghton Mifflin, 1965), Chapters 9 and 10. A more thorough treatment is found in S. Goldberg, *Introduction to Difference Equations* (Wiley, 1960).

Edward F. Denison, *The Sources of Economic Growth in the United States and the Alternatives Before Us* (Committee for Economic Development, 1962). A comprehensive effort to estimate the sources of economic growth in the United States during the period 1909–1958. Denison separated the sources of economic growth into the following categories: labor, capital, education, economies of scale, and advances in knowledge. According to Denison, advances in knowledge, or technological advance, accounted for 20% of the total annual growth rate during the period 1929–1957. One of his particularly surprising discoveries is that capital inputs accounted for only 15% of the growth rate during this period.

Charles E. Ferguson, "The Simple Analytics of Neoclassical Growth Theory," *Quarterly Review of Economics and Business*, Vol. 8 (Spring 1968), 69–83. In this paper, Ferguson presents graphically, and in terms of elementary mathematics, a comprehensive analysis of the one-sector neoclassical model of economic growth. The virtue of the presentation is its simplicity—in contrast to other literature on the topic, which is quite heavily mathematical.

Much of our Chapter 18 is devoted to a review of the "neoclassical" approach to growth theory. If you want to delve further into this approach, you should read Charles E. Ferguson, *The Neoclassical Theory of Production and Distribution* (Cambridge University Press, 1969). You might also want to read a few reviews of the book—one appeared in nearly every major economic journal—to catch the flavor of the pro and anti-neoclassical factions in economics. This is *not* a policy disagreement (i.e., it is not a Keynes versus the "neoclassical" school type of debate). It is a debate centered on whether or not it is proper to employ the neoclassical production function, with all of its attendant implications for other areas of economics (e.g., distribution theory). An excellent survey of this debate is given by G. C. Harcourt, "Some Cambridge Controversies in the Theory of Capital," *Journal of Economic Literature*, Vol. 7 (June 1969), 369–405.

Lester B. Lave, *Technological Change: Its Conception and Measurements* (Prentice-Hall, 1966). A thorough study of technological change. Among other topics, the book includes a review of the important studies that have been conducted on technological change, an elaboration of the difficulties in measuring it, the effects of technological change on economic theory and on public policy, and a comprehensive bibliography of the literature. See also Warren L. Smith, *Macroeconomics* (Irwin 1970), 404–428; and Thomas M. Humphrey, "Productivity and Its Measurement," *Federal Reserve Bank of Richmond Review* (June 1971), 2–10.

D. Meadows et al., *The Limits to Growth* (Universe Books, 1972). A controversial report on economic growth, arguing that growth cannot be sustained because natural resources will soon be exhausted, and technology will not be able to provide continuing solutions.

E. J. Mishan, *Technology and Growth: The Price We Pay* (Praeger Publishers, 1969). Mishan's provocative views on the impact of technological advance on the quality of life are spelled out in detail in this volume. This book is intended for the layman, and is highly readable.

National Bureau of Economic Research, *Economic Research: Retrospect and Prospect*, Volume 5, *Economic Growth* (Columbia University Press, 1972). This volume contains the paper by William Nordhaus and James Tobin, "Is Growth Obsolete?," which considers the relationships among economic growth, the environment, and economic welfare.

Myron H. Ross, *Income: Analysis and Policy*, 2nd ed. (McGraw-Hill, 1968), Chapter 12. Ross' chapter on business cycles, a subject in macroeconomic dynamics which we have omitted, provides an excellent introduction to that topic. See also Stanley Bober, *The Economics of Cycles and Growth* (Wiley, 1968).

Paul A. Samuelson, ed., *Readings in Economics*, 6th ed., Part 6 (McGraw-Hill, 1970), 281–307. This section is devoted to elementary readings on the economics of growth. See also Heinz Kohler, ed., *Readings in Economics* (Holt, Rinehart and Winston, 1968), Part 3; Shelly M. Mark, ed., *Economics in Action*, 4th ed. (Wadsworth, 1969), 347–438; and

Dennis R. Starleaf, ed., *Economics: Readings in Analysis and Policy* (Scott, Foresman, 1969), Part XVI.

Sam H. Schurr, ed., *Energy, Economic Growth, and the Environment* (Johns Hopkins University Press, 1972). Contains papers presented at a conference conducted by Resources for the Future, Inc., including papers by Walter W. Heller, Barry Commoner, and Kenneth E. Boulding.

Amartya Sen, ed., *Growth Economics* (Penguin Books, 1970). A collection of major articles on growth theory. The introduction by Sen is an excellent overview of the subject. See also Joseph E. Stiglitz and Hirofumi Uzawa, eds., *Readings in the Modern Theory of Economic Growth*, MIT Press, 1969; and F. H. Hahn, ed., *Readings in the Theory of Economic Growth* (London: Macmillan, 1971). For another worthwhile book of readings, in which the public policy aspect of growth is emphasized, see Edmund S. Phelps, ed., *Economic Growth*, rev. ed. (Norton, 1969).

David L. Sills, ed., *International Encyclopedia of the Social Sciences*, Vol. 4 (The Free Press, 1968), 395–429, "Economic Growth." The articles under this heading give several views of the process of economic growth. The first is an "overview" of economic growth by Richard A. Easterlin. An excellent, relatively nontechnical presentation of the "theory" of economic growth is presented in the second essay by Gustav Ranis. The third essay is a survey of "mathematical" growth theory by Michio Morishima. The fourth is a summary of the "noneconomic aspects" of growth by Bert F. Hoselitz. Three other relevant summaries in this encyclopedia are "Business Cycles," Vol. 2; "Statics and Dynamics," Vol. 15; and "Income Distribution," Vol. 7.

Warren L. Smith, *Macroeconomics* (Irwin, 1970), 373–440. Part IV of Smith's book is a good introduction to the theory of economic growth. See also Paul A. Samuelson, *Economics*, 9th ed. (McGraw-Hill, 1970), Chapter 37; and K. C. Kogiku, *An Introduction to Macroeconomic Models* (McGraw-Hill, 1968), Chapters 7 and 8. For more detail, see R. G. D. Allen's, *Macroeconomic Theory* (St. Martin's Press, 1967), Chapters 3, 15, 16, 19, and 20; or Thomas F. Dernberg and Judith D. Dernberg, *Macroeconomic Analysis* (Addison-Wesley, 1969), Chapters 7–12. An excellent, easy-to-follow treatment of mathematical models of economic growth, which emphasizes the practical applicability of the models for actual planning purposes, is found in Jan Tinbergen and H. C. Bos, *Mathematical Models of Economic Growth* (McGraw-Hill, 1962).

Robert M. Solow, "A Contribution to the Theory of Economic Growth," *The Quarterly Journal of Economics*, Vol. 70 (February 1956), 65–74. The model presented in this paper is basically neoclassical in nature. Solow investigates the implications of economic growth by considering in his model variable factor proportions, monetary factors, and technological change.

Robert M. Solow, *Growth Theory* (Oxford University Press, 1970). An excellent, short summary of growth theory. In recent years a number of growth-theory textbooks have appeared, reflecting the strength of economists' interest in the subject. See, for example, Edwin Burmeister and A. Rodney Dobell, *Mathematical Theories of Economic Growth* (London: Macmillan, 1970); Daniel Hamberg, *Models of Economic Growth* (Harper & Row, 1971); and Henry Y. Wan, Jr., *Economic Growth* (Harcourt Brace Jovanovich, 1971).

Input-Output Analysis

Anne Carter, "Changes in the Structure of the American Economy, 1947 to 1958 and 1962," *The Review of Economics and Statistics* (May 1967), 209–224. In this article Carter shows how slowly technological change alters the technical coefficients, a_{rc}.

Hollis B. Chenery and Paul G. Clark, *Interindustry Economics* (Wiley, 1959). A clear discussion of basic input-output theory. Chenery and Clark devote considerable space to projections of economic structure in the United States and several other countries, and describe the use of input-output analysis for interregional analysis.

Conference on Research in Income and Wealth, *Input-Output Analysis: An Appraisal* (Princeton University Press, 1955). This is Volume 18 of the National Bureau of Economic Research's *Studies in Income and Wealth*. It includes an essay by Wassily Leontief on basic problems of empirical input-output analysis, as well as essays reviewing its use in the American economy. This volume is essential for anyone seriously pursuing the subject.

Walter Isard and Thomas Langord, *Regional Input-Output Study: Recollections, Reflections, and Diverse Notes on the Philadelphia Experience* (MIT Press, 1971). The application of input-output analysis to regional economies is described in this volume through the case-study approach, using the Philadelphia metropolitan area.

Wassily Leontief, "Environmental Repercussions and the Economic Structure: An Input-Output Approach," *The Review of Economics and Statistics*, Vol. 52, No. 3 (August 1970). Using simple examples, Leontief shows how input-output analysis can be applied to environmental issues.

———, *Input-Output Economics* (Oxford University Press, 1966). This book consists of a collection of eleven essays written by Leontief over a twenty-year period. Although the development and application of input-output analysis is the common theme of the book, the level of treatment varies greatly from one essay to another. Essay 7, "Input-Output Analysis," and Essay 8, "The Structure of the U.S. Economy," are particularly accessible to the beginning student.

William A. Miernyk, *The Elements of Input-Output Analysis* (Random House, 1967). This is a lucid, non-mathematical introduction to input-output analysis.

David L. Sills, *International Encyclopedia of Social Sciences*, Vol. 7 (Macmillan, 1968), 345–354, "Input-Output Analysis," by Leontief, surveys a field which he developed. Pages 345–350 of Leontief's article parallels our presentation; however, price equations are added so that relative prices can be determined. The remainder of the article deals with the theory of dynamic input-output systems. Some knowledge of matrix algebra is required.

C. G. F. Simkin, *Economics at Large* (London: Weidenfeld and Nicolson, 1968). A brief presentation of inter-industry accounting and the input-output analysis on which much of Chapter 19 is based.

U.S. Department of Commerce, *Survey of Current Business*, November 1969. The results of the 1963 input-output study of the U.S. economy by the Office of Business Economics is summarized. "Input-Output Structure of the U.S. Economy: 1963," explains how the input-output table is constructed, and presents summary data. The complete picture is available in three volumes, in *Input-Output Structure of the U.S. Economy: 1963 Transactions Data for Detailed Industries.*

U.S. Department of Labor, Bulletin No. 1536, "Projections 1970: Interindustry Relationships, Potential Demand and Employment," (1966); Bulletin No. 1672, "Patterns of U.S. Economic Growth: 1980 Projections of Final Demand, Interindustry Relationships, Output, Productivity, and Employment," (1970); Bulletin 1733, "Projections of the Post-Vietnam Economy, 1975," (1972). Studies published by the Bureau of Labor Statistics during the last few years which utilize interindustry relationships. These studies are a source of data as well as a source of descriptions of the techniques used.

   For national planning designed to insulate sectors from the economic hardships of potential shifts in the economy, some of which may originate in the government sector (such as defense) and others of which may originate in the household sector (such as changing tastes from durables to services), it is critical that we be able to evaluate employment effects. Input-output analysis can be used to shed light on this issue. The following articles illustrate how this can be accomplished. Jack Alterman, "Interindustry Employment Requirements: A New Table That Permits Manpower Analysis of Changes in Initial Demand," *Monthly Labor Review (MLR)* July 1965; Charles T. Bowman, "Report on Employment Related to Exports," *MLR*, June 1969; Richard P. Oliver, "Employment Effects of Reduced Defense Spending," *MLR*, December 1971.

Chiou-shuang Yan, *Introduction to Input-Output Economics* (Holt, Rinehart and Winston, 1969). Ms. Yan introduces and utilizes matrix algebra in her exposition.

INDEX